Introduction to African Literature

An anthology of critical writing

Edited by Ulli Beier

Longman

LONGMAN GROUP LIMITED
London

*Associated companies, branches and representatives
throughout the world*

© Ulli Beier and Mbari, 1967, 1979

First published 1967
New edition 1979

ISBN 0 582 64228 0

Printed in Great Britain by
Lowe & Brydone Printers Ltd, Thetford, Norfolk

Contents

Acknowledgements

We are indebted to the following for permission to reproduce copyright material: The author for extracts from 'Rediscovery and other poems' by George Awoonor-Williams; Dr. S. A. Babalola for extracts from his translations of *Ìjálá* verses; Ulli Beier for extracts from his translations of Yoruba verses; Bookman Associates Inc. for lines from 'Selected Poems of Claude McKay'; the author for lines from *Barbare* from 'Soleil Cou Coupé' by Aimé Césaire; the author for lines from 'Poems, 1962' by John Pepper Clark; Carl Cowl, on behalf of the Estate of Claude McKay, for lines from *To Winter* and *Rest In Peace* from 'Spring in New Hampshire', and lines from *Hard Times* from 'Songs of Jamaica' by Claude McKay; Editions Gallimard for lines from 'Les Armes Miraculeuses' by Aimé Césaire; Carl Hanser Verlag for *Amalia* and *Wir proben den Schlangentanz* by Marcelino Arozarena from 'Rumba Macumba—Afro-cubanische Lyrik', selected and translated by Janheinz Jahn; Michael Joseph Ltd. for lines from *The Emigrants* by George Lamming; Réné Julliard for lines from *L'Adventure Amgiguë* by Cheikh A. Kane; Alfred A. Knopf, Inc. for lines from 'Selected Poems' by Langston Hughes; The London Magazine for 'African Writers of the Eighteenth Century' by O. R. Dathorne; Library of Congress, Music Division, for lines from *I'm going to leave here walking, going down highway 61* . . . ; Editorial Losada, S.A. for *Sensemaya* from 'Songoro Consongo' by Nicolas Guillén; Gerald Moore for his translations of *What invisible rat, The black cow* and *Here she is* by Jean-Joseph Rabearivelo; Thomas Nelson and Sons Ltd. for extracts from *Igbo Olodumare* by D. O. Fagunwa, translated by Ulli Beier; the author's agents and Hutchinson & Co. Ltd. for an extract from *Blade Among the Boys* by O. Nzekwu; Christopher Okigbo, on behalf of Mbari Publications, for lines from 'Limits' and 'Heavensgate' by Christopher Okigbo, 'Icheke' by O. G. Nwanodi and 'Sirens, Knuckles, Boots' by D. Brutus; Henry Owuor and Gerald Moore for their translations of Luo songs; Oxford University Press for lines from *The Raft* by John Pepper Clark from 'Three Plays' and *A Dance of the Forests* by Wole Soyinka from 'Five Plays', and for *Le Totem* and *Nuit de Sine* by L. S. Senghor from 'Selected Poems of L. S. Senghor' edited by J. Reed and C. Wake, and *In Memoriam* by L. S. Senghor from 'Senghor: Prose and Poetry'; Penguin Books Ltd. for lines from *Woman* by Valante Malangatana, and *Over the Vast Summer Hills* by Mazisi Kunene from 'Modern Poetry from Africa' edited by Gerald Moore and Ulli Beier and for lines from *On me dit que là-bas* by André Breton from 'The Penguin Book of French Verse—4: The Twentieth Century'; the author for lines from 'Poems' by Dr. Lenrie Peters; 'Présence Africaine' for a poem by Lamine Diakhate published in Vol. II, No. 3a, for *Casino* by Paul Niger published in Vol. 12, 1951, and for lines from 'Les Chiens se Taisaient' and 'Cahier d'un Retour au Pays Natal' by Aimé Césaire; M. Solofo Rabearivelo for lines from the poems of Jean-Joseph

Rabearivelo; Miss Iris Salas for *Tango No. 2* by Virginia Brindis de Salas, and Editions du Seuil for *Visite* by L. S. Senghor, and for *Aux îles de tous vents* from 'Ferrements' and lines from *Le Griffon* and *Sommation* from 'Cadastre' by Aimé Césaire.

Every effort has been made to trace the owners of copyrights, but in a few cases this has proved impossible; the publishers would welcome any information that would enable them to do so.

Writers and Commitment

EZEKIEL MPHAHLELE

If you set out deliberately to make one-sided statements to a mass audience in order to advocate a point of view, then you are making propaganda. This should be distinguished from such closely allied uses of communication as instruction, information, and inquiry. You are advocating something if you select material from some channel of communication which is meant to influence attitudes on controversial issues. When the government distributes a pamphlet on what to do to help combat illiteracy, the act is instructive, it is not propaganda, unless the need for mass literacy is in question. It is inquiry, not propaganda to analyse controversial doctrines like capitalism or Communism for the sake of enlightening others.

What we hear and what we see make the most effective media of propaganda. You see a drawing or a painting or a poster that shows the ravages of a disease or the agony of forced labour, or a rioter holding a firebrand and shouting: 'Burn, baby, burn', or you hear a speaker urge you to go on strike. You feel that the message in either case comes direct and registers in quick time. Drama combines both the visual and the oral. It is conceived in terms of presentation on the stage. It is accordingly a most effective weapon in educating for an immediate end.

George Bernard Shaw, John Galsworthy, Brecht, Jean-Paul Sartre, Ibsen, Chekhov, and then the crop of angry playwrights of the late 1950s and the early sixties such as John Osborne, Arnold Wesker, Wole Soyinka and so on . . . all these were concerned with the predicament of man in a hostile environment and with the sickness that we all see in highly developed societies. They dramatise this predicament, showing us in the process a portion of life on the stage.

Are they propagating a doctrine or belief, or advocating a point of view? To a very large extent they are doing this, but in different ways. Some, like Shaw, tell us more or less what they stand for in long prefaces so that we understand more fully what they mean in their dramatic presentations. Others are more subtle, but the message registers. It may be the irrelevance or death of aristocracy as Chekhov represents; or the woman's assertion of her independence as in Ibsen; or the courage of woman as in Brecht; or it may be a portrayal of the working class as a community that feels life at its most basic and real levels, as in the kitchen-sink playwrights; or the loneliness of the intellectual, or the futility and cruelty of class or religious snobbery; or the loneliness of the political prisoner as in Wole Soyinka; or the brutality of American race attitudes as in Lorraine Hansberry and James Baldwin.

Perhaps it is a measure of a dramatist's success as an artist when he can move us and pleasurably teach us without any offensive propaganda, precisely because this is a medium which lends itself easiest to the propagating of ideas. For at his most naive, he merely needs an explosive situation to represent and then simply to talk through his characters. Yet, for reasons I cannot pretend to understand, blatant propaganda in itself seldom if ever offends when served up from a theatre stage, while it offends easily in fiction and verse. When it does not offend, it is boring or embarrassing.

Propaganda is always going to be with us. There will always be the passionate outcry against injustice, war, fascism, poverty etc. It will keep coming at us, reminding us that man is as wicked as he is noble and that the mass audience out there is waiting to be stirred by passionate words. African literature, like the other literatures of the world, is never going to be totally free of propaganda. But to say this is not to say propaganda is necessarily conducive to great literature no matter *how* it is served up. It was Brecht who said:

> I have noticed that we frighten many people away from our doctrines, because we appear to have an answer to everything. Should we not, in the interests of our propaganda, draw up a list of those problems that we consider totally unsolved?

Indeed in great literature propaganda cannot be easily separated from the world that is conceived by the author and the manner in which he presents it.

Before we talk specifically about African literature, let us look at various aspects of commitment as it prompts propaganda. Commitment need not give rise to propaganda: the writer can make his stand known without advocating it openly or in two-dimensional terms, *i.e.* in terms of one response to one stimulus. People tend to suspect political commitment. Yet politics are a human activity. In ancient Greece and in the Middle Ages there was not this dividing line between politics and other areas of human activity.

Every writer is committed to something beyond his art, to a statement of value not purely aesthetic, to a 'criticism of life'. Existentialist philosophers regard liberty as an integral feature of the human condition itself. Man is freedom. Jean-Paul Sartre, one of the leading French philosophers and writers, and himself an existentialist, insists that this view of liberty should be an important factor in literary criticism.

> The writer, a free man addressing free men, has only one subject . . . freedom.

The writer assumes a respect for human freedom even as he writes. But Sarte is not content with this as a mere attitude: it needs a political purpose. Literature must be made to serve a political purpose. For him literature, truth, democracy and other human values are bound up in a kind of programme. The question is—and the same question may well be posed in connection with that wing of Communist culture in Russia that insists on a social and political programme for the writer and artist in general—whether the respect for freedom and mankind as the absolute entity towards which all things must move can always be contained by literature and its other concerns like structures, its forms, its styles? Can Sartre's kind of discipline and aims for literature become inviolable rules for a craft that is always breaking rules, breaking down myths?

Somehow Sartre's thoughts about commitment did not take root in England, even in the late 1940s when he was most prominent. Perhaps this was because most of Sartre's works were not yet translated into English; it may be that something native in the English intellect or creative spirit resisted Sartre's kind of discipline, and generally the French habit of interpreting literature in philosophical terms. Instead of his influence, we see the new Left growing out of new alliances and affiliations. This comprised Raymond Williams, Richard Hoggart, John Osborne, Arnold Wesker etc. But its commitment was sociological: it was concerned with a new vision of society. It was not philosophical or literary. The writer on the other hand managed to contain in his craft a number of beliefs and ideologies that were opposed to one another even while he took a stand on the whole question of the national diffusion of culture, because he rejected the idea of culture as a privilege of the elite.

For some strange reason Sartre excluded poetry from his scheme of commitment. Poetry was 'opaque', 'non-communicative' while prose was 'transparent', 'communicative', and used words as means, as distinct from poetry that used words as an end. So prose was best suited as a tool for the committed writer. And commitment for the existentialist comes out of a sense of responsibility. To be committed means to be responsible.

Yet Sartre in his introduction, *Orphée Noire*, to Senghor's anthology of African and Malagasy poetry encourages by implication the negritude movement as anti-racist racism. He seems to recognise African poetry as a fit vehicle to propagate a creed. After Sartre, several people have claimed that African literature is 'functional', meaning, I believe, that this writing advocates the black man's cause and/or instructs its audience. This claim indicates a dangerous tendency, which is to draw a line of distinction between a function in which an author vindicates or asserts black pride or takes a socio-political stand and a function in which he seeks to stir humanity as a whole. At any rate it is dangerous for literature, which even while it particularises, literature takes in wider circles of humanity. The functions overlap, and the bigger the rift between them, the more stridently its propaganda yells out, the more life's ironies and paradoxes are overlooked, and the more the reader feels his sense of belonging assailed or unduly exploited. It is not that protest is necessarily faulty: indeed all art that humanity identifies itself with is a kind of protest, a criticism of life. Much depends on the writer's vision and the way he protests.

All the same, in spite of Sartre's sanctions, Africans have found poetry more readily available as a weapon of propaganda than prose fiction or even the essay. The following two examples will show how badly propaganda can be handled. Kwabena Akyeampong, a Ghanaian, writes in his *Mother Africa's Soliloquy*:

> Did they brand me dark
> Through ignorance or infatuation
> Did they call me primitive
> Through sheer spite or hate?
> Through misjudgement or mistake?
>
> Did they tag me backward
> Despite my agelong knowledge of civilization
> They disdained me
> In spite of my verdant lands and radiant sunshine
> They called me dark
> Notwithstanding my rich traditions and cultures
> They termed me primitive . . .

And then:

> I know I am an eagle; mighty bird by nature,
> Whose abode is nowhere but the lofty place . . .

This sounds naive, but not as tiresome as *The Blackman's God* by Francis Parkes, another Ghanaian, otherwise a fine poet and more sophisticated:

> Our God is great
> Who dare deny it?
> Our God is great
> Powerful and dark
> Peering through ages
> Healing, killing, guiding along.
>
> Our God is black
> And like any goddamned god
> Guiding when loving
> Killing when angered.
>
> Our God is like all gods
> Slow to anger when fed fat on yams
> And of great mercy when suckled on blood
> Brothers, blackmen, unbelievers
> Our God is like all gods
> Powerful and blood-loving.

This poem is only valid if the poet is talking with his tongue in his check, or if he is saying in effect: if we *must* have a God, it doesn't matter which one he'll be: we've had it anyway. But if he is serious, and he is actually upholding the black man's traditional gods because they are 'black', the verse crumbles as a propaganda piece. It purports to answer all the questions about God. It assumes the need for a God straight away, and the poet pretends to know everything about the intentions of his moods, when and how he wants to punish and reward. As a reader I feel imposed upon and bullied. The poem is killed by its tone.

Even before negritude or Negrismo was coined, W. E. B. Du Bois was singing:

> I am the Smoke King
> I am black
> I am darkening with song,
> I am hearkening to wrong;
> I will be black as blackness can
> The blacker the mantle the mightier the man.

Other American Negro poets hammered out the same theme to counteract their rejection by whites. Negritude caught on with the Caribbeans and then with the Africans. And now that colonialism has receded, even though its trappings remain, the Afro-Americans have taken it back as it were and are producing volumes of verse vindicating their black pride, using propaganda in a most sophisticated and often angry, incisive and moving idiom. These Afro-American poets have mastered the language of 'felt thought'. They do not try to use rhetoric to do their feeling and thinking for them in the way so much of our African black-pride verse does. The poignancy that we read in the American and Caribbean poetry of alienation shows again and again that this is where negritude began; that it was not mere gesturing; alienation was felt deep down to the marrow; that so much of it in Africa was derivative and rode on a rhetoric that flew like flakes at a second reading.

There are some fine voices of propaganda to be heard in African poetry which either bring out the distilled essence of negritude because it is beyond mere gesturing, or expresses the agony of white oppression. Senghor can say in his *Prayer to Masks*:

> For who else would teach rhythm to the world that has died of machines and cannons?
>
> For who else should ejaculate the cry of joy, that arouses the dead and the wise in a new dawn?
>
> Say, who else could return the memory of life to men with a torn hope? . . .
> They call us men of death
> But we are the men of the dance whose feet only gain power when they beat the hard soil.

Kofi Awoonor speaks of the moment of rediscovering ourselves:

> It cannot be the music we heard that night and still lingers in the
> chambers of memory.
> It is the new chorus of our forgotten comrades and the halleluyas
> of our second selves.

Gabriel Okara, on himself as the meeting point between two modes of
life—piano and drums:

> And I lost in the morning mist
> Of an age at a riverside keep
> Wandering in the mystic rhythm
> Of jungle drums and concerto.

Mbela Sonne Dipoko makes a beautiful statement about our growing
up, our passage from the life of uncles and fathers and mothers, from our
'world of greenness', to the world of today:

> And the mind soon flung pebbles at the cranes of the off-shore
> island.
> But today
> Floods flee the rising sun
> And the owls hoot from the edge of the dark song
> Like cripples blinded by sandy winds
> Dreams drift under the low sky of our sleep
> And our hearts listen to the voice of days in flight,
> Our thoughts dusting the past.

Dennis Brutus on the police raids that harass him and his fellow-blacks
in South Africa:

> Investigating searchlights rake
> Our naked unprotected contours;
> over our heads the monolithic decalogue
> of fascist prohibition glowers
> and teeters for a catastrophic fall;
> boots club on the peeling door.
> But somehow we survive
> severance, deprivation, loss.
> Patrols uncoil along the asphalt dark
> hissing their menace to our lives,
> but somehow tenderness survives.

Brutus's voice here is harsh and hard. But it mellows into strains
reminiscent of the Imagist poets:

> The sounds begin again,
> the siren in the night
> the thunder at the door

the shriek of nerves in pain
of faces split by pain
the wordless, endless wail
only the unfree know

Importunate as rain
the wreaths exhale their woe
over the siren, knuckles, boots;
My sounds begin again.

Because of the very nature of prose narrative, the novel does not *directly* express a state of mind like poetry. Although we talk prose, poetry more closely approximates the human voice as an expression of feeling and state of mind; as long as we do not try to let rhetoric do this for us. And yet the sense of commitment is no less sharp among the novelists. They document even as they dramatise. The abler kind of novelist allows for a free use of irony too. The following themes are very African:

(a) the conflict between new ways of life, new beliefs and the old (Chinua Achebe; Onuora Nzekwu)
(b) the homecoming of the black man who has been schooling overseas (Lenrie Peters; William Conton; Camara Laye)
(c) agitation against ruling white settlers (James Ngugi)
(d) the politics of independence (Camara Laye; James Ngugi)
(e) humiliation set in a colonial situation (Ferdinand Oyono; Achebe)
(f) labour upheavals (Sembène Ousmane; Peter Abrahams)
(g) black childhood and schooling (Laye; Bernard Dadié)
(h) the black servant (Oyono; Mongo Beti)
(i) the student in metropolitan capitals of colonising countries (Dipoko; Dadié; Aké Loba)
(j) city life (Cyprian Ekwensi; Wole Soyinka)
(k) snobbery among the enlightened blacks (Soyinka)
(l) oppression by whites, urban squalor, physical violence, police terror etc. (Alex la Guma; Peter Abrahams; Bloke Modisane; Richard Rive)
(m) themes drawn from mythology (Amos Tutuola)
(n) traditional life and the coming into consciousness of the village boy (Legson Kayira; Adhambi Asalache)

All these writers reflect a sense of commitment: the writer is committed to the African setting; he does not show any indication of wanting to flee from his African origins in preference for the Western world. He does not imagine a world of fantasy as an escape from his real environment. If he has to lead the life of an exile, his creative instincts still drive him to African themes that demand his commitment, or those in which he has already taken a stand. He is often nostalgic. We do not yet have a Frank Yerby in

Africa. Propaganda is subdued in our fiction, with the outstanding exception of *The African* (William Conton) which obviously advertises African values, and *Wand of the Noble Wood* (Nzekwu).

We do not yet have in African fiction anything like George Orwell's manner of thrusting his prejudices and hates into the open. I think this spoils his fiction. That *Animal Farm* and *1984* have stood the test of time can only be due to the fact that the political situations the propaganda in these works is aimed at still exist today. The prevailing political moral of the books still holds. We do not yet have a George Orwell in Africa perhaps because the writer here is still by and large ambivalent in his attitude towards Western values, and by the same token his experience is richer. Even when we advertise Africa or lash out at white oppression, our commitments tend to shift slightly when we are not simply documenting, even our stand on South Africa being at bottom only relatively firm. A self-avowed Marxist like Alex la Guma writes more like Gorki and the American Negro than Orwell. He documents and 'shows', without throwing in asides to let his voice be heard (except at few unguarded moments). And yet you know where La Guma stands. You know he wants to demonstrate the wickedness of a social system in which the black man is trapped. This is the social realism we have become accustomed to in Negro-American literature which portrays a similar human situation.

I have tried to show the various distances and degrees of commitment without attempting to be categorical about whether propaganda should or should not enter a work of art. Yet I do not even think this is the question: rather it is the manner in which the writer uses propaganda that decides the literary worth of a work. The question of the audience also comes in. For instance, poetry inspired by negritude is for an elite, because only the elite are plagued by the problem of identity. Such a poetry is only meant to be read by such people and appeal to them. It does not speak to or about the unassimilated masses, except in a romantic idealistic way. But in the Caribbean and the United States I can see how relevant such poetry is even for the masses. Because, especially in the U.S., the Negro is in a state of siege culturally. He has to locate himself as a Negro with a double commitment: to share in the life of the Americans as a whole, and to assert his cultural importance, so that he is not integrated into the white culture on the white man's terms.

As we find ourselves eventually talking about commitment, Leon Trotsky's incisive and perceptive remarks in his *Literature and Revolution* come to mind:

> Our Marxist conception of the objective social dependence and social utility of art, when translated into the language of politics, does not at all mean a desire to dominate art by means of decrees and orders.
> It is not true that we regard only that art as new and revolutionary which speaks of the worker, and it is nonsense to say that we demand that the poets should describe inevitably a factory

chimney, or the uprising against capital! Of course the new art cannot but place the struggle of the proletariat in the centre of its attention. But the plough of the new art is not limited to numbered strips. On the contrary, it must plough the entire field in all directions. Personal lyrics of the very smallest scope have an absolute right to exist within the new art. Moreover, the new man cannot be formed without a new lyric poetry. But to create it, the poet himself must feel the world in a new way ... No one is going to prescribe themes to a poet or intends to prescribe them. Please write about anything you can think of! The form of art is, to a certain and a very large degree, independent, but the artist who creates this form, and the spectator who is enjoying it, are not empty machines, one for creating form and the other for appreciating it. They are living people, with a crystallized psychology representing a certain unity, even if it is not entirely harmonious. This psychology is the result of social conditions.
The creation and perception of art forms is one of the functions of this psychology ...

The proletarist has to have in art the expression of the new spiritual point of view which is just beginning to be formulated within him, and to which art must help him give form. This is not a state of order, but an historic necessity. You cannot pass this by, nor escape its force.

I should like to think that African negritude propaganda, even in its limited framework and with its special audience, has at least prompted, in a social context, those who need it to search for a new spiritual point of view which we need to give artistic expression while at the same time we strive to explore the human situation in general. Black pride need not blind us to our own weaknesses: in fact it should help us to perceive our weaknesses. Also, I do not care for black pride that drugs us into a condition of stupor or inertia. I do not care for it if leaders use it to dupe the masses so that they forget to clamour for the bread and decent shelter and education they have a right to.

Can the major concerns of Africa merge at any point with the universal major concerns like war, poverty, fascism, the insolence of power etc.? Must they indeed merge? It is quite obvious now that the African writer (even outside South Africa) has arrived at the 'threshold of pain' where he can already begin to feel the muscle of political authority in his own country. And so the Russians and the South Africans are not alone. I hate to think that one of these days we are going to sink to the degenerate level of Afrikaans writers in South Africa who have always censored themselves and not dared to challenge the government, because it has Calvinist Boer origins, like themselves, because they are all of a tribe.

What Trotsky has to say about the Russian situation has relevance to Africa, although things in his country are not what he had hoped for. The Russian proletariat would be a parallel of our illiterates and semi-literates, urban or rural. Russian proletarian poets could be paralleled by our new intelligentsia writing today, using the language and craft of the former colonial power. Trotsky says that the proletarian poets used versification as a means of complaining of one's sad fate, or expressing revolutionary passion. During the revolution they wrote to a march, which was quite simple. After the tension of the civil war, these poets had to approach poetry as an art and as a craft. But they did not have the background of the bourgeois intelligentsia who had appropriated literature and created a tradition in it. The proletarian poets were not artistically prepared. Their poems still read like revolutionary documents. When they were faced with the problems of craftsmanship and art, they began to seek for themselves a new environment. 'It does not look as if the present groups of worker poets are destined to lay immutable foundations for a new great poetry. Maybe distant generations, yes. For there will be plenty of ideologic and cultural deviations, waverings and errores for a long time to come!' This is Trotsky's assessment.

I cannot agree with Trotsky's prescription that the new art should be incompatible with pessimism and 'all other forms of spiritual collapse'. Also, I am not sure how, if we must, we can make our art 'virtually collectivist'. What we do know is that we have not yet adopted a view of the world as we see it in Kafka, which the Marxist critic Georg Lukacs despairingly refers to as being 'from the perspective of a trapped and struggling fly'. 'This experience,' he adds, 'this vision of a world dominated by angst and of man at the mercy of incomprehensible terrors, makes Kafka's work the very type of modernist art . . . Kafka's angst is the experience par excellence of modernism' (vide *The Meaning of Contemporary Realism*). No black hero in Negro-African fiction is stricken with *angst* which makes him dash about like a trapped fly. Perhaps he is the typical hero of Western literature, perhaps he is the supreme example of modern man as modern literature sees him, because the Western world today is a disintegrated because differentiated one. So it produces disintegrated personalities. We have not yet created societies like this in Africa, and the heroes of our fiction cannot yet be seen as possessing what one may call the intensive 'other individuality' of a Kafka or Camus hero. The African hero is still very much part of a communal world. I can't even be sure that we shall stay out of Kafka's and Camus's world for all time. I am inclined to stake a lot on the dialogue that is continuing between the stream of modern life in Africa and the stream of its *living* traditions. Each is informing and criticising the other, and this dialogue may yet determine the idioms of the literature to come. At the moment our literature in the European languages is of a frontier kind. We are pioneers at the frontier, seeking a definition of ourselves and the past from which we have come. The frontier lies between us and the white man's technology, religion, mores, economics. We try to address him and ourselves at the same time.

All the same I go along with the rest of Trotsky's thesis. I think we need to think seriously about what he has to say about culture also. In traditional society where culture is a process of growing up and is not a thing separate from human activity in general, comfort and abundance would not be necessary for the growth of culture. But we have poverty and illiteracy, wealth and literacy are unequally distributed. So Trotsky's formula for the Russians may very well be ours as well. He wrote in 1924:

> Culture feeds on the sap of economics, and a material surplus is necessary, so that culture may grow, develop and become subtle. Bourgeoisie laid its hand on literature, and did this very quickly at the time when it was growing rich. The proletariat will be able to prepare for a new socialist culture and literature, not by laboratory method on the basis of present-day poverty, want and illiteracy, but by large economic and cultural means. Art needs comfort, even abundance. Furnaces have to be hotter, wheels have to move faster, looms have to turn more quickly, schools have to work better.

Bibliography

I am indebted to the following sources among others:

LEON TROTSKY, *Literature & Revolution*, Ann Arbor, Paperbacks, University of Michigan Press.

GEORGE LUKACS, *The Meaning of Contemporary Realism*, Merlin Press, London.

G. V. PLEKHANOV, *Art and Social Life*, Lawrence Wishart, London.

JOHN MANDER, *The Writer and Commitment*, Secker and Warburg, London.

Part 1

The Oral Traditions

Ewe Poetry

GEORMBEEYI ADALI-MORTTY

The Ewe country makes exacting demands on its people. From the sweat of their brows, the Ewes eke out their bare livelihood. Their part of the country has no gold and diamonds and timber as have some parts of Ghana.

But the people have an extraordinary gift for music and drumming and dancing. How, otherwise, could the people of Eweland have maintained such good humour and optimism in the face of hardship?

The poems which follow are words of folk songs. Not mummified folk songs dug out from an archaeological pile; but living songs which, like farmers of old, the farmers of today are singing at work, as they clear the bush, plant the crops and harvest them; while they weave the cloths they wear, carve the stools they sit on or build the houses they live in.

They are above all songs which are sung to honour a departed one, and to mourn his loss.

When were they composed, these songs? And who composed them? No one knows. What is known is that they are almost as old as the Ewe people themselves. Containing some of the richest literary pieces in the Ewe language, the songs are highly charged with emotion and, in Shakespeare's words, with 'wise saws and modern instances'. And the thoughts are condensed in terse language, making their translation into English a hazardous venture!

The choruses have a definite, recognisable pattern; but the solos are such that there is wide room for creative improvisation.

> Nye m'be drɔ̃ kum mele ɖee,
> Drɔ̃ʃenyawo ɖia de kodzogbe   (bis)
>   Atamgbaɖee Drɔ̃ʃenu:
>   'Drɔ̃ʃenya metsia 'me si o.
> Adze ɖaa wole!'
> Nenye drɔ̃ʃenyawo ɖeɖe e,
>   Ne menya ahaliʃenyawo vɔ!
> Nye m'be drɔ̃ kum mele ɖee,
> Drɔ̃ʃenyawo ɖia ɖe kodzogbe . . .

This is a poem in classic Ewe. I shall try to give its approximate meaning: I can do no more, and can merely suggest the atmosphere and the background without which even an Ewe, well versed in the language, would miss the meaning.

3

Here it is:

> Methinks it's been a dream;
> But the dream has come to life!
> Atangba's son, Drofenu, says:
>> Believe them not:
>> A dream's a dream.
>>> No more!
> Truly, had dreams been real,
> Death, I'd have fathomed death.

A study of Ewe traditional songs is a study of the philosophy of life, and of the values of the Ewe people. Above all, it is a study in sweet sorrow. Underlying rural life is a vague, all-pervasive sadness. The fields may laugh in the rain and the sunshine, but they adjoin the brooding woods and hills. The birds twitter with glee on the treetops, but below them the moody four-footed animals prowl in dread through the thickets. To man and animal alike there is the haunting uncertainty of the day to come; the fear of the future; the sudden disaster; the caprices of the weather; the deep mystery of natural phenomena—all this finds an echo in the songs.

Here is a poem which exemplifies what I mean. It tells the story of a man who has lost his relatives through death. He alone of the clan is left behind. He bemoans his fate. But behind his moaning lies stoical strength and fortitude.

> Ame vɔvɔe botoe mexe - e.
>> Nasi agble botoe ne mevu lo!
>> Yã mewua 'me, dzi gakua 'me o!
>>> Yã wu amea ɖewo vi
>>> Dzi le wokuu dzi.
>>> Hlɔ̃vɔvɔɛ dzunamelawo,
>>>> Mibia miaƒe agbediƒiawo sea?

Chorus: Ne medo wome asi mɔ nu ɖe,
Dze maku, mayɔwo ɖe?

> Last remaining, last to go:
> A border mark I stand.
> Were I a boundary post
> On the farm's edge,
> I'd heave myself
> Aside and free me.
> What can't be cursed must be endured.
> Some folk unwisely fret
> Under ills they can't prevent.
> You who mock my loss of kin,
> Know you the will of Fate?

If you could follow the Ewe version you would notice a good deal of sophistication in the use of rhythm and rhyme, metre and stress.

The following song is about a certain man who has learnt, perhaps too late, that a brother is like an animal trap—one of those traps like a tilted raft which fall upon any beast that strays beneath them. You cannot stand in the distance and know the real condition of a trap. How do you know that its lever has not become entangled? Seen from afar, the trap, now defective, might appear to be in good order. In human terms, a brother is much too dear to be kept at a distance. You can only know the real needs of a person by living intimately with him. It may be too late to help a distant brother.

Here are the exact words:

Amenɔvi azã ye:
Womenɔa adzɔge
    Henɔa ekpɔ o lo.
        Wolegbe tse eda xixa,
        Ayrumawo!

The next song is an allegory told around the figure of an army of driver ants. We all know that few animals, snakes included, can fall among driver ants and survive the experience, so destructive are these creatures.

The song tells of a person who, having the misfortune of finding his way into an army of driver ants, gets bitten by a snake—the least likely company in which to encounter a snake!

Medɔ alɔ̃lɔ̃wo me xe da ɖum lo!
Womedɔa alɔ̃lɔ̃wo me da gaɖua 'me o.
    Nye ya medɔ alɔ̃lɔ̃wo me xe da ɖum,
    'Lee mawɔe o, naviwo.
        Mm-m-m.

The next poem is 'Adzia tso-tɔ-ɖo mewɔa lã o'. The child who is brought up under a father's supervision has no cause to grow to be a fool. 'Why,' enquires the songster, 'not being orphans, why do some folk behave so foolishly?' The actual words are:

Adzia tso-tɔ-ɖo mewɔa lã o!
Tse ta 'me 'ɖewo tso tɔ ɖo. tso nɔ ɖo
    Kafe gale lã wɔɔ le dza'
        Nye, Patipre-nɔvi gototro anumnyam'
Yã gbã ye: ame 'ɖewo tso tɔ ɖo, tso nɔ ɖo
Kafe gale lã wɔɔ, koiba lo!   Aã-aa!
Naviwo, milɔ̃e nam dzro'   Aã-aa!
Hexowo gbɔa lo!   Aã-aa!

In traditional folk songs the words are given prominence over the sound. Though the melody may be charming, it is kept very simple. The sound gives colour and depth to the words. The sound embellishes the ideas, and gives them a pleasing background.

5

In the following song you will notice a shift of emphasis. The rhythm has become more definite and more pronounced. It is a song which compels the accompaniment of a drum. The very words themselves are clearly emphatic:

> Ati tɔ hexoawo ʃʼaɖe.
> Miyɔ ha yeyewo neva . . .

> A stick has pricked the tongue of the
> celebrated singers.
> Call forth younger singers to sing us new songs!

I am not able to analyse the form of these poems in terms of Western poetry. Yet they certainly have form; they adhere to certain conventional patterns. And yet these songs are not sung exclusively by specially endowed and trained people. Everybody joins in the refrain. It is a complex art practised and enjoyed by ordinary people.

Pleasing language, worth-while ideas, balance of arrangement, measured form—these then are the qualities we find in the poems. The songsters of our 'rude forefathers' knew how to choose the colourful, the rich, the refined word and phrase, and to place them in juxtaposition so that the final product is genuine poetry.

It is true that a string of words can be poetical without having much to say: like traditional cradle songs and nursery rhymes—both of which abound in our various communities in West Africa. But our ancestors who composed and sang funeral, farming and hunting songs were concerned with the deepest things in life—the profound feelings which moved them. All around them was a wealth of material—life as they led it, death, the cycles of the farm year, animals and trees, the supernatural agencies, love and hate, kindness and cruelty. The allusions and imagery of the poems were drawn from this rich environment and from the social background of the people.

These poems can be sung only on the appropriate occasion. One does not sing a mourning song unless a death has actually occurred. Even to sing a farming song at home in the village, or to sing a hunting song without a cause, one has to apologise first to the gods. It is sacrilegious to sing these when feelings have not been aroused or when it is not intended to arouse feelings.

Whatever differences we may find between these poems and Western poetry, one unmistakable quality links them together—beauty of language and discipline of form, and the combination of these in such a way that they are capable of evoking emotion.

Let us analyse some of these poems:

1	Dzodzo 'ʋãlã nye tu ɖee	a
2	Afɔ mato yi ʋua dzi ɖee?	a
3	Amenɔvi-ŋutsu, glimetie:	a
4	Ne mele asiwò o	b

5	Gliwò mũ lo!	b
6	Amenɔvi-nyɔnu, aɖadzaɖoe ye	a
7	Ne mele asiwò o	b
8	Avuvɔ wɔ wò kpoo.	b
9	Tɔkɔ mele ŋunye o;	b
10	Nɔkɔ mele ŋunye o	b
11	Mee madó nyanyeawo na o?	b
12	Navie!	a

Where did the accents fall? As in most of our traditional music, the tune is complex double time. Some of the beats have one, some have two and some have three syllabic units. But, in Ewe, the units as such are of equal accentuation. Therefore, the English accented and unaccented syllable pattern does not apply. Neither does the metrical arrangement depend on a regular form of high-and-low sounds. The rhythm of the spoken piece, spoken in the dialect of the locality from which the song derives, is as follows:

Lines 6 to 8 repeat lines 3 to 4 with a minor variation in 8.

The tempo then slows down considerably, and the metrical pattern changes to:

Tɔkɔ mele ŋunye o
Nɔkɔ mele ŋunye o

7

The rhythm of the last line, slower still, is a pathetic symbol of resignation: 'Mee madó nyanyeawo na o!'—'In whom shall I confide?'

The rhyming pattern is: a a a b b b a b b b b b a. The sound 'o', as an ending to the lines, predominates. Nor is this its only rôle. 'Os' are to be heard in every line. Has this any significance to the theme of the poem? Turn to the English version for a moment:

1 My wings are plucked; woe's the day
2 Shall I ascend the tree by foot?
3 A buttress—that's a mother's son:
4 If you haven't it,
5 Down falls your house.
6 All-purpose cloth, a mother's daughter is.
7 If you haven't it,
8 You're cold-exposed.
9 Relations on the father's side,
10 Relations on the mother's side,
11 None. In whom shall I confide?
12 Oh, brother!

A song of lament. Here is a lonely soul, without relations on the mother's or on the father's side. Can you imagine a calamity graver than that in a traditional African community? The song mourns this fact. And the one sound that predominates over all others in vocal mourning in Eweland is 'o'.

Note how the ideas have been arranged in pairs: 3 and 6, 4/5 and 7/8, 9 and 10. Also the rapid succession of metaphors: the 'wing', the 'buttress' (no doubt of a mud wall), the all-purpose (loin) cloth—all these are likened to the rôle a brother or a sister plays in one's life.

We shall next analyse another piece, one of the most touching poems of lament that I know.

Na ye e e!
 Na mumũa na 'mela
 Ɖaɖa na 'mela
Na mlenuɖee
Na yɔ mele!
 Azi favi megbea na yɔɔ o.
 Mele na yɔɔ metɔa nam o.
 Dzre wɔɔ mîle dzã?

Mother dear!
Mother, who freely gives of what she has:
 fresh food and cooked meals alike.
Mother, who never deserts the hearth,
Mother, hearken to me!
The crying child will call after its mother.
How is it that mother does not answer me when I call?
Are we quarrelling?

Pathos is engendered by use of 'Na' (Mother) in all but the third and last lines, which evokes the idea of a helpless child, yearning for its mother. More than any other of these poems, the rhythm of this one is so varied from line to line that it conveys a jagged impression. It seems that the anonymous bard made the rhythm deliberately uneven in order to emphasise the gasping, choking wail of a person bereaved; and yet the rhymes of the couplets serve to bind the irregular rhythm together.

A mother is here presented to us as the Giver. She is mirrored as sharing food in the farmstead, in the hut back home and then we are made to picture her in the kitchen.

This is done by a highly compressed use of language:

> *mumuanamela*—a giver of the food that can be eaten raw;
> *dadanamela* —a giver of the cooked food;
> *mlenudee*   —one who sits by the cooking stove.

In contrast with these images of a living mother is that of a mother present but unseeing, unhearing, unheeding. 'Are we quarrelling?' the singer asks the corpse. The superb touch of a skilful composer lies in the manner in which all this is subtly conveyed—'I'm calling mother! She heeds me not!' And then the simple heart-breaking line: 'Are we quarrelling?'

Let's take another look at the first poem quoted, which also illustrates this condensation of thought and expression.

'Methinks it's been a dream . . .' That's to say, what was feared has come to be; that which was merely imagined has turned out to be a reality; the news I hoped would prove untrue is a fact, alas! Like many poems of this nature, the various concepts and metaphors are not given a chance to fade smoothly one into the other: they are introduced, as it were, in flashes, in clearly defined abruptness, in sharp contrasts. The flight of thought and emotion is expressed by these sudden alternations of metaphorical *motifs*.

In this poem, however, the metaphor of a dream theme has been sustained throughout, broken by the conflict between what is generally believed: *dreams are a fantasy*; and the deviation from it: *a dream has come true*. And yet, the speaker still feels that if all he had known in dreams were the reality, he would have known all there is to know about the hereafter. The hereafter, *ahali*, has been personified in order to heighten the vividness of the conception. *Ahali* is an affectionate name for death.

Here is another poem which, while telling a story, also probes the philosophical foundations of life.

> Nye ya mezu aɖa denutɔme:
> > Menye nono ta ɖe meva o lo!
> Miatsi (miagblɔ) na naviwo be
> > Tsɛta wosea 'haha!'
> > Henoa sisii le dzã!

Miatsi na wo be
'Haha!' meɖua 'me o lo!
Nye ya mezu aɖa denutɔme
Menye nono ta ɖe meva o,
Akpiniawo!

The setting is a wooded country, watered by a stream. On the banks are a few grass plants. Imagine a grass plant bending over the water, as it flows over a river bed strewn with pebbles and stones. Momentarily, as the stem of the grass sways in the breeze, the tip of the hanging blade of grass bobs and dips in and out of the water. And, as if making sure that its intentions are not misconstrued, the grass says, 'You know full well that a plant doesn't drink through its leaves. If then my leaves should dip in the stream, know I am not selfishly assuaging my thirst. I'm only a blade of grass in a stream.'

Literally translated, the poem continues, 'Do ask my people, why it is they flee by hearing a mere 'haha' (alarm).' The onomatopoeic word 'haha!', the sound used by a person to scare another, has been used instead of a word like 'threat', 'bark', or 'intimidation'.

A blade of grass in a stream, no more;
I haven't come to drink.
From mouth to mouth pass down the word—
No need to flee at mere alarm.
Mere noise devours no one.
I'm no more than a blade of grass
A-laving in a stream, not come to drink.
Akpiniawo!

The general feature of these poems is that they are short and extremely economical in the use of words. And the words used often conjure up associations with tribal usage, history, values and physical environment. There is frequent use of quotations from celebrated minstrels and people reputed for their wisdom. Even the prattling bird Patipre's relation 'Anikagro' has been quoted. While the themes are philosophical in character, the treatment of them is rather secular—employing as they do practical situations and material objects. When reference to the spiritual world is made, the singer immediately returns to the material world.

The field from which I have drawn these songs is a deliberately limited one. The songs are those sung among the people inhabiting the valley and the plateau of the Togoland range of mountains some twenty miles in radius around my village, Gbledee, from where these collections were made. The means of travelling in this area is still by bush paths, though some of them have recently been widened to permit an occasional truck to venture over them. Only as recently as my boyhood days, these people produced most of their own food and shelter.

10

The wealth of our past in song and dance and customary usage has not yet been lost entirely. But time is running out, both in my country and in the other West African societies. There is much left which we can still retrieve, if we tackle now the job of study and research and collection. There are many precious pieces in folk tales, there are madrigals, songs sung by children at play in the moonlit village squares, drum songs and drum language, hunters' songs, lullabies and cradle songs, songs for out-dooring a maiden, songs to illustrate stories, songs of *asafos* (youths' warrior organisations) and songs of battle, songs of challenge and of abuse, words of libation, religious prayers and songs.

It is out of these materials that modern creative writing can be built, if it is to be distinctly original and West African. There is a form of West African poetry—we must find it out.

All this confronts us with a challenge. There is, too, the challenge posed by our dependence on foreign books for our schools. Foreign books, we must read; but, to make textbooks meaningful to our children and new literates, the background must be familiar. In the matter of general litera-ture, too, we owe it to our country and to the world to make our own distinctive contribution. The task of interpreting ourselves and our culture can best be done by ourselves.

Ìjálá

The Traditional Poetry of Yoruba Hunters

ADÈBOYE BABALỌLA

Ìjálá is speech-like song which is part of the traditional oral literature of the Yoruba people. It is chanted by talented men and women at the religious social gatherings of the devotees of Ògún, the Yoruba god of war and of iron implements. So it is understandable that blacksmiths and hunters predominate among the chanters of ìjálá, but of course they are inevitably farmers also. It is for the purpose of social cheer and hilarity that the chanting is done, while palm-wine and maize beer are freely drunk by all those present. It often follows sacrifices offered to the god of war at his shrine. The women involved are wives or relatives of the men.

Other occasions of ìjálá chanting are during the periods of hard work by farmers on their farms. Ìjálá then serves the purpose of 'music-while-you-work', cheering the farmer, making him work faster and longer, and helping to make his work not a burden but a delight for him: be it the removal of weeds, the clearing of a fresh farm plot in the forest, the making of soil-mounds with the hoe, the harvesting of crops, or the tapping of the palm trees for wine.

Long narrative ìjálás are rare. At least that is so in the area of my own limited research, namely: my hometown, Ìpetumodù, and at Yábă and Igbóbì near Lagos. In Yorubaland as a whole, long narrative ìjálás may be more frequent. Most of the ìjálás that I have heard and written down merely express one odd thought after another about almost anything in the life of the Yorùbá, but especially about forest birds and animals and domestic human relations, and they may include admonitory words for correct conduct in society, character portraits (usually flattering) of friends and acquaintances, and traditional mythology.

A large number of these ìjálás seems to belong to the common oral heritage of the Yorùbá proper—those speaking the Ọ̀yọ́ dialect—though from place to place differences in their wording can be observed due to differences in local dialects. But a large number of ìjálás is composed impromptu from day to day by the talented men and women at their social gatherings, with the lavish aid of alcoholic drinks. To my surprise, one ìjálá chanter told me bluntly: 'No one can chant ìjálá commendably without drinking some wine or beer in the process.'

Ìjálás can truly be termed poetry. They are produced by a spontaneous overflow of powerful emotions—they are an expression of strong feeling from the depth of the poet's personality. Moreover, the euphony of the words of ìjálá and the associated rhythm of the chant further qualify ìjálá for citizenship in the realm of poetry.

12

I admit that I have not yet succeeded in discovering the various rhythm-patterns in *ìjálá*, but it is obvious that the rhythm is always there and to my mind it is most likely based on the tonal variations in the pitch of the vowel sounds: middle tone, high tone, low tone, and combinations of these.

It is usual for the end of one *ìjálá* which, as I have explained, is speech-like song, to be marked with a short, real-song refrain introduced by the chanter and joined in by the entire audience before the next *ìjálá* begins. It is only thus that real music is associated with *ìjálá*, and the short song may be accompanied with drumming.

These songs are usually quite short, and their subject-matter is not necessarily connected with the preceding *ìjálá*: Here are some examples, of which the first may be sung to greet the arrival of another *ìjálá* singer:

> Ọ̀hànhàn arrives from the farm of laughter.
> A jester arrives.
> Ọ̀hànhàn arrives from the farm of laughter.

> Ògún is a god.
> Anyone who knows Ògún
> Must not jest with Ògún.
> Ògún is a god.

> Come on, lead the way to your home!
> Come on, lead the way to your home!
> It's wrong to keep someone's company
> Without a visit to his home some time.
> Come on, lead the way to your home!

> Lálálákùbérú!
> Thus the Arabic Moslem prayer sounds to my ears.
> Were I a Moslem man,
> I should top my class in prayer-saying.
> Lálálákùbérú!
> Thus the Arabic Moslem prayer resounds.

> Death never makes friends with anyone
> So just go on eating anything you have.
> Death never makes friends with anyone.

To chant *ìjálá* well is a matter of natural talent, though training and practice are important. There are subtle differences between the voice tone of *ìjálá* and those of other forms of Yoruba song such as *rárà* (chants in praise of a noble citizen) *ègè* (laments for great men) *ọfọ̀* (magical incantations) *ògèdè* (a kind of *ọfọ̀*, supposed to be most efficient) *ewì ogun* (songs for the god of war) and *oríkì* (praise names). It is quite common to hear a good *ìjálá* singer say without apology that he does not have the voice for *ègè* or *ògbérè*.

Translating *ìjálá* is not an easy task. Many words used by the chanters are obsolete, and others, particularly names, are untranslatable. Take for

13

example a name like 'Alégóńgópẹtuẹ̀báọ̀nà'. This can be split up into the following components:

> *a* —a prefix meaning 'he who'
> *lé góńgó*—'crouches sportingly'
> *pẹtu* —contracted from *pa ẹtu*, 'to kill an antelope'
> *ẹ̀bá ọ̀nà* —the side of the road.

It is of course not possible to build up an English compound noun as complex as this.

A further difficulty is that it is often impossible to find the English equivalents of the names for plants and animals of the bush that abound in the hunters' poetry.

Yoruba poetry has neither rhyme nor regular metre. The 'line' of *ìjálá* poetry is the sense group and its length varies. It was therefore considered that English blank verse might be the best medium of translation. The longish sense-groups of *ìjálá* could hardly be contained in a shorter line than the decasyllable.

Kújọ̀wú and the Elephants

> Kújọ̀wú is the son of Ọ̀tẹ́rọ̀, the son of a man
> Who always puts an *ẹtu* limb among
> The offerings of his sacrifice to idol-gods.
> His wife once told him that she wished to have
> An ivory neck-chain such as all farmers' wives possessed.
> So Kújọ̀wú dipped his hands into a pot
> Of specially concocted herbs and snails,
> Several times repeatedly, to invoke
> Good luck upon himself. Then he left home,
> And quick, to hunt within the thickest jungle bounds,
> He pursued his way along footpaths,
> Chanting hunters' ballads as he went.
> News had reached his ears that the elephant
> Did sometimes have its meals at Àróòpo;
> He had also heard that in Àrôbàdàn
> The elephant was sometimes seen to feed.
> Yet he first sought the elephant with care
> At Rẹ́fúrẹ́fú, but he missed it there.
> Therefore he went next to Rẹ̀fùrẹ̀fù;
> But even there he missed the elephant.
> Then he shifted ground and went far away
> Till he reached Àróòpo at which place
> He found two elephants both eating leaves
> Of *mọ̀dúmọ̀du* trees.
> At once the elder of the elephants

14

Called Kújọ̀wú by his name,
Kújọ̀wú the son
Of Arápáẹranṣèkúnlẹ̀ Ọya.
And then it bade him seek no elephant,
Reminding him that elephants were called
Láyíko Ọ̀rọ̀kúlábẹ̀bẹ̀jà;
Ọ̀rọ̀ṣẹ́giwówòwógbẹ̀gilọ.
Kújọ̀wú replied that he would not desist
From hunting them; that if they rushed on him
Within the forest heart, he would flee from them
By being metamorphosed into a tree.
If they pursued him to savannaland,
He would become a tall grassplant and so escape.
And if they chased him to an anthill land,
He would become a chief among the ants.
The elephants then warned Kújọ̀wú repeatedly.
They spoke and spoke but Kújọ̀wú did not leave.
He stood there still and presently he said:
'As the gourd we eat shoots forth many creepers
But instead of wagging them aggressively
It keeps them very passive on the ground,
And as the tẹ̀tẹ̀ vegetable-shoots,
When longest, trail themselves upon the soil,
And also as a young boy fails to root
Efficiently from earth in garden-plots
Many weeds that are by name ọ̀ṣẹ́pòtu,
So may you elephants feel incapable
As you try to injure me, and so may you
Be made inactive by my spell.'
The elephants now changed themselves to baobab-trees,
And in despair Kújọ̀wú went back home.
There he quickly summoned all his wives to him
And charged them with the sin of adultery
Committed while he was away from home.
His first-wed wife then said
She knew the charge was cruel and wholly false.
She would divorce Kújọ̀wú and go elsewhere,
Especially as up till then she had
Not the ivory neck-chain that she ought to have
Being, as she was, a hunter's first-wed wife.
So Kújọ̀wú dipped his hands two times again
Into the pot of choice decocted drug,
And at once went back to see the elephants.
Again the beasts forbade him to draw near,
Re-telling him their attributive names:
'Erin Láíko Ọ̀rọ̀kúlábẹ̀bẹ̀jà'.

And instantly the senior elephant
Made three high heaps of earth,
And told Kújọ̀wú, 'Don't dare to climb on these!'
Kújọ̀wú replied by climbing on the first.
At this the beast spoke with a human voice,
'Though you have dared to climb on that first heap,
Be not so bold to climb the second one.'
Yet Kújọ̀wú once more disobeyed the beast.
So for the third time the elephant gave
Decree: 'Kújọ̀wú, if you dare to climb
And cross my third heap, I will strangle you.'
Then Kújọ̀wú scaled the third.
Immediately, the elephant, enraged,
Caught hold of him with its powerful trunk,
And Kújọ̀wú sang to it a pleading song:
'Erin Láíko, I now submit to you,
Let mercy carry me to town,
And not to your retreats in forest bowers.
This is my humble plea because I want
My wives to know my present wretched plight.'
To this the elephant replied in song:
'The Elephant is climbing Àlọ̀ Hill,
And as he walks on, he will snort at will.
The Elephant is climbing Àlọ̀ Hill.'
So to the Lion's house the elephant
Soon brought Kújọ̀wú for penalty deserved,
Before the Lion, king of all the beasts.
The King told Kújọ̀wú to stand on guard
Before the main gate of his palace-wall.
There Kújọ̀wú is still alive today,
A guard on duty at the Lion's gate,
Wearing a scarlet cloth as his official dress.
This Kújọ̀wú, it is believed by all, was born
At Àgọ́-Òwu in Ìkirè Town.

Mystery at Ẹ̀rìn

Of Ẹ̀rìn in Moje district I sing;
Of a giant tree, very tall and large,
Which crashed and blocked a salient footpath at Ẹ̀rìn,
And so prevented the slaves of Ẹlẹ́rìn,
The king of Ẹ̀rìn, from going to work on his farm.
It also confined his sons and daughters
To the town, making it impossible
For them to go and play on the demesne.

One day, one of the Councillors disdained the tree
As soon as he saw it, and he declared,
'I will go home and fetch my wonder-working axe,
And with it I will return immediately
To make a useful tunnel-road straight through the tree.'
With arrogance unparalleled he spoke.
And as if to humble him, this great tree,
Before the man returned, transformed itself
Into a long, colossal tree of brass,
An *agogo* tree having round its stem
Sixteen thick creepers tightly interlaced.
(In case you think that this is not authentic,
Ask about it from anyone you see,
From anyone you come across at Èrìn,
And I am sure that he will bear me out.)
In their perplexity, the people of Èrìn,
With reverent homage and appropriate rites
Invoked their gods—all twenty minus four
Near that mysterious tree, beseeching each
To cut it up and clear it off for them.
Of these Powers-that-be, the first fifteen did not succeed.
It was the sixteenth god who did the trick.
Thus came the various gods and goddesses:
Olúfọ́n reached there first, but, alas, he failed.
Erinlẹ̀ reached there next, but, alas, he failed,
Ògìyán reached there next, but, alas, he failed,
Ọ̃ṣà Ọṣun reached there next, but, alas, she failed,
Ọ̃ṣà Òbé reached there next, but, alas, he failed,
Ọ̃ṣà Ọya reached there next, but, alas, she failed,
Ọ̃ṣà Ṣàngó reached there next, but, alas, he failed,
Oníkónkótó next came, but, alas, he failed,
Òrìṣà Òkè next came, but, alas, he failed,
Àgbọ̀nnà next came, but, alas, he failed,
Òrìṣà Ògún next came, but, alas, he failed,
Ọsányìn was the helpful god that day—
Ọsányìn the one-legged, man-like god.
In token of their gratitude to him,
The King, Councillors, and People of Èrìn
Presented to Ọsányìn two hundred slaves,
Two hundred children, two hundred women,
And two hundred men; also two hundred snails,
Two hundred tortoises, two hundred goats,
Two hundred sheep, and two hundred chickens.
To their benefactor all these they gave.
And so Ọsányìn became a very wealthy god.

The Elephant

About the elephant of whom you speak,
Please forgive my interposing a few words.
The elephant is, undoubtedly, not
Quite like what you have made him out to be.
Ah! the elephant whom we also call
Oríríbobo Orìrìbobo,
Orìrífǫwǫ́mǫ́wèwájúwe;
The elephant whom man respects perforce,
And points towards with all his fingers ten.
Just as builders roof a house but not its yard,
So hunters treat the elephant in manner
Different from that they use for other animals,
The elephant to whom we also give
These attributes: Erin Gbágbálóro
Abìrìntìkò, in acknowledgment
Of his royal gait, grave, erect, and slow.
The elephant who has white arrows of bone
For teeth; the husband of Àbádàtù—
Half a word is sufficient for the wise!
Now, please sing the chorus of this song with me.
'Not yet enough' are the choral words.

Solo	Chorus
My abuse of you will soon be enough.	Not yet enough.
Mucous are your nostrils, like an old man's.	Not yet enough.
Two large wallets of flesh hang from your neck.	Not yet enough.
Because you eat broad beans voraciously	Not yet enough.
Your cheeks are distended laterally,	Not yet enough.
Very much like those of the big bush rat.	Not yet enough.
My abuse of you will soon be enough.	Not yet enough.

It was not I who made this dainty song.
It was my friend, Ògúnrìndé of Ǫwènà,
The son of Jǫ́síre, who taught me that
I should never work too long on the farm
Since I am not a slave; nor should I there
On any day do only such work
As would make me get back to town too soon,
For I am not of sluggard parentage.
Instead, I should daily return from farm to town
Just at a decent time in the evening.
He also taught me saying, 'My friend, please note
Whenever you are going with me, your halting friend,
Along a forest trail or a bush path,
Walk neither before me nor behind me,
For it's unwise to walk immediately

Following or preceding a lame-footed man.
If you precede him, you thereby tempt him
To imitate wood-peckers and peck you,
And if you dog him, you thereby tempt him
To fall backwards on you, in languishment.
Therefore you must see to it that you're not
Closely before or behind a halting man.
If you have to walk in such a man's company,
Closely walk abreast with him by his side.'
And, now, may I finish with another song?
 'You girl, who say I've stayed too long from town,
 Know that your cheeks are rough like dry bean-cakes.'

He Says it is All Right

He says it is all right, it's surely right;
For the foolish man does not mind at all
Receiving as a gift things which have been
Already placed as sacrificial dues,
Sprinkled with palm oil in bowls of calabash,
Deposited for gods at a crossroads
Or before a boulder-altar in the streets.

The courage of a boy is never such
As to embolden him to meet the god of fate.
Neither is any boy ever so bold
As a man who fearlessly takes and eats
Any good food that he finds left as sacrifice
By the highway side; and yet such a man
Is far less daring than Èṣù is.

Oh! Look there! The masquerader Òlóló
Is returning to his vestry in his shrine,
Òlóló Agbágòoyè, the masquerader
Who parades the streets at the ceremony
Of installation for a new town chief.
The truncheon that he bears is made from *ẹdun* wood,
Ẹdun, that tree which grows so very high
In its old age, and whose wood has been nicknamed
'Baba Mobòomi' which, interpreted, means
'The Father of all sinkers.'

A song which is now in vogue throughout our town
Has words of timely warning for all thieves:
'You have burgled first a Christian's home,
And, next, you have robbed a hunter's home,

Unless you now reform, you will soon fall
Into that temptation which will be your death—
Attempts to steal even from the god of fate himself.'

If perchance you wish to know how best to make
A hunter give some of his kill to you,
You will do well to learn these words of mine,
With which I greet my hunter friend, Òjó,
Father to Ìlọrí, whene'er I see him go
A-hunting in the forest anywhere:
'Bí ẹ bá mbọ̀, ẹ ṣe mi 're,
Bàbá 'Lọrí t'ó pẹ́sẹ̀ òyà bí ẹni pẹ́sẹ̀ àgbàdo.'
That is a plea that he be kind to me
On his returning from successful hunt,
But notice that I also give him praise
For the diligence with which he pursues
The tracks of beasts for game, walking as slowly
As one would walk in furrows on a farm
While planting maize at the rainy season's start.
And notice too that I delight his heart
By addressing him as 'Father to Ìlọrí'.

Will you agree with me in this belief
That, by and large, our present reigning king
Is indeed a sovereign wise, good and firm?
Witness in particular the pleasing fact
That in his reign our harvests have been large,
And almost all of us have had prosperity
So that we've built more houses in the town
And our comforts have been growing gradually;
And we have made, at his command, good streets
Which beautify the town; and, moreover,
By his decree, old dunghills have become
Market sites, better assets to our town.

On the motor-road which leads to Ìbàdàn,
A gang of highwaymen, 'The sons of Ọ̀tẹ̀tẹ̀',
Are certainly bedevilled human beings;
Just yesterday they were arraigned in court
For their sixth charge, but, as before, they won.

One day, on my way to Ilé-Ifẹ̀,
Ifẹ̀ Oǹdáiyé, that ancient town so named
Because the earliest settlers there belonged
To one single family inhabiting
Only one compound, which has, as it were,
Since then expanded and formed the present town,
And because, as many current legends say,

The first man-and-wife were made there by God—
As I was saying on my way to Ilé 'fè
En route to Àjĕ, where my wife's relations live,
(Àjĕ, a district of tall oil-palms
Totalling twenty thousand at the least—
But, alas, in any harvest season,
Only half of them bear fruit satisfactorily)—
As I was going, I overtook a group
Of merry people who were also walking
To Àjĕ and at their request I joined them.
Soon, to my surprise, they burst out singing
As follows:
'Our home is at Àjĕ,
And since it's wrong for us to walk with you
Without your having told us where your own home is,
We now ask you, "Where is your own home, friend?"
Our home is at Àjĕ.'

Have you heard the news that in Ìrèsà
The average housewife seldom stays at home
During the day, and so evades the work
Of cooking lunch for her husband and her lord,
If he is then in town, doing no farm-work,
But doing some other work or doing none at all?
The excuses that she gives are multiform—
Reasons honourable! A hundred and one!
'Today, I'll make palm oil from oil-palm fruits,
Tomorrow, I shall wash the palm-fruits' peels.
Today, I'll collect newly ripened oil-palm fruits,
And tomorrow is my day for cracking nuts
To get the kernels from the palm-fruits' seeds.'

You must know, if you don't already know,
Of my friend Onírèsé Ajíṣọlá,
The son of Awòìrà and Kéléògún,
For he's a man of copious generosity.
Whenever I am passing through his town.
Pursuing my way to my Ìrèsà home,
I cannot but call upon him at his house
To enjoy his bounteous hospitality,
And so my strength recoup and spirits raise
To undertake most happily the rest
Of that long walk from here to Ìrèsà,
Ìrèsà, a town founded by a prince who was
By name Ọmọ-Ọba Agúdúlépo—
Bĕmoroọ̀mìnìjoyè Arèsà,
Whose first offspring was dark in complexion,

But whose second son was light-yellow-skinned,
And who attributed this discrepancy
To the ill-health of his first-born, in infancy,
Which he considered due to the darkness
Of the infant's skin, and therefore he desired
That his next child should have an orange hue
To guarantee good health for it continuously.

Akan Poetry

KWABENA NKETIA

The development of the poetic tradition of the Akan people appears to have followed four distinct courses, each one giving rise to a distinctive style of arrangement or delivery.

Spoken Poetry

First there is tradition of poetry which is recited and not sung. The greatest use of this is in connection with chiefship. At state functions special poems of praise are recited by minstrels who also act as masters of ceremonies to paramount chiefs. In these poems allusions are made to past successes in war, particularly the decapitations of enemy chiefs and potentates in which these masters of ceremonies are interested as state executioners. They are intended to remind the chief of his former enemies or the enemies of his predecessors, to remind him of his power as war leader, and to incite him to similar deeds of bravery.

> The chief is one who has an oath that should not be taken lightly.
> He is one who hates to see an enemy return victorious.
> He delivers old and young from the ravages of war.
> He is one of whom armies of enemies get tired.
> He is bullet-proof: when you fire at him, you waste your ammunition.
> He is so powerful as to be able to bring the divinations of priests to naught.
> He catches priests and snatches their bells from them.
> He cannot be caught and decapitated at the battle front.
> He is like the tough trees, as well as the old, wet, half-dead tree, neither of which can be cut.

The delivery of the poems is very dramatic and expressive. There may be an introductory exclamatory lead: 'He is the one' (*ono no*), or a simple interjection for calling attention: *odee e!*

Where the poem begins with a name or appellation it may be followed by a prolonged exclamation on the particle of address—*ee*. This opening may be repeated.

The rest of the poem follows straight on in short or long utterances, some of which are dramatically hurried or spoken very deliberately according to the dramatic effect required. The person reciting the poem half covers his mouth with his left hand as he points the sword in his right hand to the chief in front of whom he stands. This heightens the dramatic effect.

The actual patterns of the poem may be in the form of cumulative utterances or a dialogue.

23

He is the one!
O father wake up.
What is it, my child?
It is the Toucans crying.
Really!
You are good boy to mistake the horns of
    Amaniampong for the crying of Toucans.
Don't be too quick to shoot at a great man.
Before you can fire, he snatches your powder.
He says: Help! Help!
He says: Akosua, Adwoa!
    Quick, get me my torch.
What is it, she asks?
He replies, Is it not what happened the other day
    that has happened one more?
Again? This child is really a child!
When I was a mighty one, I could not overthrow him.
The mighty one could not overthrow him.
The entangling one could not overthrow him.
Aku that eats the snails of little children.

When each such poem is being recited, there is always a tense atmosphere which is relieved at the end of each poem by drums and horns which play an interlude while the minstrels get ready to recite the next.

Recitative

The second tradition is that of verse which is half spoken and half sung—the recitative style used in dirges and the poetry of hunters' celebrations.

In dirges and in the elegies of court minstrels (*Kwadwomfoo*) a number of references are made which are grouped around a few themes: the theme of the Ancestor, the theme of the deceased or any particular individual, the theme of place of domicile. To these are added a number of reflections and messages such as the following:

What were your wares that they are sold out so quickly?
This death has taken me by surprise.
When father meets me, he will hardly recognise me,
For he will meet me carrying all I have:
A torn sleeping mat and a horde of flies.

The interesting thing about the dirge is that there is a set of poems suitable for every Akan person according to his clan or immediate kinship affiliations or the name he bears which in the past indicated his *Ntoro*. For example, Boakye, Boahene, Dua would be Bosompra group, while Apea, Apea Kusi would be Bosomtwe. Another example may be of interest.

24

This poem emphasises the theme of The Ancestor:

> Grandsire Opon Sasraku,
> I ask you to help me in clearing the forest to make a farm.
> Then I ask you to help me in felling the trees on the farm.
> Then I ask you to help me in making mounds for the yam seeds.
> But for harvesting the yams, I do not need your help.
> Your subjects, male and female alike, are terrible suckers.
> Opon's grandchild who hails from Danyase and drinks Tefufu and
> Akonoma.

The recitatives of hunters' celebrations are partly dirge-like and partly heroic, for the celebrations usually take place in connection with the funerals of elephant hunters, or on occasions when hunters succeed in killing elephants. The delivery is usually fast, the emphasis being on the continual flow of utterances which need not be linked by any apparent intellectual thread, but which are united by their cumulative emotional effect. The recitative ends with a little refrain which is taken at a much slower pace. The sequence of utterances may be simple or they may be in the form of a dialogue.

> Father has asked me to come with him:
> Grandfather, please, arm me.
> Grandfather has asked me to come with him:
> Father, please, arm me.
> Little wise one, what are you doing
>   up on the roof tumbling things down?
> I am looking for salt and pepper.[1]
> Whatever for?
> To win honour.
> It is for winning honour that one takes salt and pepper.
> Gyaakyeamo![2] I am calling Kwasi Febriri Kae.
> Dependable, I shall accompany him,
> Yentemadu[2] is his name.
>   Hail him.
>   One who says and does it,
>   It is father.

Lyric Poetry

Most of Akan poetry is in the lyric tradition: the use of the song as a vehicle for poetry. Some songs are fragmentary though sometimes such fragments are terse and poetically interesting. It is difficult to translate them briefly so as to convey their implications. Here is an example:

[1] i.e. The commodities which a hunter requires while living away in the forest.
[2] Strong name of the hunter Kwasi Febrisi Kae. For the relevance of such names see NKETIA, J. H. K.: 'Funeral Dirges of the Akan People', Achimota, 1955, pp. 30–33.

What good is the woodpecker to be used in the soup?
A great bird has been left behind on the other side of the river.
Wayside palm tree, I have grown a multitude of branches.
Who will reap my nuts when I am dead and gone?
Little beetle,
My head has no thinking-cap.
I have searched for one, but without avail.

The structure of lyric poems is greatly influenced by the musical requirements. Songs performed by individuals tend to have a sustained verse form with the minimum of repetitions, whereas those sung by solo and chorus tend to have some phrases repeated over and over again.

In general the sequences of 'utterances' closely follow the musical phrases. In some songs this is regular; in others, however, phrases of unequal lengths are used.

Examples of the poems in this tradition will be selected from various lyric types.

SONGS OF PRAYER, EXHILARATION AND INCITEMENT

The lyrics in this group are performed by bands of women on occasions when chiefs are deposed or installed and in times of war and other emergencies.

Let us pray to God for the King.
Let us pray for a shower of blessing.
Chief of the Ring Wing and kinsman of
    Boaten of Woonoo, Akuamoa of Kyerekyere,
When he was opening his new palace,
He caused cattle to be slaughtered
    for inhabitants of the town.
He gave to the women presents of sheep.
Guard of the roads that lead to Sekyere,
Hunter, Baa Asiemmiri, father the watch dog,
Brother of Tonsa and Badu,
I shall never cease to thank him.
Owusu that knows something,
Let us pray to God for him.
Amankwaa,
Kinsman of the lord of Botoku
    for whom the Mpintin drums play,
Is Amankwaa not coming to sing for
    Chief Adu, the generous giver?
My eyes are looking at the roads in expectation.
What are my ears going to tell me?
Amankwaa,
Kinsman of Tuo Brobe of Sekyere,

Is Amankwaa not coming to sing for
   Chief Adu that scatters presents?
My eyes are looking at the roads in expectation.
What are my ears going to tell me?

CRADLE SONGS

In these songs there is always scope for the reflections of the mother or
nurse, for allusions to the co-wife of a polygamous marriage, allusions to
the treatment meted out to the woman by the husband. Cradle songs,
therefore, can be as satisfying to the mother as to the child.

> Someone would like to have you for her child
> But you are my own.
> Someone wished she had you to nurse on a good mat;
> Someone wished you were hers: she would put you on camel
>   blanket;
> But I have you to rear you on a torn mat.
> Someone wished she had you, but I have you.

> Who took away my child?
> Is the one who took away my child a woman or a man?
> If a woman, she would know what it means to deliver a baby.
> Kwakye's child,
> I am anxious and troubled.
> Kwakye's child,
> I am anxious and troubled.

SONGS FROM FOLK TALES

The poetry of song interludes in folk tales is interesting. Some of the verses
are short, sometimes with lines of nonsense syllables thrown in on account
of their prosodic interest. Others are long and specially constructed to
provide commentary on the story or to continue the theme of the story.
The long poems are usually composed in the recitative style.

   Elephant and Antelope are said to have made very good friends in the
forest. Elephant, being the stronger and the wealthier of the two, was able
to lay on sumptuous meals every day to which he invited Antelope. One
day he expressed the desire to visit Antelope in his house. This embarrassed
Antelope, for he also wanted to give him a good meal. It occurred to him
after failing to get any meat that Mother Antelope was the answer, so he
caused her to be killed and used. When Elephant arrived he was greatly
surprised by the delicious meal and asked to see Mother Antelope. But
Antelope succeeded in putting this off. After the meal, however, Elephant
again asked for Mother Antelope and Antelope replied in a song as
follows:

Elephant, please don't worry me.
Have you ever seen a poor man
And a wealthy man exchange things equally?
Elephant Akwaa Brenkoto that commands his destiny,
Elephant that plucks the tops of trees on his right,
King of musketry, father and king,
Birefi Akuampon, mighty one to whom all stray goods
    are sent to be used,
Yes; let us proceed.
Mother Antelope, I have stewed her.
Yes, let us proceed.
Mother Antelope, I have used her to redeem myself.
Yes, let us proceed.

MAIDEN SONGS

In Akan society maiden songs are sung on moonlight nights by women who form themselves into little performing groups for this purpose. The women stand in a circle and clap their hands as they sing. Each one takes a turn at leading the verses of each song.

The songs are used mainly for praising or making references to loved ones, brothers or other kinsmen or outstanding men in the community. In the past anybody who was thus honoured was supposed to give the women presents the following day.

He is coming, he is coming,
Treading along on camel blanket in triumph.
Yes, stranger, we are bestirring ourselves.
Agyei the warrior is drunk,
The Green Mamba with fearful eyes.
    Yes, Agyei the warrior,
    He is treading along on camel blanket in triumph,
    Make way for him.
He is coming, he is coming,
Treading along on sandals (i.e. on men).
Yes, stranger, we are bestirring ourselves.
Adum Agyei is drunk.
The Green Mamba, Afaafa Adu.
    Yes, Agyei the warrior,
    He is treading along on camel blanket in triumph.
    Make way for him.

WARRIOR SONGS

Warrior organisations form part of the political organisation of Akan states. These organisations have their own songs which they use on important occasions such as festivals, political ceremonies and, in the past, in times of war. The songs include songs of defiance, incitement, insult, songs of mourning (used when conveying the body of a dead captain back home) and other types.

> Hirelings adamant to rain and scorching sun,
> Members of the Apagya company,
> There was a cannon mounted vainly on top of the fort,[1]
> The cannon could not break us,
> The trusted company that engages in battle.
> Hail the helper.

The Poetry of Horns and Drums

A great deal of our heroic poetry is conveyed through the medium of horns, pipes and drums whose rhythms often have a verbal basis.

The poetry of horns and pipes tends to be in the lyric style, as you will see from the following example:

> Conqueror of Kings,
> The great silk cotton tree has fallen down.
> In its place has sprung the small *osesea* tree.
> There is a big river flowing in the valley,
> But it has no deposits of gold.
> Asono Gyima that never retracts his words,
> Noble and tall Osafo Gyamfi Agyei,
> Osafo, father of Osee of Amanten,
> Master of the path, I am exposed to fire.
> Master of the path, I am exposed to fire.

Finally, the poetry of drums. Although drums are used in Akan society for making a limited number of announcements, they are also vehicles of literature. Indeed, in view of the radio, the newspaper and other modern means of communication, there would be no hope for the talking drum if its only function was to give information. On state occasions they drum poems of special interest to the chief and the community as a whole. These poems run into many scores of verses and fall into four groups:

First there are the poems of the drum prelude called the Awakening *Anyaneanyane*. When a drummer is playing these poems, as he has to on the approach of the Adae festival, he begins by announcing himself, closing the opening with the formula:

> I am learning, let me succeed,
> or I am addressing you, and you will understand.

He then addresses in turn the components of the drum—the wood of the drum, the drum pegs, strings, the animal that provides the hide of the drum: the elephant or the duyker.

[1] British fort on the Ghana coast; a reference to the British Ashanti Wars.

Next he addresses the Earth god, the witch, the cock and the clock bird, ancestor drummers, and finally the god Tano, saying:

> The path has crossed the river.
> The river has crossed the path.
> Which is the elder?
> We made the path and found the river.
> The river is from long ago,
> The river is from the Creator of the universe,
> Kokon Tano,
> Birefia Tano.
> River-god of the King of Ashanti,
> Noble river, noble and gracious one,
> When we are about to go to war,
> We break the news to you.
> Slowly and patiently I get on my feet.
> Slowly and patiently I get on my feet.
> Ta Kofi, noble one,
> Firampon condolences!
>   condolences!
>   condolences!
> Ta Kofi, noble one,
> The drummer of the Talking Drum says
> He is kneeling before you.
> He prays you, he is about to drum on the Talking Drum.
> When he drums, let his drumming be smooth and steady.
> Do not let him falter.
> I am learning, let me succeed.

The next example from the drum prelude *The Awakening* is about the deity traditionally revered above all others:

> Otweaduampon Nyame, the Ancient God.
> The Heavens are wide, exceedingly wide.
> The Earth is wide, very very wide.
> We have lifted it and taken it away.
> We have lifted it and brought it back,
> From time immemorial.
> The God of old bids us all
> Abide by his injunctions.
> Then shall we get whatever we want,
> Be it white or red.
> It is God, The Creator, the Gracious one.
> Good morning to you, God. Good morning.
> I am learning, let me succeed.

There is another group of drum poems which are in the nature of panegyrics or eulogies. Abridged forms incorporating the names, praise appellations of individuals and greetings or messages are used in social situations—for example in a dance arena. The chief use of these eulogies, however, is for honouring kings and ancestor kings on ceremonial occasions when their origin, parentage and noble deeds are recalled against a background of tribal history, as in the following example recorded at Kokofu in Ashanti:

> Slowly and patiently I get on my feet.
> Slowly and patiently I get on my feet.
> Osee Asibe, noble ruler,
> Firampon, condolences, condolences, condolences!
> Osee Asibe throws away,[1] throws away, throws away,
> Throws away to the remotest corner,
> Osee Asibe,
> Child of Adu Gyamfi Twere.
> Tweneboa Adu Ampafrako,
> Child of the Ancient God,
> Dress up and let us go.
> Dress up and let us go.
> Child of Noble Adwoa Seewa,
> Ruler of Kokofu Adu Ampoforo Antwi,
> Child of the Ancient God,
> Lifter of towns, noble ruler and last born . . .
> The hunter that provides for all,
> That gives the vulture its carrion,
> The vulture says it thanks you:
> Give it its carrion.
> It thanks you, mighty one.
> It thanks you, gracious one.
> Firampon, condolences, condolences, condolences!

A third group of poems is those used for heralding the movements of a chief, for greeting people, for announcing emergencies and so on. For example when a chief is drinking at a state ceremony, the drummer drums a running commentary. If it is gin, he drums as follows:

> Chief they are bringing it.
> They are bringing it.
> They are bringing it to you.
> Chief you are about to drink imported liquor.
> Chief pour some on the ground.
> He is sipping it slowly and gradually.
> He is sipping it in little draughts.
> He is sipping it in little draughts.

[1] That is presents, gifts of money.

If the drink is palmwine, he drums the following alternative:

> Chief they are bringing you cool and refreshing drink.
> They are bringing you palmwine.
> He has got it. He is drinking it.
> He has got it. He is drinking it.
> He is sipping it in little draughts.
> He is sipping it slowly and gradually.
> The residue remains. It is poured out.
> Well done, gracious one, well done!

Lastly, proverbs. These may be played separately or they may be incorporated into other poems, or they may be incorporated into drum pieces intended for dancing. Dances like *Akantam, samrawa orosee* make use of these proverbs. Here for example are some proverbs of the Akantam dance.

> *Duyker Adawurampon Kwamena*
> *Who told the Duyker to get hold of his sword?*
> *The tail of the Duyker is short,*
> *But he is able to brush himself with it.*
> 'I am bearing fruit', says Pot Herb.
> 'I am bearing fruit', says Garden Egg.
> Logs of firewood are lying on the farm,
> But it is the faggot that makes the fire flare.
> *Duyker Adawurampon Kwamena*
> *Who told the Duyker to get hold of his sword?*
> *The tail of the Duyker is short,*
> *But he is able to brush himself with it.*
> 'Pluck the feathers off this tortoise'.
> Tortoise: 'Fowl, do you hear that?'

Conclusion

Our poetry has tended to give prominence to persons, interpersonal relationships and attitudes and values derived from our conception of the universe. We do not spend time on the daffodils or the nightingale, the night sky and so on as things in themselves, but only in relation to social experience. Our poetry is full of animals and plants, but these are used because they provide apt metaphors or simile, or compressed ways of reflecting upon social experience.

In group life, the use of poetry is more or less organised. There are men set aside in the state to convey poetry on drums. There are others set aside to convey it through horns and pipes, and others set aside to convey it by word of mouth. Similarly among popular bands and associations there are leading singers who are able to bring into the song a variety of poetic expressions appropriate to the occasion.

The poetic tradition is still being maintained, though not to the same degree. Some types of poetry, particularly those associated with the Court, are not nearly as well known as they used to be only a few decades ago. Many people, particularly those who have had the benefit of school education, cannot make any bold claim to a knowledge of the traditions. Nevertheless, poets and custodians of the tradition are still to be found creating and re-creating traditional poetry in appropriate contexts.

Hausa Poetry

DON SCHARFE AND YAHAYA ALIYU

The past of Hausa literature can be seen in the words of Mungo Park, speaking of 'votaries of the Muses' heard in his travels through the West African interior. They could well apply to the poets of Hausaland.

> They consist of two classes; the most numerous are the 'singing men' called *jilli kea*. . . . One or more of these may be found in every town. They sing extempore songs, in honour of their chief men, or any other persons who are willing to give 'solid pudding for empty praise'. A noble part of their office is to recite historical events of their country. . . . The other class are devotees of the Mahomedan faith, who travel about the country, singing devout hymns and performing religious ceremonies, to conciliate the favour of the Almighty, either in averting calamity, or insuring success to any enterprise. Both descriptions of these itinerant bards are much employed and respected by the people, and very liberal contributions are made for them.

These two classes of oral poetry still exist in Hausaland, and there is also a considerable tradition of written verse. Literacy, however, has been for a minority, and it is the art of the spoken language which has predominated, and which we shall consider first.

The Oral Tradition

There are certain kinds of rhythmic utterance which one would hesitate to classify as poetry, yet which are clearly related to it, and which illustrate the linguistic and social bases of the oral tradition.

Among the Hausa each individual has what is known as a drum rhythm. It identifies him, and almost always has attached to it a series of words that either describe him, or form themselves into a characteristic epigram. This is at the base of the oral tradition. Similarly each class of individuals in the society has songs composed to be used at work, or as identification. Men are set this task according to talent, and while the changes in the social structure are weakening this system, it is a rare individual who cannot phrase words to a pattern with some degree of success.

Most of the poems have a chant-like substructure which is varied only slightly from verse to verse. Rhymes are regular; and punning, as well as vowel-consonant play, is expected. Often the lines are punctuated by a rhythm word which anchors the form of the song, and gives the singer, if he is improvising, a moment for consideration of the song's development.

One such song, recited by a twelve-year-old girl, is filled with the expected

34

patterns, and stock sentences. Not meriting full reproduction, it gives clues to the form of oral poetry as a whole, beginning with its orthodox 'I start in the name of God, I start in the name of God' and going on rather more secularly to 'I am going to praise my beloved, I am going to praise my beloved who is handsome in the Bale shoe'. It is interspersed with such aphorisms as 'Women are men's slaves unless there is individual respect, a woman is good if patient, a man is good if sensible', and when thought is unsure, time is gained by the lines, 'I have a secret in my mind, I am going to say it even if it kills me'. The whole of the thirty or forty lines is punctuated by a regular refrain of a breathed 'Eh', giving pause and a form to the whole. It is a song also filled with seeming irrelevancies, a factor inevitable in any form of improvisation.

More consistent oral poets are the begging classes, both those who are somehow disabled, and those who choose to make a living through song. In a sense they are professional, but perhaps this term is best reserved for those whose achievement is both original and artistic. The songs of these men are largely repetitive reminders to the community of Islam's insistence on the duty of alms-giving. The verses sung are rarely original; generally they come from Arabic devotional pieces, or from the learned works of one of the literary poets of the society, such as Aliyu Na-Mangi.

As one might suspect, even from Park's description, the true professionals of the oral tradition group themselves around the still affluent hierarchy of Hausa society. These are the extempore praise-singers, the oral historians, the social commentators. Satire in song has a popular base, and it is perfected by these men whose wit can cut as soon as praise, and who form a line in the political ranks of the day. The mercenary base of much of this can be seen in the fact that it is the office rather than the man who attracts singers. Praise requires patronage, and an office brings with it the responsibility of maintaining the poet.

Depending on their accustomed hearers, the poets are accompanied by a variety of instruments. Hausa is capable of expression through the talking drum known as the *kalangu*. Similarly the reed instrument known as the *algaita* expresses tones that an experienced ear can translate, and is often used in songs for the upper classes. Singers use these instruments to form a verbal and musical counterpoint to their own verses, and often have a vocal chorus to repeat and emphasise verses. Men like Narambada, a retainer of the Emir of Gobir, and Sarkin Kotson Daura have become identified with the open-ended *kalangu* known as the *kotso*, while Mamman Sarkin Taushi, a singer of the Emir of Katsina, and one Jan Kidi have stressed the small talking drum known as *taushi*.

But by no means all of the professional poets are tied to the aristocracy or political classes of the Hausa. Some are affluent, itinerant singers whose patronage is from the people. The most famous of these rootless men is Mamman Shata, originally of Katsina, who sings of social concerns and of his travels, the latter class of poems becoming increasingly popular as the consciousness of the society extends.

35

The Literary Tradition

In Hausa the word for song is the same as that for poem, *waka*. The transition from the oral to the written is thus relatively simple as far as Hausa categories are concerned. In many ways the literary poet is merely an oral poet who has learned to write, or who has had his songs written for him. The art of the literary poet is perhaps more intricate than that of the oral, but it is safer to say that his art is different, and requires care in areas which the spontaneous creator can ignore. A more interesting distinction is made between secular and religious poetry, the word *wake* being used in reference to the latter.

In dealing with the oral tradition it has been possible to leave unmentioned the educational patterns that have evolved in Hausaland. But here the language group becomes more important. There is a temptation to view the Hausa as a part of tropical West Africa, but it must be emphasised that culturally the country is orientated to the Middle East. Arabic has been the significant influence on the Hausa, as it followed the conversion of the people to Islam centuries ago. Mecca is the region's spiritual centre.

The coming of the European did not have the effect on the North that it had on the other regions of the country. The civilisation of the West has taken longer to prove its worth and if schooling has at last decisively turned from the Koranic, the process has been gradual. To a large extent, in literary circles, no adjustment to Western forms has been necessary, and Arabic continues as a second language among intellectuals of the region.

The very fact of literacy elevates the written poet in the society above the oral. The wandering-scholar tradition is evidence of the respect shown the educated even hundreds of years ago, and literate men were sought and supported by the rulers, even as they are today. Patronage was then and is now an important lure for the skilled writer. Often the aristocracy itself composed literary works, and works by the Hausa ruling class form an important, perhaps *the* important, part of the written tradition in poetry.

Initially, learning meant knowledge of Arabic, the language of the Koran, and Islamic tradition. Gradually a form of nationalism arose, and the local languages of various areas were put into written form, making use of the Arabic alphabet. Where sounds did not exist in Arabic they were added, and the resulting script of Hausa was known as *ajami*. Many poets use it to this day.

The most influential of the *ajami* poets was Mohammadu Na Birnin Gwari, who lived at the time of the founder of the Sokoto Dynasty, Uthman dan Fodio. Like many, he had been educated at Timbuctoo, to the north-west, and brought his knowledge to the service of the nineteenth-century reformers of Islam. Arabic was the accepted language, but Mohammadu did much to establish *ajami*. His letters to Malam Haji of Zaria were written in the language, and his poems initiated a tradition.

Isa, son of Uthman, was moved by the Hausa poems to translate the works of his father from their pure Arabic into *ajami*. Similarly, the daughter

36

of Uthman dan Fodio, Nana, began writing poems in this script. Her subject-matter was restricted generally to the place of woman in Islamic society.

As can be imagined, the arrival of the British was received with a degree of disdain by the leaders of the area. White outsiders, if militarily superior, were hardly to be credited with a civilisation that could contribute much to that which had been achieved by the tradition-conscious Fulani moulders of the Hausa. It is interesting that one of the first breaks with orthodox poetry was caused by the arrival of the British. Aliyu dan Sidi, Emir of Zaria at the time of Lugard's appearance, wrote a long poem first in praise of himself and his reign—how peaceful, how prosperous it was—and secondly on the dangers of allowing the white man to take over the administration of the country. It is difficult to fight poetry, and he was later deposed by Lugard and sent to Lokoja.

From a linguistic point of view Aliyu's poetry was important in establishing *ajami* as a dominant literary form, replacing the Arabic that had dominated the nineteenth century. More traditional in subject matter, but also serving to establish *ajami*, was the work of Shehu na Salga, who wrote at the same time. He framed an epic of how the Haɓe (Hausa) founded the dynasty of Kano, entitled *Bagauda*, or *Bakandamiya*, after the first pagan chief of that city. To a large extent he succeeded in purifying his Hausa of Arabic.

Contemporary topics also had appeal. Ibrahim Nalado of Katsina wrote short poems on the importance of education, calling on the people to seek knowledge wherever it might be found, echoing the Prophet Mohammed who said that people should seek knowledge and wisdom even if the journey should take them to China. Technically the importance of his verse is in its use of alliteration, a device that had been largely ignored until his time. The influence of his style is still felt today.

Some of the poets expressed fears for the future of the traditions of Hausaland. Nagwamatse of Kontagora composed a pure Hausa poem on the struggles between the Europeans and the Northern Emirs, and not surprisingly ended with his fears for the liquidation of the Islamic religion in the North. He saw European education as essentially Christian, and its influence therefore negative. To a large extent he was responsible for the state of mind which greeted the reformers who arose in the name of a changing society.

Obviously the result of the West's colonization has been to replace the influence of the Middle East. If Arabic is still the language of the traditional Hausa intellectual, English is that of his more recently educated counterpart, and the influence of English on modern Hausa is little less pervasive than was that of Arabic a hundred years ago. An academy-like Hausa language board tries to control the process of adoption of terms, English and Arabic, with only partial success.

For the literary poet the problems are many. If he is to encompass the past of his language, he must not only become immersed in Arabic and the

37

Islamic writings of earlier centuries; he must also comprehend the new largely scientific education that has come with secondary-school development. He must be at home in the culture whose centre is Arabia, and in that of the West as well.

Of recent poets none exemplifies this attempt so well as Sa'adu Zungur, originally of Bauci. Writing first in *ajami*, he later changed to the Roman script Hausa, prevalent since colonisation, and he became one of the most respected of the modern poets. He is of interest as one of the first Northerners to attend Yaba College in Lagos, and, as a poet, to bring the tensions facing Northern society into articulate expression. The most famous of his poems—*Maraba da Soja*—is a welcome to a soldier returning from the Second World War, considering that war and its import. Its form is traditional, its subject-matter far from being so. The isolation of the past had been shaken by the arrival of the European; it was even more threatened by the reality of world politics in which Hausa men were being forced to play a part. Sa'adu's poem is in the tradition of praise for valour in war. Its setting is far from familiar.

> Kai, Atom bomb, ya yi shema   Can a Birnin Hiroshima,
> Gobara har Wakayama,   Har ta miƙa Yokohama,
> Can arewa da Fujiyama,   Har Tanega da Kagoshima,
> Sai ka ce harshen Jahima,   Wannan bom babu dama,
>   Ka ji ɗam bom mai ragargazawa.

> Kai, what this atom bomb has done to the city of Hiroshima.
> The outbreak of its fire reached from Wakayama as far as
>   Yokohama,
> And to the north of Fujiyama, then to Tanega, and Kagoshima,
> Like the tongue of fire from Hell, this bomb is an awesome
>   piece of work,
> Which can smash everything to pieces.

The technical intricacy of the poem is considerable, rhyming as it does within the stanza. The refrain line rhymes are the same throughout the forty-three stanzas which follow; the poem, like oral works, requires to be read with a slightly repetitive tune.

The most significant of his poems is *Arewa Jumhuniya ko Mulukiya*, considering the claims of monarchy and republicanism on a North that is faced not only with a regional movement, but also with social upheaval. Sa'adu Zungur died in 1958, having brought to the written tradition of Hausa poetry a contemporary intellectualism.

More traditionally Islamic, and therefore more popular, is the work of Aliyu Na-Mangi. His works are recited throughout the region. Blind, as more than one great traditional poet has been, his *Waƙar Imfiraji* is easily the best-known poem among all classes in Hausaland. Still incomplete, the work had been published in both its original *ajami* and in transliterated Roman Hausa form. The rhythm is said to have come from a pattern he heard his daughter using while pounding yam or grinding corn, a rhythm

38

identifiable as *cagi* and often used by beggars. The first stanza establishes the tone that follows throughout.

> Bismillahil Majidi
> Nai nufin waka jadidi,
> In yabon Manzo Hamidi
> Zushafa yaumal mi'adi
>   Mai sonsa ba zai baƙin ciki ba.

> In the name of God, the most generous,
> I intend to sing a new song,
> In praise of the beloved messenger,
> The saviour at the day of judgement;
> Who loves him will never suffer.

The organisation of the poem is impressive. The first book is essentially praise, the second on the Prophet, the third about general problems of life in this world, the fourth on corruption and bribery; and so on to the projected conclusion at the end of twelve books. That this work should be so well known, so completely accepted, shows the depth of the Arabic/ Hausa tradition that is still at work. As Sa'adu Zungur thrust his verse into the political present, Aliyu Na-Mangi has taken orthodox refuge in the past. He is certainly one of the last manifestations of the *ajami* school of writers. Others, like Muzzu Hadeja of Kano, find themselves somewhere between the orthodox and the modernising.

The changes that manifest themselves in the near future will no doubt be considerable. The oral tradition seems secure in the tireless voice of radio. It is the written that will perhaps be most affected, reflecting as it does a community's perceptions. As students emerge from the region's secondary schools, grounded in an education far different from that of their past, their verse obviously will be influenced. The effects of federation should also be significant on a region that has been largely cut off from its tropical countrymen. One hopes that the culture of Islam will prove able to incorporate the Western educational system without losing its traditional integrity. In Kano one passes children inking the complex alphabet of Arabic. At the secondary school children memorise a *waka* by a new singer who also does the twist. To maintain the unity of past culture is a primary task of Hausaland. The poets have a rôle to play in the attempt. That the region's university should separate its departments of Arabic and Islamic studies from the main centre of instruction hardly bodes well. The Hausa poets of the future must know the invading secularism at first hand, not through isolated instinct.

> Rabbi na nufi wagga waƙa
> Ta yabo nasa ba nifaƙa,
> Taimake ni ka ban hazaƙa,
> In yi waƙa mai zalaƙa,
>   Ta yabo nasa ba da kuskure ba.

God; I intend to make this poem
In praise of Him, without pride.
Help me and give me intelligence
So that I may sing a zealous song,
In his praise without error.

The tradition of Hausa poetry is a live one, and the pattern of Hausa poetry is varied, from the oral traditions of the street to the learned works of the literate. In the range of its influence may lie its strength.

Swahili Poetry

JAN KNAPPERT

The Swahili live along the East African Coast from Southern Somalia down to Mozambique, and on the adjacent islands. As traders they spread their language inland so that it is now understood throughout the eastern part of the Congo and in parts of Zambia.

The Swahili are the only African people south of the equator who reduced their own language to writing. Muslims since the early Middle Ages, they employed the Arabic alphabet to write their own Bantu tongue.

The Swahili of old were fishermen, traders and plantation-owners. Their culture is in many ways unique among that of their neighbours. Apart from the art of writing, they are famous for their wood-carving and ship-building, for silverwork and embroidery. They dress in long robes and live in stone houses of two storeys. Their commercial activities take them to the shores of Arabia and India in their elegant dhows, and to the interior of the Congo. Before the advent of the Europeans they were the only traders in East Africa. In the Congo, their language is still spoken in some of the towns: Ki-Ungwana, the language of the Wa-Ungwana, the free men or noblemen. This is what the Swahili called themselves; the name Swahili, 'Coast-people', was given to them by the Arabs.

The Beginnings

The earliest Swahili manuscripts that have been preserved are from the beginning of the eighteenth century. These are the *Hamziya*, a poem of 460 stanzas in praise of the Prophet Mohammed, and the *Tambuka* or *Herekali*, a poem of 1150 stanzas in a different metre. Both the prosody and the elaborate rhyme scheme, and the skill with which the poets handle their language and their poetic images, show that their craft was then already the fruit of a long poetic tradition. We may therefore place the origin of Swahili poetry tentatively in the sixteenth century.

The *Hamziya* is a translation from Arabic, but for the *Herekali* no Arabic original is known. Metrically, Swahili poetry seems to be based on Indian rather than on Arabic models.

From the second half of the eighteenth century, we have the *Inkishafi*, a poem of 79 stanzas, again in a different metre. It describes the many ruins of old palaces in Swahili country with such refinement that one has the impression that in that age Swahili culture had already passed its peak; it was already an ancient culture. The sight of this decay of regal glory is an inducement for the poet to admonish his fellow men to lead a virtuous life. All earthly greatness is transient, nothing in this world will last. Let us therefore search our hearts and turn away from the vain pleasures of the

41

flesh. Soon we shall have to face our Maker who will ask us: Did you pray to Me? Did you seek enjoyment or did you direct all your thoughts towards Me?

> Where are the palaces of the Emirs?
> where are the court-rooms of the grand-viziers?
> where are the officers and noble peers?
> they are all dead and buried in the dust.

Religious Verse

This set the theme for the Swahili poetic tradition up to the present. Still today all the poets of an Islamic background (there are only one or two Christian poets of note) remind us that death is every day on our doorstep, that there is no lasting satisfaction in luxury and voluptuousness, that we must live a saintly life of spiritual exercises.

We must rise in the middle of the night and pray, repeating God's Holy Names; we must fast and abstain from filling the stomach. Physical love is rarely discussed, and then only to say that prayer is better. Love between man and wife is compared to the love between brother and sister or between mother and son. Love for one's neighbour on the other hand is repeatedly praised as the mainspring of good actions. All Muslims are brothers and must help each other; they are all equal in the eyes of God and whether they are rich or poor is unimportant, for does not God create all wealth as well as all poverty? Therefore, those who spend most of their time in the mosques concentrating their thoughts on God will be nearest to Him, and will rise highest after this brief life, for they are dearest to God, even if they were destitute lepers. For does not God create leprosy and all the other diseases in order to test us, and does He not take them away whenever He wills?

Money and other earthly riches will only hinder us on the road to Paradise; it is much better to give them away to the poor, for all the money which we give away in charity will be noted in the great Book of our deeds. It is, as it were, an advance payment to ensure us a place in Heaven. Rather than buy pleasures in this world we should buy the eternal bliss of the Other world for our money. It will be well spent. It is unnecessary to hoard money out of fear that one might need it later, indeed it would be a sign of distrust in the providence of the Lord. Can we extend our lifespan by one day? And if God has decided that we shall live for a given period, would He not provide at the same time for our sustenance? The food we are going to eat tomorrow and the clothes we shall need next year, everything has been planned many centuries in advance. We do not have to look for them, they will look for us. There are special angels appointed by God whose duty it is to see that we get everything in time. If we do not, if we suffer from hunger or some other visitation, then this too is the will of God; we must be patient until it is over. It is much better to suffer and pray than to

42

defile our souls with greed and ingratitude. For to complain is to accuse God, to grumble about our lot is to doubt God's justice and wisdom. Do we know His purpose? Will it not be for the good of all of us except the infidels? Did we create the world? Can we alter the colour of our eyes? Let us rather be grateful when God has made us pious and God-fearing and thereby apparently destined us for Paradise. If God decides that we must go to Hell, He will make us apostatise, neglect our prayers, fornicate, rob and murder, for nothing happens which He did not decide a long time in advance.

This total dependence on the decisions and provisions of an otherworldly Power has the effect of turning the attention of the traditional Swahili poets away from this earth, because it is only a temporary abode, a testing ground. There are no descriptions of landscape in Swahili poetry, the glittering beauty of the Indian Ocean is never admired. The splendid beaches of the African coast, the colourful formations of coral rock, the silver surf in the sunshine, leave the poets unaffected.

Ruins of ancient palaces are not described because one finds there the red flowers of the wonderboom-tree, or the deep shade of the dark-leaved mango. Morality is the only purpose of these poems. One is strongly reminded of the European situation in the Middle Ages, when Gothic Cathedrals were built by people who themselves lived in mean huts, when nature was only admired in order to illustrate God's omnipotence, but never for its own beauty. The word beauty in traditional Swahili poetry is used to describe only the appearance of the Prophet Mohammed, from whose face the Light of divine wisdom shines forth, the Light which all hope to find in Paradise, the Light of the divine Presence. Again, it is the Light of the Other world that is admired and longed for, not the light of this earth, because it will pass away. The Muslim on the east coast of Africa is not satisfied with less than eternal enjoyment, and, perhaps more important, he is terrified by the descriptions of Hell so often found in Swahili poetry. The tortures of the infernal fire are so atrocious that anyone who believes in them must lose his taste for the vain pleasures of this earth and spend all his time thinking of his religion.

Songs

Next to the pietistic poetry which forms the majority of the body of poetic work in the Swahili language, there is also a considerable number of songs (*nyimbo*) and serenades (*tumbuizo*) which are composed in a metre of their own, in which pious poetry is never written. These songs belong to the profane world and are never written down in the traditional form—there are no manuscripts of them in the Arabic script. Collections of songs have been made by European investigators, records are being made of them in our technological and secular age, but for the devout poets of the upper classes, the traditional Swahili, they are *infra dig*.

In so far as these songs can be called traditional, they belong to the

43

ngoma, the traditional dances of the 'low-class' Swahili. These dances go on through the night, very much as in many other parts of Africa. 'Low-class' in this context means that these people are only superficially islamised. The population of Africa's east coast includes a substantial proportion of recent (up to second- or third-generation) immigrants from other parts of Africa, from the 'interior'. Their Bantu background induces them to indulge in things that for pious Muslims are anathema, such as alcohol. It is almost as if the two classes of the same nation live in two different worlds, each with its own interests and its own set of rules.

It is very difficult to record dance songs; all the dancing is done at night and the presence of onlookers is strongly resented, probably because the participants are well aware of the fact that the upper classes of their society frown upon these activities. A few songs, however, have been recorded:

> I want to give a burden to the daughter of the moon.
> Welcome! The crescent shines forth like the full moon.
> When she wears coloured cotton she fancies herself;
> Better is blue calico, like rain clouds.

In spite of its typically African context, this song shows again that Swahili poetry is actually Oriental in form and content. This song, like so many Arabic, Persian and Indian poems, conceals erotic allusions wrapped in flowery language. The daughter of the moon is a girl who has begun to menstruate. A burden is a frequent euphemism for a pregnancy. The crescent, the new moon, is welcomed every month; the same word can also mean a hole in the ground for planting (in the rainy season), or a gully gouged by the rains; here it is doubtless an allusion to the female body. Coloured cotton mantillas are worn by Swahili girls; married women wear them in dark blue. Here the poet again reinforces his reference to the fertility of the rainy season. So, in decoded non-poetic language the meaning of the song is:

> I want to marry the adolescent girl and have children with her.
> Her shining body will swell up and become rounded like the moon.
> She will no longer wear fancy dress but the dignified colours of
> her status.

To compare a girl to the full moon is very complimentary in most Oriental languages, and is often done in Swahili poetry. This song shows how language and culture are interwoven, and how familiar one has to be with both before one can learn to appreciate the poetry of a people, which is the confluence of their language and culture.

The love songs are expressions of the individual poet's emotions versified on the spur of the moment. Some of these songs may catch on and be sung by many people along the Coast, others may die and never be heard again. They are not traditional in the sense that the religious poems are traditional. The latter are carefully preserved, the literal text is written down or memorised, and handed down for many generations. The songs however are

44

'children of instant love', they are ephemeral as the flowers when the rains come. Even the metre is freer though there are stricter rules for their composition than has hitherto been assumed. Among the Swahili several women have become poetesses of repute, as well as the men. The following couplet was sung by a woman while plaiting her friend's hair:

> Sweet bananas are very expensive these days:
> I lost a jewel as large as an egg.

The sweet bananas or sugar bananas are especially sought after in Swahili country. She uses it here as a metaphor for her beloved husband whom she lost. A loss harder to replace than a jewel as large as an egg!

Modern Swahili composers of secular verse are strongly influenced by Western ways of expression, like the following from which only three stanzas will be quoted:

> Love is a poison, a poison that kills
> Love is like madness, it staggers when it goes
> Love is delicious, when you love each other.
>
> Love is a poison, a lethal poison
> Love is a sweetness, sweet for the body
> Love is a sweetness, if two are together.
>
> You are the antidote, you my sweetheart
> I have no other one, will you remember!
> I am yours for ever, for ever and ever.

(O. SHARI)

This language is understandable for European readers, it does not require the explanatory notes of the philologist. Like all traditional forms of expression in Africa, Swahili poetry is moving in a Western direction.

Shairi

The *shairi* metre is used for the type of poetry that comes nearest to our lyrical verse, though it also has other uses. It may have originated from the game of *kufumbana*: two poets try to 'tie each other in knots'—one poet composes two lines of a verse which the other must complete by two lines in the same metre and rhyme, giving the answer to the implied question in the same veiled language. If one knows that each line must have sixteen syllables, with a caesura after the eighth syllable, using only two rhymes throughout the verse, one at the end, one in the middle of each line, one can appreciate that this is a highly developed skill which requires a long training and a refined feeling for the virtually unlimited possibilities of the Swahili language! The *diriji*, the festive occasion at which these word-artists performed, are now a rarity. In the old days a wealthy merchant would hold a *diriji* in order to acquire kudos as a man of erudition. Since

45

it was customary to invite the whole town for supper and soft drinks, these *diriji* are now too expensive. The custom, like the poetic metre, may well derive from India.

The *shairi* metre is now in use for virtually all non-narrative poetry that is a little more serious than the songs. Though mostly secular, this *shairi* poetry has always a serious undertone; it is philosophical, though the philosophy is shrouded in images that seem to suggest other, lighter, even amorous subjects. This symbolic language makes the *shairi* as obscure and difficult to interpret as the dance songs though they are sometimes each other's opposite: the former try to hide their seriousness, the latter their frivolity.

The following is a typical example of the *shairi*:

> I wandered in a certain town by day; the sun was hot.
> I saw a lovely palace where I would have liked to rest;
> The walls were white and flowers bright hung from the windows,
> But O! when I had found the door, a snake attacked my leg.

> I planted once a garden full of every flower and tree.
> There were roses, there was jasmine, all in fragrant bloom.
> Once upon an early morning I went in to breathe the odours;
> Look, there was an ugly baboon, he had scattered all the
>   petals.

> I had furnished my house with exquisite carpets,
> With colourful silken cushions impregnated with incense,
> With rubies and emeralds, with china and glasswork;
> There came a muddy swine and rolled on the rugs.

> One day in the virgin forest I found a pomegranate tree;
> Reaching high I could pick a fruit with my hand,
> But a worm had bored his way through its fresh flesh.
> I turned back never to see the forest again, never to remem-
>   ber.

This clearly Oriental-influenced language is accessible to Western taste; the poet is lamenting the fact that he married a beautiful girl only to find that she had been spoiled by a despicable individual.

The *shairi* metre can be used to embroider upon some proverb or other aphorism; in Swahili the majority of the poetry is still didactic; in the West it is no longer good taste to couch one's wisdom in verse form, though it is still *en vogue* to quote proverbial lines from Shakespeare. Swahili poets like to comment on such topics as: 'He that was not taught by his mother, the world will teach him', explaining that if a child has been spoilt by his mother, he will tend to be conceited, but the world with all its harshness will soon cut him to size.

46

Narrative Poetry

The largest part of Swahili poetry, in volume, is narrative. The narrative poems vary in length; the shortest have less than a hundred stanzas of four lines each, the longest one has over six thousand stanzas. They also vary in strength of poetic expression, some of the passages reaching the very peaks of epic diction. The majority of these epics, including the longest ones, deal with the heroes of early Islamic history, in the first place, of course, with the Prophet Mohammed himself, the miraculous events that accompanied his birth, his death, his ascension to heaven.

Other heroes are his son-in-law Ali bin Talibi and his successors Abu Bakari and Omar. Their exploits in fierce battles against villain infidels, hideous monsters and satanic demons are narrated in great detail. It is here that one finds some true examples of epic descriptions, especially in the narration of the heroes' battles:

> They swooped down like vultures on their prey condemned to
>   death;
> they were like ferocious buffalo angered by a pack of jackals,
> ready with their mighty horns to rend the bodies apart;
> they were like the spotted leopard, swift and deadly with his claws
> hitting in one swing and not missing.

(BW. MWENGO, 1741)

Of course it is not possible to do justice to the typical epic language of Swahili poetry in an English translation. In Swahili this passage takes about half the number of words, each word loaded with its own special meaning that will call forth the expected reaction from the listeners.

Though this poetry may seem long-winded to Western taste, the Swahili never get bored listening to recitals of these poetic stories.

This art reached its apogee in the nineteenth century, but it is still widely practised, and not even all the titles of long epics are known. New ones turn up every year, now written in school copybooks, but still in the calligraphic Arabic characters, sometimes done in black and red. Some poems are recited traditionally on festive occasions of the Muslim calendar. Some of them, written around the turn of the century, deal with the wars against the Germans in Tanganyika, but as far as I know this *genre* of historical narrative was never further developed.

The future of Swahili poetry looks very bright indeed. Of course the taste of the people in East Africa changes as it does in all countries. There will be less religious poetry and more secular, amorous, humorous and other poetry. But the fact that Swahili has become one of the two official national languages in the Republics of Kenya and Tanzania has already caused many poets to try their hand at Swahili poetry who would otherwise never have written anything at all, for English is rather difficult for aspiring *littérateurs*. This potentially unlimited reservoir of writers may well, in the future, yield new generations of poets that outnumber the Coast-born

Swahili-writers. For East Africans, to be able to write good Swahili is just as conducive to prestige as it is for Europeans to write good English or French. In all the Swahili newspapers one can find poems written on the occasion of some important event such as the death of a master-poet or to celebrate some national commemoration, or even to express some political thought. This may motivate a political opponent to frame *his* political concepts in verse-form. More than once this has given rise to a versified debate on the poetry page, which always enormously amuses every East African who has an interest in politics. Obviously the more competent poet can say more in his metaphoric language than his opponent and will therefore win more readers for his point of view. Once an elderly poet stepped in and wrote in a more conciliatory tone:

> The clocks of here and the clocks of there
>   are not in harmony with everywhere . . .

Naturally the veiled language of astute poets is accessible only to insiders, so that they can use poetry as a safety valve to ventilate discontent that would otherwise have to be bottled up.

In many Western countries poetry has become the privilege of the few; a limited group of self-styled connoisseurs has the exclusive right to write *belles-lettres*, so that modern poetry in English for instance does not have the interest of the general public. Swahili poetry, however, is so much in the centre of common interest that several men in high office are poets of renown.

To conclude, here is a small love poem, supposedly written by a girl for her lover. The reader will by now be able to 'read between the lines' and perceive the true meaning of the words:

> If only I could be a bird,
>   a pigeon soft of down,
> I would unfold my graceful wings
>   and fly into the sky;
> I would alight upon the crossbeam of your roof.
>
> I have given you the key
>   of my little box of jewels;
> though I realise its value
>   never did I hesitate.
> If you have some real wisdom, bring it here to me.
>
> Captain, tell the steersman
>   to hold the steering-wheel well
> so that the trembling needle stays
>   straight in its round box.
> If the ship is in the harbour, see that it stays safely there.
>
> (ANON.)

These are only a few lines out of a much longer work. Indeed, Swahili literature is so extensive that no one knows all the titles of even the major works, let alone the separate poems. The literature is now growing faster than ever, as more and more East Africans choose Swahili as the medium of expression for their literary talents. The Swahili writers have a deep and sincere love for their language which they show by treating it with great care and dedication. No doubt it is this proper use of Swahili that has given the language in the past such a crystal clarity. No doubt this care will remain a guarantee that in the future the language will maintain its purity and clarity and that foreign elements will be absorbed and integrated to keep Swahili poetry the art of beauty and harmony it has always been.

Luo Songs

HENRY OWUOR

The Luo are a tall Nilotic tribe inhabiting the eastern shores of Lake Victoria Nyanza in Kenya. They have not been in their present area for more than two centuries, but they have brought with them a culture and language very close to that of other Nilotic people still living farther north, in Northern Uganda and in the Sudan. They are ceremonious people and very fond of music. The eight songs printed here are all *oigo* songs and represent only one of the many musical traditions in Luo country.

The *oigo* are love songs which were sung by girls of marriageable age when they went to visit the young men with whom they were courting. This was often called 'visiting the *simba*'. The *simba* was the hut in which young men slept and entertained their guests. The visit was usually carefully organised at or near the full moon. As the girls walked to their destination, they sang the *oigos* either individually or as a group, maintaining the performance all the way by singing in turns. There was no formal order of singing; the more musically gifted girls or the more effusive took the leading part according to their mood.

Meanwhile the young men were waiting and listening intently until the first faint *oigo* melody reached their ears. Then one of them stood on a raised piece of ground just outside the gate of the homestead and announced at the top of his voice: *Ogoree, omolo* (the landing has taken place, they have arrived).

At the gate the girls stopped moving but continued singing the *oigos* until a grandmother of the compound, who had placed herself near by, offered them gifts—metal ornaments, beads or rings. As part of the evening's entertainment the young men smoked a gourd-pipe of opium or played enthusiastically on a reed flute while the girls sang the *oigos*. Often the hosts would have invited a lyre player as well.

The *oigos* were also sung while girls collected firewood or were going to draw water, but this was regarded as a kind of rehearsal. Girls who were close friends were often known by their favourite *oigos*. Late in the evening, while travelling to a gathering at a lyre performance, they would decide to follow different paths (the longer and more tortuous the better) shouting the *oigos* at each other. The girls also used the *oigos* to introduce themselves to the lyre player before addressing him. This beautiful custom has unfortunately died out completely over the past thirty years, and all the songs translated here were recorded by elderly women who remembered them from their youth.

The style of *oigo* singing is extremely distinctive. The singer trills in a bird-like voice and conveys an impression of being possessed by the stream of song within her, breathless and helpless. The emotions expressed are

50

often sorrowful and almost hysterical, yet the singer exults in her ability to sing endlessly like a bird (as in *Atimo Hono*). Her accomplishment will be judged by her skill and power in this *redo* style, refrains such as *doree ree yo* being much more repetitive than can be conveyed in these translations. In *Pod Aredo* and *Atimo Hono* the singer conveys very well the possessive nature of the *oigo*. *Simba Mwalo* refers to the custom of starting the *oigo* on a distant path, so as to have the longest possible journey to the *simba*; hence the singer begins her lament 'down in the reeds'. *Nyagwenda Ywagore Tok Dala* again stresses the sorrow of the *oigo* singer, but *Okot Kiyiengi* and *Nyagwe Gune* stress another side of her nature; wilful, impulsive and unpredictable, liable to break the taboos of ordinary life. The bell referred to in *Okot Kiyiengi* is probably a ceremonial bell hanging on the reed walls of a grain store, which the young would be forbidden to touch. *Nyagwe Gune* also gives us a moving glimpse of a Luo family starting off on a visit, led by their favourite bull, who symbolises and embodies the whole family or clan. The singer has been running ahead to keep up with the bull, and this accounts for the pain in her chest.

Yala ere Yala is a modern song in the *oigo* style, in which the singer mocks at the new-fangled fashions introduced by the shops. Yala is a small trading centre in Luo country, and this song probably dates from the time when the first overseas goods were being offered for sale there. Her satire plays over the young clerks, the bicycle-owners and the new printed cloths. *Aloo Ogo Oigo* is really a lyre-player's song, which would be sung in the *simba* while the girls were visiting. The lyre-player's *sim* is his musical assistant who has stayed at home, and he compliments the *oigo* singer by saying that she is as good as an assistant to him, while all the men are simply lolling in their chairs half dead and doing nothing.

The word *oigo* seems to mean slightly different things in different localities, and so a true evaluation of the songs would have to take these into account. I have not been able to do this. Nevertheless, the following conclusions can be based on the songs printed here.

The girl in the *oigo* songs is a type representing only certain characteristics of girlhood, as expressed within the special culture of her tribe. She lives in a dreamland, though much tempered by the idealised rôle she longs to fill in the community. By implication, singing is regarded as a good thing, especially when it is powerful—so that everybody can hear it—and persistent. As with a bird, singing appears to be the natural outpouring of the life force itself. The prestige of clan and family depended not only on the prowess of its young men but also on the zealous way in which its women represented its interests in song and dance. For a group of girls the *oigo* was a means of announcing their presence and of differentiating themselves from the older, married women; for an individual a way of expressing her idiosyncrasies. Educationally, the *oigos* were an amusing way of criticising flagrant breaches of conduct. The *oigos* are, however, more reflective and less excited than the insistent *ree* theme would suggest; they are simple, rather repetitive but nevertheless delightful tunes.

51

Atimo Hono

I am possessed,
A bird bursting on high with the *ree* lament,
I am the untiring singer.
Dear bird, let's sing in rivalry
Our *doree ree yo.* . . .
It is my wayward self,
Singing in rivalry
The *doree ree yo*;
I am the untiring singer
That rocks far-off Mombasa
With the *aree ree yo*;
It is the voice crying the *doree*

That rocks far-off Nakuru;
I am the compelling *Ondoro* drum,
The bird bursting with the *doree*'s plaintive tones;
I am the untiring singer
Choking herself with the *doree ree yo*.

Pod Aredo

I'm still complaining,
Crying the *ree ree ree*,
I'm still complaining,
Ever tearful with the *ree ree ree*,
I'm still complaining;
The *redo*-singer's unceasing complaint,
Scion of young women
Still complaining,
Ever tearful with the *ree ree ree*,
I'm still complaining.

I am in love with the *oigo*,
I cry the *ree ree ree*
Infatuated with the *oigo*;
The *redo*-singer's unceasing complaint
Blasting Amimo's hearth
With constant complaining;
Ever tearful with the *ree ree ree*,
I'm still complaining.

Nyagwe Gune

Our bull is starting off for Holo,
The Kapiyo clan have fine cattle.
Our bull is starting off for Holo,
The Kapiyo clan have fine cattle.

Then the giggling one said,
Then the playful one said,
(How amusing)
The impulsive *ree* singer
Is a forest creature lamenting the pain in her chest;
The forest creature lamenting the pain in her chest,
The spirited one lamenting the pain in her chest,
The giggling *ree* singer
Is a forest creature lamenting the pain in her chest,
The *Nyagwe Gune* lamenting the pain in her chest,
The impulsive *ree* singer
Is a forest creature lamenting the pain in her chest.

Our bull is starting off for Holo,
The Kapiyo have fine cattle;
The Kadulo clan is a bull which starts off for Holo,
The Kapiyo have fine cattle.

Okot Kiyiengi

The *ree* for Ameli, daughter of Omolo,
She is the Achichi who goads the encircling crowd;
Sing *oyiyoree*.
Sing *oyiyoree*.
She is Achichi who goads the encircling crowd:

Shaking the bell.
Shaking the bell
I dare you to shake the bell
The forbidden bell,
The one who dares shake the bell,
The girl who shakes the bell,
It's the naughty one who longs to tickle the bell;
Tickling the bell.
I dare you to tickle the bell
The forbidden bell,
Who dares shake the bell
The girl who shakes the bell,
It's the naughty one who longs to shake the bell:

53

The *ree* for Ameli, daughter of Omolo,
She is the Achichi who goads the encircling crowd;
Sing *oyiyoree*
Sing *oyiyoree*.
She is the Achupa who goads the encircling crowd.

Simba Nwalo

Sing the *ree*,
I am starting my lament down in the reeds
Down in the reed country
I am starting,
I, the *nyaredo rere reyo*;

Sing the *ree*,
I am starting the lament down in the *simba*,
Down in the *simba*
I am starting,
I, the *nyaredo rere reyo*;

Sing the *ree*,
I am starting my lament down in the reeds,
Down in the reeds
I have gone into the reeds,
I, the *nyaredo rere reyo*;

Sing the *ree*,
I am starting my lament down in the *simba*,
Down in the *simba*
I am starting,
I, the *nyaredo rere reyo*.

Nyagwenda Ywagore Tok Dala

My chick laments its life in the tree behind our home,
Crying *Chiyo*;
The kite has carried away my chick,
The little cock lamented its life.

So would I shout in distress,
Would flap my hands mournfully,
Flapping in imitation.

My chick laments its life in the tree behind our home,
Crying *Chiyo*;
The kite has carried away my chick,
The little cock lamented its life.

54

So would I howl inconsolably,
Yes, stumble with sorrow,
Stumbling in invitation.

My chick laments its life in the tree behind our home,
Crying *Chiyo*;
The kite has carried away my chick,
The little cock lamented its life.

Yala ere Yala

Yala, O sing the *ree* for Yala,
Sing the *eree ree yo*,
These coming days the clerks will be writing,
The skirt of Adore, the daughter of Disa,
Is printed with boards on one side,
Plain cloth on the other;
Amara's mother cannot afford a bike—
She travels on foot,
But the Kamnara gambol on wheels;
Even Oloo the musician of Nyabondo village
Has forsworn travelling by train;
How can a mere musician fly in an aeroplane?

So Yala, I sing the *ree* for Yala,
Sing the *eree ree yo*,
These coming days the clerks will be writing.

Aloo Ogo Oigo

The *ree ree*
Aloo has sung the *oigo*,
The *ree*, O Odera,
Aloo has sung the *oigo*.

The *yoo ree*
My *sim* is staying home,
Odera's *sim*
Staying home to reflect in tunes.

The *yoo ree*
This is Gol, son of Were,
The *yoo*, O Odera
Who is Gol, son of Were.

In his chair
Almost smothered by the chairs,
Nyagudi of the Kogalo clan
In his chair
Almost smothered by the chairs.

In their chairs,
Almost smothered by their chairs,
Our neighbours the Kogalo clan
In their chairs
Almost smothered by their chairs.

So the *ree ree*
Aloo has sung the *oigo*,
She is Obiero's daughter
Aloo has sung the *oigo*.

These songs were translated by Henry Owuor and Gerald Moore.

Ojebe Poetry

ROMANUS N. EGUDU

Traditional African life in general is rich in poetic expressions, and these expressions are poetic in a sense that is far-reaching, for they are not only spontaneous and realistic, but also beautiful, musical, and profound in diction and imagery. The funeral ceremony of an important Ibo man, for instance, vindicates the elegiac qualities of the eulogy pronounced on this hero and his feats. Much of this poetry is not either recorded or translated, for it is rightly believed that once any song or poem is translated from the vernacular into, say English, it loses its essence. This is true though only to the extent that the particular piece sheds the rhythm, the linguistic tricks and figurative devices which form the aesthetic equipage of most African languages; but it is not true to insist that no 'meaning' can be retained by such translation.

Ulli Beier has noted this problem of translation from African languages, but still finds the task worth undertaking, illustrates the case for its utility by referring to the 'Akan Funeral Dirges' translated by Kwabena Nketia,[1] and Adeboye Babalola's 'Ijala'[2] as indicating 'that the effort is worth while, because our knowledge of African life and thought is greatly enriched'.[3]

Though the difficulty of translation exists, considerable successful work has been accomplished in this connection. Besides the works already referred to above, studies in Ewe Poetry and Akan Poetry have been done by Geormbeeyi Adali-Mortti and Nketia;[4] and it is the aim of this essay to add to the corpus already realised, by a study of the poetry of one section of the Ibos—Ojebeogene Clan.[5]

Invocations

These are poems sung by Idol-priests, hunters, and most of the elders. The Idols are usually called Ugwu (Hills), and almost every village has at least one such Ugwu. In Ebe, for instance, there are *Ugwu-Akuma*, *Ugwu-Omelum*, *Ugwu-Abazi* and so on. The verse addressed to *Ugwu-Akuma* runs thus:

[1] See *The Funeral Dirges of the Akan People*, Achimota, 1955.
[2] Published in *Black Orpheus*, September 1956, pp. 5–16.
[3] Bakare Gbadamosi and Ulli Beier trans., *Yoruba Poetry*, Ibadan, 1959, p. 6.
[4] See 'Ewe Poetry', *Black Orpheus*, Oct. 1958, pp. 36–45; and 'Akan Poetry', *Black Orpheus*, May 1958, pp. 5–11.
[5] Ojebeogene is the name of a clan in Udi Division, Enugu Province, in the Eastern Region of Nigeria. It comprises seven villages (towns as they are sometimes called): Ebe, Abor, Ukana, Awhum, Okpatu, Umulumgbe and Umuoka.

57

Ugwu-Akuma, king living in the wilderness,
Guide of your people,
Dispenser of justice,
Ugwu, the hero that is dreadful,
The hero that is fearless,
Protect your children
From friends and foes.

This is sung by the priest of this particular Ugwu, and he uses a special kind of horn—'opi' for doing so. At the end of such a poem is often appended a prayer or petition.

The hunters also invoke their god to help them kill a lot of game:

My god, hail,
I am in your hands
For today's hunt.
The hungry child
Runs to his father for food,
So I run to you for today's meat.
The Red sun of the sky,
Please, please, doo . . . doo . . .

And when the hunter kills any animal during the hunt, he intones jubilantly:

My god, I salute you, o o o . . .
I thank you, o o o . . .
I kneel before you, o o o . . .
May the killer kill again, o o o . . .

The third kind of invocatory poetry is the early morning prayer that every respectable elder says as soon as he wakes up. It comprises the normal invocation, an offertory and a petition. The man, after washing his hands and face, takes up his holy staff (Offor) and brings out cola nuts which are to be offered, and, as in the particular case studied, says:

Agu, my father, come.
Take cola and chew.
The Tree that shelters his brothers,
The cola is come: it is for you.
Okaibe and Ogbuagu, you caused
The cola tree to grow and produce
Fruit; come and have the biggest share.
Ezenna, you the father of all the above and me,
You will come last, for the father eats
Only after his sons have fed—here is
Your own cola.
All the Hills and Valleys in Ojebe Clan,
The cola is come, it is come, it is come
In great abundance; take it and chew.

Protect me and my family—my wife and children.
I wish no man evil,
But if anyone says I have lived too long,
Let him go before me to see what it is like
In the land of spirits.

The names mentioned in this poem are those of the singer's ancestors: Ahu, Okaibe, Ogbuagu and Ezenna. The Hills and Valleys are the various idols which are also believed to have great influence on the lives of the people, and therefore some claim on the votive rites of the people.

Pronouncements of the dead

In this group the masqueraders' verse represents the voice of the dead. In Ojebe clan, the Odo is the best known masquerade, very powerful, full of wisdom, representative of the dead—in fact regarded as the dead come to life again—and therefore is supposed to know the past, the present, and the future. The minstrel Odos are so philosophical, musical and dignified in their verse that, to me, the poetry they produce epitomises the meaning, depth and scope of life in this part of Ibo land.

This poetry varies from one singing Odo to another, but the general pattern is roughly the same—ranging from the rehearsal of the ritual of the Odo cult, to the tracing of the history of the people, especially the heroes and the Ozo-titled men, who in the past had been renowned for their marvellous activities, and whose present sons must inevitably inherit this heroic blood. This is expressed in Ibo as 'Ani-na-efu-Ngwu', and that is to say 'The-Land-That-Breeds-The-Ngwu-Tree'. The Ngwu tree is sacred and mystic; it is a symbol of magic and supernatural power. Another feature of this poetry is that it generally consists of a number of proverbs so strung together that one not only explains, but also reinforces the other:

I live by the Ngwu tree
Near the Nkwo market.
He who hastens to a fight
Knows not his death awaits him there.
Remember, my sons, the day
You called upon me for help,
Remember the wilderness
Where I encountered the foe:
It is for you to say what happened.

You have needed an increase of wealth,
I gave it before you asked.
I knew you had no male issues last year,
Today their cries are heard in your compounds.

When I was living my name struck fear in my mates,
My deeds shone everywhere.
Now in the land of the dead,
My place is higher still.
My sons, let not the light go out in your time;
When a blind man mistakes a lump of earth for food,
It is his brother that is ashamed, not himself.

The Odo goes on to other matters; but the tone is throughout that of declaration in a spirit of triumph and exultation.

Another type of declaratory poetry is the Ozo-title poetry. On the day the Ozo takes the title, he sings aloud, in a mood of heroic pride, a list of names by which people will henceforth address him. These names are usually a series of proverbs rich in imagery and metaphorically couched, detailing the feats he performed, the difficulties he surmounted in his pursuit of the means for carrying out the costly title-taking ceremonies, and pointing to the various sources of his entire wealth. At this moment of the title-taking, he will, as a victorious chief, add some names signifying the opulence and social dignity that have become his. In the process, one person, often the female relation of the man, will be calling on him in a musical tone to give his names, and in response, he gives such names as the following:

I am:
The Camel that brings wealth,
The Land that breeds the Ngwu tree,
The Performer in the period of youth,
The Back that carries its brother,
The Tiger that drives away the elephants,
The Height that is fruitful,
Brotherhood that is mystic,
Cutlass that cuts thick bushes,
The Hoe that is famous,
The Feeder of the soil with yams,
The Charm that crowns with glory,
The Forest that towers highest,
The Flood that can't be impeded,
The Sea that can't be drained.

Each of the names is a metaphor. As the camel brings wealth home to the owner, so the Ozo brings wealth home to his people. As the Ngwu trees are very important ones, the land that breeds them is highly regarded. This man compares himself to this land because by taking the Ozo-title, he has continued the tradition of his forefathers; for the land that grows the Ngwu trees never fails to produce them. Some of the names refer to the man's sources of wealth. He is 'Height that is fruitful'. This means that one of the most important sources of his income is the tapping of palm-wine. He has to climb to a great height to get the palm-wine, which he sells

60

for money. Farming is another occupation of his. This is indicated by the names 'Cutlass that cuts thick bushes', 'The Hoe that is famous', and 'The Feeder of the soil with yams'. His status is now such that he is comparable to a 'Forest' which has grown higher than the surrounding bushes, the 'Flood' which is so voluminous that its flow cannot be stopped, and to the immensity of a sea that cannot be emptied of its water.

Ever after the time of the title-taking, the man goes by those names. Anyone desiring to hear some of them has only to 'tune' the Ozo by saying to him: 'Your own, Ozo?' This is the cult way of saying 'How are you called, Ozo?' In response, he would often begin with 'I am', and then give as many as the inquirer is patient enough to hear, or as many as the Ozo can remember at the time. However, the names are so much part and parcel of his life that he always has them at the tip of his tongue.

Incantations

The verse sung by the fortune-tellers is primarily a kind of incantation. It begins in the form of a soliloquy full of questions and answers. Then the fortune-teller reflects on his power and that of his ancestors in this profession, and prays the gods and spirits of his forefathers to give him the power of vision which he needs. This poetry reads something like this:

> What will it be today?
> Success or failure?
> Death or life?
> Ha! the flood cannot run up the hill.
> What is the evil spirit that throws his shade
> Between me and the truth?
> I hold my sacred staff against it.
> Here is the east, there is the west;
> Here the sun rises
> See the truth come riding on the rays of the sun.
> The Sky and the Earth keep me company,
> And can my tongue go zig-zag? (i.e. Can I tell lies?)
> The grey hair is an enemy of lies.
> Come, the spirits of my forefathers,
> Stand by your son.
> Let us show this client of ours what we can do.
> We have been known for this power:
> If one cuts the Ngwu tree by noon,
> It mocks him with a new shoot
> Before the sun falls. (i.e. before sun-set.)
> Speak, speak to your son.
> Show the way
> There, there, it comes, the truth comes!

61

At this point he has seen what he is looking for. He then addresses the client, and after asking him a few questions, tells him the solution to his problem by prognosticating future events. One such fortune-teller was reported to have foretold the use of aeroplanes in Nigeria even before any were seen in the country.

Laudations

This group parallels what Gbadamosi and Beier call 'Praise Names' in Yoruba poetry;[1] but while in the case of Yoruba poetry these names are addressed to the gods and the chiefs mainly, in Ojebe poetry, they are addressed to the chiefs and any other persons who have done something remarkable. Here such names have become so much a mere social phenomenon that one does not need to do any heroic action before earning them. For instance, a boy or girl who is hairy may be known and addressed as 'Hair is the spice of beauty'. This is one kind of laudatory poetry in Ojebe clan. It is also attributive, and a man or a woman can have as many as he or she has praiseworthy qualities. In some areas, the reverse of this poetry becomes condemnatory and denunciatory. A man can be known as:

> The Lizard that spoils his mother's funeral,
> Head is bigger than body,

and so on. The first name means that the man cannot help himself when others are willing to help him. The second is descriptive. He has a head that is out of proportion to his body; so it is said to be bigger than his body.

The most popular of the laudatory poems are heard at the funeral ceremony of a deceased Ozo-title holder. In this case, the daughters and sons of the dead man rehearse his cult names, and add flourishes of their own to suit the occasion. As special drums are beaten, and amid the boomings of gun-shots, one hears these daughters and sons say in praise of their dead father:

> You are King
> The king who is a tiger,
> The king that guards the town,
> The hand that breaks the hill,[2]
> Wealth that imbues with wisdom,

and all the other titles the man has been known by. At the same time the peers of the deceased sing his praises using their musical horns. Incidentally, these horns are also used to summon the people, especially the Ozos and the elders, to a gathering of the clan or the village.

---

[1] *Yoruba Poetry*, p. 14.
[2] The line implies that the man has been famous as a farmer: 'breaks' means 'tills'.

62

Praises sung during community labour are also popular. One man usually stands by the workers and inspires them to greater action by singing out their praise names. He knows the praise names of all of them, and addresses them one after the other. This is one of such songs addressed to one man:

> You have wedded your hoe to the soil,
> You uproot trees with bare hands,
> You are the hero who does not care
> That to fight is to die,
> The sun and the rain are the same
> To you when the soil must be tilled,
> Yours are the hands that harrow the soil:
> The time is come again
> Show us now if you are still the man
> That you have ever been.

Hearing this, the man addressed will shout out passionately in answer to the singer, brandish his hoe for some time, and then demonstrate with the hoe that he is still as strong in tilling the land as he has always been known to be.

Didactic and satiric poetry

This kind of poetry is calculated to satirise social mischiefs either of the high or the low. In Ebe, for example, there was the 'Iyo' singing group, now replaced by the 'Omaja' group. Their objective is the same, which is to teach good manners by exposing the offenders in matters of social and ethical codes. The victims of this criticism include young men who beat or insult their parents, married women who are unkind and unfaithful, spinsters who through their misdemeanours and general irresponsibility fail to get married, and are thus living until their death in their fathers' homes (a real blot on the escutcheon of such fathers), and the Ozo-titled men who eat cassava (strictly forbidden by the cult of the Ozo group). Such songs are often full of pithy, sarcastic, yet humorous sayings, and in the clan their effects of the nature of redeeming evil, and instilling moral and ethical consciousness into the people, have been wonderful.

The three songs given here below are collected from Abor and Awhum villages:

> Woman, you enter everyman's room,
> By night and by noon,
> You must remember what our people say—
> A thing that is sweet can kill the eater;
> So retrace your footsteps
> Or meet your doom.

This song satirises the woman who, though she is married, goes to meet other men. It is a warning to her, reminding her of the implications of her action, and the probability of danger.

Another song from the same village deals with the theme of unkindness on the part of a woman who does not like to give food to other people. The woman is supposed to be cooking, and there is somebody present, who, though he is not invited, would wish to be asked to the table. The woman purposely leaves the cooking pot on the fire for a very long time, even though the food has been done, and this is to make the man feel tired of waiting and so quit. But the man is quite ready to wait for as long as the pot is kept on the fire. The singing group takes up the idea floating in the waiting man's mind and satirises the woman in the following words:

> Woman, though you cook without ending
> And leave your pot on fire till evening,
> Though you let the food burn into charcoal
> That is as black as the coal
> Mined at Enugu,
> The waiting man stays without going,
> Stays even unto midnight without sleeping!

The singing group may be girls, as is the case in Awhum village. There was a particular incident of a spinster who was impregnated in 1958. The girl tried to effect an abortion, but without success. It was reported that she drank all sorts of concoctions prepared by the local herbalists, and ran long distances so as to dislodge the foetus. In the end she was doomed to carrying her shame about:

> You may drink the root-juice
> From today till tomorrow;
> Go to the dibias young and old,[1]
> Collect from them the herbs of the bush
> And make a meal of these day and night,
> Run up the hill, run down the hill:
> The foetus still sticks fast, very fast!

Lullabies and private songs

Under this heading will be included all those songs in Ojebe clan, which range from the songs of the baby-sitters and the morning songs of a girl sweeping her father's compound, through the meditative as well as the lyrical pieces sung by women as they spin threads, thresh beans, or peel cassava, to the historical narrative verses sung by men as they build fences or train the vines in thier farms, commemorating their own, or their ancestors', heroic performances in the past. The lullabies are the more universal verses in the clan. A girl taking care of a baby sings such a song as

[1] Dibia is the Ibo word for a herbalist.

64

the following, especially when the baby becomes restive and is crying, to soothe the child:

> Mother is gone to Egede market,[1]
> Mother is there to buy you a hen,
> The hen will be as white as chalk,
> Stop crying and look at your hen,
> The fox has come to eat your hen.
> Stop crying and let's drive the fox away.

Generally the lullabies are not very significant semantically, but they are musical and produce magical effects on the babies, which is all they are meant to do.

Elocutionary poetry

Some poems are meant to exercise the people on speaking fluently and remembering the sequence of facts without halting on the way, and to give them general pleasure by the special arrangement of the words of the poems. Such poems are usually recited in one unbroken breath:

> Give me pear pear for parrot
> Give me parrot parrot for money
> Give me money money for land
> Give me land land for farming
> Give me farming farming is wealth
> Give me wealth wealth makes enemies.

In this kind of poetry, it is not so much the sense as the sound that counts. The rhythm is regular; the last word of a line is sung twice at the middle of the next line, and the initial phrase 'Give me' runs through the lines, so that the whole song sweeps rapidly from the beginning to the end, where the last line wittily clinches the entire piece: '. . . wealth makes enemies'. The repetition, which would otherwise have been boring, is sufficiently forestalled by the cannon of unbroken breath ensuring high speed, the obedience to which the song demands.

In another poem of this group, the whole movement is structured on the word 'crooked' which appears in all the lines. Like the former piece, it moves very fast, and should be read rapidly:

> I entered a crooked bush
> And cut a crooked stick
> For staking a crooked yam
> To be harvested by a crooked man
> With a crooked digger,
> And given to a crooked woman
> To cook with a crooked pot
> For celebrating a crooked feast.

[1] Egede is a neighbouring village to Ojebe clan.

65

All these poems from Ojebe clan are handed down orally from generation to generation. They are not yet recorded; but the old men in the villages are reliable repositories for most of them, as they are very willing to give an inquirer as many as they know; and they know quite a bit. The spirit of poetry therefore runs down deep into the roots of the being of the people, as is the case in other parts of Africa, and as has been pointed out by Israel Kafu Hoh, among other people, we should respect 'the thoughts and feelings of our forefathers as they are shown in our poems', and endeavour to emulate them.[1]

[1] *Voices of Ghana: Literary Contributions To The Ghana Broadcasting System* 1955–57, Accra, Ghana, 1958, p. 93.

Part 2

Poetry

Aimé Césaire

An Approach to his Poetry

ABIOLA IRELE

Aimé Césaire is best known for his long poem, *Cahier d'un retour au pays natal*,[1] in other words, as the poet of the Negro Revolt. Indeed, the militant character and the exceptional energy of his writing in the fervent advocacy of the cause of his race do suggest a preoccupation with a public theme which seems to preclude a more individual awareness of the world and a more intimate poetic tone. His poetry is manifestly dominated by the racial theme in which his personal experience and emotions are situated within a more embracing collective feeling.

Nonetheless his poetry does move distinctly at two levels: it is the reflection of a strong personal involvement with social and political realities, the expression both of a collective and of a personal drama.

The point of departure of all Césaire's poetry remains, of course, the objective fact of the race question in general and the colonial situation in particular. It is impossible to understand his poetry outside this definite context; it is equally impossible to measure its full significance without an understanding of its particular impact on the poet as an individual. The historical situation of the race touched Césaire so directly and so immediately as to constitute for him the framework of his poetic destiny. The most obvious character of his poetry is thus its acute race consciousness, the awareness of the poet of belonging to a 'fallen race':

> my race pitted with macula
> my race ripe grapes for drunken feet
> my queen of spittles and of lepers
> my queen of whips and of scrofulas.[2]

His indignation is aroused by the prostration and the abjection to which the race has been reduced, first in slavery—

> And they sold us like beasts, and
> they counted our teeth[3]

—then as an object in the service of the material interests of the oppressor, furthered at the expense of suffering and humiliation:

> London, Paris, New York, Amsterdam
> I see them all assembled around me like
> stars, like triumphal moons
> And I want with my cursed eyes, my rotten
> breath, my blind-man fingers in a keylatch
> to measure

[1] Revised edition, 'Présence Africaine', Paris, 1956. [2] *Ibid.*, p. 77.
[3] *Et les Chiens se taisaient*; p. 92, revised stage version of the poem, 'Présence Africaine', 1956.

69

Ah to measure
what it has required of my nervousness
of my panic
of my eternal beggar's cries and
of the beads of sweat on my oozing face to build
that . . .[1]

His poetry gives voice to the resentment of the black against the moral and economic alienation to which he has been submitted by white domination.

But more than his consciousness of the social injustice and indignities suffered by the black man, Césaire feels deeply about the spiritual disruption of the black race, 'a people fed on insults', disorientated and unable to relate itself meaningfully in a hostile world. Centuries of denigration have demoralised the black, making him unable to live either within himself or without, as a full man. Against the denial of the humanity of his race, Césaire realises the contradiction of 'assimilation' by which he is singled out by the oppressor and refashioned in a foreign image:

I salute the three centuries that
uphold my civic rights and my blood
minimised.[2]

A dominant theme in his poetry is consequently his sentiment of frustration and tension within an imposed culture, his sense of deprivation and of the division in his self-awareness. For his personal predicament takes its place for him within the general framework of the negation of his race by the white; the price demanded from him in order to be accepted as a human being has been the renunciation of his authentic self, the diminution of his fullness:

I am a remembrance that does not attain the threshold and wanders in the limbos where the gleam of absinthe when the heart of the night blows through its mustiness moves the fallen star where we ponder our lot.[3]

The personal sentiment of loss and exile appears then as the corollary of the alienation of his race.

A livid anger runs through the poetry of Césaire like a consuming brush fire. Seen against the background just evoked, in which the poet's objective involvement with the situation of his race is seen to mark his sensibility, it is not surprising that his poetry should be a reflection of the violent turmoil of his inner state. Césaire identifies himself with the race, for as he says, 'a sea of sorrows is not a proscenium, for a man crying out is not a bear dancing'. He defines himself by reference to the historical condition of his race. His commitment, total and irrevocable, makes him the vibrant embodiment of a people:

[1] 'Chiens', p. 101.   [2] 'Cahier', p. 65.
[3] 'Cadastre', p. 15, Paris, Editions du Seuil, 1961.

```
my family name   :  offended
my first name    :  humiliated
my status        :  rebel
my age           :  the age of stone.¹
```

His poetry acquires the character of a testimony, becomes a cry of indignant protest and refusal:

> Let me be he who refuses the unacceptable
> . . . .
> the bird-clear monument of Refusal.

His reaction takes the form of a violent denunciation of his oppressors—

> each one of your footsteps is a conquest
> and a spoliation and a misconstruction and an
> assassination²

—and an incrimination of the society that permits colonial exactions by its tacit complicity:

> Arrest that innocent man. He carries my blood on his shoulders.
> He carries my blood in his shoes. He hawks my blood in his nose.³

His accusation of Western society is linked with an explicit moral outlook; it is an exposure of the spiritual decay of a society that has lost its humanity. He concludes a poem inspired by the summary lynching in the United States of Emmet Till, a Negro youth, with this parody of the presidential report on the state of the union:

> 20 years of zinc
> 15 years of copper
> 15 years of petrol
> and in 180th year of these states
> but in the heart an unfeeling clockwork
> nothing, zero
> of blood not a drop
> in the rank white disinfected heart⁴

Thus in Césaire's poetry we have, at many points, a straightforward statement of his revolt as a social and political attitude. His poetry is a direct attack on Western society as the oppressor of his race. But Césaire's revolt takes another form which is more indirect, in which this attitude is given a symbolic representation.

Anger is an important emotional springboard for the poetry of Césaire; thus his poems brim over with an internal tension and an eruptive violence which translate his mood of defiant rebellion. It is in this connection that his surrealist technique acquires a particular significance, for it serves to carry an elaborate system of symbols with which his fantasy of aggression is realised in poetic form:

> my desire, a hazard of tigers surprised armed with sulphur⁵

¹ 'Chiens', p. 68.   ² *Ibid.*, p. 8.   ³ 'Cadastre', p. 10.
⁴ 'Ferrements', p. 78, Editions du Seuil, 1960.
⁵ 'Les Armes Miraculeuses', p. 26, Paris, Gallimard, 1946.

His poetry becomes the 'miraculous arms' of the Negro revolt, of a general insurrection of the black rising against domination:

> and the mines of radium buried in
> the abyss of my innocences
> will burst into grains
> in the manger of birds.[1]

The poet creates the vista of a violent 'progress of perturbations', of a generalised disturbance rising to a vision of a total Apocalypse:

> Clouds, derail on the reed! Rain violent maiden spin out your lint-shreds! Wounds of the sea, settle down whistling! Craters and volcanoes break adrift! On the stampede, mad deities! Get your brains blown off! Let the fields be torn up with the trident and the pearl-fishers hurled right up to the sky . . .[2]

A dream of desolation and catastrophe is a natural one to the rebel, whose consciousness is permeated by violence. In Césaire's poetry, his picture of destruction is reinforced by images drawn from the natural world, of fire and its many variations, of serpents, and poisonous plants and dangerous animals, and from the human world bullets, poisons, knives and the like. The poet in his revolt arms himself with all the agents of destruction, allies himself with all the violent manifestations of the natural world so that he acquires the primordial strength of an elemental force—

> It is me singing with a voice still held
> in the stutter of the elements[3]

—and he presents his revolted brothers endowed with the same primordial power:

> And by my gills conspired in a gnashing of teeth
> and of rockets syncopating harsh uglinesses
> behold the hundred thoroughbreds neighing with
> the lust of the sun in the midst of stagnation[4]

This combative mood is dramatically realised in the symbolic presentation of the antagonists—'white dog of the North', 'black serpent of the South'—and in a series of images of opposition—'night and day', 'darkness and light', 'white and black'—which acquire definite values, the one set appearing as the antithesis of the other. Césaire reverses the ordinary associations of words in the French language for his own purposes. This appears clearly in the following passage where he evokes the memory of the hero of the Haitian revolution, treacherously vanquished by Napoleon:

> a solitary man imprisoned in white
> a solitary man who defies the white cries of white death
> TOUSSAINT TOUSSAINT LOUVERTURE
> He is a man who bewitches the white hawk of white death
> He is a man alone in the sterile sea of white sand.[5]

[1] *Ibid.*, p. 8. [2] 'Ferrements', p. 48. [3] 'Cadastre', p. 47.
[4] 'Armes', p. 10. [5] 'Cahier', p. 46.

The negation of Western values and the reversal of the concepts of Western society form an essential part of Césaire's technique. His disaffection for Western society prompts his violent assault on its spiritual foundations and becomes an aggressive iconoclasm. Morality is the 'obsidional currency of towns deprived of water and of sleep'. Reason and order, for him synonyms of constraint and repression, are swept away. A strongly anti-clerical attitude is also a part of his revolt.

Thus, a significant aspect of Césaire's poetry appears to be its nihilism. But this is not unrelated, for his revolt is logical and motivated, nor is it absolute, for it is amply counter-balanced by a more constructive vision.

Rebellion and refusal, however strongly accentuated, are only the obvious aspects of a more profound desire, moments in the more significant aspiration that has its roots in the poet's personal sentiment of exile. At a more intimate level, they appear as a personal project of salvation:

> I force the vitelline membrane which
> separates me from myself.[1]

The rejection of Western values is a preliminary in his quest for fulfilment. Again, the technical resources of surrealism become the instruments of this process of disalienation. The negation of reason, for example, is the discharge from the poet's veins of the 'parasitic worms' of Western culture, forced by the 'lucid crack of unreasoning' and complemented by a new insight into the depths of his authentic self—

> the birds will sing softly in the sweep of salt
> the Congolese lullaby that the jailers have taken
> from me but which the very pious sea of cranial
> boxes preserves on its ritual leaves.[2]

—and by a more penetrating vision, undreamed of by his acquired logic, of the 'essential landscape' of the universe. And it is this descent into himself that reveals to him a quality more natural, and more essential than his acquired but 'inauthentic riches':

> for me I have nothing to fear I am before
> Adam I belong neither to the same lion nor to
> the same tree I am of another warmth and of
> another cold
> O gleams, O dew-drops, O sources,
> O remains of starry towns,
> my infancy milk of glow-worms and thrill of reptile.[3]

And it is by virtue of this quality that the poet re-orders the world. From his 'great flesh of night with grains of day', he wills the elevation of things to a 'gaseous level of the organism' in which opposites have been abolished, to bring forth a new image of a total reconciliation in the universe:

> Void of day
> Void of night

[1] *Ibid.*, p. 56.　　　　　[2] 'Armes', p. 44.　　　　　[3] *Ibid.*, p. 32.

> a soft attraction
> In the very flesh of things
> splinters forth
> nocturnal Day
> diurnal night
> exuded in Fullness[1]

Césaire's surrealism goes beyond a play of words; it is rigorously functional, the vehicle of a poetic vision. It is the poetic tool with which he reveals the positive irony and the profound constructive purpose of his movement of revolt:

> and our faces beautiful
> as the true operative power
> of negation.[2]

Complementary to this is the other function of his technique to which reference has been made, namely as an instrument of disalienation, as a means of unfolding his interior self, of bringing to the surface his suppressed African nature. It is important in this connection to consider his Caribbean origins in order to assess this side of his poetry.

Aimé Césaire is the foremost poet of the Caribbean not only in the literary quality of his work but also in his sentiments, in his imagery and in the total atmosphere of his writing. A feeling of and for the West Indian islands pervades his poetry.

His attachment to his native country is a particular aspect of his racial consciousness. His indignation is moved directly by the lamentable conditions of the West Indies, its physical and moral misery. The opening pages of *Cahier* are a long and bitter evocation of the material and spiritual desolation of his people; of the

> monstrous globe of night sprouted from our
> debasement and our renouncement.[3]

The same particularity appears in his movement of revolt against white domination:

> And the sea lice-ridden with islands
> breaking under rose fingers
> flame shafts and my body
> thrown up whole by the thunderbolt.[4]

An even more distinctive theme of his poetry is the memory of slavery. The Middle Passage and the degenerate traffic to which his ancestors were submitted are a haunting presence in his poetry. The 'carcan', the 'chain', 'the whip' as well as associations like 'pursuits' and 'shipwrecks' recur with striking regularity in the imagery of his poetry, for the memory of slavery has become a palpable part of his consciousness:

> 'I hear swelling up from the holds the chained maledictions, the
> last gasps of the dying, the noise of a man being thrown into the

---

[1] *Ibid.*, pp. 19-20.   [2] 'Cadastre', p. 56.   [3] *Ibid.*, p. 31.   [4] 'Armes', p. 25.

sea . . . the baying of a woman in childbirth . . . the scratching of nails looking for throats . . . the mocking tones of the whip . . . the swarming of vermin in the midst of weariness.[1]

Colonial domination appears as a continuation of slavery, so that his protest is often framed in terms of slave revolt. *Et les Chiens se taisaient* is a dramatic presentation of this characteristic of Césaire's revolt. This aggressiveness is also projected in images and symbols drawn from the fauna and flora of the islands. A particularly significant example is his frequent use of 'volcanoes' and 'eruptive forces', a direct reference to the volcano which is a striking feature of the landscape of Martinique, his native island. So closely tied up with his different moods and attitudes are these local images that his poetry results in a deepening of local colour and becomes the expression of an organic union of the poet with his natural habitat. This telluric strain in Césaire's poetry is also fundamental to his view of man as a whole.

But perhaps the most significant theme in his poetry in connection with the West Indies is his sentiment of rootlessness, which appears as a variation on the theme of alienation, his most profound personal sentiment. Here he displays a keen awareness of the spiritual consequences of the uprooting of a considerable section of the black race from the original home and its transplantation in new surroundings; hence his accompanying sense of separation. Césaire has called himself the poet of the Diaspora, and the analogy with the dispersal of the Jews is reflected in the religious note which he strikes with this description of the West Indies (in terms of its own flora)—

> dwelling made of undoings
> dwelling made of quick hulls
> *dwelling made of Passion Flower*,
> dwelling a hundred times made and unmade . . .[2]

His preoccupation with this theme also conditions his imagery. His wish for fulfilment is often expressed in terms of a plant growing, of a striking of roots. Yet it is his awareness of incompleteness and frustration that dominates.

The very idea of the island becomes for him the physical symbol of a diminution, of a separation from a larger whole:

> Island of the blood of sargassoes
> Island nibbled remains of remora
> Island backfiring laughter of whales
> Island specious word of mounted proclamations
> Island large scattered heart
>
> . . . .
> Island illjointed, island disjointed
> All islands beckon
> All islands are widows[3]

[1] 'Cahier', p. 62.   [2] From 'Soleil Cou Coupé', p. 30, Paris, Editions K, 1946.
[3] 'Cadastre', p. 90.

It is in this particular respect that the African theme assumes its significance in his poetry. For apart from the sentiment of rootlessness which requires a palliation, there is also present in his Caribbean mind a conflict arising out of his suppression of his African origins in the face of a diminishing Western culture. Africa, though present in the popular culture of the Caribbean, is the 'unavowed continent'; a situation which has created an unfortunate complex in the West Indian and given rise to a difficult social problem. Césaire's poetry has a social purpose in this connection: to render back to the West Indian that sense of pride in his racial origin which is necessary for him to reconcile the two parts of his divided self:

> the irresistible purity of my hand calls out
> from afar, from very far, from the hereditary patrimony
> for the victorious ardour of the acid in the flesh of life[1]

Africa is the ultimate source of Césaire's poetic inspiration. All the elements of his poetry—the themes and sentiments as well as the formal modes of his poetic expression—take on a final meaning with reference to Africa.

In the circumstances that produced Césaire's poetry, his sense of Africa is a direct consequence of his racial consciousness. It is clear enough that the poet's turning to Africa, the home of his persecuted race, is a reaction against social and political realities and in particular against the long denigration of the black continent:

> I have hailed my gods by dint of denials[2]

Along with this is his refusal of 'assimilation' and his claim to an inner quality that is preserved in him, despite the disfiguring effect of Western culture:

> You may paint the tree's trunk white,
> the force of the bark cries out from under[3]

His resentment against domination and alienation, and his need for identity provoke a yearning for a richer experience of himself and of the world:

> I the carrier of burdens am also a carrier of roots[4]

Thus Africa appears as his source of strength, and his poetry as a long backward movement for the recovery of this essential force. In the light of his emotional need, his poetry becomes a means for the rehabilitation of the black continent (hence his references to its ancient civilisation) and a restoration of its values:

> Your solar tiara with butt-strokes driven full to the hilt
> they have made into a yoke; your deep sigh
> they have blinded in the eyes; shamed your pudic face;
> muzzled, shrieking that it was guttural,
> your voice that spoke in the silence of the shades[5]

---

[1] 'Armes', p. 24. [2] 'Chiens', p. 37. [3] *Ibid.*, p. 38.
[4] 'Cadastre', p. 81. [5] 'Ferrements', p. 79.

It is possible, therefore, to speak of Césaire's emotional identification with Africa in his poetry as a compensatory counter-balance to his experience of the West. But, however valid, such a view is at best a superficial assessment of the real import of his poetry and misses the true direction of Césaire's aspiration.

In the first place, Césaire's poetry is wedded to a revolutionary cause—the liberation of Africa from colonial rule and the freedom of the race—as a pre-requisite for the *spiritual regeneration* of black people:

> Liberty my only pirate, water of the new year my only thirst[1]

The political cause dictates the need for a *deliberate* self-consciousness on the part of the black, for a self-affirmation in terms of values that do not enter the sphere of those by which he is oppressed and negated by the white; in other words, in terms original to the self. Thus, in the face of a humiliation that threatens to provoke his spiritual extinction, the black redresses himself and recovers his dignity in these celebrated lines from *Cahier*:

> my *négritude* is not a stone, its deafness hurled against the clamour
> of the day,
> my *négritude* is not a speck of dead water on the dead eye of the
> earth
> my *négritude* is neither a tower nor a cathedral
> it thrusts into the red flesh of the soil
> it thrusts into the burning flesh of the sky[2]

Césaire's definition of *négritude* in the last two lines is a reference to a Bambara symbol depicting man in intimate union with the earth and with the sky. Thus in terms of an authentic African humanism what has been denounced as an excessive romanticism becomes in reality a reaffirmation. In other words, Césaire's Africanism is a genuine rediscovery of the spiritual values of the black continent, and a reappropriation, through his poetry, of a personal ancestral heritage.

Once again, the surrealist technique is used as an instrument for this process of revaluation and personal identification. In the poem *To Africa*, Césaire addresses the African peasant in these lines:

> Peasant the wind where hulls glide fixes around my face
> the distant hand of a dream
> your field in its pillage bursts open with sea monsters
> that I am helpless to ward off
> And my gesture is as pure as a forehead of oblivion
> Strike peasant, I am your son . . .[3]

In another poem, again to Africa, his personal symbolism is combined with the image of fertility to express his own hankering after his origins and for a rebirth to nature

> and by the spark of Woman through which I seek
> the road to bracken ferns and to the Fouta Djallon
> and by Woman closing upon a longing unfolding . . .[4]

---

[1] 'Armes', p. 90.   [2] 'Cahier', p. 71.   [3] 'Cadastre', p. 40.   [4] *Ibid.*, p. 50.

His imagery and the structure of his poems reflect an African influence, either directly or through his West Indian connection. The baffling difficulty of much of his poetry imitates the esoteric character of African ritual incantations, reinforced with images and symbols drawn from nature.

Even where it is possible to trace the influence of Césaire's conscious study of African ritual customs in his poetry, nothing other than the poet's temperament bearing a particular cultural imprint can explain the rhythmic strength of his poetry. It seems to me perfectly logical to explain the muscular vigour of his verse not only by the violent nature of its emotional inspiration, but also as an expression of the rhythms bequeathed to West Indian popular culture by Africa. A poem like *Batouque*[1] is a veritable drama in rhythm, something unique in French poetry.

In short, the surrealist revolution, by breaking down the conventional forms of French poetry, gave to Césaire a ready tool for providing an individual accent to his poetic expression, for restoring within the literary tradition of an imposed culture 'the upright majesty of [his] original eye'.[2]

In Césaire's poetry, then, we have the translation of an historical experience into a human situation. His poetry is public in so far as it relates directly to objective realities, properly introspective in as much as his inner state reflects outside events and transforms them into an individual subjective experience: that of a spiritual progress. And what gives unity to his themes is his aspiration towards an Absolute.

On the one hand, Césaire's personal themes show the efforts of a singular sensibility to bring together the disparate elements from his three cultural horizons—Europe, the Caribbean, Africa—and to integrate them into a new harmony within his personality:

> Space conquered Time triumphant as for me, I love
> time time is nocturnal and when Space which betrays
> me gallops,
> Time returns to deliver me
> Time Time
> Oh trap without prey calling to me
> integral
> natal
> solemn[3]

On the other hand his commitment to a cause expresses his concern for the salvation of his people as a condition for universal brotherhood. His poetry contains numerous expressions of his confidence in the advent of this purpose, for as he says in *Cahier*, 'there is room for all at the rendezvous of victory'.

But even beyond these direct concerns, his poetry as a whole expresses a more essential ideal, that of the regeneration of mankind. It is the vehicle of a primary vision of a world in which man, restored to nature in an immediate union, will find 'the rock without dialect, the leaf without keep, the fragile water without femur'.[4]

[1] 'Armes', pp. 81–90.　　[2] 'Cadastre', p. 66.　　[3] *Ibid.*, p. 86.　　[4] 'Armes', p. 45.

Langston Hughes

Ezekiel Mphahlele

Here is a man with a boundless zest for life. Now that sounds trite. But who could say less of Langston Hughes? He has an irrepressible sense of humour, and to meet him is to come face to face with the essence of human goodness. In spite of his literary success, he has earned himself the respect of young Negro writers, who never find him unwilling to help them along. And yet he is not condescending. Unlike most Negroes who become famous or prosperous and move to high-class residential areas, he has continued to live in Harlem, which is in a sense a Negro ghetto.

Since 1926, when his first volume of verse, 'The Weary Blues', appeared, Langston Hughes has loomed progressively larger on the North American literary scene, and he has stayed top among Negro writers.

Hughes is a most versatile writer: poetry, fiction, plays, jazz lyrics, librettos, books about jazz, Negro history, and so on. We are here concerned with his verse.

There was quite a chorus of Negro voices in the 'twenties, and the then 23-year-old Hughes was one of the chorus. Among the others were Countee Cullen, James Weldon Johnson, Angelina Weld Grimké, the Jamaica-born Claude McKay, Jean Toomer, Paul Laurence Dunbar, Sterling Brown, Arna Bontemps and Georgia Douglas Johnson. Journals like 'Crisis' and 'Opportunity', which catered specifically for Negro culture, gave a terrific spurt to creative talent.

As might be expected, a large volume of the verse that was turned out was very close to the Negro situation; the fact of oppression, the fact of the black man's rejection by the white man, the fact of rootlessness. This protest swayed between surrender and self-pity at the one end and a stiff-necked self-justification at the other. We hear Angelina Weld Grimké say in *Surrender*:

> Uncrowned,
> We go, with heads bowed to the ground,
> And old hands, gnarled and hard and browned.
> Let us forget the past unrest—
> We ask for peace.

Countee Cullen in his *Protest* says he does not long for death:

> But time to live, to love, bear pain and smile,
> Oh, we are given such a little while.

'We shall not always plant while others reap', Cullen holds forth, echoing Shelley. Although the Negro is dark-skinned he harbours a certain loveliness.

> So in the dark we hide the heart that bleeds
> And wait and tend our agonising seed.

And yet it was he who reiterated so often that he wanted his verse to be taken as poetry, without the implications of race.

In the same idiom Langston Hughes sings:

> I, too, sing America.
> I am the darker brother.
> They send me to eat in the kitchen
> When company comes
> But I laugh,
> And eat well,
> And grow strong.
> Tomorrow,
> I'll sit at the table
> When company comes.
> Nobody'll dare say to me,
> 'Eat in the kitchen,'
> Then.
>
> Besides,
> They'll see how beautiful I am
> And be ashamed—
>
> I, too, am America.[1]

Again, The night is beautiful,
So the faces of my people.

All his life the fact of Hughes's Negro-ness (he has actually a light complexion) has aroused in him a desire to challenge those from the other side of the colour line that reject it:

> My old man's a white old man
> And my old mother's black.
> My old man died in a fine big house.
> My ma died in a shack.
> I wonder where I'm gonna die,
> Being neither white nor black?

It is unfortunate that blunt protest, inevitable in circumstances of race discrimination which often expresses itself in lynchings or slow murder, seldom lifts poetry above the level of sickly, mawkish versification.

Naturally, this colour-consciousness had, at a certain point, to look for its roots, or rather try to feel Africa as the Negro's cultural cradle. In 1923 Hughes met and heard Marcus Garvey exhort Negroes to go back to Africa to escape the wrath of the white man, and Hughes became one of the many poets who thought they felt the beating of the jungle tom-toms in the Negro's pulse. Their verse took on a nostalgic mood, and some even imagined that they were infusing the rhythm of African dancing and music

---

[1] All the poetry by Langston Hughes quoted in this essay is taken from his 'Selected Poems', New York, Alfred A. Knopf, 1959.

80

into their verse. They were called, half-sarcastically and half-enviously, the 'Rhythm Boys'. Professor Stirling Brown of Howard University, who was a young poet then, regarded the movement as a mere faddism. Dr. W. E. B. Du Bois roared at Carl Van Vechten, a white author, for portraying in his novel, *Nigger Heaven*, Harlem cabaret life as a show of savage, primitive passions in the rhythm of its dance and music.

This romantic mood very rarely produces powerful poetry. Only when it was dispersed and was fused with other thoughts could it result in a sober poem like Hughes's *The Negro Speaks of Rivers*. He wrote it on his way to Mexico to see his father who hated 'niggers', although he was a Negro himself. This worried the son a great deal, and the poem is a fusion of thoughts about the father, Negroes, himself, slavery and African ancestry.

> I've known rivers:
> I've known rivers ancient as the world and older than the
>   flow of human blood in human veins.
> My soul has grown deep like the rivers.
> I bathed in the Euphrates when dawns were young.
> I built my hut near the Congo and it lulled me to sleep.
> I looked upon the Nile and raised the pyramids above it.
> I heard the singing of the Mississippi when Abe Lincoln went
>   down to New Orleans, and I've seen its muddy bosom turn
>   all golden in the sunset.
> I've known rivers:
> Ancient, dusky rivers.
> My soul has grown deep like the rivers.

He came to Africa. As with most things, Langston Hughes took this continent casually, with a sense of fun. Not as Richard Wright was to take it years later when he came here and gave an account of his experiences in *Black Power* (1954). Wright took himself too seriously and expected Africans to warm to his approach immediately simply because he was black. He assessed the value of African cultures as he observed them in Ghana by Western standards and summed them up as inadequate (in spite of his own admission that he could not strike a medium for mutual understanding between him and the Ghanaians). He did not have Hughes's humility and sense of adventure.

'My Africa, Motherland of the Negro peoples! And me a Negro! Africa! The real thing, to be touched and seen . . . !' Hughes exclaimed. To him the people were 'dark and beautiful'. But he was sad, because 'the Africans looked at me and would not believe I was a Negro. You see, unfortunately, I am not black!'

The vogue for primitivism put Langston Hughes in an embarrassing position at one time, which, however, he came out of with grace. He had found himself a patron in the person of a rich white woman. She kept him comfortably in food and clothing so that he could write 'beautiful things', things that came out of his 'primitive soul'. One day he wrote something

81

angry against the luxurious newly-opened Waldorf Astoria, the symbol of plenty surrounded by so much poverty and toil. Hughes simply did not know how to satisfy his benefactor. He writes:

> She wanted me to be primitive, and know and feel the intuitions of the primitive. But, unfortunately, I did not feel the rhythms of the primitive surging through me, and so I could not live and write as though I did. I was only an American Negro—who had loved the surface of Africa and the rhythms of Africa—but I was not Africa. I was Chicago and Kansas City and Broadway and Harlem. And I was not what she wanted me to be.

This experience hurled Hughes into another emotional crisis. The first one had been that time when he was in Mexico and felt he hated his father. Desperately ill, he went to his mother and stepfather in Cleveland.

Langston Hughes left the African theme for a long time. Now that Africa has begun to take on a new significance for the American Negro, he has reviewed the old poems with their drumbeats and nostalgia. He has written new ones, and handled the lot as part of *The Poetry of Jazz*, a series of readings Hughes does, accompanied by drums. The following is in the new mood:

> Africa,
> Sleepy giant,
> You've been resting awhile.
> Now I see the thunder
> And the lightning
> In your smile.
> Now I see
> The storm clouds
> In your waking eyes:
> The thunder,
> The wonder
> And the new
> Surprise.
> Your every step reveals
> The new stride
> In your thighs.

The Negro's recall of the slave days piles up imagery in such poems as *Trumpet Player*; and the 'black' theme is elevated from the shallows of self-justification. There is a muted voice of protest here, coming out like the plaintive tones distilled from a muted trumpet. Here are four stanzas from the poem:

> The Negro
> With the trumpet at his lips
> Has dark moons of weariness
> Beneath his eyes

Where the smouldering memory
Of slave ships
Blazed to the crack of whips
About his thighs.

The music
From the trumpet at his lips
Is honey
Mixed with liquid fire.
The rhythm
From the trumpet at his lips
Is ecstasy
Distilled from old desire—

The Negro
With his trumpet at his lips
Whose jacket
Has a fine one-button roll,
Does not know
Upon what riff the music slips
Its hypodermic needle
To his soul—

But softly
As the tune comes from his throat
Trouble
Mellows to a golden note.

It is not often that Langston Hughes's anger mounts to a pitch. When it does, especially when he writes on the South, his protest comes straight from the shoulder, and he throws in tense and turgid word-pictures. In *Third Degree* he says:

Slug me! Beat me!
Scream jumps out
Like blow-torch.
Three kicks between the legs
That kill the kids
I'd make tomorrow.

Bars and floor skyrocket
And burst like Roman candles.

Again, there is the poem, *The South*:

The lazy, laughing South
With blood on its mouth.
The sunny-faced South,
    Beast-strong,
    Idiot-brained.

83

The child-minded South
Scratching in the dead fire's ashes
For a Negro's bones.
    Cotton and the moon,
    Warmth, earth, warmth,
    The sky, the sun, the stars,
    The magnolia-scented South.
Beautiful, like a woman,
Seductive as a dark-eyed whore,
    Passionate, cruel,
    Honey-lipped, syphilitic—
    That is the South.
And I, who am black, would love her
But she spits in my face.
And I, who am black,
Would give her many rare gifts
But she turns her back upon me.
    So now I seek the North—
    The cold-faced North,
    For she, they say,
    Is a kinder mistress,
And in her house my children
May escape the spell of the South.

He writes much in lighthearted vein, skimming the surface of things, presenting the externals of a situation to suggest the inner meaning to the reader, never posing as a thinker. His abundant sense of satire reinforces everything he touches in this manner. At one time he will say:

I don't mind dying—
But I'd hate to die all alone!
I want a dozen pretty women
To holler, cry and moan.

A man returns to his lover whom he left a long while ago. The woman says:

I looked at my daddy—
Lawd! and I wanted to cry.
He looked so thin—
Lawd! that I wanted to cry.
But the devil told me:
    Damn a lover
    Come home to die!

In a roaringly funny satirical poem, *Life is Fine*, a man is driven by some love problem to thoughts of suicide. He goes to a river and jumps in:

I came up once and hollered!
I came up twice and cried!
If that water hadn't a-been so cold
I might've sunk and died.
   But it was
   Cold in that water!
   It was cold!

He takes a lift sixteen floors up a building, to jump down. He yells and cries because if the building hadn't been so high, he might have jumped and died. 'But it was high up there! It was high!' So he decides to go on living. He might have died for love, 'but for livin' I was born'. And,

   Life is fine!
   Fine as wine!
   Life is fine!

Finally, in more pensive vein but with Hughes's deep chuckle down there at the base of his questionings:

   What happens to a dream deferred
   Does it dry up
   Like a raisin in the sun?
   Or fester like a sore—
   And then run?
   Does it sink like rotten meat?
   Or crust and sugar over—
   Like a syrupy sweet?
   Maybe it just sags
   Like a heavy load
   Or does it explode?

Langston Hughes still talks about the beauty of being dark-skinned. He may yet help to supply the artist's answer to the dilemma in which the American Negro finds himself these days: political, economic and social integration with whites—yes; but can the Negro retain his cultural identity and avoid being swallowed up by the American mainstream? Some Negroes of culture think they want to do both. There is a good deal of talk among them about *négritude* and the enchantment it holds out to them. One Negro writer said recently at a conference of writers that, with the general improvement of the coloured man's position in the United States, it was going to be hard for those apprenticed in protest writing of the 'lynching tradition' —especially the older men—to re-adjust themselves. Langston Hughes is in no such predicament. It is a long time since his poetry outlived dead-pan protest. And Hughes was never preoccupied with a two-dimensional protest.

McKay's Human Pity

A Note on his Protest Poetry

ARTHUR D. DRAYTON

Outside Jamaican and Negro literary circles in the United States, the late
Jamaican poet, Claude McKay, is known best and often only for his race-
conscious verse, sometimes only by his much-quoted sonnet which Sir
Winston Churchill helped to popularise during World War II. For many
people, in the same way that *The Negro Speaks of Rivers* is Langston Hughes,
so this particular sonnet is McKay.

> If we must die, let it not be like hogs
> Hunted and penned in an inglorious spot,
> While round us bark the mad and hungry dogs,
> Making their mock at our accursed lot.
> If we must die, O let us nobly die,
> So that our precious blood may not be shed
> In vain; then even the monsters we defy
> Shall be constrained to honor us though dead!
> O kinsmen! we must meet the common foe!
> Though far outnumbered let us show us brave,
> And for their thousand blows deal one deathblow!
> What though before us lies the open grave?
> Like men we'll face the murderous, cowardly pack,
> Pressed to the wall, dying, but fighting back!!!¹

G. R. Coulthard has described his protest verse as 'bitter and violent',
and has observed that 'his best poems are characterised by a racial hatred,
or even a challenge, of the most violent kind'. Bitter and violent; a challenge: yes. But the charge of racial hatred is difficult to support; and unless
we are to argue a complete change in McKay between this later protest
verse and his earlier dialect poems, it is a strange assertion. For, quite apart
from the evidence of the protest verse itself, it assumes a new dimension if
one is familiar with McKay's two publications of dialect poems before he
left Jamaica to take up residence in the United States.

But it is not surprising that McKay should have won recognition through
his verse written around the theme of Negro suffering in the States. For this
has the virility one might expect of a Caribbean poet shocked by what he
discovers in America. Coming from quite a different kind of experience of
Negro degradation in Jamaica, McKay was fired by what he saw in the States
and helped to give to American Negro poetry a distinctly different voice.

As we shall see, McKay's early years in America coincided with crucial

¹ In 'Selected Poems', New York, Bookman Associates, 1953.

86

years for the Negro cause, and the virility of his verse was in keeping with the prevailing atmosphere. But, looked at closely, this virility reveals itself as based on something more than mere bitterness; it includes and depends on a certain resilience—perhaps stubborn humanity would be better—on the part of the poet. And this in turn is to be traced to McKay's capacity to react to Negro suffering, not just as a Negro, but as a human being; to react to human suffering as such. For there is a certain danger which is inherent in the Negro situation, one which can lead to great human tragedy, and has no doubt done so times without number in individual cases. It is that the Negro, because of the injustices which he has suffered and continues to suffer, reacts quite rightly as a Negro to the degradation of the Negro; but he is called upon to react in this way so continually, and at times so violently, that he is in danger of losing his capacity to react to suffering in a way which rises above this and includes it, to react simply and primarily as a human being. White bigotry has become so insistent that it is difficult to ask this of the Negro, and he is left in danger of not being touched by human suffering outside the Negro context, or outside a situation which closely resembles his own. And yet, if he is not to abdicate his humanity, he must retain his capacity for this larger and more basic reaction, since to be without it has frightful implications for his emotional growth and his stature as a human being.

For the poet, especially one handling 'racial' material, to lack it would be anathema. If he does not have it, he may as well go off and write about daffodils and lakes. But if by identifying himself with his own community or race he can proceed to that greater and more meaningful identification based on his humanity, he is qualified to handle 'racial' material. McKay always had this qualification, and it imparted to his verse a certain universal significance. Thus the sonnet *If we must die* was written after and relates to the Washington race riot of 1919. Sir Winston Churchill, however, could use it to whip up defiant courage during World War II because it is essentially a cry of defiance from the human heart in the face of a threat to man's dignity and civilisation, a threat which was and is true of Nazism and the hatred of the Negro alike.

To the White Friends is a slight poem, apologetic in tone and coming near to romanticising the black man. But as in the sonnet, *If we must die*, the poet's pride of race is sublimated. Here he claims for the black man a superiority over the white in the former's refusal to out-savage the latter and in this divine mission to save mankind—

> Thy dusky face I set among the white
> For thee to prove thyself of higher worth;
> Before the world is swallowed up in night,
> To show thy little lamp: go forth, go forth![1]

The poet, in these poems and in others, is moved by what he sees as a noble duty devolving on the Negro to save not just himself but the human

[1] *Ibid.*

race; to restore, if necessary through the Negro's very sacrifice, the dignity of man. It is a sentiment, in brief, informed by a sense of responsibility to mankind, the sentiment which today pervades James Baldwin's writing on the Negro situation. This is one reason why, as Coulthard has pointed out, 'his poetry has not aged'. This, then, is one way in which he escapes the blight of racial hatred which would have been fatal to his humanist concern.

Sometimes, too, there is a certain poignancy as he attempts to reconcile his reaction as a Negro with his larger reaction as a human being. To see his verse in terms of mere racialism is to miss this quality, and a return to his earlier work is instructive in this respect.

We may trace this quality, using McKay's own phrase, to his human pity. In *The Desolate City* he was to write:

> My spirit is a pestilential city,
> With misery triumphant everywhere,
> Glutted with baffled hopes and human pity.[1]

No doubt the baffled hopes were to accumulate gradually, but the human pity was there from the beginning and evident in his early dialect verse. Its source lies in the poet's tender, gentle spirit. And both in his early and later verse it saves him from racial extremism.

It is not that McKay did not have pride of race. The dedication of his first volume of poetry to the Governor of the island is proof of his consciousness of and love for his race; but it is also evidence of the overriding insistence of his social conscience which is not circumscribed by the limits of race. For the dedication is to the Governor 'who by his sympathy with the black race has won the love and admiration of all Jamaicans'.[2] The reference to *all* Jamaicans is not mere rhetoric; for there is something here of that typically Jamaican national pride, a pride that seldom appears elsewhere in the Caribbean as fiercely as it does in Jamaica, and certainly never appeared elsewhere in the region that early.

Max Eastman, who knew him well, has written about the poet's early knowledge of his ancestors.

> He learned in childhood how a family of his ancestors, brought over in chains from Madagascar, had kept together by declaring a death strike on the auction block. Each would kill himself, they vowed solemnly, if they were sold to separate owners. With the blood of such rebels in his veins, and their memory to stir it, Claude McKay grew up proud of his race and with no disposition to apologise for his colour.[3]

However apocryphal this may seem, if we grant that McKay accepted it we may expect to find a keen sense of race in his early work. But this is not the case. An undercurrent of protest is always there, but it is social protest—though in the context of Jamaica in the first two decades of the century this

---

[1] *Ibid.* [2] 'Songs of Jamaica', Kingston, Gardener & Co., 1912.
[3] 'Selected Poems', p. 110.

inevitably meant protest on behalf of the black man. To write about those who suffered was to write about the black man, and the fact that they were black must have quickened McKay's interest in them. However, one does not get the impression that his protest emanates primarily from a sense of race, but rather from his shocked sense of fair play, ultimately and instinctively from that very characteristic trait of McKay's to which reference has already been made, his tender, gentle spirit that was appalled at human suffering.

Claude McKay was born in 1889 in the Clarendon Hills of Jamaica, for which he always retained a deep affection. On the evidence of his poetry he was one of those wanderers who have an undying attachment to the place of their roots. If such later pieces as *Flame Heart* and *The Tropics in New York* revealed his nostalgia for Jamaica when he lived abroad, in his early dialect verse there are also nostalgic references to the Hills. He had moved down to the plains to join the Police Force, having begun life as a wheelwright. It would come as no surprise to a West Indian that his naturally gentle disposition should have received its first great jolt in the Force. For in those days the West Indian policeman was recruited for his brawn rather than his brain, and was expected to honour and celebrate this fact every hour he spent on the beat.

The Police Force was therefore the last place for a man who was always uneasy in the presence of human suffering, and McKay's experiences there have been recorded in his second volume of dialect verse. However, his first volume, *Songs of Jamaica*, does not deal with these experiences but was written to relieve his feelings while in the Force. Here then was a situation that might have produced one of two elements or both, anger and sentimentality. Of the latter there is very little; and nowhere in this volume is there any anger in McKay's voice, although over and over again he is reprimanding those responsible for social injustices to his people. No doubt McKay, writing to relieve his feelings, must have sought for redeeming features in the dark picture. So that while his gentle nature led him to pity his people's suffering and to protest against this, his need for relief must have compelled him to celebrate their cheerfulness and other such qualities. That is to say, what emerges from this volume is not only his keen sense of suffering, and his people's suffering, but also his deep knowledge of what sustains them and makes them interesting and vital as human beings, their cheerfulness and good humour in spite of dispiriting conditions.

Instead of the note of anger, then, there is the celebration of the sense of duty which characterises the labourer's resignation. In *Quashie to Buccra* he sings of the toil and sweat which the 'naygur man' must put into his field, toil and sweat unknown to and unappreciated by the 'buccra' (the white man). It is, in fact, the attempt by 'buccra' to cheat 'quashie' of his due reward that is the starting point of the poem:

> You want a basketful fe quattiewut,
> 'Cause you no know how 'tiff de bush fe cut.

89

And he returns to the theme in his last verse:

> You tas'e petater an' you say it sweet,
> But you no know how hard we wuk fe it;
> Yet still de hardship always melt away
> Wheneber it come roun' to reapin' day.[1]

But he never allows the protest to overshadow the peasant's resignation and pride in his work; and the poem appropriately ends with a reference to the joy in the rewards of labour, which is what the poet here makes of the old habit of the New World Negro of forgetting his hardships on pay-day in a bout of rollicking fun.

In *Whe' Fe Do?* and *Hard Times* situations which could easily have led him to racial protest come to rest instead on a note of resignation. After complaints about taxes, poverty, sickness, nakedness and the following verse—

> De picknies hab to go to school
>   Widout a bit fe taste;
> And I am working like a mule,
> While buccra, sittin' in de cool,
>   Have 'nuff nenyam fe waste . . .

comes the key verse in *Hard Times*—

> I won't gib up, I won't say die,
>   For all de time is hard;
> Aldough de wul' soon en', I'll try
> My wutless best as time goes by,
>   An' trust on in me Gahd.[2]

Thus a complaint about the inequality of the distribution of wealth is tempered by his observation of the determination to try, against all the ordained odds. So too in *Whe' Fe Do?* as he mourns the hard lot of the Negro and sees the social injustice inherent in the polarisation of the world into black and white, he sees it as the way of the world and celebrates instead the imperturbable cheerfulness of the socially victimised Negro:

> And though de wul' is full o' wrong,
> Dat caan' prevent we sing we song
> All de day as we wuk along—
>   Whe' else fe do?
>
> We happy in de hospital;
> We happy when de rain deh fall;
> We happy though de baby bawl
> Fe food dat we no hab at all;
> We happy when Deat' angel call
> Fe full we cup of joy wid gall:
> Our fait' in this life is not small—
>   De best to do.[3]

---

[1] 'Songs of Jamaica.'   [2] *Ibid.*   [3] *Ibid.*

Of course, we must be careful not to ascribe to the poet personally the various attitudes struck in these verses. It is more than likely that the poet is articulating commonly held folk views and attitudes, and that he intended this to be part of the appeal of the volume. Thus there is self-denigration when in *Hard Times* he writes:

> De peas won't pop, de corn can't grow,
> Poor people face look sad;
> Dat Gahd would cuss de lan' I'd know,
> For black naygur too bad.

Or there is the pervasive fatalism and the paradoxically concomitant reliance on God in such poems as this and *Whe' Fe Do?*. Or again the habit of blaming the government:

> You hab all t'ings fe mek life bles'
> But buccra 'poil de whole
> Wid gove'mint an' all de res',
> Fe worry naygur soul.[1]

This presentation of commonly held views contributes to the humour of the pieces—and twice over. For there is first of all the verbal humour; and then there is the humour of situation arising out of the West Indian capacity for making fun of himself. But it is also part of his way of achieving a subtle criticism of the white man and those responsible for the suffering of his people. For belonging as he does to the victimised segment of society, he has earned the right to make fun of their views. By contrast the 'buccra' has not. So he accomplishes this criticism by stating the superficial position of 'buccra' and contrasting this with his more authoritative voice. Thus he criticises 'buccra' for wanting to cheat 'quashie', but he dismisses 'buccra' and goes on to sing of the hard-working 'quashie'. Or he criticises the tourist who is intrigued by the water-carrier but who doesn't give a thought to the suffering and hard work involved.

> De pickny comin' up de hill,
> Fighting' wid heavy gou'd,
> Won't say it sweet him, but he will
> Complain about de load:
> Him feel de weight,
> Dem watch him gait;
> It's so some of de great
> High people fabour t'ink it sweet
> Fe batter in de boiling' heat.[2]

But the poet will nonetheless go on to celebrate the joy of the water-carrier.
The technique which is used is to make the suffering of his people the starting point, often by criticising those responsible for it or oblivious of it,

---

[1] *My Native Land, ibid.*   [2] *Fetching Water, ibid.*

91

and then without inconsistency to proceed to sing of the cheerfulness and glory of the victims. This conflict between suffering and cheerfulness is there, both in the people forming the subject of the poems and in the poems themselves, even in poems where he is not explicitly criticising anyone; in the latter it is always resolved in the unstated authority of the poet to sing of both, having shared in both. This right to complain and rejoice is denied the 'buccra' and the tourist who have not shared in their suffering and have no deep knowledge of their life. In the early poems this right is merely implied arising out of the conflict which heightens the interest. Later—and this is some measure of how far McKay had moved in the direction of racial protest—this right becomes explicit:

> Only a thorn-crowned Negro and no white
> Can penetrate into the Negro's ken,
> Or feel the thickness of the shroud of night
> Which hides and buries him from other men.[1]

So both early and late McKay evinces a sensitive identification with his people, whose suffering is his suffering, whose joys are his joys. He is proud of his race, and is hurt by the wrongs they suffer. And yet in his early work there is no strident racial protest. A further clue to this is to be found in one or two places in the first volume of dialect verse. Two poems carry footnotes explaining their origin. *Jim at Sixteen* is the story of a lad arrested by the author. The tight handcuffs make a raw wound on his wrist, but 'he was so patient, saying that he knew I could not help it. Although it was accidentally done, I felt so sad and ashamed.'[2] The second, *Strokes of Tamarind Switch*, was written after the author had seen a judicial flogging. 'I could not bear to see him—my own flesh—stretched out over the bench, so I went away to the Post Office near by.'[3] The boy had not cried during the flogging but broke down later while talking to the author, who was moved to give him tickets for his train journey. Clearly this is evidence of a gentleness of spirit which from the point of view of the policeman then (and even now, perhaps) is softness, unmanliness and sentimentality; but which also makes possible the finer verse (though this latter poem is flaccid) based on an instinctive feeling of sympathy for a suffering people, and no less for an individual. What we have here is primarily not a racial poet but someone whose human pity finds ample scope in the social and economic inferiority of his people. When he takes up residence in the United States amid the welter of human suffering, he will quite rightly be concerned first of all with the victims of it, the Negroes; but this will not prevent him from seeing other implications, terrible and far-reaching, for those who are guilty of the evil, for mankind as a whole, and not least for himself as a poet and as a human being.

That the poet coming face to face with human suffering and injustice must work out the implications which the experience holds for him as poet and human being is too commonplace to require further comment. He is of

---

[1] *The Negro's Tragedy*, 'Selected Poems'.
[2] In 'Songs of Jamaica.'   [3] *Ibid.*

course no real poet if this exercise degenerates into maudlin self-pity, and will have no claims on the interest of his fellow-men. McKay wrote his first volume of verse to relieve his feelings, to avoid self-pity; and in doing so he celebrated precisely those qualities on which people must fall back if they are to avoid it. In his second volume of Jamaican poems, *Constab Ballads*, he faces his personal dilemma more squarely; nor does the question of self-pity arise, since he recognises that his dilemma does not exist in isolation.

For his displeasure with the Force may derive from the suffering which as a policeman he has to inflict on his own people and which will lead to his forfeiture of their love:

> 'Tis grievous to think dat, while toilin' on here,
>   My people won't love me again,
> My people, my people, me owna black skin—
>   De wretched t'ought gives me such pain.[1]

Or it may arise from the insults to his dignity and what this does to him as a human being:

> 'Tis hatred without an' 'tis hatred within,
>   An' I am so weary an' sad;
> For all t'rough de tempest o' terrible strife
>   Dere's not'in' to make poor me glad.[2]

But it is in large part also due to chagrin occasioned by a variety of disillusioning experiences—the sight of another policeman disgracing himself, or that peculiar view of the debauched world which the policeman gets, and so on. For these ballads represent a wide variety of moods, and as the poet catalogues the different kinds of suffering which it is the lot of the policeman to encounter, it is as though he is recording his disappointed hopes for mankind. It is, in a word, his human pity which directs him from his personal dilemma to a more universal one.

When in 1912 McKay left Jamaica for the U.S.A., it was inevitable that this should lead to an eruption of Negro verse from his pen. For here was a man with a proud sense of his race, who had seen his people suffering in Jamaica and had—

> ... fled a land where fields are green
> Always, and palms wave gently to and fro,
> And winds are balmy, blue brooks ever sheen,
> To ease my heart of its impassioned woe.[3]

And he goes to America to meet Negro suffering such as he must have heard of but could never have envisaged. He has told us that rather than

---

[1] *The Heart of a Constab.*, in 'Constab Ballads', London, Watts, 1912.
[2] *Ibid.*
[3] *To Winter*, in 'Springi n New Hampshire and other poems', London, Richards, 1920.

return to the 'less demanding' life of Jamaica, he felt a compulsion to remain and join the struggle, for he was—

> ... bound with you in your mean graves,
> O black men, simple slaves of ruthless slaves.[1]

And no wonder. For in addition to what we know of McKay, we must remember the nature of the time of his early years in New York: a time of growing racial bitterness, with the stiffening of the South; Negro disillusionment with Booker T. Washington and a consequent adjustment of the Negro attitude; the increase in white hysteria and violence, which was to become even steeper after the war; the dashing of Negro hopes after the war which had been fought by them as well in defence of democracy; and the rise of Garveyism and the hostility between Garvey and the N.A.A.C.P. and others—all of which factors and others combined to bring about the Negro Renaissance.

But if McKay were simply a racial poet it would have been a short step, in these new conditions, from his Jamaican verse to bitter race-conscious work. Instead, however, we find for a long time a sober reaction to his new and disturbing environment. However much this new environment was dominated by the race question, it is clear that McKay, like Countee Cullen after him, was determined that the dignity of the poet's calling was not to be sullied. He refused to allow the quality of his reaction as poet to be warped; and equally he refused to allow his ambitions and status as a human being to be destroyed. All this affected his poetry, and explains the apparent ambivalence in his love–hate relationship with America.

About America and the experience of the Negro there McKay had no illusions; but he could at the same time pay her the tribute which she deserved:

> Although she feeds me bread of bitterness
> And sinks into my throat her tiger's tooth,
> Stealing my bread of life, I will confess
> I love this cultured hell that tests my youth![2]

In paying her this tribute there is a triumph, however; and it lies in the successful resistance to the threat of spiritual corrosion which America's 'hate' threatens to start within him:

> Yet, as a rebel fronts a king in state,
> I stand within her walls with not a shred
> Of terror, malice, not a word of jeer.[3]

Or, as in *Through Agony*, he refuses to meet hate with hate:

> I do not fear to face the fact and say
> How darkly dull my living hours have grown;
> My wounded heart sinks heavier than stone

---

[1] *In Bondage, ibid.*   [2] *America*, 'Selected Poems'.   [3] *Ibid.*

94

> Because I loved you longer than a day!
> I do not shame to turn myself away
> From beckoning flowers beautifully blown,
> To mourn your vivid memory alone
> In mountain fastnesses austerely gray.[1]

Through Agony may well have a more personal and private application, but surely it also refers on a symbolic level to McKay's continued admiration for America despite the pain which she caused.

This is integrity to self. There is also integrity as a poet. In *The Lynching* he approached the agonising subject if not in a dispassionate mood (how could any Negro?) in a disciplined one; in a mood which allows him to see more than one painful aspect. The poem proceeds in a subdued tone, and because of the subdued tone, the terror mounts and the poem ends on a note of sheer horror. This horror arises not only out of the deed, which is horrible enough, not only out of the hard inhumanity of the doers; but on top of all this, the dark prospects for the next generation:

> And little lads, lynchers that were to be,
> Danced round the dreadful thing in fiendish glee.[2]

Thus McKay sees not only the violence done to his own people, but the violence which the whites inflict on themselves as well. This, then, is McKay refusing to be stampeded into hysterical protest, served well by his breadth of vision which his capacity for human pity had strengthened. He can still be touched by misery pure and simple, as in *The Castaways* where, standing in a beautiful park, he is attracted not by the 'visible delight' of nature but by 'the castaways of earth', the lonely and derelict, and turns away in misery.[3] And it is not clear if they are black or white and it does not matter. In *Rest In Peace* it is his tender heart that is responding to the suffering of his people as he bids farewell to a departed friend:

> No more, if still you wonder, will you meet
>   With nights of unabating bitterness,
> They cannot reach you in your safe retreat,
>   The city's hate, the city's prejudice![4]

It is not that McKay is not reacting to Negro suffering. It is rather that he is meeting America's challenge as man and poet. He meets the challenge which America's hate sets for his humanity, and in his resistance he flings back his challenge to the forces of hate in America. As poet and man he must discipline himself, and this gives to his pain a dignity through which his verse sometimes transcends racial protest and becomes human protest.

But however much McKay might

> . . . possess the courage and the grace
> To bear my anger proudly and unbent

[1] 'Selected Poems.'   [2] 'Spring in New Hampshire.'   [3] *Ibid.*   [4] *Ibid.*

however much he must

> ... search for wisdom every hour,
> Deep in my wrathful bosom sore and raw,
> And find in it the superhuman power
> To hold me to the letter of your law![1]

the tide of violence and injustice to the Negro was too insistent for him to be in danger of becoming a moral Canute. Hatred never really becomes a characteristic of his poetry, but there came a time when it crept in occasionally. In *O Word I Love To Sing* he declares an undisguised 'hatred for the foe of me and mine', and regrets that the poem is an inadequate vehicle for his hatred.[2] McKay must have realised that poetry is too fragile and too sacred a vehicle for the kind of bitter hatred into which racial bigotry and its violent inroads on human freedom could compel the gentlest of men.

But if his poetry did not quite reflect the hatred which must have been eating into many a Negro breast at the time, it certainly reflected another aspect of Negro reaction, a new consciousness of the African connection. For however much the intellectuals might have resented Marcus Garvey's success among the masses with his appeal of 'Back to Africa' (which at first did not have the radical implications which it gathered to itself in his later years), intellectual Negro poetry was moving nearer to Africa spiritually. Garvey's call for a black man's religion was paralleled in sophisticated verse and so was his insistence on the past glories of the Negro race, and so was the new pride he encouraged in Negro beauty and indeed in everything black. Garvey himself put some of his ideas into rather indifferent verse, romanticising Africa and Africans. In better verse McKay does the same. In *Harlem Shadows* black prostitutes fetch from the poet this cry:

> Ah, stern harsh world, that in the wretched way
> Of poverty, dishonour and disgrace,
> Has pushed the timid little feet of clay,
> The sacred brown feet of my fallen race![3]

The Harlem dancer, in the poem of that name,

> ... seemed a proudly-swaying palm,
> Grown lovelier for passing through a storm.[4]

In *Outcast* he confesses to a spiritual oneness with Africa:

> For the dim regions whence my fathers came
> my spirit, bondaged by the body, longs.
> Words felt, but never heard, my lips would frame;
> My soul would sing forgotten jungle songs.[5]

When we recall that in his very first book of verse in Jamaica, McKay had only one poem about Africa, *Cudjoe Fresh from de Lecture*; and that

---

[1] *The White House*, 'Selected Poems'.   [2] 'Selected Poems.'
[3] 'Spring in New Hampshire.'   [4] *Ibid.*   [5] 'Selected Poems.'

96

in this poem McKay goes no further than the contemporary West Indian view of Africa, we can measure how far in racial protest he has travelled by now. In *Cudjoe*, after Cudjoe has expressed his surprise that in a lecture on evolution the Negro had been given a place in the scheme of things, we get:

> Yes, Cous' Jarge, slabery hot fe dem dat gone befo':
> We gettin' better times, for those days we no know;
> But I t'nk it do good, tek we from Africa
> An' lan' us in a blessed place as dis a ya.
> Talk 'bouten Africa, we would be deh till now,
> Maybe same half-naked—all day dribe buccra cow,
> An' tearin' t'rough de bush wid all de monkey dem,
> Wile an' uncibilise', an' neber comin' tame.[1]

As observed before, McKay was probably doing no more than dramatically representing a widely held view, one that even Marcus Garvey shared, if we read between his lines.

To romanticise Africa he must have relinquished such a view, if he ever held it himself. But as we see in the poem *Africa*, he could strike a balance between this romanticism and realism. In fine verse he pays a tribute to Africa's past glories, but he ends:

> Yet all things were in vain!
> Honour and Glory, Arrogance and Fame!
> They went. The darkness swallowed thee again.
> Thou art the harlot, now thy time is done,
> Of all the mighty nations of the sun.[2]

And in *Exhortation*, in a burst of Communist fervour, he called on Africa, 'dreaming for dim centuries', to awake and 'to the East turn, turn your eyes'.[3]

So at a time of romanticising he does not lose his sense of realism; at a time of hatred he does not lose his sense of balance nor his breadth of vision. Fully sensitive to the Negro plight, sharing in it and bitter about it —'what I write is urged out of my blood'[4]—he nevertheless contrives to maintain his equilibrium while protesting vehemently. It is sometimes a protest on behalf of humanity, for he is a poet. But he was also a black man in the United States, and it is more often a protest on behalf of his people, and for this he reserves a language that is often bitter and violent. But he never loses his temper; his poetry does not become undisciplined because of anger; he can achieve his effect through the dignity of his pain, through the controlled power of an image. When, for instance, he sees the white man's oppression in terms of primitive, animal concern for self he can write with dignity and force: 'The white man is a tiger at my throat'.[5]

---

[1] 'Songs of Jamaica.'   [2] 'Selected Poems.'   [3] 'Spring in New Hampshire.'
[4] *The Negro's Tragedy.*   [5] *Tiger*, 'Selected Poems'.

He does not seek to hide his bitterness. But having preserved his vision as poet and his status as a human being, he can transcend bitterness. In seeing, as he does, the significance of the Negro for mankind as a whole, he is at once protesting as a Negro and uttering a cry for the race of mankind as a member of that race. His human pity was the foundation that made all this possible.[1]

[1] Attention is drawn to McKay's autobiography, *A Long Way from Home*, New York, Furman, 1937.

His prose works are:
Home to Harlem, New York, Harper,1928
Banjo; a story without a plot, Harper, 1929.
Ginger Town, Harper, 1932.
Banana Bottom, Harper, 1933
Harlem: *Negro Metropolis* (Essays), New York, Dutton & Co., 1940.

Rabearivelo

ULLI BEIER

One of the greatest French-speaking African poets is undoubtedly the Malagasy Jean-Joseph Rabearivelo. His work has been much less boosted than that of some other French-speaking poets (he has been almost ignored by translators, so far), presumably because his writing does not seem to fit into the now fashionable *négritude* movement.

Rabearivelo died in 1937, which is two years before Césaire published his famous 'Cahier d'un Retour au Pays Natal'. The poet died tragically by taking his own life. His death came as a complete surprise to most of his friends, and the mystery that surrounded it has never really been solved. He was only thirty-four years old.

Rabearivelo left behind him seven volumes of poetry.[1] It is only in two of these, 'Presque Songes' and above all 'Traduit de la Nuit', that he liberated himself completely from French models. The volumes were first published in 1934 and 1935 respectively, and were reissued in Tananarive in 1960.[2]

Nothing could be further removed from the themes and images of current French African poetry than the writing of Rabearivelo. Colonialism and the African personality do not figure in it. There are no tom-toms, palm trees, and black nude women. There is no oppression and no revolution. In fact Rabearivelo is not concerned with the everyday issues of here and now.

Rabearivelo is a poet of cosmic visions. The themes of his poems are death, dissolution, catastrophe and sometimes resurrection. But he does not give us his personal heartbreaks; he writes a kind of depersonalised, anonymous poetry.

The poet himself hardly even figures in his poems, certainly not in his *good* poems. In fact human beings rarely occur. His basic images are: stars, birds, trees, seaweeds, lianas, fishes, cows. Where human images occur they never describe individuals but rather cosmic, semi-divine beings like 'She who was born before the light' or 'The black glassmaker, whose countless eyeballs none has ever seen'. or 'She whose heels are planted in the sea and whose sticky hands rise from it full of corals and crystals of shining salt.'

[1] 'La Coupe de Cendres', Tananarive, Pitot de la Beaujardière, 1924.
'Sylves', Tananarive, Imp de l'Imerina, 1927.
'Volumes', Imp. de l'Imerina, 1928.
'Presque Songes', Imp. de l'Imerina, 1934.
'Imaitsoanala—Fille d'oiseau—Cantate', Tananarive, Imp. Offic., 1935.
'Traduit de la Nuit', Tunis, Editions de Mirages, 1935.
'Lova', Tananarive, Imp. Volamahitsy, 1957.
[2] 'Poèmes', Tananarive, Imp. Offic., 1960.
   For English translations of some of the poems see 'Twenty-Four Poems', tr. Gerald Moore and Ulli Beier, Ibadan, Mbari, 1962.

The world Rabearivelo describes is a strangely unreal world. There is an extremely tantalising quality about these poems, because on the one hand he can make us see his visions so clearly—and on the other he destroys them again by removing them right out of our sphere of knowledge and experience. Thus he speaks of 'blind light'; or 'insipid salt'; these are images that destroy themselves and produce a sudden shock in the reader. On the whole Rabearivelo is careful to remove his poems from the sphere of everyday existence. Occasionally he mentions his native land, 'Imerina', but more often he locates his action near the 'frontiers of sleep'. Nearly all of his images suggest to us that we move in strange, unexplored zones: 'all seasons have been abolished in those unexplored zones that occupy half of the world', or 'soil which is neither hot nor cold, like the skin of those who rest far from life and death'. Rabearivelo speaks of 'leaves which no wind can shake' or 'unidentified trees' or 'unknown flowers of no climate'. The strangeness and super-real quality of this world is accentuated by the strange metamorphoses that take place. Berries are turned into crystals; crystals are turned into a 'forest of flutes', and so on.

Rabearivelo's world is a world of extreme strangeness and also of extreme loneliness. We seem to be invited to an experience we cannot share with others and the cosmos we see is full of 'paths deserted by goats, and roads frequently by silence'. A recurring image is that of 'birds that have become strangers and cannot recognise their nests'.

A sense of deep frustration bordering on despair underlies all his writing. His poems abound with images like: 'dumb birds'; 'fingerless hands', 'rootless trees', 'dissolving stars', 'Fingers of Wind', 'nude sailors whose tongue has been cut out'; 'birds with eyes of glass'; 'round berries like blocks of quartz, that cannot reproduce themselves on earth'.

The dominant vision of Rabearivelo is a vision of death. The most frequent verbs in his poetry are 'killed', 'scattered', 'dissolved', 'fled', 'caught'. The death he sees is not a specific individual death; it is a cosmic, universal death. Many of his poems read like ancient myths. There is that magnificent poem, for example, that opens with the line: 'The hide of the black cow is stretched'. It is one of Rabearivelo's most powerful images of death. But we are not told who the black cow is, or who killed it. Equally haunting is the poem in which the 'invisible rat' destroys the moon and 'tomorrow morning, when it has gone, there will be bleeding marks of teeth'. And again, anonymous, the image of death which opens the poem *Valiha*:

> Crystals of pointed emerald,
> risen from the soil,
> cutting through the flowering grass
> and resembling innumerable horns of young bulls
> buried alive by moonlight.

Often the poet has visions of some great final catastrophe: he speaks of the 'ebbing of oceanic light', of a bird that 'wounded the lone eye of the sky', of birds that 'strike their bright wings against the sombre rocks' and other frightening omens. In a fearful poem he sees an enormous black spider slowly drawing his net across the entire sky. In another uncanny poem a 'bird without colour or name' breeds 'cocks, of all the villages that will be conquered and dispersed'.

In all this gloomy, frightening vision, there is only occasionally a gleam of light, a hope of salvation or resurrection. Thus we hear the black cow will live again, 'white and pink, before a river of light'.

The dominant note, in spite of such brighter moments, is one of doom, death, frustration, loneliness and destruction.

Superficially, but only very superficially, Rabearivelo resembles some of the French surrealist poets. But there are very essential differences. Rabearivelo is not concerned with producing a shock for its own sake. His poetry is no mere intellectual game. There is no self-conscious attempt to expose oneself to the chaos of the subconscious.

Rabearivelo's poems are clear and precise visions of a strange and personal world. Like Baudelaire, his favourite French poet, Rabearivelo had a disgust of reality. In his poetry he has destroyed and dismembered reality. And out of the fragments he has built a new mythical world; it is a world of death and frustration, but also transcended by a sad beauty of its own.

> Slowly
> like a lame cow
> or a powerful bull,
> hamstrung,
> a large black spider emerges from the earth
> climbs up the walls
> balances precariously on the tree tops
> throws its net, which is carried by the wind
> weaves a cloth that touches the sky
> and stretches its web across the azure.
> Where are the colourful birds?
> Where are the songsters of the sun?
> Their eyes are dead with sleep
> in the swinging lianas.
> Yet their sparkling light
> revives dreams and echoes
> in that evanescence of fireflies
> that becomes an army of stars
> to baffle the spider's ambush:
> The net
> That will be torn by the horn of a leaping calf.

The hide of the black cow is stretched
stretched but not set to dry,
stretched in the sevenfold shadow.
But who has killed the black cow,
dead without having lowed, dead without having roared
dead without having been chased
over that prairie flowered with stars?
She who calved in the far half of the sky.
Stretched is the hide
on the sounding box of the wind
that is sculptured by the spirits of sleep.
And the drum is ready
when the new-born calf,
her horns crowned with spear-grass,
leaps
and grazes the grass of the hills.
It reverberates there
and its incantations will become dreams
until the moment when the black cow lives again
white and pink,
before a river of light.

What invisible rat
come from the walls of night
gnaws at the milky cake of the moon?
Tomorrow morning,
when it has gone,
there will be bleeding marks of teeth.
Tomorrow morning,
those who have drunk all night
and those who have abandoned their cards,
looking at the moon
will stammer thus:
'Whose is that sixpence
that rolls over the green table?'
'Ah!', One of them will add,
'Our friend has lost all
and killed himself.'
And all will snigger
and staggering, will fall.
The moon will no longer be there:
The rat will have carried her into his hole.

A bird without colour and name
has bent its wings
and wounded the lone eye of the sky.
She rests on a tree without trunk
all leaves
Which no wind can shake
and whose fruit
one cannot pluck with open eyes.
What does she hatch?
When she will continue her flight
cocks will emerge:
the cocks of all the villages
that will be conquered and dispersed
the cocks that sing in dreams
and feed on stars.

Ebbing of oceanic light, the devil fish in their flight
blacken the sand
with their dense slime;
but innumerable little fish
that look like silver shells
cannot escape,
they flounder:
caught in the nets spread by shadowy algae
that become creepers
and overgrow the rock of the sky.

A purple star
evolved in the depth of the sky—
a flower of blood unfolding on the prairie of night.
Evolve, evolve,
Then become a kite, abandoned by a sleeping child,
It appears to approach and withdraw at the same time.
It loses its colour like a drooping flower,
becomes cloud, turns white, dissolves:
is nothing now but a diamond point
cutting across the blue mirror of the sky
which is reflecting now
the glorious decoy
of the nubile morning.

Here
is she whose eyes are prisms of sleep
and whose lids are heavy with dreams
she whose feet are planted in the sea
and whose sticky hands rise from it
full of corals and crystals of shimmering salt.
She will pile them up in little heaps near a misty bay
and until the rain falls
she will distribute them to nude sailors
whose tongue has been cut.
Then she can no longer be seen
and only her hair will be visible
dishevelled in the wind
like a knot of sea weeds that disentangles itself
and perhaps like grains of insipid salt.

All seasons have been abolished
in those unexplored zones
that occupy half of the world
and adorn it with unknown flowers
of no climate.
Pushed by ephemeral blood of plants
in an entanglement of gloomy lianas
all movement of living branches is strangled.
Confusion of birds that have become strangers
and cannot recognise their nest
they strike their bright wings
against sombre rocks
which is neither hot nor cold
like the skin of those
who rest
far from life and death.

Translations: 'What invisible rat', 'The black cow' and 'Here is she' were translated by Gerald Moore and Ulli Beier; the rest by U.B.

L. S. Senghor

The Theme of the Ancestors in Senghor's Poetry

ULLI BEIER

Those African poets who most strongly assert their *négritude* are often the most sophisticated and—on the surface at least—the most assimilated Africans. One might ask oneself, therefore, whether this new proclamation of *négritude* is a genuine rediscovery of African attitudes and values in the poet's soul, or whether it is merely a deliberate, selfconscious intention, a kind of cultural manifesto. Since *négritude* has become a kind of literary and cultural movement some people will no doubt suspect that when Senghor makes use of Balafongs and Khalams in his poetry, when he speaks of the princess of Elissa and the night of Maghreb, when he envisages the Lamantines drinking at the source and the procession of the dead on the beach—that all these are merely picturesque trappings intended to provide atmosphere and an African flavour to his poetry.

In the following I shall attempt to show that this is not so. Senghor's poetry is not artificially folkloristic; it is genuinely African, because it expresses genuine African attitudes on very basic questions. One could no doubt analyse the reactions of the poet to love, politics and a great many other subjects and examine to what extent the outlook is specifically African. Here I shall confine myself to an examination of Senghor's treatment of the ancestors and the dead in his poems.

The African attitude to death is fundamentally different from the European one. The European has almost lost his belief in survival after death altogether, but even where it still exists the separation between the living and the dead is believed to be final. The dead never return to this earth and they do not continue to influence the living community from beyond. As if to symbolise the finality of this separation we bury our dead outside the town in secluded and walled-in places. Even in the Middle Ages, when belief in eternal life was strongest, the popular image of death was one of horror, as many revolting images in medieval churches show.

In Africa, on the other hand, the idea of death is not associated with horror. The living and the dead are in continuous contact and a large part of the religious life of the African is devoted to establishing a harmonious contact with the dead. The ancestors are the guardians of morality among the living community; they are guides and protectors. Through priests and masqueraders a constant communication is maintained with the dead. Nor is their state final. An ancestor can be reborn in the same family and many African names denoting 'father has come back' or 'mother has returned' testify to this belief. It is significant that in Africa the important people are buried in the compound or even inside a room. It is a common sight in

Africa to see children play around the tomb of their grandfather—something quite unthinkable in Europe.

When we look at Senghor's poetry the first thing that strikes us is the important part played by the dead. In European poetry, too, there may be poems about death, but Senghor's poems are not really *about* death. Senghor writes about life and love, but whatever he does, the dead are near and he is conscious of their presence.

Life and death are not separate spheres to him, but flow into each other. They have no clear boundaries. A poem in his latest volume *Ethiopiques* begins:

> I do not know when it happened, I always confuse childhood
> and Eden,
> And I mix up death and life—who are joined by a tender bridge.[1]

These lines also contain another very African idea: the closeness of the child to the ancestors. The very small child is often treated with great reverence in Africa, because it has only just come from the other sphere, where it was in contact with the revered ancestors; where, in a sense, it *was* an ancestor. Therefore a little bit of the awe reserved to the ancestors attaches to it. So conscious is the African of this perpetual cycle of life and death that in Benin a very old man is addressed as 'my child'.

It is because of this belief in the great cycle of birth, death and rebirth that the idea of death holds no horror. Death is *familiar*, because everyone has moments of vague memories of the country from which he has come:

> In the evening I dream of the lost land where the dead and kings
> were my relatives.[2]

The familiar dead are friends rather then horrors; more often than not they appear as an image of peace and gentleness:

> Because their smile is gentle like the smile of our dead who dance
> in the blue villages of the Fata Morgana.[3]

The dead are always present, there is no separation, no 'death' in the European sense:

> O you dead, who have always refused to die, who have always
> resisted death.[4]

There is an exquisite little poem entitled *Visite* in which Senghor describes the mystic hour in which communion with the dead, with 'his' dead, is established. We can quote it here in full:

> I dream in the intimate semi-darkness of an afternoon.
> I am visited by the fatigues of the day,
> The deceased of the year, the souvenirs of the decade,

[1] From *Je ne sais* in 'Ethiopiques', Paris, Editions du Seuil, 1956.
[2] From *Lasse ma tête* in 'Chants pour Naëtt', Paris, Seghers, 1949.
[3] From *J'étais assis, ibid.*
[4] From *In Memoriam,* in 'Chants d'Ombre', Paris, Editions de Seuil, 1945.

Like the procession of the dead in the village on the horizon
of the shallow sea.
It is the same sun bedewed with illusions,
The same sky unnerved by hidden presences,
The same sky feared by those who have a reckoning with the dead.
And suddenly my dead draw near to me . . .[1]

But there is much more to Senghor than this feeling of presence and communion. Without any self-consciousness at all the poet addresses himself to the dead, to the ancestors and invokes their help. His famous poem *Prayer to Masks* begins with an invocation to the masks, symbol of the ancestors:

Masks, Oh Masks!
Black mask, red mask, your black and white masks,
Rectangular masks through whom the spirit breathes,
I greet you in silence!
And you too my pantherheaded ancestor.

And he demands their help in this hour when the new African is to be born:

Now turn your immobile eyes towards your children.[2]

And again in the poem *In Memoriam* he calls on the dead to protect and guide his life:

Protect from the Sine to the Seine, and in the fragile veins my
inextinguishable blood,
Protect my dreams, like your sons, the longlegged migratory
birds.
O you dead, protect the roofs of Paris in the Sunday fog,
the roofs protecting my dead,
And forbid me to descend from my dangerously safe tower,
To my brothers with blue eyes
And hard hands.

But the dead are not only protectors and guides. It from them that we learn the true secret of life. It is only through mystic unification with the dead that we can understand life in its depth and live it with intensity. Thus Senghor concludes his poem *Night of Sine*:

'Let me listen in the smoky hut for the shadowy visit of
propitious souls,
My head on your breast glows, like a *kuskus* ball smoking
out of the fire.
Let me breathe the smell of our dead, let me contemplate and
repeat their living voice, let me learn
To live before I sink, deeper than the diver into the lofty depth
of sleep.'[3]

[1] *Ibid.*
[2] *Ibid.* A translation of the whole poem appears in 'Black Orpheus', No. 1.
[3] *Ibid.*

All these references to the dead in Senghor's poetry are not conscious statements or pronouncements of belief. These are, on the contrary, images that rise in his mind not because he is asserting his *négritude* but because he *is* an African and he allows himself to be one. This matter-of-fact presence of the dead in a man's life and thinking, this natural communication with the ancestors is something non-existent in European poetry. Senghor is conscious of this; he is aware that here is one of the things that differentiates him basically from European culture and which is therefore a potential cause of misunderstanding. This is what he expresses in his short poem *The Totem*:

> I must hide him in my most secret veins,
> The ancestor whose storm skin is furrowed with lightning and
>   thunder.
> My guardian animal, I must hide him,
> Lest I break the barrier of scandals.
> He is my loyal blood demanding loyalty
> Protecting my naked pride against
> Myself and arrogance of luckier races.[1]

Thus, as this poem also implies, even the most sophisticated African still carries his 'guardian animal' in his 'most secret veins'. However much he has absorbed of European culture, however much he may have assimilated it outwardly, he remains an African in some of his most basic human attitudes. His conscious identification with the movement of *négritude* merely allows him to acknowledge these emotions and responses, which he might otherwise try to suppress.

Senghor, then, is not merely a Frenchified African who tries to give exotic interest to his French poems; he is an African who uses the French language to express his African soul.

[1] *Ibid.*

Night of Sine

L. S. SENGHOR

Woman, rest on my brow your balsam hands, your hands
    gentler than fur.
The tall palmtrees swinging in the nightwind
Hardly rustle. Not even cradlesongs.
The rhythmic silence rocks us.
Listen to its song, listen to the beating of our dark blood,
    listen
To the beating of the dark pulse of Africa in the midst of
    lost villages.
Now the tired moon sinks towards its bed of slack water,
Now even the peals of laughter fall asleep, and the bards
    themselves
Dandle their heads like children on the backs of their mothers.
Now the feet of the dancers grow heavy and heavy grows the
    tongue of the singers.
This is the hour of the stars and of the night that dreams
And reclines on this hill of clouds, draped in her long gown of
    milk.
The roofs of the houses gleam gently. What are they telling so
    confidentially to the stars?
Inside the hearth is extinguished in the intimacy of bitter and
    sweet scents.
Woman, light the lamp of clear oil, and let the children in bed
    talk about their ancestors, like their parents.
Listen to the voice of the ancients of Elissa. Like us, exiled,
They did not want to die, lest their seminal flood be lost in
    the sand.
Let me listen in the smoky hut for the shadowy visit of
    propitious souls;
My head on your breast glows, like a *kuskus* ball smoking
    out of the fire.
Let me breathe the smell of our dead, let me contemplate and
    repeat their living voice, let me learn.
To live before I sink, deeper than the diver, into the lofty
    depth of sleep.

Translated by Ulli Beier

Surrealism and *Négritude* in the Poetry of Tchikaya U Tam'si

GERALD MOORE

Introducing Tchikaya U Tam'si's fourth book of poems, *Epitomé*, M. Senghor has written his own answer to the question implied in my title. After a brief account of U Tam'si's style and imagery, he writes:

> Surrealism, some will say. Certainly, like the poetry of Césaire, whose images explode from the heart, whose passion is a lava that flows straight upon its way, carrying all, burning all with its fervour and transforming it into pure ore.
>
> Jean-Paul Sartre has said of Césaire, nothing is accidental here; this is not automatic writing. A single passion constantly and tumultuously offered. A single passion; to bear witness to *négritude*.
>
> Tchikaya is a witness whose sole end here is to manifest *négritude*. We have seen that he has all the negro virtues. But above all he assumes the mingled hope and despair of the negro, the epical suffering, the *passion*, in the etymological sense of the word.

This statement is very much in line with what M. Senghor has written elsewhere on the subjects of *négritude*, style and *surréalisme*. Its adjectives are carefully chosen, and it both invites and deserves a deliberate analysis. To make such an analysis we shall have to consider not only the poetry of U Tam'si but that of Césaire and of the avowed *Surréalistes* themselves.

One thing is certain; U Tam'si is a poet of some importance and the most prolific black poet of French expression to appear since Césaire. Over the seven years 1955–1962 he has published four volumes of poetry, distinguished by a consistency and continuity, but at the same time a marked development, of style. We are not asked to assess him on the basis of a handful of lyrics but of an *œuvre* remarkable for a man of only thirty-one. Apart from their consistency of style his poems exhibit a complex system of interdependent imagery, so that the particular images of each poem often feed the significance of those in surrounding poems. This characteristic makes each of his books very much a whole, to be read and evaluated as such.

However, our time here does not permit such a leisurely exercise, and we must make a preliminary test of these definitions by the examination of a few selected poems. Let us begin with the fourth poem of M. U Tam'si's fine book 'A Triche-Cœur' which appeared in 1960.

The first three long poems in that volume have already familiarised the reader with a certain imagistic *geography*, a geography which makes much use of those fundamental symbols around which human imagination has

110

perpetually revolved: the tree, the bird, the river, stars, sun and moon, the sea, the breaking of bread; and a vocabulary often recalling the insignia of Passion, Death and Resurrection. The first poem, *Agonie*, traces a mysterious dialogue between a boatman and a bird in which the black boatman, whose arms are *ouverts en croix* and who seeks *un amour tonique* to unloose his arms, carries the bird across a river. In reward for this the bird will tell his name to the boatman and so unpinion his arms. The boatman guesses 'quail' but the bird denies it and leaves him with words of doubtful comfort:

> I am your soul farewell
> my dark body farewell
> your arms will unloose themselves[1]

The language of the poem continually touches upon associations of love, despair and death by crucifixion. The second poem is full of intensely sexual imagery mingled with a curious comic violence:

> above a herd of ruttish buffaloes shines
> a moon narrow as a virgin's cunt
> the ship of my loves sank deeper
> between two grins of a caressing dawn
> the winds sat down on my sister's knees
> laughing at the knife thrust between them[2]

The third poem, which is the title-poem *A triche-cœur*, echoes the laughter and violence of the second and develops further the hints of a 'Last Supper' which first sounded there:

> I have not known how to eat
> the bread I have broken
> take it from my mouth
> eat my crumbled bread
> you have failed
> you will save your soul
> and win joy

and later

> at the last judgement
> with the sword break the bread
> offer the hand make love

It also introduces the image of the poet as a sterile tree which at the end is thrown down from the place where it stood in the wind. This of course ties up with the crucifixion imagery of the first poem.

The fourth poem, entitled *L'étrange agonie*, begins this way:

[1] From *Agonie* in 'A Triche-Cœur', Paris, Oswald, 1960.
[2] From *Etiages, ibid.*

sweating the languor of a blues
from head to foot
listen I shed my pain at every step
I abandon all my limbs
I leave my heart again
I go my way
my head in my legs
the better to knot my destiny
to the grass of the pathways

After the passive suffering of the previous poem, the poet is suddenly on the move again. But the poem soon develops into a strange interplay between movement and reminiscence, an interplay introduced in the very next stanza:

I go
and I remember that one summer
sitting before a fashionable beach
I learnt much from the ladybirds

It fills with images of isolation and rejection which take up the *sans baggages* theme of the opening stanza:

soul and body naked
I am a man without history

and the poet comes unusually near to defining his position (or *a* position) with regard to the religion whose symbols rack his soul and body:

a christian could never understand
what is evoked in me
by saint george and his intimate verse
shadow the pagan no longer remembers
we were foolish among the vines
and stroked the seas in order to weep
between the pine needles
her agony my agony our agony oh virgin
but love not being a christian virtue
I have given joy to none
my face to the backs of men
all christians tactically
thrusting at me the cross of a god betrayed
whom I betray to remain faithful
to the shadow

As in this passage, so again and again in the poem, the poet is physically *behind* all human experience he encounters, '*face au dos des hommes*'. His reverie on the '*plage mondaine*', to which he returns several times in the poem, leads only to this new vision of exclusion mingled with a sort of pinioned sensuality (one remembers Leopold Bloom in *Ulysses* making hot eyes at Gertie McDowell on the beach at Howth):

> I have dreamt that she she I will love
> will have seven vehemences
> on the flesh of her pink back
> one close to the neck
> for delight
> I have already seen the back of more than one girl
> when my ladybirds took flight
> leaving me spent on the fashionable beach

And in the most frantic passage of the poem, which follows upon his rejection of the cross in order to remain faithful to the shadow, he creates a weird savage tableau whose ranks of '*derrières fourbus*' suggest Courbet but whose other elements would have scandalised Salvador Dali. Nothing in the mocking but rather wistful passage that precedes it prepares us for the deliberate violence of this:

> face back to face
> ten bottoms with knocked up buttocks
> of women with heads upright
> behind these women
> a woman lying in childbirth
> cracks her pelvis dilates her sex
> all this filth
> in front of ten other women
> back to front upright
> then setting their buttocks down
> and having no joy or pain
> one of them licks the litter
> somewhere between anus and penis
> a deluded angel sings
> he is born the holy child

Looking back over these first four poems one is struck above all by the exploration of imagery that is found there. Let us take for example the image of the man-tree, which glimmers in and out of so much of U Tam'si's writing. In 'A Triche-Cœur' we meet it in the very first poem, where the nature of the imprisonment of the boatman's arms is only made clear to us by the final couplet:

> do not die awaiting me
> arms opened in a cross

I shall take it that the crucifixion image here evoked is simply a phase of the immemorial identification of man and tree; or, if you will, a manifestation of Christ as Tree-God.

A little later, in the poem *A triche-cœur* itself, we have a rejoicing in

113

passive impotent suffering, which to some extent carries on the crucifixion or castration idea:

> I have had the promise
> to be a sterile tree
> I have played with the bitter winds
> played and lost my sex

This is followed by the introduction of a wild boar (this brings Adonis into the mind) who twice in the poem appears in the role of *overthrowing* the tree, whose sap and seed remain nevertheless mingled with the earth, ensuring its resurrection. In the next poem comes the addition of a parrot who jabbers in the branches of the tree and so causes it to be spared, in a poem otherwise full of images of death:

> the tree turns the storm aside
> because a parrokeet babbles upon a branch

and this seems to hint at the immortality of the poet *despite* his mortality. Can we then identify the tree with man's materiality and the man-or-bird figure itself with his spirituality? However, the poet is determined to keep us moving, for soon afterwards we find:

> a motionless hearse stands there
> which must pass
> before the tree of which I am a leaf

and soon after this the tree becomes a 'family tree', a genealogy, and an instrument of the poet's search for his own identity:

> I met nothing but trees
> which carried each other's fruit
> trees none the less
> but no one of my family
> upon their branches

In the last poem of the book, *The Hearse*, the tree *rejoices* to have its bark scorched and seared by the lightning, while the storm knocks down its fruit *in vain*:

> sometime during the night
> the lightning showed its joy
> in scorching the tree
> which the storm had plundered in vain

These last hints are taken up again in U Tam'si's latest book, 'Epitomé'[1]. Here the first poem develops both the genealogy aspect of the tree and the concept of the poet as a single leaf upon it, a leaf destined to fall without ever fully knowing what has fed it:

---

[1] Oswald, 1962.

> o my absurd genealogy
> from what tree do I come?
> what flowers did that tree
> shed before the funeral bell?
> who sounded the bell?
> at the summit of a hill a tree
> lifts like a candle a branch of blood
> the branch carries in its fist a green leaf
> image of flame against the soft yellow daylight
> hooted by demons!

And in the following poems the poet begins a search through the forest for the very tree that has shaped his life:

> whence comes this arborescent madness?

Later in the book a great part of this constantly shifting and interacting group of tree-images is invoked in a single short poem. The poet has found a bunch of withered flowers in his letter-box. He rages at the normality of life in Paris, including his own, while the terrible events of 1960 unroll themselves in the Congo. And now the tree becomes not only an image of unknown growth and secret origin; of life, death and regeneration; but of cultural purity and impurity. At least I take this to be the meaning of these lines, where U Tam'si appears to re-enact the hate affair with 'assimilation' which Damas and Senghor have played out before him:

> it is likely enough
> false growths upon the roots of my tree
> poison my utmost branch
> I no longer know the essence of my soul
> all the doors open into shut houses
> my hands crinkle already
> like dying flowers.

This particular group of images could be pursued much further through the strange landscape of U Tam'si's imagination, but I hope we have travelled far enough to establish that this young poet is distinguished not only by *élan* and energy and the startling power of his invention, but above all by the intensity with which he explores, eviscerates, rearranges his vocabulary of images.

And this brings me to the comparison with Césaire which we are required to make. Certainly U Tam'si occasionally echoes Césaire, as in these lines with their play upon light and darkness:

> that woman spat fire into her idleness
> her black looks were the sun of black days
> my days too white too black of the long poisonous winters

Césaire too has certain favourite poetic landscapes—in particular one of sea-girt islands with great waves eating at their cliffs—and a similar richness

115

and wildness of imagery. But in reality we are dealing with two very different temperaments. M. Senghor's description of Césaire's language, already quoted, gives an accurate idea of its headlong movement; *'une lave qui coule droit son chemin, entraînant tout, brûlant tout de sa fervour et le transformant en or pur'*. There is a breathless quality about much of Césaire's poetry; not simply the breathlessness of astonishment, but the breathlessness of trying to keep up with the incessant flow of new images which springs from his pen. Where U Tam'si occasionally astonishes by the impact of his invention, Césaire continually does so by the sheer speed of it. This passage from *A l'Afrique* is typical:

> peasant so that there may spring from the mountain's head
>   that which wounds the wind
> that a cloth of bells may warm themselves in her throat
> which will show forth as crows as skirts as piercers of isthmuses
> so that my wave may spend itself in her wave and bring us again
> to the beach in the drowned torn flesh of guavas
>   in a draughtsman's hand in beautiful seaweeds in
>   flying grain in bubbles in memories in tree
> let your gesture be aware that flings
>   and withdraws itself in the crutch
> of the rocks to bring a rebellious isle to birth[1]

Even this passage is enough, I think, to convey the onward rush of Césaire and make a contrast with the more inward, spiral, exploratory movement of U Tam'si, with what Senghor calls *'ses rédites qui ne se répètent pas, ses parallélismes symétriques, ses enjambements, ruptures et retournements'*.

Earlier in the same passage Senghor claims that this quality is something which U Tam'si has simply retained from traditional African poetry; *'La poésie de Tchicaya a donc gardé les vertus de la poésie nègro-africaine la plus authentique. Et d'abord cette syntaxe de juxtaposition qui fait sauter les bonds de la logique. Une syntaxe qui déraisonne.'*

Now *'une syntaxe qui déraisonne'* is actually a very fair description of what the *Surréalistes* were aiming at; much fairer than M. Senghor's rather too easy dismissal of *'ecriture automatique'*. No one really supposes that writers like Paul Eluard, Robert Desnes, André Breton and Louis Aragon achieved their fine early poems by a process of automatic writing. Such freaks were safely left to the Dadaistes. But they *did* attempt to set words free to dance directly at the will of the reader; to free them from the sort of patterns which the mind otherwise imposes by habit. They did this partly by their choice and arrangement of words, and partly by the apparently superficial device of avoiding all punctuation and capital letters, so that the reader has to find his own way round the poem without the signposts on which he has come to rely. And this stylistic device, apparently so trivial and in reality so essential, is precisely the one which both Césaire

---

[1] In 'Soleil Cou Coupé', Paris, Editions K, 1946.

and U Tam'si have adopted, for apparently very similar reasons. This aspect of *Surréalisme* was expressed by Aragon when he wrote '*Le Surréalisme n'est pas une forme poetique. Il est un cri de l'esprit qui retourne vers lui-même et est bien décidé a broyer désespérément ses entraves.*' A good formula, one would have thought, for an African poetry of revolution and self-discovery. When M. Senghor writes of U Tam'si's technique '*Mais celle-ci ne fait que traduire les mouvements même du cœur,*' he is not far from Aragon's meaning. And for the practice of it we could look at these lines of André Breton:

> behind you
> shooting its last dark rays between your thighs
> the earth of a lost paradise
> ice of darkness mirror of love
> and lower towards your arms which open themselves
> to the proof by the spring
> AFTERWARDS
> of the non-existing evil
> all the flowering appletree of the sea[1]

Given the cold, rather classical quality of Breton's imagination, the words here, I think, enjoy the same kind of 'freedom of association' that we find both in the major *Surréaliste* poets and in the work of Césaire and U Tam'si. The mind in reading moves them to and fro upon the page, so that in effect they *do more work* than they could do in a more rigid context.

On the other hand, I find it difficult to assess M. Senghor's claim that there is much of Bantu poetic tradition informing U Tam'si's style. The field indicated seems to me a little too vast and vague for useful comparison. But I can think of a specific quality which U Tam'si's imagery has in common with that of a particular vernacular poetry that is slightly known to me. In Yoruba poetry we find often a cryptic juxtaposition of images; a refusal to *explain* and to build easy bridges for the reader from one part of the poem to another; coupled with an extreme power and conciseness in the images themselves. For example, in one of the *Orikis* of Shango we find a long sequence of hints, attributes and images which all help to create the worshipper's total impression of the god simply by juxtaposition:

> Fire in the eye, fire in the mouth, fire on the roof.
> He walks alone, but he enters the town like a swarm of locusts.
> The leopard who killed the sheep and bathed in its blood.
> The man who died in the market and woke up in the house.[2]

And later, at the most terrible moment of the poem, this picture of the god kneeling in the morning fields:

[1] From *On me dit que là-bas* in 'The Penguin Book of French Verse', ed. Hartley, A., Harmondsworth, 1959.

[2] From 'Yoruba Poetry', ed. and trans. by Gbadamosi and Beier, Ibadan, Black Orpheus special publication, 1959.

He kneels down like a collector of vegetables.
Shango does not collect vegetables,
He is only looking for the head of the farmer.[1]

Coupled with this abrupt and cryptic power, we often find images of amazing range and boldness. The Yoruba hunting songs (*Ijala*) contain many of these, of which this from a song to Erin (the Elephant) may stand as an example:

> With his one hand
> He can pull two palm trees to the ground
> If he had two hands
> He would tear the heavens like an old rag.[2]

Let us, then, return to the basis of our enquiry. To evaluate the rôles of *surréalisme* and *négritude* in U Tam'si's poetry we shall need first of all to determine the precise nature of each. Is *surréalisme* an indivisible programme of writing, a technique which can be used for only one purpose: '*broyer désespérément ses entraves*'? This is definitely stated in André Breton's early manifesto; '*Le Surréalisme n'est pas un moyen d'expression nouveau ou plus facile, ni même une métaphysique de la poésie. Il est un moyen de libération totale de l'esprit et de tout ce qui lui ressemble.*' But can it nevertheless be isolated as a literary technique and employed in the service of a particular ideology? Again, is *négritude* itself a programme, an ideology or, as M. Senghor has insisted elsewhere, a style?

It seems clear that *surréalisme* cannot by its nature be didactic, since didacticism would imply throwing new fetters upon the words just set free. On the other hand, by a particular choice and juxtaposition of words within a context of maximum freedom, such as we find in Césaire's poetry, certain particular effects can be achieved. Works like 'Cahier d'un Retour au Pays Natal' and 'Et les Chiens se Taisaient' seems to me to be didactic to this extent. On the other hand, a great deal of Césaire's work in volumes like 'Les Armes Miraculeuses' and 'Soleil Cou Coupé' seems to be pure *surréalisme* and to establish Césaire as probably the greatest of the *surréaliste* poets. As for U Tam'si, he manifests himself in his first four books as a totally undidactic poet, a poet who would not dream of bullying words into the service of any external purpose whatever.

But if *négritude* itself is not a programme but a *style*, what can we usefully say about a style which poets as various as Léon Damas, Aimé Césaire, Léopold Senghor, David Diop and Tchikaya U Tam'si are supposed to have in common? At this point the enquiry becomes a trifle mystical. The poetic landscape of U Tam'si, the materials of his imagination, his whole sensibility, the very music of his life, have all been shaped by Africa. To that extent we can certainly speak of his *négritude*. And to precisely the same extent we could speak of the Anglitude of Shakespeare or the Francitude of Racine. The great River Congo flows through U

---

[1] *Ibid.*   [2] *Ibid.*

Tam'si's poetry, swarming with canoes and crocodiles. The tree that grows in his head is an African tree, '*parce qu'un perroquet badine sur une branche*'. But many things, I believe, have helped to shape this poetry: the inspiration of Césaire, and beyond him the technique and example of the *surréalistes*; the sculpture, music, dancing and poetry of the Congo; and not least, his own unique genius. There is surely no need to deny the part played by any of these unless we are asked to regard *surréalisme* as 'a false growth upon the roots of this tree'?

A Study of Six African Poets

Voices Out of the Skull

PAUL THEROUX

In this essay I shall be concerned with the work of six African poets.[1] If these poets were all members of a particular school of writing, using similar literary techniques, I might have written it differently. But they are of different ages and regions and temperament, and so must be considered as individual voices. If there is a common concern it is the common concern of all good poems, and that is freedom, the liberating experiences of reading and writing well. The theme of artistic progress dominates but exhibits itself in many ways, and so must be considered separately.

There are shortcomings in some of the poems: the language is sometimes stilted and archaic, the pathos prefabricated, the metrics diffuse, and the hyper-emotionality hard to bear. I have not concentrated on the faults of the poems—one can easily be preoccupied with such things. People grow, the façade falls away and nothing the critic says has much to do with the speed with which these affectations are dropped. Usually I have tried to find the very best examples of what I supposed to be the writer's intentions, and then concentrated on his best writing. Clark presents a different problem, so I have looked a bit into his unsuccessful poems.

I know only the essential things about these poets; I have no idea what they look like or where they are presently employed. The poems themselves have supplied all my information: their aspirations, their joys and disgusts. All clues to my interpretations were in the poems, and maybe the clues were not intentionally thrown out. But if one finds scales on the ground it is up to the finder to tell whether they came from a fish, a fowl or a snake. And it is the finder's personal madness that determines the choice.

DENNIS BRUTUS

Speaking of the writer living in this bloody bungled world, Albert Camus says he 'cannot hope to remain aloof in order to pursue the reflections and images that are dear to him'. Every act must be seen as a result of the times, as a function of tyranny or of tenderness; the work must be 'inserted into its time'.[2] Obviously, the writer in Alaska might possibly be more aloof

[1] All published by Mbari, Ibadan.
　　Dennis Brutus: 'Sirens, Knuckles, Boots', 1963.
　　Lenrie Peters: 'Poems', 1964.
　　Okogbule Glory Nwanodi: 'Icheke', 1964.
　　George Awoonor-Williams: 'Rediscovery and other poems', 1964.
　　John Pepper Clark: 'Poems', 1962.
　　Christopher Okigbo: 'Heavensgate', 1962; 'Limits', 1964.
[2] Camus, Albert: *Create Dangerously*, essay in 'Resistance, Rebellion and Death', New York, Modern Library, 1960.

than his counterpart in South Africa, but it will be up to the Alaskan to determine what his comrades aspire to, to make the way plain.

The South African writer is in a very special position. With Britain, the United States, Germany, Japan and countless other countries pouring money and industrial schemes into the country, it takes a strong voice and a skilful hand to unravel the gorgeous South African travel brochure, shout in the faces of the Great Powers and touch the brutalised nerves beneath it all.

To continue with Camus: 'Every artist today is embarked on the contemporary slave galley . . . like everyone else, [he] must bend to his oar . . . go on living and creating.' But the black South African writer on the slave galley, rowing his guts out, up to his eyes in bilge, is not only a slave to the régime but also a slave to the régimes of the most powerful countries in the world. It would be odd, therefore, if a writer in South Africa were not concerned where his particular slave galley was going. And the 'reflections and images that are dear to him' are farther out of reach than those of any man on earth.

Brutus is constantly nagging, condemning, lamenting. He says in his opening poem:

> A troubadour, I traverse all my land
> exploring all her wide-flung parts with zest
> probing in motion sweeter far than rest
> her secret thickets with an amorous hand:
>
> and I have laughed, disdaining those who banned
> inquiry and movement, delighting in the test
> of will when doomed by Saracened arrest,
> choosing, like unarmed thumb, simply to stand.

But reading through the book we find that, however lovely it is to think of oneself as a troubadour, laughing at the gross-booted policemen, probing injustices in flight with beautiful gestures, this is not what happens in the poems which follow. There is very little trace of 'an amorous hand' in the lines:

> So here I crouch and nock my venomed arrows
> to pierce deaf eardrums waxed by fear
> or spy, a Strandloper, these obscene albinos
> and from the corner of my eye
> catch glimpses of a glinting spear.

Amorousness is something that is dear to Brutus, but something that is out of reach. So Brutus concentrates on the emotion that will lead to amorousness—the way is through tenderness, to love:

> Somehow we survive
> and tenderness, frustrated, does not wither.
> . . . .

121

> most cruel, all our land is scarred with terror,
> rendered unlovely and unloveable;
> sundered are we and all our passionate surrender
>
> but somehow tenderness survives.

The tenderness, the faith that Brutus places in it, may be a result of the terrible rage of the previous poem quoted above with its bowman spying on the 'obscene albinos'. Here is an angry man; the vitriol of the words 'obscene albinos' matches that of James Baldwin in the United States. During the second-act intermission of *Blues for Mister Charlie* the white-liberal segment of the audience stayed in their seats, were ashamed to go into the lobby of the theatre for a cigarette and risk the further contempt of the Negroes present. J. P. Clark, who has criticised Brutus, is right in saying that Nigerian poets do not write lines like 'obscene albinos'; but Nigerians are not murdered or imprisoned because they are black; they are not considered the black stinking lubrication that helps the huge cogs of the economy to run smoothly. Brutus is whipped and he lashes back furiously. It is true that sometimes his punches are wild, sometimes he misses, but he swings enough times for us to see what he is aiming at.

Brutus, speaking for the millions of black South Africans, has been frustrated and turned away and confined and shot at and still nothing has changed. And so he continues to rage. Other poets in other places may write poems about their wives to celebrate their beauty and their wondrous functions. Brutus, separated from his wife, speaks of her as if she were dead. There is a fat white hand between him and his wife; that, and many miles:

> It is your flesh that I remember best;
> its impulse to surrender and possess
> obscurely, in the nexus of my flesh
> inchoate stirrings, patterns of response
> re-act the postures of our tenderness.

Here is tenderness without rage, but more often it is a mixture of rage and tenderness that prevails in Brutus' poems. The poems are not easy to read, his book cannot be taken in one gulp—it would hurt too much. Here, as an example, is another of Brutus' love poems

> A common hate enriched our love and us:
>
> Escape to parasitic ease disgusts;
> discreet expensive hushes stifled us
> the plangent wines became acidulous
>
> Rich foods knotted to revolting clots
> of guilt and anger in our queasy guts
> remembering the hungry comfortless.

> In draughty angles of the concrete stairs
> or seared by salt winds under brittle stars
> we found a poignant edge to tenderness,
>
> and, sharper than our strain, the passion
> against our land's disfigurement and tension;
> hate gouged out deeper levels for our passion—
>
> a common hate enriched our love and us.

Here is the rebuttal to all who clamour for silence; the 'discreet expensive hushes' will undo the poet or the lover. It is piteous, the view of the lovers loving within the system of hate and even enriching themselves by it. But this is also one of Brutus' most brilliant poems, for in it he combines all the themes of love, rage and tenderness, and all the stark ugliness and terror of living in a bitter land. The poem is not a commitment to hate but to rage—rage in love and in living. The nine poems which follow this one are similar in tone. Sex in these poems is frightening; images of love-making are contrasted with images of death and dying:

> . . . you pressed my face against your womb
> and drew me to a safe and still oblivion,
> shut out the knives and teeth; boots, bayonets
>   and knuckles . . .

Or:

> Desolate
> Your face gleams up
> beneath me in the dusk
>
> abandoned:
>
> a wounded dove
> helpless
> beneath the knife of love.

There is horror in these poems, but it is not the horror of a man skittering in a high wind away from white ghosts stalking him with Sten-guns. It is rather the horror of a man seeing love nourished in bad soil, in a country made ugly by hatred. Perhaps Brutus likes to picture himself in flight, but I read these poems differently. He is not moving (living furiously does not mean bobbing around); he is staying, suffering the phantasms, and he is recording them faithfully. This takes great strength and dedication; he has escaped the decayed language of revolt, the clichés of the man oppressed. If the poems are depressive in their raging tenderness it is because Brutus is being hammered from within his soul and from without: the sirens in his ears, the knuckles and boots against his body.

It is hard to refuse to detach and to descend from metaphysics to exist among the most miserable and unhappy in his country, identifying with

123

all the injustice and lust and criminality; yet Brutus makes the descent, a descent which is the only means of resurrection:

> Under me
>> your living face endures
>>> pools stare blindly
>>> muddied by ageless misery:

> descending to you
>> in a rage of tenderness
>>> you bear me
>>> patiently.

LENRIE PETERS

From the horror of Brutus' nightmare we pass to the untroubled phantasies of Lenrie Peters and Okogbule Glory Nwanodi. These two poets write short unthundered poems which have the virtue of occupying more space in the mind than on the page. The following poem by Lenrie Peters is a good example.

> Parachute men say
> The first jump
> Takes the breath away
> Feet in the air disturbs
> Till you get used to it

But not total breathlessness, dizziness without direction, for when the parachutist lands:

> The violent arrival
> Puts out the joint
> Earth has nowhere to go
> You are at the starting point.

It is the simplicity of these lines that is attractive, their meaning which is immediately made plain:

> Jumping across worlds
> In condensed time
> After the awkward fall
> We are always at the starting point.

What characterises this and others of Peters' poems is the wonderment he feels at suddenly discovering he is among the living and capable of loving —the wonderment of the discovery and the wish to share it. Peters extends his hand in *She Came in Silken Drapes* and says

> Let me lead you
> Through the dense crowd,

And over the phallic mound
To the crystal spring
Where I have found
The purest living thing.

In this poem Peters is emerging from a confused dream which is only shattered when he asserts his love, promises to share a secret. Both of the poems above start without fanfare and build to a point near the end which provides a shift in the point of view. The parachutist drifts aimlessly in flight until at the end of his flight (and at the end of the poem) he does more than strike the ground—he discovers earth. *She Came in Silken Drapes* builds from a series of images (Artemis; 'Poison of the Coral Snake'; 'Gentle Winged Butterfly'; 'chambered Monuments') to the next-to-the-last stanza, where love is pondered as the 'misused' word, falsified by man. In the last stanza comes the selfless assertion of love and the secrets it will hold.

The poet will lead the way. In these poems the words are carefully chosen, hard transparent shapes of glass. The flow of the poem is determined immediately and we do not stop until the final assertion is made. Peters shows himself, through his poems, to be a patient man; this provides him with a pure view of the world. His is not a childish optimism but a conscious hope mixed with a strong desire to see the pure triumph:

Open the gates
To East and West
Bring in all
That's good and best ...

On this point it is interesting to contrast Peters with Brutus. Peters condemns by mocking the charlatans or quietly describing the hypocrisies; Brutus suffers the charlatan and describes his own suffering. The torturer is seen through the wounds of Brutus; Peters describes the torturer at work—our view here is bloodless, exact, detached. Both views are effective, though Brutus' is the most painful to read since we identify with the victim.

Although Peters' love predominates over passion, acceptance over disgust, he is fully equipped to describe the lower depths. In *Clawed Green Eyed* a series of lustful images ('feline of night', 'worm tunnelled sod') culminates in the poet seeing himself as a

Friend of the falling star
Victim of the lonely bed.

Our last glimpse is not of lust but of loneliness and the hallucinations which that state can produce in us. Peters' most grotesque poem similarly ends with a feeling of purity. After lines like

Fog strangles
With wet hands

125

and

>   ... the brains of drowning men
>   Oozing down nostrils

and

>   Rancid old women
>   Cough their Haemorrhoids out

the final lines are:

>   The ghost has gone
>   Leaving the nuptial dew.

This is not quite enough to eradicate the earlier images, but it does make a basis for the beginnings of a way of hoping for purity, however ephemeral that purity may be. Ironically, Peters' next poem is about 'camping out in space', which, like 'Parachute', ends on earth and in the company of men.

More than anything else, Peters asks dignity of men, and exemplifies this by writing with dignity. In *We Have Come Home* Peters speaks of

>   That spirit which asks no favour
>   of the world
>   But to have dignity.

It is strange that a doctor (which Peters is) should be concerned with the spirit of man and not the body, though it is understandable. Peters demonstrates that he knows the spirit of man is contained in man's body. And the man who asks for dignity is asking more of himself than of others. In this is Peters' devotion and commitment to a time when man will realise finally that he and his love can combine to form 'the purest living thing'.

OKOGBULE NWANODI

This vision is shared by Okogbule Nwanodi in his book 'Icheke'. Nwanodi is still growing as a poet, still learning the craft, so often the purity of the idea is obscured by the movement of the poem. We get experiments that don't work, such as the 'Moonlight Play' section of *New Days*:

>   Banana stands mask
>   Marshes' fair futility;
>   Furtive fare would feign
>   Magic turns of turgidity;

And:

>   Bustle, scuffle and ruffles!

126

But these concocted and self-conscious lines are in the same poem that contains the lines:

> We start afresh
> Until the touched turns searcher.

The former are examples of a poet discovering words, feeling for meaning among the sounds; the latter lines are an example of the language found. The final two lines of the poem are great indeed and proof of the growth.

I find Nwanodi's little poem *Harvest*:

> walk over the hills
> and pick the seeds
> that shall flower
> these brown plains
>
> Walk over the hills
> and the harmattan
>   will soon be over.

or his poem *Night Talk*:

> we dreamt in the day
> of peaks falling on spades
> and we slept at night

much better than the long (seven-part) title poem of the book, with its clotted imagery and flabby praises and condemnations. There is not much point in writing a seven-part poem like *Icheke* when a seven-line one, like *Harvest*, would do. It is rare that a person can handle a very long poem —and I am speaking of the reader as well as the writer.

Nwanodi at his best does not dwell on a scene but brings us quickly up to it. The vision that causes hope to be born cannot be put into the words of a poem. It can only be hinted at, and the prolonged view—even of hopefulness—will be, in the end, depressing. By relating the experience of talking at night, of the 'enclosed nativity', and of the seeds that 'shall flower these brown plains' Nwanodi is granting us the chance to test our own vision.

GEORGE AWOONOR-WILLIAMS

Christopher Okigbo, as we shall see, passes through a succession of Heavensgates. George Awoonor-Williams waits at 'hellgate', not to pass through but to be 'delivered' from his place of waiting to a pleasanter spot. The fascination that Awoonor-Williams has with things basic, mysterious, such as death or the ritual acts of love or worship leads him to the temporary rediscovery and fleeting recognitions that he desires. He reminds one of Okigbo because he goes on and on with the purifications and is as dissatisfied with the 'purified' state as Okigbo. But, unlike Okigbo's poetic litanies, Awoonor-Williams' poems are single moments selected out of a pattern of rediscovery. The points of crystallisation are recorded—both low and high, the moments of inglorious desire, the moments of discovering the strengths that his own soul possesses. Okigbo presents the notes and feelings of the entire journey; Awoonor-Williams selects the moments of greatest importance, ones which have a significance beyond themselves.

Awoonor-Williams' great achievement is his use of 'extended rhythms' and, in this, he is as skilful as Ezra Pound or the William Carlos Williams of *Paterson*[1]. The most common poems are those in which the rhythms are self-contained. This evokes the mood of a single poem, but of course ends when the poem ends (the rhythm ends; the idea stays). Reading both Awoonor-Williams and Okigbo one passes from poem to poem and the experience is enlarged by the repetition of words and phrases, the music swells. In *To Her Afar* Awoonor-Williams says:

> Cannot I remember the profile
> That thundered in virgin gaiety
> Refusing the chastity belt of family
> And watching the heart that watched.
> Six years have passed since we thought
> We knew what the throbbing hearts of youth
> —age has not come as yet—
> Demanded in those demanding gestures of wanting . . .

Some hint of the rhythm of repetition is given in the lines 'watching the heart that watched' and 'Demanded in those demanding gestures'. Five poems later, in *Lover's Song*, he says

> Shall I fold mine and say I am cheap
> Returned unsold from the market?
> If they marry a woman don't they sleep with her?
> Isn't it seven years now since you went away?

In *To Her Afar* the loss of recognition is realised and this is tied up with the theme of death:

> For we know maybe the final drum beat shall sound
> And we shall have to identify one another.

In *Lover's Song* it is not the loss of recognition but the incomplete remembrance of desire and the wish for physical contact—the lament in the first poem is turned into a feeling of degradation in the second

> . . . cheap
> Returned unsold from the market . . .

[1] Williams, W. C.: 'Paterson' Books I–IV, New York, New Directions, 1946–48.

The repetition can be seen again in the poem *The Anvil and the Hammer*

> Sew the old days for us, our fathers
> That we can wear them under our new garment,
> After we have washed ourselves . . .

and *The Years Behind*

> Sew the old days for me, my fathers
> sew them that I may wear them
> for the feast that is coming

or in *The Longest Journey*:

> By the rivers of Babylon there I sat
> and watched the dancing girls gyrating to the drums
> That have been muffled by the dead drummers' anguish

and in *My Song*:

> Shall I sing the chorus?
> It's a long long way and we couldn't hear the music.
> By the rivers of Babylon there I sat
> and watched my joyful hours.

Awoonor-Williams extends his rhythms by extending the lines into other poems. As we have seen he can make large pregnant pulsations that work in counterpoint. He is not 'writing the same thing' as the similar lines might lead one to believe, but enlarging his theme by repetition in depth. Anyone who has read the Bible knows that Awoonor-Williams was not the first to sit 'by the rivers of Babylon', but he puts this theft to work for him. And this also adds to the symphonic effect of the body of poems.

Next to what I consider a rather inconclusive theme of Christianity, the most important single theme in the book, 'Rediscovery', is that of death. The feelings towards death are mixed, but the mourning returns, as Whitman says, 'with ever-returning spring'. Seeing the 'consummation' as birth it is not odd that Awoonor-Williams is haunted by thoughts of death. The examples in 'Rediscovery' are numerous and carefully spaced:

> For we know maybe the final drum beat shall sound
> *To Her Afar*

> Doom, Doom, Doom, you said the funeral drums said
> The funeral drums beat from the eastern houses.
> *Salvation*

> After the final identity
> and the drum beat summons us to our songs
> will you receive the wounded soul I bring?
> *The Drum Beat Summons*

129

> And sing of lost souls redeemed by the agony of death.
> *Come, Let Us Join*

> Flesh weakens before the agony of death
> *That Which Flesh Is Heir To*

> This flesh shall melt in the melting pot
> of receding clay and the flesh shall peel off
> and be used to muffle the funeral drums.
> *In My Sick Bed*

In the early poems he sees death as finishing off the man and making him into a purer substance; in the later poems death is seen still as a redeemer, but a terrible one—'the flesh weakens'. He is ambivalent, fearful, since the passage through death to the other state is a painful process of leaching and peeling. The completion will come when all have heard the drums and have consented to join in the ritual:

> Come all ye faithless and bring your drums along
> For the noon day of fulfilment is here
> The ceremony of oneness is near.

The conflict in the early poems comes when he is trying to 'get born' without first dying—he seeks birth through desire, sexuality, excess. The reminder of death predominates over all our physical acts, so sexuality inevitably leads us back to thoughts of death. Awoonor-Williams broods thus throughout the book, the drums always in his ears. A complete acceptance of death is not achieved even at the end of the book, although at the end we are a lot closer to discovering what it is in death that will redeem us, or the poet.

Awoonor-Williams is waiting for the strengthened and confident second self to emerge and make an assertion. Until this happens the two selves will continue to grapple, the soul will shrink and expand, the flesh will weaken and tumesce. In the recollection of the glorious birth that came about through a previous deadly sex-act and agonising gestation is the key. The title poem *Rediscovery* gives us this insight:

> It cannot be the music we heard that night
> that still lingers in the chambers of memory
> It is the new chorus of our forgotten comrades
> and the halleluyahs of our second selves.

JOHN PEPPER CLARK

Affected language and precious syntax work to John Clark's advantage in his plays. The tense atmosphere of *Song of a Goat* and *The Raft*[1] profits by the convolutions of language, lends a brittle quality to the movement. But

[1] Clark, J. P.: 'Three Plays', O.U.P., 1964.

130

language can be an irritant and, where the whole edifice of a play stands up because of the brittleness, the tiny structure of a poem is not enough to support it.

The first stanza of Clark's *Easter* is striking, austere:

> So death
> being the harvest of God
> when this breath
> has blown uncertain above the sod,
> what seed, cast out in turmoil
> to sprout, shall in despair
> not beat the air
> who falls on rock swamp or the yielding soil?

'Sod' may be a bit archaic, but this is a highly successful stanza. The rest of the poem is a failure:

> O! hear the reaper's cry! the rap
> of his crook on the door—
> but the poor
> dupe! op'ning, shall find bats far gone with my sap.

The hysteria of the exclamation mark does little either to excite or to convey the anguish of death. This unfortunate last stanza, with the 'reaper', the 'crook', and 'op'ning', is what strikes me as the irritant that defeats the careful imagery of the first stanza.

As long as poets continue to write good poems using traditional forms it is foolish to say that the metrical rhyming poem is out-moded. One of the great *villanelles* of all time was written by Dylan Thomas ('Do not go Gentle into that Good Night') and some of Robert Frost's best poems are fractured sonnets. Clark cannot be criticised for using the forms—he must be criticised for misusing the forms or for not meeting the demands of the forms he appears to be attempting.

T. S. Eliot, writing on Pound, says, 'In *Ripostes* and in *Lustra* there are many short poems of a slighter build . . . equally moving, but in which the "feeling" or "mood" is more interesting than the writing. (In the perfect poem both are equally interesting as one thing and not as two.)'[1] It is the writing that intrudes in the early poems of Clark. If the writing does not openly irritate, it distracts. Here are three examples from three different poems:

> Up the laughing stream
> We raced down the sun.
> Who there thought such fun
> Could end? We held one steam.

[1] Introduction to Ezra Pound: 'Selected Poems', London, Faber & Faber, 1933.

131

And:

> Give me your water whole
> And slake slake my soul
> The irresistible blight
> Spiriting in the night . . .

And:

> A tree has broken in the lull,
> The most buoyant in all the forest!
> No lightning split past its hull
> Nor any wind shook its crest;
> But the hand of a woodster . . .

Again, these are dismal stanzas from good poems, although the last, *Tree*, approaches the melon-headed sentimentality of 'Woodsman! Spare that Tree!'. The concentration on the plumping and patching of metre and rhyme, choosing words like 'steam', 'irresistible blight', 'hull', 'woodster' and two slakes, prevent any of the real effects from coming through. These stanzas are collections of various effects, each working separately. There is no integration of the language or metrics and so the imagery collapses and no clear idea is conveyed.

In contrast to these poems of Clark that don't come off there are the poems that succeed on many levels. Clark's poor poems are few, but he has thought them important enough to include in a book and so they must be considered as seriously as any of the others. Clark's best poems either crush us or lift us up with simple words, as in *Streamside Exchange*:

> Child: River bird, river bird,
> Sitting all day long
> On hook over grass,
> River bird, river bird,
> Sing to me a song
> Of all that pass
> And say,
> Will mother come back today?
>
> Bird: You cannot know
> And should not bother;
> Tide and market come and go
> And so has your mother.

The poem asks a simple question with simple words; the reply is a crushing statement of the loneliness that men must bear. Also the rhyme is not intrusive. It is a quiet poem but leaves us with a mood that cannot be shaken off.

Despite the many exclamation marks that Clark uses in his poems, he still seems to be a writer of extremely quiet poems. The effects are heightened by the simplicity and quietness and, as in *Streamside Exchange*, there is often great intensity in the writing. Usually, Clark is content to set a scene, make a picture or describe a drama without acting in it or having a 'dramatic movement'. It is a brilliant stroke to have the 'bird' end the poem above; the child may or may not be silent, but his further questions must be our own. The dramatic action takes place after the poem has ended; the reader is responsible for the drama. In setting the scene well Clark has given us all the ingredients of the drama without telling us what we should think, how we should act our part. It must be difficult for a writer of dramas to leave off so early; it may also be the reason for his failure in other poems where, by trying to create dramatic action, he loses control and founders in his own language.

Another example of the quiet powerful poem is *Pub-Song*. Again it is someone talking naturally, matter-of-factly, that creates the tension:

> So that is what they say?
> That I walk the house of bawds
> Who bathe my feet from gourds
> Raising smoke between me and day?
>
> Well, if that's all you meant
> Now the myth is broken
> And I wild in the open
> What is there left to repent?

There is an anxious moment right after the first stanza which is dispelled in the second immediately, as it would be in the quick exchange of conversation. But the last line leaves us with the impression that there *is* something to repent, and the poet, 'wild in the open', must find that which must be atoned for. Since 'the myth is broken' what remains is reality, the real guilt, the real transgressions. After the light moment ('What is there left . . .'), after the poem has finished we are left to ponder.

In the often-anthologised *Ibadan* the scene is set delicately:

> Ibadan,
>   running splash of rust
> and gold—flung and scattered
> among seven hills like broken
> china in the sun.

Poets compare cities to women (Paris, the raped whore; New York, the long-legged neon blonde, and so forth). Clark's poem on Ibadan presents an image that is both vivid and new. Ibadan flashes before us. I have never seen Ibadan, but when I read this poem a city materialised before me, a city of dazzling light, of both randomness and order. The sun stands out in the poem and dominates as it must in that city. The poem is interesting as one distinct visual experience, the mood and the writing fused.

I think John Clark's best poem is *Night Rain*. There is a natural rhythm

133

in *Night Rain* which the subject demands (unlike the imposed rhythms in the poems I criticised earlier). Not only does the subject, rain, demand rhythm, it also gets it in the best possible way. There is no metrical pattern in *Night Rain*, yet there is metre; there is no regular rhythm, yet there is the rhythm of rain, irregular as the rain's rhythms are.

> What time of night it is
> I do not know
> Except that like some fish
> Doped out of the deep
> I have bobbed up bellywise . . .

Clark goes on to describe the drumming of the rain, although he has already set the mood of drumming by the ingenious rhythms in these first lines. He traces the path of the raindrops from the sky to the roof, compares them first to fruits, then to prayer beads breaking in wooden bowls. The rain's sound rouses his mother, and these are the two images (the drumming, the mother) that persist to the end of the poem:

> I know her practised step as
> She moves her bins, bags and vats
> Out of the run of water
> That like ants filing out of the wood
> Will scatter and gain possession
> Of the floor.

The entire movement is seen by the narrator lying with others on the floor. The mother moves, the rain continues to fall, the spell is set:

> So let us roll over on our back
> And again roll to the beat
> Of drumming all over the land
> And under its ample soothing hand
> Joined to that of the sea
> We will settle to our sleep of the innocent and free.

The images of the sleeper conscious of the rain and waiting, of the rain joining with the sea-water to rise and purify are deftly handled. I have not quoted the entire poem. Read in its entirety this poem sets a mood that lulls with a peacefulness and acceptance that is very rarely matched in modern poems. The rain that soothes also makes people move, that washes clean also washes things away. It is a prayerful poem but cannot be called a strictly religious poem; it is peaceful but not monotonous. It is difficult to place this poem in correct thematic relation to Clark's other poems. It can be said, however, that the most successful poems in 'Poems 1962' are the ones in which the narrator is unmoving, observing the patterns that exist in nature and in man's nature. Clark writes on many themes, not all of them consistent with the efforts in his best poems. Fulani cattle bother him because they appear inscrutable; but in describing the exterior of the cattle he has given us enough information to lead us to the place where conjecture must begin.

There is a thin line between Clark's good poems and his bad ones. The poor poems are obscured by the use of pyrotechnic and imprecise language. The good poems are illuminated by simple and direct language. Ambiguity exists in both kinds, although it is hard to take in the poor poems. If Clark has a 'general theme' it has escaped me. This is not a weakness in Clark. It shows him to be a far more curious and hungry individual than one might suppose. There is something to be said for the poet giving in to every impulse and indulgence in his poems, but it must be admitted that neither randomness alone nor symmetry alone makes art out of the substance of the poet's impulse.

CHRISTOPHER OKIGBO

Ordeal. Ending on the edge of new agonies. Beginning again. And the poet wrapped only in nakedness goes on, deliberately, mostly conscious because he is half-carried by the nightmare winds, half-carries himself with his own home-made, wild, tangled-wood tales.

'Logistics,' says Okigbo in the *Initiation* section of 'Heavensgate', 'which is what poetry is'. The art of movement, says the dictionary. And here is the key—Okigbo's art is in moving, movement, being moved, a lived-through victimisation full of symbol and logic and accident and the poet's own plots. It is pure motion because he does not presume and force himself over the ordeal, but suffers it and summons at the end all his energy to resume and carry us all on to continuous illuminations all along the way to death.

At the beginning Okigbo finds himself before the 'watery presence' of *Idoto*. He is naked, a supplicant, offering himself as a sacrifice to his own poetic impulse; he is prepared to suffer creation.

And again, in *Passage*, there are the classical 'Dark waters of the beginning,' 'Rays . . . foreshadow the fire that is dreamed of,' and

> On far side a rainbow
> arched like boa bent to kill
> foreshadows the rain that is dreamed of.

The rainbow, the Covenant, is seen as a snake, capable of both leading and devouring the poet. The symbol that will lead the poet is seen as the embodiment of good and evil. The dual vision of Okigbo's occurs all through his journey; the saint would see only the rainbow, the profligate would see the snake—but the visionary Okigbo sees both.

O. R. Dathorne wrote in *Black Orpheus 15*, 'Christopher Okigbo's poetry is all one poem; it is the evolution of a personal religion.' Dathorne goes on to say that Okigbo's poems are narrating the 'progress towards *nirvana*'. But, although Okigbo speaks of being cleansed and desires the 'cancelling out', it seems he is acting on a larger desire to work himself

135

through the ordeal of accepted religiosity and mythology to a new way of seeing, rather than to evolve 'a personal religion'. It is not so much evolution of a religion as the *sublimation* of religion in himself that he seems to seek. Surely he begins with all the religious trappings, but the objective is to be released from them, and this can only be had by a complete acceptance and understanding of them. The very fact that Okigbo is always left on the edge seems to indicate that he will never finish 'the eight-fold path' towards true *nirvana*. At the beginning of *Distances*[1] he says:

> I was the sole witness to my homecoming

Yet, many lines later, the last line of the poem is

> I am the sole witness to my homecoming.

This seems proof that there is more than one home and that the poet is doomed always to be the only witness to his arrival at a temporary state of perception. There are different layers of perception, but they must be continually obscured or the poet will be paralysed with all the new rituals of his 'religion'. Once found, the perception must be abandoned.

Okigbo has to conspire with God to reach a state of perception, but always it is the act of writing that serves to release him:

> Stretch, stretch O antennae,
> to clutch at this hour,
>
> fulfilling each moment in a
> broken monody.

At the beginning of *Newcomer* he has begun to assume a new identity:

> Mask over my face—
>
> my own mask
> not ancestral—

He has thrown off the curses and blessings of the ancestral identities and says, simply, 'Time for worship' several times in this first section of *Newcomer*. The most meaningful and direct lines in the book come next:

> O ANNA of the panel oblongs,
> protect me
> from them fuckin angels,
> protect me
> my sandhouse and bones.

Those 'fuckin angels' that have become love-locked in a death-grip with so many believers *must* leave him alone. The strength of the above lines comes from his confident examination of his powers as a seer in the previous section, *Lustra*. His spirit is 'in ascent' and with confidence he muses:

[1] In 'Transition', *4*, no. 16, Kampala, 1964.

136

> I have visited,
> on palm beam imprinted
> my pentagon—
>
> I have visited, the prodigal . . .

Throughout the poem he views himself as a prodigal, yet he returns again and again to confirm this in order to release himself in the confirmation. His visitations meditated upon in *Lustra* give him the strength to cry out in *Newcomer*. The voice in *Newcomer* comes from a newly realised identity.

He has not become a 'newcomer' without sacrifice. He has been, as Dathorne says, crucified (*Initiation i*—the repeat of the crucifixion image, the impossibility of forgetting 'the scar of the crucifix') after becoming 'newly naked', and finally he ends the *Initiation* section with the explicit:

> And he said to the ram:
> disarm.
>
> And I said:
> except by rooting,
> who could pluck yam tubers
> from their base?

Dathorne calls the reply 'the pain of self-knowledge'. It is the knowledge of lust's presence spoken in reply to a severe command. The ram can only become innocent, lamb-like, by disarming; the disarming of the ram means the removal of his horns—the poet's reply shows us that he understands, for in both the command and the reply there are different castration images. The destructive and distracting sexual appurtenances must be removed. The poet replies in parable: he can only rid himself of 'yam tubers' by 'rooting', dig in order to pluck, immerse himself deeply in his own glands. This process of disarming would not be acceptable to the adherents of conventional religion who are supposed to pluck out the eye if it offends. The poet in *Initiation* will pluck by digging, which implies a concentration on the damnable fixtures (Augustine stares at the sour flesh of a fat whore and achieves sainthood in the rejection of it). Okigbo is guilty of all the things he is *capable of doing*. A blind man can hardly be praised because he is not a peeping-Tom.

The next section is a '*Bridge*' in the metaphorical-religious sense and also in the jazz meaning of the term—some music between the main choruses in the piece. And then

> in the teeth of the chill Maymorn
> comes the newcomer.

Most of the symbols Okigbo has established in 'Heavensgate' are repeated in the first section of *Siren Limits* (the first part of 'Limits'). He is at the edge, 'talkative'

                    like weaverbird
            Summoned at offside of
                dream remembered
            Between sleep and waking

And:

            Queen of the damp half light,
                I have had my cleansing,
            Emigrant with air-borne nose,
                The he-goat-on-heat.

The ordeal has ended at 'offside of dream remembered' yet he is sure of
only his nose being 'air-borne'. His feet are planted on earth as he is aimed
at a vague idea of perception. Certainly the cleansing is real (the best
poems in 'Heavensgate' come after the disconnected images of the vision
fragments; he assumes the new strength immediately after purification),
but the 'he-goat-on-heat' is the ram disarming himself in his own way (the
ram trying to wrench his horns free in his moment of heat, oestrous). And
he goes on 'feeling for audience'—both the audience of listeners that will
not be present at his homecoming, and the 'audience' with the force that
drives him on, up into his head.

   With the new cleansing comes new agony. The poet does not let us
forget:

        & the mortar is not yet dry . . .

            Then we must sing
        Tongue-tied without name or audience,
        Making harmony among the branches.

        And this is the crisis point,
        The twilight moment between
            sleep and waking;
        And voice that is reborn transpires
        Not thro' pores in the flesh
            but the soul's back-bone.

The agony is again partially resolved, in the old way with a new consequence: the traditional groves of *Heavensgate* bathed with the hard light
that he has realised in his passage. No one will watch, he must accept the
anonymity of the artist and visionary. Okigbo demands humility of himself and so, soon after the 'crisis point', he calls for us to 'Hurry on
down—'.

   In the last section of *Siren Limits* we glimpse how incomplete the
cleansing has been.

            an image insists
                from the flagpole of the heart
            The image distracts
                with the cruelty of the rose . . .

138

Desire has led him back through the 'soul's back-bone'. Sexual baggage, the pole, the rose, insist on the memory of 'my lioness', the same image as in *Watermaid ii* of 'Heavensgate': 'Bright with the armpit-dazzle of a lioness', she answers:

> Distances of your
>   armpit-fragrance
> Turn chloroform,
>   enough for my patience—
> When you have finished,
> and done up my stitches,
> Wake me near the altar,
>
> & *this poem will be finished.*

In these eight lines Okigbo plunges backward into *Heavensgate* (the lioness) and forward into *Distances* where the last four lines are used as an epigraph. The lioness, the whole sexual operation, haunts the sensually anaesthetised poet. In realising that it is an image that has insisted and in giving way to this insistence he is again granted the perception. This perception turns into disappointment because no one is capable of sharing it. In *Fragments out of the Deluge*

> He stood in the midst of them all
>   and appeared in true form
> He found them drunken, he found none
>   thirsty among them.

And later,

> They cast him in mould of iron,
> And asked him to do a rock-drill:
>   Man out of innocence—
> He drilled with dumb bells about him.

The 'Man out of innocence' drills through experience. 'Dumb bells' can be interpreted as the set of weights that strong men lift to show they are strong; or as morons (American slang); or as instruments capable of producing sound, now silent. In the context it is actually *all three*!

In section vii of *Fragments* he has reached the high point of the poem; the rest, as he says in 'Heavensgate', is 'anagnorisis'. In this section comes the deification,

>   which is not the point;
> And who says it matters
>   which way the kite flows,
> Provided movement is around
>   the burning market,
> The centre—

The wisdom that he has practised throughout the poem comes upon him in a phrase, consciously; the logistics of staying near the flame no matter what the mask. This is more than an approach to sexual action—it is a commitment to it. So we are not surprised to find in the vision of ix ('Then the beasts broke . . .') the careful preparation and final orgasmic violence ending in division and death. Neither does the final ambiguity of the return of the 'Sunbird', mixed with the image of 'Guernica', startle. He has entered 'the burning market' as he predicted. After it, a quiet moment:

> The Sunbird sings again
> From the LIMITS of the dream,
> The Sunbird sings again
> Where the caress does not reach

Quiet, though mixed with unspoken torment, for it is this 'caress' of the Sunbird (no longer the Lioness that he can devour) which he cannot manage that will release him from the 'Limits' and press him into the 'Distances' where

> At this chaste instant
> of delineated anguish,
> the same voice, importunate,
> aglow with the goddess
> . . . .
> strips the dream naked,
> bares the entrails;

The Sunbird still out of reach agonises him. And the litany:

> I have fed out of the drum
> I have drunk out of the cymbal
> I have entered your bridal
> chamber; and lo,
> I am the sole witness to my homecoming.

The repeated pattern all through *Silences*, *Heavensgate*, *Limits* and *Distances* has shown the concern for movement *through* and not necessarily a movement *to*. The fat state of perceptivity has been gained, he is 'symbiotic with non-being' (Dathorne) but it is a 'chaste instant', impermanent, and it is this short-lived purity that delivers him again into the pain of the 'homecoming', and that will continue to deliver him into pain.

It is impossible to do justice to Okigbo's erudition in such a short space. His sources can be found in Ibo mythology, the Bible, Allen Ginsburg's *Howl*, Pound's *Cantos* and in his own impeccable craft coupled with a soaring imagination. Okigbo, poet, prophet, prodigal; the consistency of his vision is apparent throughout his work.

He passes 'from flesh into phantom', from holy groves to the hospital bed. This is *nirvana*? No. It is a hell of revelation in which the reader sees Okigbo become a disembodied existential eyeball scorching itself on the

140

ordeal. He cannot be picked up at random and thumbed through; we have to follow his progress from pain to perception and back to pain. Okigbo can be considered from the point of view of all theologies, mythologies—each yields an interpretation. But better we too suffer the ordeal, ending on the edge of new agonies. Beginning again.

> *after we have formed*
> *then only the forms were formed*
> *and all the forms were formed*
> *after our forming . . .*

Agostinho Neto

To Name the Wrong

W. S. MERWIN

Agostinho Neto, a Negro from Angola, has spent a good part of the years since 1952 in Portuguese prisons. In July 1962, however—after this article was written—he managed to escape and is now leading the Angolian liberation movement MPLA.

It is possible for a poet to assume his gift of articulation as a responsibility not only to the fates but to his neighbours, and to feel himself obligated to try to speak for those who are in circumstances resembling his own, but who are less capable of bearing witness to them. There are many kinds of dangers involved in any such view of what he owes himself and his voice. There is, for instance, the danger that his gift itself, necessarily one of the genuinely private and integral things he lives for, may be deformed into a mere loudspeaker, losing the singularity which made it irreplaceable, the candour which made it unteachable and unpredictable. Most poets whom I have in mind would have considered this the prime danger. But there are other traps which have claimed their victims. Where injustice prevails (and where does it not?) a poet endowed with the form of conscience I am speaking about has no choice but to name the wrong as truthfully as he can, and to try to indicate the true meaning of justice in terms which the victims of injustice, among whom he lives, can understand. The better he does these things the more he may have to pay for doing them. He may lose his financial security, if he has any, or his health, his comfort, the presence of those he loves, his liberty, or his life, of course. Worse, he may lose, in the process, the faith which led him to the decision, and then have to suffer for the decision just the same.

Put at its simplest, and with its implications laid out all plain and neat: the decision to speak as clearly and truthfully and fully as possible for the other human beings a poet finds himself among is a challenge to obscurantism, silence and extinction. And the author of such a decision, I imagine, accepts the inevitability of death. He finds a sufficient triumph in the decision itself, in its deliberate defiance, in the effort which it makes possible, the risks it impels him to run, and in any clarity which it helps him to create out of the murk and chaos of experience. In the long run his testimony will be fragmentary at best. But its limits will have been those of his condition itself, rooted, as that is, in death; he will have recognised the enemy. He will not have been another priest or ornament. He will have been contending against that which restricted his use and his virtue.

I have to talk about Agostinho Neto as though he were dead. I mean that, after I have read what poems of his have found their way into print, and what

142

information about him has managed to evade the obscurantists who govern his country, I have to accept my remaining ignorance of him and of his situation as though it were final. He is a man whose vocation it is to articulate, to say, to make sense out of language; yet as far as the man himself is concerned I must rely to a great extent upon inference, as though he were incapable of saying anything more on his own account. I infer, to begin with, that he is a poet who, early in his life, made the decision I have been trying to describe, and adhered to it.

But that much is easy. Neto's crime was an articulate objection to Salazar's cynical and brutal use of the Angolan people—a transgression which is scarcely surprising. The plight of the people of Angola is not a school for indifference, and one of the dominant themes of Neto's poetry is the relation between his personal predicament and the experience of the people among whom he grew up. Such a preoccupation has led some poets towards propaganda; they have employed their talents in the making of public announcements. As far as I can tell, that is not Neto's temptation. Rather, in the best of his poems about Africa, he is at pains to reveal his own situation as he glimpses it in the lives of other Africans. It is best to give an example:

Night

I live
in the dark quarters of the world
without light, nor life

Anxious to live,
I walk in the streets
feeling my way
leaning into my shapeless dreams,
stumbling into servitude.
   —Dark quarters,
      worlds of wretchedness
where the will is watered down
and men
are confused with things.

I walk, lurching
through the unlit
unknown streets crowded
with mystery and terror,
I, arm in arm with ghosts.
And the night too is dark.

To keep to what is known about him (this time to factual information obtainable from the Conference of Nationalist Organisations of the Portuguese Colonies, 6 rue Paul Tirard, Rabat, Morocco), Agostinho Neto was born in September 1922, in Icolo Bengo, Angola, and went to school in Luanda, in that country. He had to interrupt his studies in order to work.

143

From 1944 to 1947 he served in the Department of Health in Angola, and than an Angolan working-men's organisation made it possible for him to go to Portugal and continue his medical education at the University of Coimbra. In 1948 some of Neto's poems were published for the first time, in Luanda, where a national cultural movement representing the young generation of Angola had just come into existence. He was at once acclaimed. Some of those for whom he was speaking recognised a voice.

In Lisbon he and other Angolan intellectuals came together to work out some means of protest against Salazar's colonial régime. There was a petition. Neto helped collect signatures. Here I am indebted to an editorial appeal in *Africa Today*, February 1962. Canvassing a poor section of Lisbon, he knocked on a door and had presented his request before he noticed (he is apparently not one who looks at people's feet when he is talking to them) that the man wore policeman's boots. He was arrested, for the first time. That was in 1952. It was not a long sentence, the first one.

On his release, he returned to his studies, to his writing and to his efforts on behalf of the liberation of Angola. He became a leader of the African students in Portugal, and represented them in Paris, in December 1953, at at the annual congress of the Fédération des Etudiants d'Afrique Noire en France, where he spoke of the wretched conditions of the native peoples in the Portuguese colonies, with special reference to the vast inadequacies of the educational facilities. Probably no one was astonished when, in 1955, Neto was again arrested by Salazar's PIDE (Policia Internacional de Defesa do Estado) on a charge of subversive activities. But by that time his name and his character were known outside the Portuguese-speaking dominions, and François Mauriac, Louis Aragon, Georges Duhamel, Jean-Paul Sartre, Edouard Pignon, Simone de Beauvoir, from France; Nicolas Guillén from Cuba; Diego Rivera from Mexico; André Kebros from Greece, and many others, demanded his release. Nevertheless his second term in prison lasted from December 1955 until June 1957, and before he was released he was condemned to the loss of all political rights (whatever that phrase may mean in Portugal) for five years.

He managed to finish his medical studies, and in 1959 returned to Angola, and to political activity—this time as one of the leaders of the Movimento Popular de Libertacao de Angola. His importance in this work was conceded by the Portuguese government; when he was next arrested, on June 9th, 1960, it was the Director of the PIDE himself who came to Neto's office in Luanda to take him into custody. Neto was sent to Lisbon, to prison.

When the news of his third arrest became known in Angola, his native town of Icolo Bengo organised a peaceful demonstration of protest. The Portuguese troops fired on the assembly, killing thirty and wounding 200.

Once again Neto's arrest was deplored and his release demanded by organisations and individuals from many parts of the world. Whether or not such protests influenced the Portuguese government, Neto, with his wife and children, was banished to the Cape Verde Islands, where he was kept

144

under surveillance until September 21st, 1961. Then he was again arrested and taken back to Lisbon, to the Aljube Prison. According to the authorities, his most recent misdemeanour consisted in showing friends a photograph of Portuguese soldiers assembled around a spear adorned with the head of an Angolan nationalist. No doubt the authorities were right that such exhibits are apt to create an unhappy impression. They took no pride, either, in the publication of the same photograph in newspapers in Belgium, Tunisia and Morocco, nor in its display, along with many others of the same nature, in the United Nations Building.

Even if the Portuguese authorities were deaf to all other considerations, they might reflect on the possible consequences of giving the people of Angola a martyr just at this point and, especially a martyr whom the Angolans already recognise as someone who speaks for them, and who acclaims

> my Desire
> transformed into strength,
> inspiring desperate consciences.

Three Poems by Agostinho Neto

African Poem

There on the horizon
the fire
and the dark silhouettes of the *imbondeiro* trees
with their arms raised
in the air the green small of burnt palm trees

On the road
the line of Bailundo porters
groaning under their loads of *crueira*
in the room
the sweet sweet-eyed mulatress
retouching her face with rouge and rice-powder
the woman under her many clothes moving her hips
on the bed
the sleepless man thinking
of buying knives and forks to eat with at a table

On the sky the reflections
of the fire
and the silhouettes of the blacks at the drums
with their arms raised
in the air the warm tune of *marimbas*

On the road the porters
in the room the mulatress
on the bed the sleepless man

The burning coals consuming
consuming with fire
the warm country of the horizons

Friend Mussunda

Here I am,
Friend Mussunda,
  Here I am,

With you.
With the established victory of your joy
and of your conscience.

—you whom the god of death has made!
you whom the god of death has made, made . . . [1]

Remember?

The sadness of those days
when we were there
with mangoes to eat,
bewailing our fate
and the women of Funda,
our songs of lament,
our despairs,
the clouds of our eyes,
remember?

Here I am,
friend Mussunda.

To you
I owe my life
to the same devotion, the same love
with which you saved me
from the constrictor's embrace.

To your strength
which transforms the fates of men.

To you
friend Mussunda, I owe my life to you.

And I write
poems you don't understand!
Can you imagine my anguish?

Here I am
friend Mussunda,
writing poems you don't understand.

It wasn't this
that we wanted, I know that,
but in the mind, in the intelligence,
that's where we're alive.

We're alive
friend Mussunda
we're alive!

Inseparable
still on the road to our vision.

[1] These two lines in the native language of Angola are part of a children's chant. Quoted in 'The Nation', 24 February 1962.

147

The hearts beat
rhythms of foggy nights,
the feet dance

The sounds do not die in our ears
 —you whom the god of death has made . . .
We are alive!

Kinaxixi

I was glad to sit down
on a bench in Kinaxixi
at six o'clock of a hot evening
and just sit there . . .

Someone would come
maybe
to sit beside me

And I would see the black faces
of the people going uptown
in no hurry
expressing absence in the
jumbled Kimbundu they conversed in.

I would see the tired footsteps
of the servants whose fathers also are servants
looking for love here, glory there, wanting
something more than drunkenness in every
alcohol

Neither happiness nor hate

After the sun had set
lights would be turned on and I
would wander off
thinking that our life after all is simple
too simple
for anyone who is tired and still has to walk[1]

---

[1] We presume that these translations are by Mr. Merwin, from poems in Neto, Antonio Agostinho: 'Colectânea de poemas', Lisboa, Ediçâo da Casa dos Estudantes do Império, 1961.

Poetry in Rumba Rhythms

JANHEINZ JAHN

The Caribbean Isles, which stretch in a vast semicircle of nearly 2,000 miles from the Mexican peninsula of Yucatan to the delta of the Orinoco and separate the Caribbean Sea from the Atlantic Ocean, have been the scene of manifold encounters, ever since they were discovered by Columbus. The first explorers met here the aborigines whom they mistakenly called Indians. A century later, around 1600, the original inhabitants of the isles had been extinguished, annihilated. The French, British, Spanish and Dutch fought for possession of the isles and the original gold hunters had by then been replaced by the planters, who grew their sugar and cotton with the help of mass-imported African slaves. Around the palatial planters' mansions one hears the whistles of the slave drivers, the hissing of the whip, the clinking of the chains, the barking of the dogs. The slaves adopted the languages of their masters, but as they were far more numerous than the Europeans they were able to retain certain elements of African culture. In 1804 a revolution brought freedom to Haiti, and gradually slavery was abolished on the other islands: in 1833 in Jamaica, Barbados and Trinidad, in 1848 in Martinique and Guadeloupe and in 1880 in Cuba. Thus the preconditions had been created from which the new hybrid cultures of the twentieth century could grow. The various European traditions—French, British and Spanish—and diverse African ones—Yoruba, Dahomean, Ashanti—blended to form a colourful new folklore, which formed the basis for a new poetry, literature and art.

In the 'twenties a number of Cuban authors discovered folklore as a theme. In 1928 Alejo Carpentier, a Cuban poet of French-Russian descent, compiled *La Rebambaramba*, a colonial-Cuban ballet. In the same year appeared Ramón Guiraos' poem *Bailadora de Rumba* (the rumba dancer) and Jose Tallet's *Rumba*. Here the rhythm of the rumba was for the first time made the basis of poetic expression.

> Zumba, mamá, la rumba y tambó!
> Mabimba, mabomba, mabomba, y bombó!
> Buzzing mamá, the rumba with its drum!
> Mabimba, mabomba, mabimba, kong-kong.
> She dances the rumba, the blackish Tomasa
> He dances the rumba, José Encarnación!
> She's rolling her right hip, she's rolling her left hip,
> He turns and he squats and he jerks his behind,
> He pushes his belly, he bows and he marches
> On one of his heels, and one drags behind.
> Chaqui, chaqui, chaqui, chaqui,
> Chaqui, chaqui, chaqui, chaqui,

The rhythm gives the poems a continuous tension; it makes the reader almost see and experience the dance, even without the aid of instrumentation. The poet attempts a precise onomatopoeic representation of the instruments, of the different sound values of the drums. Soon the theme is widened to embrace folkloristic scenes; exclamations and dialectal expressions are being used to help in the building up of the sound picture.

The first anthology of Afro-Cuban poetry, by Ramón Guirao,[1] was not only a collection of available material, it was also meant to stimulate poets to develop popular traditions into new art forms. Just as Robert Burns derived his art from Scottish folklore, so Nicolas Guillén, Emilio Ballagas, and Marcellino Arozarena have given international significance to Afro-Cuban folklore. Sensuality and humour, musicality and rhythm of the Afro-Cuban are merged in their verses with the traditional forms of Spanish poetry.

Afro-Cuban poetry is a 'black' poetry and forms part of the 'Black Renaissance', not because all of its authors are black-skinned, but because the most important elements of its style are derived from Africa. Types of literature are differentiated by style, not by colour of skin. There is no such thing as racial literature, as Afro-Cuban poetry proves. Its authors are black and white and mulattos of all shades; but style, rhythm and themes are African. They came to Cuba with the African slaves, who preserved their religious concepts through and beyond the period of slavery. Although the Africans in Cuba came perforce from the most diverse parts of Africa, it is the culture of the Yoruba that has finally survived, and whose rites and *orisha* have eventually merged with Roman Catholicism and its saints. Changó (Yoruba: Shango), the god of lightning, war, and of drums, has been merged with St. Barbara. Obatalá (Yoruba: Obatala), a bisexual god, was merged with Virgen de las Mercedes, the merciful virgin. This deity, which is known by its preference for white beads, is also called Merse, which is an abbreviation of Virgen de las Mercedes. Ogun, the Yoruba god of war, is identified with St. Peter. To Babalú or Babalú Ayé (the Yoruba Shapana) mules and dogs are sacred. He protects his worshippers from diseases and is identified with St. Lazarus. Even Changó does not perform as many miracles as he. But religious and profane life are closely interwoven. The religious feasts, whose dances aim at the state when God 'mounts the head' of the dancer, may merge into popular amusements and vice versa.

The original association with different deities dominates the character and diversity of profane dances and rhythms. The poets represent these rhythms by onomatopoeic sound groups that are varied and repeated like a *leitmotiv*. This forms the basic rhythm, which is frequently broken by a counter-rhythm. These verses should be read out aloud, so that the ear can feel the rhythmic transitions, movements and counter-movements, introduction and build-up, and the harmony of Spanish tradition with African rhythm.

[1] Ramón Guirao: 'Orbita de la poesía Afrocubana', 1928–1937, La Habana, García y Cía., 1938.

The Spanish language has been able to incorporate unbroken African rhythms and has been able to make harmonic use of African vocabulary, because, unlike French, Spanish allows a sharp accentuation; unlike German, it is rich in short sonorous vowels; and, unlike English, it has preserved the purity of vowels. That is perhaps the reason why there is no parallel to Afro-Cuban poetry in the French-speaking Haiti, although the religious concepts of its people are formed by traditions imported from the African kingdom of Dahomey. Haiti too has its sacred Vodun songs with African rhythms, but they are sung in Creole, a dialect strongly influenced by African languages and so different from French that its rhythms cannot be transposed into French poetry.

The English language is more suitable for translations, because it can carry strong accents like Spanish, and it is possible to recite even the translations to a drum. The rhythm is achieved as follows: the stressed syllables are strongly accentuated and the unstressed syllables between them—one, two or three in number—are so arranged that every second stress falls on the musical syncope. Thus in the verse 'Zumba, mamá, la rumba y tambó' there are two, then one and finally three unstressed syllables between the accents:

$$\acute{x} \quad xx \quad \acute{x} \quad x \quad \acute{x} \quad xxx \quad \acute{x}$$

If one tries to read this verse in Iambic or Trochaic metre one arrives at a line of five feet and the rhythm is destroyed.

$$\acute{x}x|x\acute{x}|x\acute{x}|x\acute{x}|x\acute{x} \quad \text{or} \quad \acute{x}xx|\acute{x}x|x\acute{x}|x\acute{x}x|x$$

In scanning this verse therefore one has to count the pauses as well, in such a way that the syllables *ma* and *bo* will be syncopated. The words *mama* and *tambó* should be followed, as it were, by an extra drum beat. This rhythm continues throughout the entire poem.

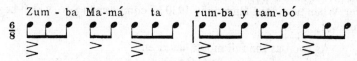

The power of Afro-Cuban rhythm has spread far beyond the island and its influence is felt in the whole of Latin America; its popularity is unique. Some poets were stimulated to write verses in other dance rhythms. Virginia Brindis de Salas writes verse in Tango rhythm:

TANGO No. 2

O what rings
under the eyes
has the night
in the hips of the tangos.

The piano
sighs and the drum
now sings in Bandonion
A dance
as the slaves have danced it
pace and the rhythm are
in the tail of the cock.

Yimbámba—yimbámba
Yimbámba—Yimbambiá
thus sound your supple hips
and thus your feet as well.
Ahéeé sings the small one
Ahóoó the piano sings.
Yumba and yumba,
yumba and yumba,
yumba and yumba,
yumba and yumba,
tchass-tchass!
O what rings
under the eyes
has the night
who is now straining her hips
in our sleepy slow Tango.[1]

Léon Damas of Guiana has even written an amusing poem in a valse rhythm.

Afro-Cuban rhythms are irresistible. In his poem *Casino*, Paul Niger tries to show how an intellectual civil servant, who disapproves of the popular art of his people because it is not 'respectable', is finally overpowered by the rhythm, in spite of his resistance.

The great Spanish poet Federico Garciá Lorca, too, could not escape the charm. When he visited Havana in 1930 he composed a Són, which begins as follows:

As soon as the full moon has risen
I drive to Santiago de Cuba
I drive to Santiago
in a cart of darkening waters.
I drive to Santiago.
There sing the roofs of the palm trees
I drive to Santiago.

The popularity of Afro-Cuban poetry in the New World has led tourists (who do not know Spanish) to believe that it is merely a kind of exotic, native entertainment. The poet Arozarena protests bitterly:

[1] Published in 'Punta del Este', Uruguay, 22 August 1953.

152

We are the folkloristic
eternally drunk
drunk of the whip and the forest and song
in the bars of rhythms
the rumba beats rum into our bodies
and tropics
The pool of the sounding isles
(musical puddles on the meadows of the Atlantic)
wraps us in cases of sextets and songs
in order to comb the tourist's dishevelled curiosity.
For eyelashes reflecting respectable pictures
the cornea, unable to seize truth by its root
our hunger is song
our culture song,
our laughter song, our weeping song, song,
song in Negroes like semi-quavers
song in Negroes like suffering oxen
that drag on their suffering life before musical carts.

A poetry that is popular, a poetry that combines surprisingly modern rhythm with gay laughter is easily thought of as insincere. Yet one should not judge too quickly! Poetry means also: to make music with language. Here a new colour is added to the rainbow (as a Caribbean poet put it), a new rhythm penetrates the world, and the demand of the African poet Senghor is fulfilled: 'I insist that a poem is only perfect when it becomes song: word and music combined. It is time to arrest the degeneration of the modern world, above all of poetry. Poetry must rediscover its beginnings, the times when it was being sung and danced. As in Greece, in Israel and above all in the Egypt of the Pharaohs. And as it still happens today in black Africa.'

Afro-Cuban poetry has taught a European language how to dance. It unites Black and White, tradition and modernity, and gives artistic expression to the Cuban soul.

Sensemaya

(Song to kill a snake)

Nicolás Guillén

    Mayombé-bombe-mayombé!
    Mayombé-bombe-mayombé!
    Mayombé-bombe-mayombé!

    The snake has eyes of glass.
    The snake appears and it winds around the post

153

With eyes of glass around the post,
With her eyes of glass.
The snake creeps without feet.
The snake hides in the grass,
Hides creeping in grass,
Creeps without feet.

Mayombé-bombe-mayombé!
Mayombé-bombe-mayombé!
Mayombé-bombe-mayombé!

Give her the axe and she dies:
Give it her now!
Don't give her the foot, for she bites,
Don't give her the foot, for she runs.

Sensemayá, the snake,
Sensemayá.
Sensemayá with the eyes,
Sensemayá.
Sensemayá with the tongue,
Sensemayá
Sensemayá with the mouth.
Sensemayá.
The dead snake does not eat,
The dead snake does not hiss,
Does not creep,
Does not run,
The dead snake does not drink,
The dead snake does not look,
Does not breathe,
Does not bite.

Mayombé-bombe-mayombé!
Sensemayá, the snake
Mayombé-bombe-mayombé!
Sensemayá does not move . . .
Mayombé-bombe-mayombé!
Sensemayá the snake . . .
Mayombé-bombe-mayombé!
Sensemayá is dead . . .

In 'Songoro Cosongo', Buenos Aires, Losada, 1952.
Translated by Akanji.

We Rehearse the Snake Dance

MARCELINO AROZARENA

Encarnasión!
Get out the box make it rattle and shake
get out this *murumba* which snaps at your feet.
get it out,
get it out,
show us the dance of the snake!
Sharpen your beak:
    'Alaalá-a-lá,
    alaalá-a-laaa . . .'
Sing without break:
'Alaalá-a-lá,
    alaalá-a-laaa,
    get out your head
    here is the snake
    the snake Mayá
    alaalá-a-laaa
    we dance, we dance the dance of Mayá . . .
Ha!
Step out with your foot
but dance very slow
as if you were stiff
as if you would fear the Mayá
and her teeth, alaalá . . .
Don't move your hips
don't move your hips
in the hips sings the fever of my love.
Encarnasión!
I walk behind your body in the harmony of the dance,
when the others look on
they see us as one
when they look from the side
they see us as two
and the song resounds anew:
    'Alaalá-a-lá,
    alaalá-a-laaa,
    get out your head
    the snake is here
    the snake Mayá
    alaalá-a-laaa . . .'
Your shoulders fall and rise
in the rhythm of your thighs
rhythmic is your step,

155

when you twirl close to me
as I come closer you evade me
and it was only a joke I see.
And the rumba Negro dancers tumba
  cumbacumba sounds the rumba
giving fire to the hips
and the partners dance and glide
like a black snake in the night—
bodies sailing free like boats
and the moving of your beads
looks like comets and like seeds—
when you tumble fall and stumble
you resemble the Mayá
don't lose the rhythm—
  'Alaalá-a-lá
  alaalá-a-laaa'
And once again
  'Alaalá-a-lá
  alaalá-a-laaa,
  get out your head
  the snake is here
  the snake Mayá
  alaalá-a-laaa,
  we dance, we dance the dance of Mayá.'

From Jahn (ed.): 'Rumba Macumba', Munich, Hanser, 1957.
Translated by Miriam Koshland and Sanders Russel.

Amalia

MARCELINA AROZARENA

Amalia dances and whirls.
— Si, Senor.
Amalia whirls and dances.
— Cómo no.
Amalia dances like flame,
like the tongue of a thirsty beast,
like a writhing snake in torment,
like a palmtree in bloom,
as if her body were a torrent,
as if,
as if,
as if . . .
Amalia dances and whirls.
— Si, Senor
Amalia whirls and dances.

— Comó no.
Amalia, holy brown woman!
Your almond eyes contain two glowworms
shining
in the black stars of your radiant pupils.
lines,
lines,
petrol lines in your hair form it to waves
and copy their sinuous course
in your body to the dance of the Batahola
Cinnamon paints your face
this face
which I love —
to pave the roads
leading
to your turgid hills
your miraculous caves,
here I leave my seed:
how much sweat to cover your hut!
Your aubergine lips bloom
in a calm voice the sounds
for my song flow:
dry is my throat
flower on ardent stems
sweeten my tongue . . .
Amalia dances and whirls.
— Si, Senor.
Amalia whirls and dances.
— Cómo no.
Amalia trembles, her feet are S's
not L's,
her eyes are fishes,
her fingers ten greyhounds
her mouth the fever of sugarcane fields
— trembling she gives them freshness,
her breasts glimmer like golden copper
and I am her mirror in the honey sea.
Amalia dances and whirls.
— Si, senor.
Amalia whirls and dances.
— Cómo no.
A whirl is her measure
burning in delight.
a whirl the conch shells
dangling on her body.
A whirl her body

gripped and lashed in the beads of her belt,
What madness!
Amalia! Amalia!
Amalia dances trembling
because she fears
her dance will become a festival
and her body and her colour
will provoke
the powerful spirit of Changó . . .
Amalia whirls and dances.
— Cómo no!

From Jahn, op. cit.
Translated by Miriam Koshland and Sanders Russel.

Casino

PAUL NIGER

Casino Casino
everything in the city
everything in the balconies and terraces
everything in the hips of young girls
everything in the people lying in their windows
everything is Casino
Casino Casino
From the trombone's piston rises the distant cry
pang-hang
through the trumpet's muzzle hua-huah
into the bitter cave of a saxophone,
a monsoon bubbles from the depth
'Moin Ka viré'
and the orchestra high on glittering platform spits,
palala spits out, the sweet temptations of the Casino.
Here I am,
A colourless official, and push
my intellectual throat through the collar's funnel,
that armour of respectability,
here I am,
Casino, dusty Casino of dusty planks
under my polished shoes.
Casino, Ah Casino,
I shall not dance, I've only come to watch,
to watch the stout, scented negresses dance,
only to watch them dance (oh the dance is the worst enemy of
   any kind of prose.)

Poetry, Poetry
I shall not be able to drink of this rum, produced by the sweat
of my rum-producing and rum-consuming
humiliated race;
these rum distillers, this sugarcane blood
made of sugarcane, this earthly song
daughters of suffering, daughters of work, daughters of the love
of the labourer, this dispossessed, impoverished
enslaved pauper
who yet labours hard
who is yet lazy
and makes music in any conceivable form
I shall not dance and I shall not drink,
Drinking and dancing is the pastime of uneducated negroes.

I do not eat this blood sausage, this undefined mixture
That makes one hot, because it's so much peppered,
That bewitches one and disarms
when it is served with rum,
when it is served with rhythms.

I shall not eat, I shall not drink, I shall not dance,
my toes lift, do not lift,
my hips swing, do not swing,
my stomach shudders and cramps,
my muscles are tense but they do not move,
Casino, you shall not get me!

In countries of cool climate, people are cool.
But even on the Atlantic the erected ship's bow is a symbol.
The white linen on my body: the soul of respectability.
I hardly transpire with the effort of remaining calm,
I hardly sigh in my immobility,
the immobility of my feet,
my dancing black feet,
in my inexplicable dance,
with my partner whom I did not see coming,
in a group which I did not see at all,
in a rhythm I hardly feel,
in a senseless tumult,
in this dust, the dust of the Casino.
Oh my feet, Oh my feet,
Casino I have come!

Published in 'Présence Africaine, Paris, No. 12, 1951.
Translated by Akanji.

Elegy of María Belén Chacón

EMILIO BALLAGAS

María Belén, María Belén, María Belén,
María Belén Chacón, María Belén Chacón,
    María Belén Chacón, — haï!
In your rounded buttocks was the coming and going
from Camagúey to Santiago,
from Santiago to Camagúey.

The constellation of your curves shall never
again be lit in the sky of the rumba.
What barking bit the tip of your lung,
María Belén Chacón, Maria Belén Chacón,
What barking has bitten your lung?

It was no barking, no claw,
It was no tooth and no hand.
The pressing iron at dawn
the iron has burnt your lung.

And then on one fine morning
they carried your beauty to grave,
your laundry and your lung,
your basket and your grace.

Let everybody stop dancing!
And even the black Andreas
has ceased to pick his fleas
and over there the Chinese
who carry their calabashes
shall also be quiet and kiss
the nails on the cross
on the sacred scaffold.
(Deliver us from evil
oh sacred mother of God!)

But never again shall my instincts
be reflected in the happy and round
bright mirrors of your buttocks,
and never again will the star
of your shining curves light up
in the sky of the beauty of women.

María Belén Chacón, María Belén Chacón—haï!
María Belén, María Belén,
in your rounded buttocks was the coming and going
from Camagúey to Santiago,
from Santiago to Camagúey.

Published in 'Mapa de la Poesía Negra Americana', Buenos Aires, Pleamar, 1946.
Translated by Akanji.

The Negro Poet and his Landscape

In poetry the rite is verbal;
it pays homage by naming.

W. H. Auden

GERALD MOORE

Now that the Negro's long debate with the West and with the condition of exile have been carried to the point where they can be left for a while, many black poets are beginning to address themselves once more to their own landscape. The way of seeing the physical environment can, I believe, be related to qualities found in the traditional arts of the Negro and can be seen as, in some sense, a return to a particular way of feeling about nature using this term to embrace everything that surrounds our consciousness, not just the conventionally beautiful.

What seems to be involved is a complete identification of the poet with the constituent features of the landscape around him. He does not so much inhabit this landscape as become inhabited by it. Its rivers flow through his veins, its branches toss in his hair, its planets burn through the bone of his forehead and irradiate his skull, its volcanoes stir and grumble in his throat. This is something quite different in order from the pantheistic ecstasies of a Wordsworth or a Shelley, who 'stand before' nature and 'contemplate' it. Whatever the philosophers of pantheism may urge, Western man simply cannot fuse himself back into a nature which he has deliberately set apart from himself in order to master it. He may see it as a complementing presence, as an antidote to the ills of urban man, or as a woman whose ravishment he at once desires and deplores. Christianity, which takes God out of nature and sets him above and beyond it, is essentially the religion of a nature-conquering or nature-transcending civilisation. The lost intimacy cannot be restored; at best it can only be lamented. Hence the note of loss or regret which haunts so much Western nature poetry. Hence also the occasional note of rather frenzied assertion in the work of a poet like Whitman, who seeks to restore the body to its central rôle in the worship of man and to walk with 'the tender and growing night'. Whitman's attempt is one of the most deliberate and aware ever made by a modern Western writer, but it is seldom free from the sense of effort. He seems always to be in quest of a lost feeling of identification, something felt once in a single moment of vision and never quite recaptured.

The Caribbean Negro poet Aimé Césaire may stand as our first example of an involvement with his landscape which makes any suggestion of 'response to nature' or 'contemplation' ridiculous. In his poem *Aux îles de tous vents*,[1] as in so much of Césaire, there is a continual interfusion of the

[1] In 'Ferrements', Paris, Editions du Seuil, 1960.

poet's physical presence with the features of his landscape, in such a way that their involvement is complete and sustained throughout the poem. There is no suggestion here of an extended analogy. The poet's gift of song is not 'like' a white gull wheeling in the blazing skies of Martinique, nor is it 'like' a knot of insult coated in bitter blood, nor a hiccup. It is all these things at one and the same time:

> From lands that leap so high
> yet never high enough to free their feet
> from the miser's clutch of the sea bellowing
>   in assault upon their ruined faces
> Hunger of men shared by mosquitoes and thirst
> for these are leaves laid out for a feast of birds
> sand hoarded against hope or with arms folded up
> to gather to the breast all who lie stretched
> in the perpetual heat.
> O justice noonday of too slack a reason it doesn't matter
> that nameless at the resinous torch of tongues
> they know not that their ashy offering
> is celebrated in this song of distant courage
>
> morning will unveil in the unknowing depth of my voice
> the bird which nevertheless it bears and noon will tell
> why it remains encrusted with the blood of my pulsing throat
>
> From these isles you will tell everyone
> how following the heart ally of dizzy birds
> long long seeking within the curtains of sand
> the wound at the centre sought by the burrowing sea
> you found within the hiccup
> the knot of insult coated with bitter blood
> which rejoicing at last at the bull blessed by the stars
> inflamed by our fevered breath and contesting
> with a sob louder than the surf we were
> crying earth clamped to the most shining wall of being
> always praising even as we die of it
> the black head parched and crinkled by the sun.

All the imagery here is busy throughout the poem, so that each picture which comes before us is immediately modified by what follows and yet continues to dwell in the mind right to the end of the poem. The absence of any barriers such as punctuation marks and capital letters assists this process, in which the poet is like some master juggler hurling one brilliant image after another into the air, while keeping all the earlier ones in motion, so that his head is ringed with a pattern of dancing forms. In this way the 'knot of insult' is able to relate not only to the poet's song and to the gull, but also to the wound at the secret heart of the island, towards which the sea is hungrily burrowing. This strengthens the identification of the poet

162

himself with the island, crouching so dangerously in the ocean. In this poem Césaire does not simply sing Martinique, he is Martinique.

There is no question of making a gesture of inclusion, of that deliberate extension of the human microcosm to embrace America, or mankind, such as we find in Whitman's *Song of Myself*. In Césaire the process is not gesture but flow. The passionate urgent stream of his poetry fuses into itself all the elements gathered in its swift career. It does not oppose one group of images to another in the interest of some purpose which extends outside the imagery. The unifying force in the poem is Césaire himself, the literal creator of his world. It is, above all, this sense of boundless creative energy at work within his poetry which makes it so often surprise and excite the reader.

A good example of Césaire's technique at its most intensive is this short stanza from the poem *Barbare*:

> Barbarous
> the dead who move in the veins of the earth
> and sometimes bruise their heads against the walls of our ears
> and the cries of revolt which are never heard
> that turn with the pitch and the measure of music[1]

Here the subtle vibration set up by the second line, which evokes the physical presence of the dead as a fructifying influence in the earth beneath us, an influence in continual motion, is greatly enriched by the next line, which suggests an identification of the earth with our living flesh, and fuses the veins of the earth with our own, which the dead equally inhabit and renew. The faint impact of the dead upon the walls of our ears at once isolates the head as the seat of individual consciousness, and reminds us that only a thin membrane separates it from the collective consciousness of all things, living and dead, that surround us. Then the circulating movement of this secret influence is carried forward in the unheard cries of revolt, finally resolving itself into a pattern of music, with all its suggestions of harmony and organic order. All this complexity of suggestion is achieved within one short stanza. Few poets since Rimbaud have been able to keep their imagery flowing so continuously through a poem, and at so many different levels, as Césaire.

If he is pre-eminent here, however, this is in part a measure only of his artistic stature in the general scene of Negro poetry. His approach to imagery and his use of it to assert the interfusing unity of existence can be closely matched in several Negro poets of a younger generation. Many instances can be found in the work of the Congolese poet Tchikaya U Tam'si, who is emerging as the outstanding African poet of French expression among those who have begun publishing since the war. U Tam'si's landscape is one of forest and river, sun and moon, earth and sea, interwoven with figures drawn from Christian ritual. At the superficial level he shares with Césaire a technique which may be called surrealist, which refuses to put

[1] In 'Soleil Cou Coupé', Paris, Editions K, 1946.

signposts and barriers within the poem in the form of punctuation and capital letters, leaving the dance of the words upon the page as the only interpreter between the voice of the poet and our ears. More significant than this is their common ability physically to identify themselves with their landscape, to again explore their own existence in its terms, or again explore that landscape itself with the vocabulary of their bodies.

U Tam'si draws an amazing range of effects from an apparently limited language of symbols. For example, the tree that haunts his imagination grows equally in the reader's mind as he progresses through the poetry, until it becomes at once the living tree of man, the crucifixion tree, the tree upon which other human sacrifices have been nailed or hung, the tree of the spirit whose branches (as in Yeats's *Byzantium*) are filling with singing birds, the tree Ygdrasil which stands at the world's navel, the tree of the poet's lost identity, and, simultaneously with all these, simply a great tree of the Congo forests, its branches swarming with monkeys, butterflies, fruit and flowers.

> How could I rejoice
> to be born all of flesh
> which is no coat of mail
> nor this wind which raps at every door that opens
> on the heart beating sky-blue sail-white blood-red?
>
> I who know nothing
> of the tree of my life
> my disgrace had three colours . . .
>
> The voyager said
> yes yes reason to live reason to die
> In that sense it was I who dreamed:
> for a superhuman voice
> to count the spasms
> of a sea in labour,
> on a crowded beach
> so that upon the savannah
> others may compose the prelude
> for a tidal wave
> but Kin sent them to me
> these flowers in my letter box
> It is likely enough
> false growths upon the roots of my tree
> poison my utmost branch
> I no longer know the essence of my soul
> all the doors open into shut houses.
> My hands crinkle already
> like dying flowers.[1]

[1] In 'Epitomé', Paris, Oswald, 1962.

It is difficult to do justice to U Tam'si without quoting at considerable length and from many different points in his work. Each of his books is unified by the constant re-working and exploration of a fairly fixed vocabulary of images which he continually places in new relations to each other. But even in this short poem from 'Epitome' (his fourth book) we can observe how the tree image is sustained and strengthened, while at the same time the suggestion of a flagpole, with the *tricoleur* of French assimilation at its head, flutters somewhere in the background. The next few lines evoke the threatening, creating presence of the sea, womb of all life on earth. In the final couplet we return completely to the physical image of the tree; the flowers which are lying in the poet's letter-box are associated at once with his hands and with the blasted 'terminations' of his life's tree. Thus the poem, as with Césaire, is not a series of images taken up and abandoned in the course of an argument, but an inter-penetration and unification of a group of images, all of which sustain their presence throughout the poem.

Another poem, also from 'Epitome', orders many of the poet's abiding preoccupations into a new pattern, in which they suddenly illuminate one another afresh.

> To you your belly is a marvel
> I am going to make there a slippery wound
> so that you will never forget it;
> the hydra in the pit of your belly makes sure
> of those she condemns to dismemberment
>
> As for you my fleshy shadow
> take back my other cheek
> mark it with your fingers
> I laugh with sorrow
> for once I will laugh at the sad gift of myself
> My cheeks were all my dignity
> I offer one to your dingy cheek,
> woman,
> dingy with the colour of three dinars
> which have betrayed me,
> I give the other to your dirty hand,
> brother,
> dirty with the colour of three histories
> My cheeks like two hills
> where the tree of my laughter could spring

The poem opens with the confrontation of an erect male threat and woman's more passive, rounded and destructive power. The word 'dismemberment' then seems to suggest a dismantling of the poet's physical presence (like that of Tutuola's Complete Gentleman) in which he divides his cheeks between the woman and the 'brother' (a figure who usually

165

evokes U Tam'si's Congolese allegiance). The woman's cheek shares the sexual associations of her round belly, while the man's hand betokens brotherhood. The 'three dinars' touch upon the idea of Christ's betrayal, but the following image of 'three histories' (in the French text there is a play upon the words 'deniers' and 'derniers') confirms that, as so often in U Tam'si, we are also concerned with the three colours of the *tricoleur*, a symbol of the poet's alienation elsewhere in his poetry. The beautiful image which closes the poem gives us again the tree of the poet's identity springing between two hills, but wedded with this is the picture of his laughter spouting upwards like a great fountain between his curving cheeks. The cheek, we divine, is an especially sensitive and exposed portion of being, because our salty tears flow over it, open to the world. This idea is immediately taken up in the next section of the poem:

> The algae glide over my cheeks
> a saltmaker drew there her ration of true salt
> The saltmaker is she to whom I give
> my other cheek.
> Anne had the foul cheek of a saltmaker!
> Ah let them take my cheeks also
> in exchange for a good easy sleep
> so that I may yet keep
> the night upon my soul!

Here salt takes on the quality of a principle of life, which commonly informs the ocean, the bloodstream and our precious tears.

These examples may be sufficient to show the sort of internal allusiveness that U Tam'si's poetry makes possible. No poem in his work stands alone, but each feeds upon and is fed by the whole body of the poetry. In particular, each book must be read as a whole.

The physical intensity with which U Tam'si explores the landscape of the world and his own being cannot be fully matched by any other poet now working in Africa, but his general relationship to the elements of landscape and his insistence on the physical and temporal unity of all experience, with energy as the uniting principles, can be found equally in the work of many other African writers.

The Gambian poet Lenrie Peters begins his *On a Wet September Morning* simply enough, with the experience of standing on the seashore with the water flowing over his feet. Then begins an extraordinary extension of his physical presence into space and time; not only, he says, do all created things reflect one another, but all are simultaneously present within the living moment, in which past and future equally inhere.

> . . .
> The sea was not the land's end.
>
> The world under the sea
> The sea under the earth
> The sky in the sea

Were elemental changes of a world
As the true life is death
    Which is the idea inside us
So distinction ends
    The plagued centuries
In a weeping jellyfish
    The pebble that will be a crown
The moon reflected in a starfish.

My amputated feet
    Buried in soft sand
Within the blue shadows
    Were already prehistoric . . .

I could not move;
    I say I could not move
My vegetable feet; . . .

Only a silent yell
    Rang through time's corridors
To the farthest end
    Where the amoeba becomes
The fire, water and air;
    Where the primeval fruit still hangs
So to the other end
    Where planets are but continents
Deep in the future
    That is darker and older
Than the past. . . . [1]

What we take to be fixed distinctions of form are in reality shifting manifestations of a single creative energy, which informs all and changes all.
The strange growing movement of the poet's feet through water and sand
into the primeval mud reminds us of a possible parallel in the visual arts of
Africa: those bronze plaques from the royal palace in Benin which show
the Oba's legs gradually sweeping outwards and downwards until they
become two huge mudfish inhabiting an aquatic world, while his wholly
human trunk stands upright and breathing in the upper air.
With the line:

Where the primeval fruit still hangs

Peters reminds us that the unity of all created things exists simultaneously
in space-time; there is no sense in which we can significantly regard these as
separate dimensions. All this, like much of the traditional thinking ex-
plored in Daryll Forde's book '*African Worlds*',[2] is remarkably close to
some of the conclusions of modern physics.

Somewhat similar is the use of the fish image in *Women*, a poem by the

[1] In 'Poems', Ibadan, Mbari, 1964.   [2] Oxford University Press, 1954.

167

Mozambique painter and writer Valente Malangatana. Here the fish precedes and includes woman, who is perpetually involved in her relationship with man, a relationship which the fish comprehends as it might a single cell internally divided but flowing within the unifying stream of creation, the river:

> In the cool waters of the river
> We shall have fish that are huge
> which shall give the sign of
> the end of the world perhaps,
> because they will make an end of woman
> woman who adorns the fields
> woman who is the fruit of man . . .[1]

The Nigerian poet John Pepper Clark gives a speech to Kengide in *The Raft* in which he discusses woman in her sexual rôle through an imagery drawn entirely from the materials of the play's landscape. The result is something which moves with equal sureness on three levels of significance at once; it gives a shrewd appraisal of three types of women as lovers, it does this entirely in terms appropriate to the setting of the play and to the imagination of the speaker, a rafting lumberman; and the movement of the speech echoes in little that of the whole play, from the cutting and dragging of timber in the interior to the journey down the spacious river, ending in the turbulence of the estuary. Although this particular speech works by means of simile rather than of extended metaphor, the way in which the materials of the imagery permeate the feeling of the whole description relates it very definitely to the sort of immediate apprehension of landscape which we have seen in the other poets:

> Women are three types. Some are like log,
> Solid and unshakable, after
> You've sweated all day lugging them into position.
> Take my word for it, run clear of wherever such
> Lie fallen. Then there are those who, like the stream
> About us now, are placid and spacious. It takes
> An unusual storm to stir them, and no passion
> However strong, can guarantee that. So you
> Just swim every market tide. And then there
> Are those who are pure billows; on them you rise
> And sink, rise and sink, and like
> The water-lettuce, you don't have to do anything.
> The woman I lost was the very crest of them.[2]

Even where the negro poet is describing landscape in more general terms, the same kind of warm intimacy can often be discerned, the same effortless movement into the elements of the landscape and out again. Whereas

[1] In 'Modern Poetry from Africa', ed. Moore and Beier, Harmondsworth, Penguin, 1963.
[2] From *The Raft* in 'Three Plays', Oxford University Press, 1964.

168

African poets of an earlier generation would rely upon a few features to evoke their African heritage from the place of exile where they stood (savannah, palm-trees, sacred grove or royal tomb often serve this purpose in Senghor, for instance), the South African poet Mazisi Kunene boldly draws upon the whole continent of Africa for the imagery of his poem *The Echoes*, yet manages to retain throughout the poem a certain warmth and ease which prevent his Africa from seeming like a construction. The poet's imagination moves easily within the physical presence of Africa to find the materials it needs, without for a moment appearing arbitary or random in the selection:

> Over the vast summer hills
> I shall commission the material sun
> to fetch you with her long tilted rays
>
> The slow heave of the valleys
> Will once again roll the hymns of accompaniment
> Scattering the milky way over the bare fields.
>
>   . . .
>
> I have opened the mountain gates
> So that the imposing run
> Of the Ruwenzori shall steal your image.
>
> The quivering waters of the Zambezi River
> will bear on a silvery blanket your name
> Leading it to the echoing of the sea . . . [1]

James Baldwin, writing of the Negro in modern America in *Letter from a Region of my Mind*, has isolated his acceptance of the fact of death, amid a white culture which implicitly denies it, as one of the most distinctive features of his culture. Finding himself in a permanent minority in a country which still denies the grandeur of his rôle in building it, the American Negro has necessarily expended much of his energy in the debate with what George Lamming has called 'the Other'. This is the opposing and challenging presence of the White, in terms of which he has constantly to define himself. Yet if we accept Baldwin's verdict on his attitude towards death, we are forced to see him as a man who still does not regard distinctions as absolute, who believes with Lenrie Peters that:

> . . . the true life is death
> Which is the idea inside us.

This would be a remarkable demonstration of the American Negro's preservation of a distinctive set of values and beliefs, even after three centuries of 'coexistence' with the white world. Perhaps the time is not far distant when he will begin to address himself to the landscape of America; when he will

---

[1] From '*Over the vast summer hills*', in 'Modern Poetry from Africa'.

begin to enter into a physical possession of it, in the fashion already hinted at in the Blues:

> I'm going to leave here walking, going down highway 61
> I'm going to leave here walking, going down highway 61
> If I run up on my no-good Joanie I declare we'll have some fun.
> I says I'm leaving in the morning, going to travel 61 by myself,
> I says I'm leaving in the morning, going to travel 61 by myself,
> So's I get killed on my journey no-one will know my death.

It may be as well at this point to turn for a moment and look at African traditional poetry, to see whether any comparable attitude to nature can be discerned there. In the very widespread literature of hunters' songs and totemic age-grade songs there is frequently a free association of animal and human characteristics which move side by side through the poetry, so that neither dominates the other. Close observation of the mannerisms and movements of animals is combined with a shrewd classification of human types, each related to their animal equivalents. This characteristic can, of course, be matched throughout the whole range of the so-called 'animal' folk-tales of Africa and in the animal masks, head-dresses and dance-movements which are so common in West Africa. An example of a totemic age-grade song in which animal and human characteristic move side by side, each illuminating the other, comes from the Buffalo Age-Grade of the Lango tribe in Northern Uganda.

> Ngore goes shaking his head
> Oh what was he like? What was he like?

> Buffaloes, eh-eh, they move in groups,
> They move in herds . . .

> Buffalo goes shaking his head
> Oh what was he like? What was he like?

Here there is a subtle implication that the young men of the age-grade also move in herds and that, like buffaloes, they draw their strength from solidarity. Also the swaying movement of the buffalo's head and heavy shoulders as he moves across the grassland is a reference at the same time to the young warrior who turns his head from side to side as he marches over the plains watching for enemies. Even the heavy shoulders of the buffalo seem to be related to the muscular vigour of the young men, while the white egret perching on the buffalo's ear, mentioned later in the song, evokes also the nodding white plume of the warrior's head-dress. Nowhere in the song is there any stated analogy between buffaloes and young men; this is implicit in the song itself and in the culture which contains it.

Lamine Diakhaté, writing on Senegalese folk poetry,[1] offers an example from Wolof praise-poetry to illustrate a particular attitude to landscape that he finds characteristic.

[1] 'Presénce Africaine', Vol. II, No. 3a.

I say:
And the moon stays her travelling
Fara Ndeud has raised her arms
a hundred and twenty thousand young marriagable girls
kneeling

I say:
the stars drive their piercing gaze through my forehead

Look! the clouds are parting
The arena is mine
Kouma Bang queen of the waters
the earth is cold
the world listens to us . . .

Here the poet is praising Kouma Bang, who is at once the moon and the patron goddess of the city of St. Louis. The picture is of the moon moving across the night sky like a bride in procession accompanied by the stars. All this depends upon the word of the poet. He can stay the whole procession, as he does in the first verse. When Fara Ndeud, mistress of the drums, raises her arms, the whole procession is stopped and everything falls silent. The moon continues to shed her light in stillness, a stillness marvellously evoked by the next few lines of the song. Poet and moon confront one another: 'the world listens to us'.

M. Diakhaté goes on from this and other examples to examine the function of the artist in African society. He isolates a particular way of feeling about the world and an ability to sacramentalise its features, even the ordinary, everyday ones, through the process of selection within an understood unity. In this way the very act of artistic selection becomes an aspect of the unity which embraces all things:

The African negro joins together, in a single lyrical impulse, God, water, stone, fire. . . . He lives the impulse to its very depths; he places himself, that is, in relation to nature. *He penetrates nature through its constituent elements.* . . . He translates this emotion by sacrifice and the word. . . . Sacrifice means fidelity to standards which have prevailed since the beginning of time in the relations between nature and man—it is Action. The word in turn answers to a certain way of ordering the Sacrifice; it brings existence down to earth by drawing an invisible thread between the sacred and the everyday. By means of the Word, the African negro converts his attitude towards nature into a reality.

Now I believe it is precisely this process of penetrating nature through its constituent elements, of drawing an invisible thread between the sacred and the everyday, which we can see at work in the passages we have examined from Césaire, U Tam'si, Peters and others. Lamine Diakhaté is disposed to interpret this as a specifically Negro characteristic. William Fagg, discussing the nature of African art in 'Nigerian Images',[1] is more inclined to the view

[1] London, Lund, Humphries, 1963.

that what we are observing is a characteristic of pre-industrial societies in general, though he does not advance convincing evidence from other areas. There is a sense, for example, in which Aztec and Inca culture were 'pre-industrial' (if by this term he means societies which have not advanced beyond a purely agricultural basis of survival). Yet the world of their more hierarchical, tensely modelled, often grim and terrifying art is utterly different from anything in a great humanistic art like that of the Yoruba, for instance. Fagg's views, however, tally closely with those of Diakhaté as to the nature of the artistic process we are observing. In discussing the quality which he discerns in all African art he writes:

> This quality, whose many forms may be subsumed under the term 'dynamism', appears to be present in the philosophical systems of all the peoples of the world except those of the 'higher' or industrial civilisations, who seem always to have abandoned or devitalised it as a precondition of embarking on the path of materialistic progress and the mastery of nature. . . . Their African ontology is based on some form of dynamism, the belief in immanent energy, in the primacy of energy over matter in all things. Thus it is energy and not matter, dynamic and not static being, which is the true nature of things. . . . Its corollary—that this force or energy is open to influence by man through ritual means—is the very basis of all tribal belief and observance.

The 'ritual means' here referred to can be equally the act of carving, of singing, of worship or of dancing. In discussing sculpture as one of these means, Fagg goes on to observe how often it celebrates increase; brought about by right influencing of primal energy:

> '. . . of all the sculptural forms given to the concept [of increase] the most striking is the exponential curve described in the growth of horns, tusks, claws, beaks, and shells.'

It may be that this concentration of interest upon the point of growth will illuminate the meaning of Demoke's act of sacrilege in Wole Soyinka's play *A Dance of the Forests.* Demoke, poet and woodcarver, plucks his apprentice to his death because he can stand upon the very top of the growing tree and carve it, while Demoke can only 'trim the bulge of his great bottom'. At the same instant as he kills his apprentice, Demoke hacks the top off the tree itself:

> Down, down I plucked him, screaming on Oro.
> Before he made hard obeisance, to his earth,
> My axe was executioner at Oro's neck. Alone,
> Alone I cut the strands that mocked me, till head
> And boastful slave lay side by side, and I
> Demoke, sat on the shoulders of the tree,
> My spirit set free, my hands,
> My father's hands possessed by demons of blood.[1]

[1] Oxford University Press, 1964.

The same point of concentration can be found in the work of another Nigerian poet, Christopher Okigbo, who builds one of his most beautiful lyrics around the exploratory movement of growth into space:

> Into the soul
> The selves extended their branches
> Into the moments of each living hour
> Feeling for audience . . .[1]

If Lamine Diakhaté relates this particular feeling towards nature to the African Negro *per se*, and William Fagg sees it as a feature of the pre-industrial consciousness in general, the West Indian Negro writer George Lamming relates it more specifically to nationalism, nationalism not as a programme of political action but as a way of feeling about one's own place in the world. There is a passage in Mark's diary in *Of Age and Innocence*,[2] Lamming's third novel, in which he writes of this feeling as it expresses itself in terms of a particular piece of earth:

> Nationalism is not only frenzy and struggle with all its nice necessary demand for the destruction of those forces which condemn you to the status we call colonial. The national spirit is deeper and more enduring than that. It is original and necessary as the root to the body of the tree. . . . It is the private feeling you experience of possessing, the being possessed by, the whole landscape of the place where you were born, the freedom which helps you to recognise the rhythm of the winds, the silence and aroma of the night, rocks, water, pebble and branch, animal and bird noise, the temper of the sea and the mornings arousing nature everywhere to the silent and sacred communion between you and the roots you have made on this island.

In the plot of the novel itself, it is only the younger generation of the islanders, the little secret society of boys, who are able to embark on the discovery of their tragic landscape in the manner which Lamming suggests.

Lamming's expression of this feeling for landscape is strikingly similar to that offered by Diakhaté, but he defines it in a way which would embrace all the people, of whatever race or origin, who find themselves now involved in the discovery of the country they have inherited. The same quest can be found as a theme in the work of the young Negro writers of the Caribbean area. Wilson Harris of Guyana has built a quartet of remarkably powerful and beautiful novels around it, novels which involve East Indian, African, Portuguese and Carib in a common movement into the heart of Guyana, hidden in its fortress of water, forest and rock. Derek Walcott of St. Lucia has expressed it in his poem *As John to Patmos*, where he renounces all 'homeless ditties' and turns the full energy of his gaze upon his own island:

> . . . So I shall range
> No more from home. Let me speak here.

[1] In 'Limits', Mbari, 1964.   [2] London, Michael Joseph, 1958.

Hence we are presented with three slightly differently explanations for a commonly observed feature in the Negro's realisation of nature. Fagg's explanation would raise serious doubts as to whether this 'dynamic' attitude towards nature and time can survive the transformation of Negro life into a pattern closer to that of modern urban and industrial living, a transformation which seems to be eagerly welcomed by the peoples concerned. Lamine Diakhaté's raises this question less directly because he does not root the Negro's attitude to nature in his past order of society. But it would savour of racial mysticism to deny that radical changes in his social living and in his relationship to his natural environment may bring about fundamental shifts in the Negro's way of looking at the world. It is precisely here that George Lamming, by offering an explanation of Negro dynamism which is itself dynamic, which is itself rooted in the process of change, of adjustment to the modern world, offers the best hope that this unique quality in Negro poetry may have a future as well as a past.

Part 3

The Novel

The Tragic Conflict in Achebe's Novels

ABIOLA IRELE

The immediate subject of Chinua Achebe's novels is the tragic consequences of the African encounter with Europe—this is a theme he has made
inimitably his own. His novels deal with the social and psychological conflicts
created by the incursion of the white man and his culture into the hitherto
self-contained world of African society, and the disarray in the African consciousness that has followed.

But a novelist deals not only with situations but also, and above all, with
individuals. And it is precisely the cycle created by the responses of men to
the pressure of events, their evolutions at significant levels of feeling and
thought, that makes the real world of the novel. The importance of Chinua
Achebe's novels derives not simply from his theme, but also from his complete presentation of men in action, in living *reaction* to their fate, as well as
from his own perception that underlies his imaginative world and confers
upon it relevance and truth.

Achebe has chosen the tragic medium in handling his theme—as opposed
to the comic treatment of the same or a similar theme in Oyono and Beti's
novels, though these two authors are in many ways no less *serious* than he.
This involves a particular dramatic ordering of events, in which each of the
situations is linked to another to reveal a tragic pattern, again, as opposed
to the comic novel in which each situation has to contain an immediate
interest for its comic effect. For tragedy implies the working out in men's
lives of a rigorous fatality that transcends the individual's ability to comprehend or to arrest its pre-ordained course of events. This approach demands
the development of the individual characters as well as of the situations. In
two of his novels, at least, Achebe succeeds in striking a profoundly tragic
note at both levels.

Things Fall Apart,[1] as the title suggests, is concerned with the dislocation
of the African society caused by impact with another way of life. The recon-
struction of Ibo village life is directed at revealing the forces at work both
inside and outside traditional society that prepared the way for its eventual
disintegration. Achebe's purpose is therefore not primarily to show its
values—though this is an undoubtedly significant side line—but rather to
show it as a living structure, as an organism animated with the life and
movement of its members: and within this framework is contained the
sphere of action which involves the personal drama of the characters themselves.

The double level of action is realised through the relationship that exists
between Okonkwo, the principal character, and his society. In many ways,
Okonkwo represents his society in so far as the society has made the man

[1] London, Heinemann, 1958.

177

by proposing to him certain values and lines of conduct. On the other hand, the man's personal disposition, his reaction to these social determinations stemming from his subjective perception of them, prepares his individual fate.

In the case of Okonkwo, he is a man who has grown up in a community which, because of its passionate desire for survival, places its faith above all in the individual quality of 'manliness'. And it is an irony of fate that makes Okonkwo start off with a disadvantage on this score—the failure of his own father to satisfy this social norm, which adds an urgency to his own particular position. It is the need for him to live down the shame of his father that compels him to an excessive adherence to the social code to an extent which in fact transforms a value into a weakness.

> Okonkwo never showed any emotion openly, unless it be the emotion of anger. To show affection was a sign of weakness; the only thing worth demonstrating was strength.

Besides, in order to justify himself, he pursues distinction with an obsessive single-mindedness that soon degenerates into egocentricity, until he comes to map out for himself very narrow limits of action or reflection:

> Okonkwo ruled his household with a heavy hand. His wives, especially the youngest, lived in perpetual fear of his fiery temper, and so did his little children. Perhaps down in his heart Okonkwo was not a cruel man. But his whole life was dominated by fear, the fear of failure and of weakness. It was deeper and more intimate than the fear of evil and capricious gods and of magic, the fear of the forest, and of the forces of nature, malevolent, red in tooth and claw. Okonkwo's fear was greater than these. It was not external but lay deep within himself. It was the fear of himself, lest he should be found to resemble his father. Even as a little boy he had resented his father's failure and weakness, and even now he still remembered how he had suffered when a playmate had told him that his father was *agbala*. That was how Okonkwo first came to know that *agbala* was not only another name for a woman, it could also mean a man who had taken no title. And so Okonkwo was ruled by one passion—to hate everything that his father Unoka had loved. One of those things was gentleness and another was idleness.

It is clear from this passage that we are in fact dealing with a psychological case. Okonkwo's way of shutting everything else out of his view, aware only of himself, is an indication that his ambition has become a blinding passion of a pathetic kind. The stage is set in the very mind of the character for a tragic career.

Outside factors afford the accessories of this tragic movement. As a result of his own mental attitude, Okonkwo's relationship with other people is thrown off balance. His own rigidity towards himself is reflected in his impatience with others, and in particular with his son, Nwoye:

Yam stood for manliness, and he who could feed his family on yams from one harvest to another was a very great man indeed. Okonkwo wanted his son to be a great farmer and a great man. He would stamp out the disquieting signs of laziness which he thought he already saw in him.

In a way, Okonkwo's way of conforming, besides being an inverted sort of nonconformity, is a perversion. The meaning he attaches to 'manliness' amounts to fierceness, *violence*. His insistence is such that he becomes a menace to his society even within the limits of its code. On one occasion he contravenes a sacred custom by beating his wife during a sacred week—he was 'not the man to stop beating somebody halfway through, not even for fear of a goddess'. And one of the elders, commenting on his action, remarks: 'The evil you have done can ruin the whole clan. The earth goddess whom you have insulted may refuse to give us her increase, and we shall all perish.'

This incident looks forward to that in which he kills another villager at a feast (though accidentally) and has to be expelled and go into an exile pregnant with consequences. But apart from the driving propulsion of his life and the consequent mental stress that this involves for him and for his immediate circle, his concern for a public image takes him to a point where his actions become a pure contradiction of the values they are meant to defend. His participation in the killing of Ikemefuna is one of the most significant events in the novel.

> As the man who had cleared his throat drew up and raised his matchet, Okonkwo looked away. He heard the blow. The pot fell and broke in the sand. He heard Ikemefuna cry, 'My father, they have killed me!' as he ran towards him. Dazed with fear, Okonkwo drew his matchet and cut him down. *He was afraid of being thought weak*.

Okonkwo has had to steel himself against ordinary human feelings, so that he becomes *dehumanised*.

On a greater scale than his passion is the struggle of the man with his fate (symbolised by his *chi*). His ambition and impatience drive him on to calculate on a larger scale than others, to demand more of his fate and to force the pace. Ironically, the reversals begin with his own son, who is the very antithesis of his father. There is an Œdipus touch to the relationship of Nwoye with his father—further emphasised by the way Achebe portrays Okonkwo's predilection for his daughter, Ezinma. In the immediate context of the novel, the conflict is created out of the gradual breakdown of a normal relationship between father and son, and Nwoye's final alienation from his father which prevents a resolution. The final breaking of the filial bond is directly related to the killing of Ikemefuna:

> As soon as his father walked in, that night, Nwoye knew that Ikemefuna had been killed, and something seemed to give way inside him, like the snapping of a tightened bow.

179

But this incident is not confined merely to the simple question of the son's reaction to his father's place in his own life and its consequences upon his sensibility, but is also related in the same passage to the wider issues of the boy's reaction to his society. Nwoye is presented all along as a sensitive young man whose psychology turns against certain customs of the village, particularly the casting away of twins into the forest. In fact, Nwoye's defection to Christianity later on has a double significance—it is at the same time an act of revolt against his father as well as a rejection of the society that he embodied; and it is essentially as such that Okonkwo himself views his son's gesture:

> Now that he had time to think of it, his son's crime stood out in its stark enormity. To abandon the gods of one's father and go about with a lot of effeminate men clucking like old hens was the very depth of abomination. Suppose when he died all his male children decided to follow Nwoye's steps and abandon their ancestors? Okonkwo felt a cold shudder run through him at the terrible prospect, like the prospect of annihilation.

Nwoye thus stands as a symbolic negation for his father, the living denial of all that Okonkwo accepts and stands for.

The disaffection and the final defection of his son is only part of a general reversal of Okonkwo's fortunes. His accidental killing of a villager and his subsequent exile from Umuofia are the workings of a blind fate crossing his path to his own conception of self-realisation. His exile, which he bears with bad grace, has not only brought him a setback, but has also added to his ambitious drive the sharp edge of frustration. But Okonkwo is a man who is prepared to grapple with his fate, to bend everything to his irrepressible will. Only at one stage, when the true propositions of his struggle appear to him, does he seem to relent:

> Clearly his personal god or *chi* was not made for great things. A man could not rise beyond the destiny of his *chi*. The saying of the elders was not true—that if a man said yea his *chi* also confirmed. Here was a man whose *chi* said nay despite his own affirmation.

His return to Umuofia when he comes back to meet new circumstances— the presence of the white man and his success in making converts—is the occasion for relaunching his struggle on a new footing. For the situation is to Okonkwo a personal issue. The fact that his son Nwoye is among the Christians is only symptomatic of the way in which the new religion strikes at his own heart, as it were; the real point is that he has to use the fight against the Christians to regain his lost place in the village. This is even easier than his inflamed passion makes him realise, and he is naturally involved in the attack on the Christian Church that leads to the arrest and humiliation of those responsible. The impact of this incident on Okonkwo's mind prepares the last phase of his tragedy:

> As he lay on his bamboo bed he thought about the treatment he had received in the white man's court, and he swore vengeance. If

Umuofia decided on war, all would be well. But if they chose to be cowards he would go out and avenge himself.

For, characteristically, he sums up the situation in terms of violence. His final action in killing the messenger of the colonial administration is in a sense his 'revenge'. And his final defeat is the utter futility of his action, his final realisation that he has gone so far beyond reasonable limits in championing his society as to have lost touch with it:

> Okonkwo stood looking at the dead man. He knew that Umuofia would not go to war. He knew because they had let the other messengers escape. They had broken into tumult instead of action. He discerned fright in that tumult. He heard voices asking: 'Why did he do it?' He wiped his matchet on the sand and went away.

Things Fall Apart is the tragedy of one man, worked out of his personal conflicts—his neurosis, almost—as well as out of the contrariness of his destiny. Yet the title is not without relevance, for the novel does have another dimension, that of social comment. Okonkwo's suicide is a gesture that symbolises at the same time his personal refusal of a new order, as well as the collapse of the old order which he represents. For Okonkwo's inflexibility, his tragic flaw, is a reflection of his society; his defect, though a deformation, derives from a corresponding trait in his society, an aspect of it pushed to its extreme logical frontiers.

It is true, of course, that Achebe presents the society as one that has positive qualities of its own. The coherence and order that make social life one long ceremonial, the intense warmth of personal relationships and the passionate energy of the religious life, all these reveal the other side of the coin. But if the social structure is carefully reconstructed—with a fondness that at least reveals, if it does not betray, the author's attachment to his social background—so also is the suddenness of the final bolt that strikes it carefully prepared for the disastrous effect it is going to have, the cracks in the edifice where the falling apart begins being carefully shown up. It is thus significant that the earliest converts should include the outcasts and particularly the mothers of the unfortunate twins. A correlative theme is here attached to the whole portrayal of Umuofia—that of the liberating influence of the new religion. Consider for example the effect of Nwoye's conversion upon the boy:

> It was not the mad logic of the Trinity that captivated him. He did not understand it. It was the poetry of the new religion, something felt in the marrow. The hymn about brothers who sat in the darkness and in fear seemed to answer a vague and persistent question that haunted his young soul—the question of the twins crying in the bush and the question of Ikemefuna who was killed. He felt relief within as the hymn poured into his parched soul.

Things Fall Apart turns out to present the whole tragic drama of a society, vividly and concretely enacted in the tragic destiny of a representative individual. This use of an individual character as a symbolic receptacle, the

181

living theatre, of a social dilemma, is what gives Achebe's novels their real measure of strength—it explains what for me is the weakness of his second novel: *No Longer at Ease*,[1] and the achievement of his third novel, *Arrow of God*.[2] *No Longer at Ease* is a sequel to *Things Fall Apart* not only in the fact that a later generation of Okonkwo's family is involved but also in the theme—it treats of the dislocation in the African psyche that followed the disintegration of a situation in which a meaningful social and moral orientation is made difficult. The first novel links up with the second much as the portent of Yeats' poem looks forward to the implication of Eliot's.

It is also the story of an individual, Obi Okonkwo, who is caught up in this situation which demands from the individual that he create a firm moral order out of the flux of values in the world in which he lives—a situation that demands an exceptional moral and intellectual initiative. Obi's dilemma is contained in the conflict between his developed intellectual insight and his lack of moral strength to sustain it.

The whole novel is built up out of the profound gulf that exists between Obi's Western education and its practical relevance to his individual place in the world. Obi is something of an aesthete, but his culture is manifest in an attachment to things that are of no real consequence. There is an unconscious irony in Achebe's presentation of this character's literary pretensions, as when he says to his girl friend, Clara: 'You know you are a poet. . . . To meet people you don't want to meet, that's pure T. S. Eliot.'

The hollow cleverness of a statement like that is made all the more devastatingly clear by contrast with the intense pulse of life around him; for instance by the overwhelming sincerity of the cyclist whom he nearly runs over—

> The cyclist looked back once and rode away, his ambition written for all to see on his big black bicycle-bag—FUTURE MINISTER.

But there is a more conscious kind of irony in the description of the conversation that Obi has with the happy-go-lucky Christopher:

> 'The Civil Service is corrupt because of these so-called experienced men at the top,' said Obi.
> 'You don't believe in experience? You think that a chap straight from the university should be made a permanent secretary?'
> 'I didn't say *straight* from the university, but even that would be better than filling our top posts with old men who have no intellectual foundations to support their experience.'

Further on, Obi explicitly links up his idea of 'intellectual foundations' with a moral stand:

> 'To most of them bribery is no problem. They come straight to the top without bribing anyone. It's not that they're necessarily

[1] Heinemann, 1960.   [2] Heinemann, 1964.

better than others, it's simply that they can afford to be virtuous. But even that kind of virtue can become a habit.'

But Obi turns out in fact to be a man with a narrow sense of values. Just as his Western education is limited to a superficial aesthetic orientation, so his application is restricted to specific delimitations, rather than to the total field, of his social situation. This constitutes his major liability in dealing with the complex problems with which he is faced.

His weakness of character is reflected in his inept handling of his human relationships and of his material problems; he is an individual with no sense of order, whose incapacity is contrasted to the strength of character of his hardly literate 'fellow Umuofians' which permits them to make sacrifices on behalf of a man who turns out to be weaker than they. Achebe indicates at one point the essential trait in Obi's character —

> He was not in the mood for consecutive reasoning. His mind was impatient to roam in a more pleasant atmosphere.

Obi is never really prepared to engage in any sort of sustained effort, with the result that he flounders through his life. Such is his mental make-up that minor problems, instead of strengthening him, carry him irresistibly to a point of dissolution.

The crisis is afforded by his disagreement with his family over his choice of Clara, an *Osu*, for a wife. Against an irrational caste system that demands of him a firm rational stand, against the pressure of a moral problem that calls for individual resolution, Obi has nothing to offer but abdication. The conflict that opposes him to his father provokes from him anger and resentment, and the unsoundness of his position does not escape him. In one of his rare moments of introspection, he manages to grasp the nature of his problem:

> His mind was troubled not only by what had happened, but by the discovery that there was nothing in him with which to challenge it honestly.

His submission on the issue of Clara, and his subsequent betrayal of her (and the cause involved in her problem) opens the wide road to his moral decline. He knows what is right, but is unable to stand up for it.

Obi's fall, then, is the result of a practical dissociation between the intellectual and the moral poles of his awareness.

The events and outside factors in his situation furnish the framework in which the conflict between the two evolves, and it is the nature of the effect of these two factors upon his individual consciousness which constitutes his tragedy. Achebe makes it clear that Obi is a man torn between two sets of values. The result is his spiritual disintegration. *No Longer at Ease* is in this sense a comment on the modern situation in Nigeria (and even in Africa): on the plight of the Westernised élite as well as on the human problems posed by the fast tempo of social change which causes a parallel instability in the spiritual framework—a picture of 'a world turned upside down'.

Yet, though the theme is potentially a tragic one, it is not given an

183

adequately tragic treatment. The main shortcoming of the novel is the in-adequate stature of the hero. Obi as he is portrayed is simply not the stuff of which a tragic character is made. He is a pathetic figure without any grain of nobility. Unlike his grandfather, he is a passive sufferer of his fate and the emotion that he inspires is not pity but antipathy.

Another reason for the failure of the novel to achieve a tragic height is Achebe's treatment of the situation. It is by all accounts too sketchy—the economy of style in the previous novel tends towards a perfunctoriness in this one. Besides, the events are not related significantly enough to each other to show their compulsion on the individual that tragedy demands. For example, Obi's bribe-taking, though foreshadowed in his psycholog-ical development, is not altogether convincing.

The other characters contribute to the weakening of the tragic effect of the novel. They are presented as individuals who are flung around and tossed about on a choppy surface, but not pulled into the vortex of a whirl-pool. Their dilemma is of a comic as well as of tragic kind: they are involved in a situation that provokes absurd behaviour, not a futile reaction against an absurd fate. It is Obi himself who sums up the situation:

> If one didn't laugh, one would have to cry. It seemed that was the way Nigeria was built.

In other words, the colonial situation is essentially a tragicomic one. Mongo Beti's understanding of this accounts for the success of his novels, particularly *Mission to Kala*. Whereas Beti paints a vast fresco of absurdity, letting the tragedy reveal itself in the degradation of human behaviour, Achebe presents degraded human behaviour in a tragic cast, but what we get rather is a picture of human misery.

For all that, *No Longer at Ease* remains an excellent novel, written with the same technical mastery as the previous novel, fashioned out of the same art that finds a triumphant vindication in *Arrow of God*.

The theme of his third novel takes up where *Things Fall Apart* leaves off. It is indeed appropriate that this should be so, for this novel is a devel-opment not only from the point of view of the human interest but also of the style. Achebe has elaborated on the previous theme in such a way as to give it a more sustained character. Consequently in this novel we have a more profound and significant treatment of character and situations than in the two previous novels.

Achebe has woven the two movements of the individual and social drama into such unity that it would be artificial to separate them: the lives of individuals meet with a combination of events to force a tragic issue. Yet the tensions at the heart of this pattern are clearly schematised. On the one hand, the internal division in the village of Umuaro is polarised around the person of Ezeulu, the chief priest of Ulu, and that of his ambitious rival, Nwaka; and on the other hand, the conflict of cultures represented by the misunderstanding that opposes Ezeulu to the colonial administration in the person of Captain Winterbottom.

184

Ezeulu, the principal character, is a memorable creation—he is a truly impressive figure, cast in a mould that is at once forceful and noble. Unlike Okonkwo, whose exterior demonstration of strength is a compensation for an internal weakness, Ezeulu's external stature reposes upon the firm foundations of a stable coherent mental structure. The strength of his moral frame is early demonstrated in his forthright stand against the 'war of blame' that his villagers plan against their neighbours.

He is also a man of superior intelligence, whose understanding of things surpasses that of his followers. He alone in Umuaro understands the nature of the dilemma posed by the presence of the white man in their midst, ushering in an age of new adjustments—

> 'The world is like a mask dancing. If you want to see it well, you do not stand in the same place.'

He towers above the other characters with such an eminent force of personality that he is set apart in a noble solitude, which circumstances and an understandably arrogant contempt of lesser men first impose upon, then emphasise.

The only other figure that is on anything like the same scale is Winterbottom. He is more of a conventional figure, though his force of character rescues him from being a caricature. But his dominant quality is not strength but nervous energy, something not innate but acquired out of stubborn application. Around these two figures are paired off two other characters who play an important part in Ezeulu's fate—Nwaka, his jealous rival, whose moral obtuseness is a foil to the bold outlines of Ezeulu, and the diffident, sensitive Clarke, Winterbottom's subaltern, whose psychological development is of great significance in the context of the novel.

The characters themselves are symbolic vehicles of the tragic movement. The uneasy rivalry between Ezeulu and Nwaka runs like a brooding dissonance through the even flow of Umuaro's history, brilliantly reconstructed —the marriages, the births, the deaths, and the other petty vicissitudes of a regular train of life. Achebe presents the picture of a total universe over which the gods Ulu and Idemili are pitched in a deadly conflict against each other through their protagonists:

> He [i.e. Ezeulu] knew that the priests of Idemili and Ogwugwu and Eru and Odo had never been happy with their secondary rôles since the villages got together and made Ulu and put him over the older deities. But he would not have thought that one of them would go so far as to set someone to challenge Ulu.

And when later he decides to carry the struggle against his rivals to avenge humiliation at the hands of the white man, it is possible for him to see the struggle as something larger than a personal issue: 'It was a fight of the gods. He was no more than an arrow in the bow of his god.'

But the Christians are at hand, whose God is also making a bid for the loyalties of the people of Umuaro. The moral of the situation is brought home with the attempt of Oduche, Ezeulu's Christianised son, to kill the sacred python. In the same way as the python is imprisoned, struggling for life, so are the gods of the land in reality circumscribed by a new order.

Achebe's symbolism is skilfully sustained throughout, from the overt dramatisation of the internal conflict to the children's innocent commentary on the situation, until the final moment in Ezeulu's divination hut:

> As Ezeulu cast his strings of cowries, the bell of Oduche's people began to ring. For one brief moment Ezeulu was distracted by its sad measured monotone, and he thought how strange it was that it should sound so near—much nearer than it did in his compound.

The new order is represented by the white man, who has brought his administration, his civilisation and his God—'The white man, the new religion, the soldiers, the new road, they are all one and the same thing,' observes one of the men. On the purely secular level, the novel represents a critique of colonisation: the overbearing attitude of Wright, the road manager, is a relevant example of its early approach. But more important than this is the emotional tangle created by the meeting of two different sets of values, the friction between two ways of thought. The incident in which Obika, another son of Ezeulu, is whipped by Wright affords an occasion for drawing out the elements of the situation—the hostile, humiliated incomprehension of the Africans, the haughty insensitiveness of the Europeans.

It is precisely because of his ranting prejudices that Winterbottom is unable to see Ezeulu as a person rather than as a 'fetish priest' who happens to be exceptional, and thus a convenient tool in the hands of the administration. His impersonal attitude to Ezeulu is contrasted to the warm confidence of the latter—'The white man and we are friends'. One source of Ezeulu's tragedy is that this is an illusion.

It is moreover a situation which has its own logic that makes no room for individual options. For it is a deliberate irony of fate that leaves Clarke, whose personal disposition is against the falsity of things, to deal with Ezeulu in Winterbottom's absence and to propose the offer of a chieftaincy warrant to the priest.

> 'Tell the white man that Ezeulu will not be anybody's chief, except Ulu's.'
> 'What!' shouted Clarke, 'Is the fellow mad?'
> 'I tink so, Sali,' said the interpreter.
> 'In that case, he goes back to prison.' Clarke was really angry. What cheek! A witch-doctor making a fool of the British Administration in public!

It is, properly speaking, an ambivalent position in which the people of Umuaro find themselves. Loyalties are shifted back and forth, compromises are made and unmade. The story of Nwodika and the behaviour of the messengers sent to arrest Ezeulu reveal the ludicrous aspect of their dilemma. More serious is the milling about of men trapped in an intolerable situation that turns them in upon themselves in violent reaction: 'It was so much easier to deal with an old quarrel than with a new unprecedented incident.' As a result of their frustration, they are left confounded in their social and spiritual awareness. Achebe has painted with remarkable insight the picture of a traumatic situation: 'We must grope about until what must happen does happen,' says one of the characters in a particular context, unconsciously summing up their total position.

And the pity of it all is that the conflict should be resolved in such tragic circumstances by Ezeulu, the only man who has tried to deal with it in an honest and intelligent way. It is a poignant moment when he realises that his foresight in sending Oduche to school—'to be my eyes and my ears' among the Christians—has resulted in his loss of the boy's loyalty. And yet this is only a minor aspect of his tragedy.

For when he turns his resentment for his humiliation at the hand of the white man against his own people, he commits a serious error of judgement. For once, he lets his personal feelings interfere with his usual lucidity. And yet, one cannot help feeling that he is right in considering himself 'the arrow of his god'. For indeed, Ezeulu has been all along an instrument of fate—the blind accessory of a monumental process that culminates not only in his own undoing, but in the fall of the gods of the land. Again, Achebe patently introduces the theme of the liberation of souls from the grip of the old order. The triumph of the Christian God is prepared and brought about by the internal weakness of the old order. In a sense, therefore, the victory of the white man is a passive one:

> It looked as though the gods and the power of events finding Winterbottom handy had used him and left him again in order as they found him.

Meanwhile, they have destroyed Ezeulu and forever deviated the course of Umuaro's history.

Achebe's three novels[1] form one continuous stream—they amount in fact to a trilogy. They are also unified by a common purpose revealed in the very nature of his narrative method.

The distinctive quality of his style is *sobriety*—not the simplicity of limited talent, but the disciplined economy of an assured artist. Within the framework of a conventional medium, Achebe creates the complexity of human situations with the slightest of means. His prose is rigorously utilitarian, and what appears as as elaborate evocation of social customs ('exoticism' to some, 'padding' to others) simply serves as a *realistic* support for the human drama, relevant to the cultural context of his novels. He is concerned primarily with individuals. His narrative method is detached, almost impassive, made of objective formulations through which the human drama is unfolded. Yet it is not impersonal, for instead of the

[1] Since this essay was written, the following novel has been published: Achebe: *A Man of the People*, Heinemann, 1966.

flamboyant colours of a heated imagination, we have rather the clear lines that compose a picture by a dispassionate observer of human destiny, who constructs a vision out of his awareness of an inexorable order.

Achebe has justly been called a chronicler, for in the last resort he is not dealing simply with the collapse of African society, but with its transformation. He is examining from the inside the historical evolution of African society at its moments of crisis, and the inevitable tensions attendant upon this process. In the final analysis, his novels reveal the intimate circumstances of the African Becoming.

Amos Tutuola

A Nigerian Visionary

GERALD MOORE

The young Yoruba writer Amos Tutuola has published three books in England[1] and has made a considerable reputation for himself throughout Europe and America. Enough material exists for some attempt at a careful and serious assessment of his work; even those who have always been inclined to dismiss him as a 'freak' will at least admit that he is now too sizeable a freak to be ignored.

The most remarkable feature uniting all three of Tutuola's books is his apparently intuitive grasp of basic literary forms. All his heroes or heroines follow out one variant or another of the cycle of the heroic monomyth, Departure — Initiation — Return.[2] In his first book, *The Palm-Wine Drinkard*, the variant form is that of the deliberate, limited quest. The whole book may best be seen as the story of the Drinkard's quest for his dead palm-wine tapster and the trials, labours and revelations he experiences in the course of it. It is thus of the utmost significance that the first of all the trials imposed upon him in his journey is the binding and bringing of Death. The naïvety and directness with which this tale is told (Death, for example, is discovered digging in his yam-garden) should not obscure its importance. It stands as a clear enough indication that the Drinkard's adventure is not merely a journey into eternal African bush, but equally a journey into the racial imagination, into the sub-conscious, into the Spirit World that everywhere co-exists and even overlaps with the world of waking 'reality'. Or, to express it mythically, he is descending, like Gilgamesh, Orpheus, Heracles or Aeneas before him, into the Underworld, there to confront death itself and attempt to carry off some trophy to the living as a symbol of his mastery over the two worlds.

Once the Drinkard is embarked on his adventure, the familiar figures of heroic myth make their appearance one by one. There are the task-masters who impose certain labours upon him as the price for giving information about the dead tapster's whereabouts; there is the ever-faithful and helpful female companion (Dante's Beatrice, Theseus's Ariadne, Jason's Medea) in the shape of the Drinkard's wife, whom he rescues from the terrible 'complete gentleman' and marries as the reward of his exploit; there

[1] *The Palm Wine Drinkard*, London, Faber, 1952.
My Life in the Bush of Ghosts, 1954.
Simbi and the Satyr of the Dark Jungle, 1955.
Since this essay was written the following have been published:
The Brave African Huntress, 1958.
Feather Woman of the Jungle, 1962.
[2] For a study of the monomyth see Joseph Campbell: *The Hero With A Thousand Faces*. Bolingen Series XVII, New York, Pantheon Books, 1949.

is the devouring monster (the Red Fish) who must be slain in order to lift the curse from a whole community and free them from the burden of annual human sacrifice. If the Drinkard encounters fewer magic helpers than his European counterpart would probably need, that is because his own 'ju-ju' powers are constantly accumulating; for this book reflects the widespread African belief that whenever a magician is overthrown his powers are immediately transferred to the conqueror. Some of the most interesting episodes, from the point of view of comparative mythology, are the birth of the half-bodied baby from the swollen left thumb of the Drinkard's wife, the meeting with Faithful-Mother in the White Tree and the Hungry Creature which swallows both the Drinkard and his wife during their homeward journey. The half-bodied baby is a very close parallel to the Tom Thumb of European folklore (the same figure is known in Yoruba as *mogbon juba* or Child-Wiser-Than-His-Father). The idyllic stay with Faithful-Mother seems a clear enough example of what Campbell calls the 'Meeting with the Mother Goddess',[1] while the White Tree may be identified as the usual tree symbol for the World Navel (Ygddrasil, the Bo Tree, the golden apple-tree in the Garden of the Hesperides, the Tree of Knowledge in the Garden of Eden). The sojourn in the belly of the Hungry Creature is certainly the familiar *motif* of the Whale's Belly from which the hero must emerge reborn, and the manner of the Drinkard's escape is also familiar: he first shoots the Creature dead from inside with a musket and then hacks his way out with a cutlass.

When at last the Drinkard reaches the Deads' Town—the lowest level of Hades—he does not, like Orpheus, enjoy even the chance of getting back to the waking world with his tapster. The tapster sadly explains to him that the dead cannot return with the living, neither can the living dwell with the dead; this is the Drinkard's real Initiation, for thereby he learns the true meaning of life and death. There is an interesting parallel in the ancient Japanese myth of Izanagi and Izanami, told in the 'Records of Ancient Matters', though there the unreturning one pursues her would-be rescuer with destructive fury till he is safely back in the land of the living. Nevertheless, the Drinkard does not return empty-handed from his quest. He wins a boon, though not the one he set out to get, for the tapster gives him a magic egg which will perform anything he asks of it (it may not be too fanciful to see in these magic eggs of folklore a regenerated version of the Cosmic Egg from which, according to many mythologies, the whole world was created). So the Drinkard, now a changed man whose past life is dead, for he has undergone his 'rite of passage' or education of the soul, sets out on the direct path to his home town. Here Tutuola gives us one of his most appalling visions, for this direct path is filled by an unending stream of deads; but the characteristic twist he gives to this Dante-like prospect is that the most terrible of all the deads are the babies, who ferociously assault everyone in their path. As the Drinkard and his wife near their home they fall in with the Mountain Creatures, who become annoyed and pursue

[1] *op. cit.*, II, 2.

them. There follows a typical example of the Transformation Flight, in the course of which the Drinkard turns himself into a pebble and succeeds in hurling himself across the river which separates them from his town. This river is, of course, the Return Threshold, and in accordance with all the rules of mythology the hero's pursuers can never cross it. It is also in accordance with the rules that the boon-bearing hero shall find his community in a state of anarchy and distress, for otherwise his whole adventure might appear wasted. The Drinkard finds his town suffering from a terrible famine and for a while he is able to relieve it by use of his egg. But soon human greed and folly defeat him and in a fit of anger he turns the power of his egg against the people. Meanwhile the real cause of the famine remains untouched, for Earth and Heaven, once fast friends, are quarrelling over the seniority, and Heaven is demonstrating his greater power by withholding all rain and dew from the Earth. The Drinkard advises that the famine can be ended only by sending a slave to Heaven with a present acknowledging his seniority. In other words, from henceforth the supreme deity will be the male Sky God and not the old female Earth Goddess, protectress of matriarchy. Thus the famine is ended. One of the most powerful moments in the book is the return of the ghost of the sacrificed slave:

> But when the slave carried the sacrifice to Heaven and gave it to Heaven he could not reach halfway back to the earth before a heavy rain came and when the slave was beaten by this heavy rain and when he reached the town, he wanted to escape from the rain, but nobody would allow him to enter his or her house at all. All the people were thinking that he would carry them also to Heaven as he had carried the sacrifice to Heaven, and were afraid.
> But when for three months the rain had been falling regularly, there was no famine again.

In this way the resolution of the Drinkard's individual development as hero is linked with the restoration of harmony between man and his gods, for it is the Drinkard's new understanding, won by the hard way of adventure, which enables him to settle the cosmic quarrel through which man is suffering.

Tutuola has managed to impose an extraordinary unity upon his apparently random collection of traditional material. The unity is that of intense vision, for Tutuola is a visionary writer and must be seen as such if he is to be understoood or effectively judged. A good deal of the criticism of his books has apparently taken it for granted that they are novels, which argues an astounding lack of literary education in the critics concerned. Tutuola's affinities are with Bunyan, Dante and Blake rather than with the Western novel, for the novel as we know it deals with man in society, while Tutuola is concerned with man alone, suffering and growing amid the images thrown forth by his own mind and by the imagination of his race. He is something much rarer and more interesting than another novelist.

There is an interesting confirmation of the visionary character of his work in Dr. Parrinder's Foreword to *My Life in the Bush of Ghosts*. Dr.

Parrinder recounts how he once asked Tutuola why he had described the various towns in the Bush of Ghosts in that particular order. Tutuola simply replied, 'Because that is the order in which I came to them.' He has *lived* through his material before ever he sets it down; the many fragments of folklore, ritual and belief embedded in it are not just things remembered (whether from individual or racial knowledge), but things already experienced; they have all passed through the transmuting fire of an individual imagination and been shaped for its ends.

The comparison with Bunyan is a fruitful one, for both writers are men of little formal education who seize upon the images of the popular imagination.

Take this passage from *Pilgrim's Progress*:

> hideous to behold, he was clothed with scales like a Fish (and they are his pride), he had Wings like a Dragon, and out of his belly came Fire and Smoke, and his mouth was as the mouth of a Lion . . .

This rises into literature from the same great sources as Tutuola's Red Fish in the *Palm Wine Drinkard*, whose

> head was like a tortoise's head, but it was as big as a elephant's head and it had over 30 horns and large eyes which surrounded the head. All these horns were spread out as an umbrella. It could not walk but was only gliding on the ground like a snake and its body was just like a bat's body and covered with long red hair like strings. . . . All the eyes which surrounded its head were closing and opening at the same time as if a man was pressing a switch on and off.

This description of the eyes is a brilliant instance of Tutuola's easy use of the paraphernalia of modern life to give sharpness and immediacy to his imagery. The comparisons with the branching stems of an umbrella frame and with hanging pieces of string are equally effective, if less striking than the switch. Perhaps the finest example of all is the Drinkard's description of the 'complete gentleman', whose beauty was such that even bombers would respect it:

> I could not blame the lady for following the Skull as a complete gentleman to his house at all. Because if I were a lady, no doubt I would follow him to wherever he would go, and still as I was a man I would jealous him more than that, because if this gentleman went to the battlefield, surely, enemy would not kill him or capture him and if bombers saw him in a town which was to be bombed, they would not throw bombs on his presence, and if they did throw it, the bomb itself would not explode until this gentleman would leave that town, because of his beauty. At the same time that I saw this gentleman in the market on that day what I was doing was only to follow him about in the market. After I looked at him for so many hours, then I ran to a corner of the market and I cried for a few minutes because I thought within

myself why was I not created with beauty as this gentleman, but when I remembered that he was only a Skull, then I thanked God that he had created me without beauty ...

If we examine the formal structure of Tutuola's second book, *My Life in the Bush of Ghosts*, we shall find that here there is no deliberate quest or definite objective. The Initiation is not sought but is imposed upon the boy-hero as the process of his development into manhood. The whole book may thus be seen as a kind of extended Initiation or 'rite of passage'. At the beginning of the story the narrator is a boy of eight and is in a state of innocence. He is just starting to know the meaning of 'bad', for he is the victim of the jealousies among his father's wives, but he does not yet know the meaning of 'good'. Fleeing from his deserted town before a slave-raiding army, he becomes separated from his brother and accidentally rushes into the terrible Bush of Ghosts, which he enters through a hole in a large mound, in a manner somewhat reminiscent of Alice falling into Wonderland. Like Alice again, he immediately undergoes a series of transformations, though his are certainly the more radical; at various times he becomes a cow, a *ju-ju* stuck in the neck of an immense pot, a horse and a monkey. As he travels or is carried from town to town, deep in the Bush of Ghosts, the boy suffers a breathless variety of experiences, mostly horrible or fearful in character. His status is usually that of a slave or, at best, a resented intruder, though he has rare intervals of peace and gradually becomes more and more contented with his extraordinary life. At one time he is even happily married to a ghostess for a few months and later he lives for four years with a beautiful Super Lady, who bears him a son, half-ghost, half-mortal, over whose upbringing they finally quarrel.

To the uninitiated European reader the word 'ghost' is likely to be rather misleading, for the ghosts of this book are not the individual spirits of those who once lived on earth; they are the permanent inhabitants of the Other World, who have never lived as mortals, but who have intimate knowledge of that life and are in constant intercourse with it. At the same time, it appears that earthly witches and wizards hold their meetings among these ghosts and that it is from there that 'spirit-children' are sent to dwell among men and act as agents for the ghost world. None of this is worked out with theological exactitude, for Tutuola assumes this kind of knowledge, but so much at least is clear.

After twenty-five years in the Bush of Ghosts the hero has become so accustomed to life there that he no longer has any wish to escape, but when at last the chance is presented to him by the Television-Handed Ghostess he decides to take it. After still further misfortunes at the hands of his long-lost, unrecognised brother, he returns to normal life with his family. Like Adam, he has lost his innocence and has fallen into a full knowledge of good and evil: he is ready to begin adult life. The closing words of the book, 'This is what hatred did', pick up again the hints of the opening pages and confirm its nature as an extended division of Initiation or Purgatory—though we must understand that this is a purgatory undergone by the living and not by the dead; a preparation for life and not a payment for its past mistakes.

Tutuola's third book, *Simbi and the Satyr of the Dark Jungle*, was published in 1955. Here the heroic figure is that of a young girl, born with conspicuous advantages of every kind, who comes to feel that these must ultimately be paid for in comparable abasement and suffering. This is a theme as universal in literature and myth as that of the deliberate quest, to whose grand object such abasement and suffering may appear as incidental and subordinate; but in reality they are two different ways of expressing the same life-renewing, regenerating experience. The belief that expense must somehow be balanced by equivalent earning of sacrifice, by a 'storing-up', is perhaps the mythic version of the Law of the Conservation of Energy, intuitively apprehended. But in myth it is seen that *man himself*, by heroic action or sacrifice, must renew the energy of his world and keep it in equipoise. This, the theme of *Simbi*, is seen particularly clearly in the great English medieval poems *Sir Gawayne and the Grene Knight* and *Wynnere and Wascoure*. For an individualist society it has lost its meaning.

Simbi, we are told, was the only daughter of the wealthiest woman in her village:

> She was not working at all, except to eat and after that to bathe and then to wear several kinds of the costliest garments. Although she was a wonderful singer whose beautiful voice could wake deads and she was only the most beautiful girl in the village.

One day her two friends Rali and Sala are kidnapped and soon after this, Simbi begins to yearn to experience the 'Poverty' and the 'Punishment' because she had known 'neither the poverty nor the difficulties of the punishment since she was born'. Ignoring the warnings of her mother and others, she consults the Ifa priest (the professional diviner of Yoruba society) and he advises her to make a certain sacrifice at that familiar starting point of mythical adventure, 'the place where three paths meet'. While she is sacrificing, the terrible Dogo comes from behind her and carries her away on the Path of Death. Then she begins to experience the poverty and the punishment with a vengeance, and immediately regrets her obscure impulse, but once embarked on the adventure she must suffer it to the finish. Dogo sells her as a slave in a far town and there she meets again with Rali and Sala and several other girls of the village, 'nameless refugees', who have been kidnapped before her. But Simbi is the only one who has voluntarily brought her sufferings on herself, and the others make her feel it. The little group wanders on from place to place and is several times threatened with human sacrifice and other dangers, but each time they are saved at the last moment by the heroic efforts of Simbi. Sometimes with her companions, more often alone, Simbi struggles on through her self-imposed agonies. When at last she wins home to her village again, only Rali is left alive to accompany her.

The central experience of the adventure is Simbi's sojourn in the Dark

194

Jungle, the empire of the Satyr. Here ends the Path of Death, and the only way of escape from the Jungle is to return by it. Simbi wanders here for a long time and has many bruising encounters with her terrible enemy the Satyr before she finally conquers and kills him by flying up his nostril in the form of a water-fly (*Iromi*) and biting him to death. The Satyr of the Dark Jungle is Tutuola's greatest creation, at once comic and terrible. Here he is talking to himself after his first humiliating brush with the resourceful Simbi:

> 'I believe, the two ladies shall come back to this jungle and I shall kill both of them at all costs at any day I meet them. It is certain, they are my meat! . . . By the way, what is the meaning of "Iro . . ."? of course, I know the meaning of "Iromi" that is an insect of water, but what of "Iro . . ." into which that lady [Simbi] said she could change? Anyhow, we shall meet again and then continue our fight.'

The use of the word 'lady' in such a context heightens the comedy of the scene. Gentility is a disease in modern Nigeria; no one is ever described as a 'woman', even by a Satyr.

The Satyr's greatest stratagem is when, knowing Simbi's love of singing, he creates a vast hall in the jungle made entirely of singing birds, so that it is literally built of pure music. Yet even this delightful trap, though Simbi falls into it all right and it rather endears the Satyr to the reader, fails to give him control of her for long. The Satyr carries her to a high rock and, after embedding her in it by turning her partially into stone, proceeds to beat her. But Simbi escapes by the aid of a magic helper and turns herself into a water-fly. Unrecognised by the Satyr, who knows that she can become 'Iro . . .', but not 'Iromi', she flies up his nose and kills him in the manner already described.

In *Simbi*, Tutuola has tightened his grasp of narrative, heightened his dramatic sense, and displayed a new speed in the handling of the big scenes. There is far more dialogue than in the earlier books, and the frequent adverbial 'stage directions' add greatly to the dramatic interest and humour of the conversation.

> 'Of course, my wish before I left our village was to seek for the "Poverty" and the "Punishment" but I have regretted it since when Dogo kidnapped me and sold me,' Simbi explained coldly. 'But before you will regret your wish will be when you return to our village,' Bako replied and then she asked sharply from the rest 'or is it not so?' 'Yes, it is so!' the rest confirmed loudly.

The occasional *longueurs* of Tutuola's earlier books arose from the whole-sale application of an oral narrative technique to written narrative. Writing of *The Palm-Wine Drinkard*, Mr. V. S. Pritchett said, 'Mr. Tutuola's first paragraph knocks one flat.' This is how Tutuola opened his first story:

> I was a palm-wine drinkard since I was a boy of ten years of age. I had no other work more than to drink palm-wine in my life. In

195

those days we did not know other money, except cowries, so that everything was very cheap, and my father was the richest man in our town.

The impact of this is that of a warm African voice beginning a tale. Tutuola wrote exactly as if he were entertaining a group of friends with his fantasies on a moonlit night. This purely oral narrative method has many advantages but some pitfalls too. The 'live' narrator who has his audience actually round him can afford (if he is a good storyteller) any amount of long-winded digression and embellishment—indeed, that is part of his art. The writer who bases his work on the same method must be much more ruthless with himself, and there were places in Tutuola's first two books where even the appreciative reader might begin to nod a little. It is all very well to knock the reader flat with one's first paragraph, but it is important that none of the later ones should render him comatose. Tutuola has now shown in *Simbi* that he can prune his exuberance fairly drastically without sacrificing any of the warmth and richness of his speaking human voice. When the *Drinkard* first appeared many were inclined to salute it as a once-for-all miracle and to raise a doubt whether even Tutuola could do it again. But in *Simbi* he has not only done it again: he has gone on to show that he can sharpen and refine the expression of his unique prolific genius.

There remains the important question of Tutuola's reputation in Africa itself. No amount of international acclaim, gratifying though it be, can count for as much in the development of such a writer as the enthusiasm and support of his own people. The progress of his reputation in Africa has been gravely hampered by the manner in which his books have appeared. The imprint of a leading English publisher, though an assistance in the London market, may even be a hindrance in the local one. His books are expensive by Nigerian standards; 10/6 or 12/6 are prices that young Nigerians may be accustomed to pay for a textbook that will help them directly in examinations, but not for 'a mere storybook'. Moreover, his publishers are a firm generally associated with the 'high-brow', in literature and the dust-jackets of these books, excellent in themselves, reflect this. For these reasons the number of Nigerians who have discovered Tutuola from the bookshelves unaided must be fairly small.[1] Last year I had the experience of lecturing to a large audience of adult students and finding that few of them had even heard Tutuola's name and not one had read any of his books. On the other hand, these same students reacted with delighted wonder and amusement to the reading of extracts from the *Drinkard* and at the end of the lecture were clamouring for copies to buy. Many educated Nigerians, however, are embarrassed by the 'mistakes' they find in Tutuola's English, which some of them seem to regard as an undeserved reflection on the African race in general. Their ears, being less sensitive than those of an Englishman to all that has become jaded and feeble in our language, are likewise less able to recognise the vigour and freshness that Tutuola brings

---

[1] Since this essay was first published *The Palm Wine Drinkard* and *My Life in the Bush of Ghosts* have been published in paperback editions.

to it by his urgency of expression and refusal to be merely correct. A similar stage to this had been gone through even by the American reading public, though to them English was their native language, and the racy American vernacular, as opposed to 'polite' English, did not become respectable till the enormous popularity of Mark Twain had made it so. In view of all these factors, a great service would be done by any publisher imaginative enough to produce cheap paperbacked editions of Tutuola's books and distribute these widely to the little bookshops in West Africa.

Tutuola's value to the rising generation of young African writers is probably that of an example rather than of a model. There are not likely to be two Tutuolas in Africa today, and to write in his manner without comparable visionary power and imaginative intensity would not only be foolish but, for a more fully educated writer, affected as well. The most valuable part of Tutuola's example is his confidence. This confidence transforms even his apparent disadvantages into special virtues, for his fragmentary education is seen to have left him in tune with the great imaginative life of his race, whilst his command of West African idiom enables him to create a style at once easy and energetic, naïve and daring. By going into himself Tutuola has rediscovered the great common soil of literature, which mere imitation of its currently branching peculiarities and variations in England or America could never have shown him. Imitativeness is the besetting temptation of Nigerian writers at present; but Tutuola has set all chance models aside and, refreshed like Antaeus by contact with his abiding Mother Earth, has forged matter, form and style again for himself.

D. O. Fagunwa

A Yoruba Novelist

Ulli Beier

When Chief Fagunwa died suddenly and tragically in an accident in December 1963, few non-Yoruba speakers may have realised that with him Nigeria lost its most popular writer. Because of the language he chose to write in, Fagunwa has had little or no international publicity. None of his works is available in translation so far, and outside Nigeria he is hardly known by name. Yet, of all Nigerian writers, Fagunwa was—and still is—the most widely read. One of his books, *Igbo Olodumare*,[1] has had sixteen reprints since 1949. The total edition of his five novels goes into hundreds of thousands rather than into thousands![2]

This unparalleled success may be partly due to the fact that Fagunwa was early in the field, and that his novels were the first story-books that could be used widely in schools.

There is no doubt that Fagunwa was aiming at a school market: the stories he tells have the atmosphere of fairy tales and every event he relates points to a distinct moral, which makes it acceptable in the most Christian of schools. And yet there is more to it than that, for Fagunwa is read by adults, and he is quoted in conversation and he is read by children to their illiterate grandparents: his appeal is universal in Yoruba country.

The least interesting aspect of Fagunwa's writing is probably his plot. *Igbo Olodumure* has a story that goes roughly like this:

The author suddenly comes across his old friend Akara-Ogun, whom he has not seen for a long time. Akara-Ogun says he has an important story to tell: namely the exploits of his late father, Olowo-Aiye, in the 'Forest of the Almighty'. He asks the author to take pen and paper and record the story.

He then proceeds to tell the story of how Olowo-Aiye sets out to the famous Forest of the Almighty in spite of the warnings of his friends. Even before he reaches that forest, a small and evil spirit called Eshu-Kekere-Ode is trying to stop him, but the spirit is overcome in a fierce fight. As he proceeds, Olowo-Aiye suddenly encounters two beautiful women walking nonchalantly about in the forest. The younger one, Ajediran, makes advances to him. Although it is clear that the women are witches, Olowo-Aiye falls in love with her and decides to marry her. Olowo-Aiye goes in search of further adventures equipped with a powerful medicine from his wife, which enables him to change himself into any kind of animal.

[1] Edinburgh, Nelson, 1947.
[2] *Trèké Oníbùdó*, Nelson, 1949; [14] 1956.
  Ogboju ọdẹ ninu igbo irunmalẹ, Nelson, 1950; [11] 1958.
  Irinkerindo ninu igbo Elégbèje, Nelson, 1954; [13] 1961.
  Àdìitu Olódùmarè, Nelson, 1961; [2] 1962.

198

When Olowo-Aiye reaches the gate-keeper of the Forest of the Almighty he is asked to swear on a large book, which contains all the sins in the world. Olowo-Aiye refuses to swear and a terrible fight follows, in which both partners transform each other into different animals. Finally Olowo-Aiye in the form of an elephant kills the gate-keeper, who is transformed into a snake. Olowo-Aiye is greatly thanked by the king of the forest for killing the wicked gate-keeper. He is feasted for three months, and the king of the Forest of the Almighty finally weds him to Ajediran.

The happy couple are about to leave the forest, but Olowo-Aiye one day goes elephant hunting and he misses his way. He misses his way for three years, and never knows that in the meantime his son Akara-Ogun is born. After frightening adventures Olowo-Aiye is consoled by his dead mother, who comes to meet him and finally he runs into Baba-Onirugbon-Yewuke, a wise old man with a very long beard. From the old man he learns much wisdom and many stories and parables. He is even taken to the fearful house of Death, who is Baba-Onirugbon-Yewuke's neighbour. When a new elephant hunter arrives at the place, the famous Ijamba Foriti, they decide to find their way out of the forest. But before they reach their homes they still have to brave Ojola-Ibinu, the king of the snakes. They are taken prisoners in the kingdom of the snakes, and only when they succeed in killing Ojola-Ibinu do they manage to escape.

Fangunwa's plot is a rambling, somewhat disorganised fairy tale. It is a succession of adventures, loosely strung together. There are elements of traditional Yoruba stories in his books, but Fagunwa does not draw as heavily on Yoruba folklore as Tutuola. Most of the stories are invented, many of them are also taken from European tradition. The true Yoruba flavour of Fagunwa's work lies not in the material he used, but in the language, in the manner and tone of his story-telling. These are the elements to which the average Yoruba reader responds with delight: for Fagunwa has the humour, the rhetoric, the word play, the bizarre imagery that Yorubas like and appreciate in their language. He impresses the reader with his knowledge of classical Yoruba ('deep Yoruba' as the phrase goes) and he is as knowledgeable in proverbial expressions as an old oracle priest. Yet he is not content with that: he uses the language creatively and inventively, constantly adding to the traditional stock of imagery and enriching the language.

Fagunwa's language is extremely visual: of a man in love he says 'love spread across his face like palm wine overflowing a calabash'; a sad man 'hangs his face like a banana leaf'; a quarrel 'sticks in the throat like a fish bone'; a liar is a man 'who has blood in his belly but spits white saliva'; when a man is afraid 'his bottom changes to water'. Fagunwa's language is enlivened by a frequent and often startling use of personification: instead of saying the hunter fired a shot he has 'the hunter called the gun—the gun answered'. When the lion queries the other animals and they dare not reply, Fagunwa says 'the question killed the reply and ate it'. His language is studded with proverbs, both traditional and invented ones. They give a fatherly, benign moral tone to the whole book and may add to the popularity of these novels among schoolmasters. They also add colour and flavour to the language:

> 'Every day is for the thieves—but one day is for the owner of property.'
> 'A matter which is as soft as a red banana does not require an answer as hard as a stone.'
> 'When the pepper and the onion meet on the bush fowl, everything will become possible.'

Fagunwa's moralising is often too deliberate and it would be difficult for the adult reader to take if it was not done with so much charm. No event takes place, no situation is described from which we are not supposed to learn something. A nauseating idea. Yet, who could object to being 'improved' in such a charming manner.

> Never aim at little things; aim at big things. Even if you do not achieve great things, it is sure that you will achieve something nearly great. Those who aim at small things will never be able to mix with great people. The man who prays for ten embroidered gowns—even if he doesn't get ten, he will surely get eight. The man who prays for six pairs of trousers—even if he does not get six, he may have five. But the one who asked God for only one pair of trousers—must he not be thankful even for two?

Fagunwa is fond of rhetoric. He likes words. He likes to pile them up, say the same thing over and over again in infinite variation. He is a master of rhetoric, who can make repetitions and variations swing in a mounting rhythm, like Yoruba drumming.

When Olowo-Aiye meets the spirit Eshu Kekere Ode in the bush, he is queried thus:

> 'Who are you? What are you? What are you worth? What are you up to? What will you become? What are you seeking? What do you want? What are you looking at? What are you seeing? What are you thinking? What is wrong with you? Where are you coming from? Where are you going? Where are you living? Where are you walking? Answer me, child of man, answer me in one word.'

Another typical passage is the one in which Fagunwa describes the diseases which Olowo-Aiye's father, who was a great doctor, could heal:

> 'And the epileptics were cured by my father, and those who suffered from guinea worm were cured likewise, and thousands of lepers became healthy people in our house. And my father punished small pox, and attacked malnutrition; he spoiled the reputation of rheumatism, and turned stomach pain into a pauper; and headache became a helpless child, and backache was speechless; cough went into hiding and pneumonia fled; the tiny itching worms kept dead silent and fever was lost in thought; dysentery bent its head, the sore wept and the stomach ulcer was disgusted; the rash wrinkled its brow and the cold cried for help.'

Such bits of rhetoric lose much in translation. The delightful sense of humour is still there, but the music of the passage is lost. Some of the purely descriptive passages survive better. Fagunwa's imagination is rich and his imagery is fresh and both come across in English. This is Fagunwa's description of Death:

'His eyes are as big as a food bowl, round like moons and red like fire; and they are rolling about like ripe fruit dangling in the wind. The teeth in his mouth look like lion's fangs, and they are bright red, for it is not yam he likes, nor bananas nor *okra*, nor bitter leaf; he likes nothing but human flesh.'

It is in passages like these that Fagunwa is closest to Tutuola. *The Palm Wine Drinkard* and *My Life in the Bush of the Ghosts* abound with descriptions like this and they may well have been directly influenced by Fagunwa.

Fagunwa's writing can be extremely vigorous. His books are full of good, tough fights. A beautiful translation of one of these fights by Wole Soyinka has been published in *Black Orpheus* 15. Here is another:

'When this fight began, Eshu Kekere tried to seize my father round the waist and press his back against a thorn tree. He tried to lift up his foot and throw my father into the dirt. But he found it difficult to punish the innocent fellow. For while he was scheming in this way, my father had his own ideas. He was looking for a way to grab Eshu Kekere by the shoulders and lift the short fellow up from the ground. He tried to carry the badluck spirit above his head and throw the brainless fellow through the air and hurl him from heaven to heaven. But this was impossible: for as he was tough like a lion, so Eshu Kekere was tough like an elephant, and huge clouds of dust rose towards the sky, and the ground began to shake, and the stamping of their feet was louder than the trampling of ten people. Their eyes were dilated. They held each other like creepers strangling a tree in the forest. They were panting like hunting dogs. It was a great day for the little ghost of the anthill whose name was Eshu Kekere Ode.

Then the wicked spirit caught my father round the waist. And when my father tried to get hold of his feet, he jumped on to his shoulders and he seized my father's neck and he slapped his ear with all his might. This annoyed my father and he grabbed the spirit and pressed him into the thorns. Eshu Kekere screamed and he jumped down from my father's shoulder. My father got hold of his ankles, and he swung him above his head and hurled him down angrily, hoping to break his skull. But this did not happen. As my father looked at him, the creature stood upright and laughed, as if the fight was only just beginning.'

Here again Fagunwa is not unlike Tutuola. But Tutuola differs from Fagunwa in two major points: Tutuola does not moralise and he is never sentimental. Fagunwa is a much more Christian writer. As we have already seen, he loses no opportunity to moralise and to improve his reader. He can also be sentimental and even sloppy. There is nothing very Yoruba about

Fagunwa's naïve, somewhat tearful sentimentality, which he displays in passages like this, where he meets his dead mother, who appears to him like an angel rather than an Egungun masquerader:

'As I was thinking all this, I noticed a large rock. I went up to it and saw a passage leading into the rock. I entered, looking for a place to rest and shelter my head from the rain. I had hardly gone six feet, when I found myself in a very large hall and it was very beautiful. Ever since I have been wandering about in this world, I have never seen such a beautiful hall. It was even more beautiful than the palace of the king of the Forest of the Almighty. In the four corners of the hall, I beheld numerous little birds that looked like swallows. They were perched in orderly lines and there were so many of them—they could not have been less than a thousand! Looking at them, they did not seem alive, because they did not stir. They were beautiful birds, red like gold, with their chests white like silver and their beaks curved like elephant tusks. As I stood and watched them they suddenly started to sing together praising Almighty God. The song was so sweet that I completely forgot where I was, I forgot all my cares and my mouth fell open in surprise and the saliva nearly dribbled out of it. But while I was listening to these sweet songs, a door opened suddenly in the wall —a door that had not been there when I entered the hall—and a fearful lion stepped out. He advanced upon me and as I turned to escape, I could not find the door again, by which I had entered. I ran here and there, finding no escape. Finally I stayed still in one corner, waiting for the lion to come and eat me alive. The lion moved close to me and roared: his body was of brass and shone, he was very beautiful. But his voice roared like a thousand thunders rumbling in the sky. Then suddenly a beautiful woman appeared. She was followed by many strange beings. They were all beautiful. Their bodies were so fresh, they were shining like new-born babes, and their robes were radiant like the afternoon sun. When the woman came near me she addressed the lion and said: "You, the creator's lion who has been commanded to guard the tombs of the dead, make way for me, for God gave me authority over you before I left heaven. I came through the black river, which is the river of indigo; I passed through the red river, which is the river of blood; and I have spoken to thousands of dead people who are expecting the judgement of God." When the woman had finished, the lion stepped back, and the woman handed over a big letter to him—surely it must have been the authority from God.

When the lion had gone she came to me with all the other beauties following her. But when I looked at her properly I saw that it was my mother! I ran forwards, to embrace her—but my arms were empty.'

Fagunwa's writing is a great deal more convincing when he draws on his shrewd and detailed observation of the everyday life that goes on around him, rather than on ideas and concepts derived from books or from his

Christian education. In the following passage Fagunwa describes how Olowo-Aiye meets two strange women in the forest and how he falls in love with one of them:

'Soon after that he looked up and saw two women walking towards him along the road. They were talking, they were laughing, they were clapping their hands in the manner of women. The two women seemed completely at home in this wild place. They were enjoying themselves in the bush and they were swaggering about as if they were in some busy market place. One of them was red skinned, large, and well built. She looked like a woman who had already gone to the house of a husband. The second one was slim, and not so tall, she was black and her teeth were white like new maize. Both were beautiful. They spoke with the confidence of well-connected people, and their gait had the self-assurance of women of the world.

When they met my father he greeted them. They answered, but with a certain modest reserve, as one greets a stranger. Then my father continued on his way and they also moved on, in the opposite direction. But my father was surprised to find such sophisticated women in such a remote forest, and he turned back in wonder to look at them. At exactly the same moment the smaller woman also looked back, and when they saw each other, they laughed. But they continued on their separate ways. When my father looked back a second time, his eyes met again with those of the woman. But he forced himself to continue on his way —even though he had no wife at the time. But when my father looked back the third time, the woman was again looking at him, and she was laughing and her teeth were shining like a white-washed wall. Then Olowo-Aiye turned round; he turned his back on the Forest of the Almighty and he walked towards the women.

Let Olodumare deliver men from troublesome women, who who push their headties provocatively into their foreheads!

When my father was walking towards the woman, she stopped. But her companion walked farther away and waited, because when a man and a woman want to exchange secret words, a third person is surely an obstacle.'

This is Fagunwa at his charming best. He is a wonderful observer of situations and has a very fine ear for speech. It is these qualities that make Fagunwa so popular with so many people.

But there is also a reaction and even opposition to Fagunwa—particularly among Yoruba intellectuals. Fagunwa is reproached with lack of realism. People say they are tired of reading about fairies and ghosts; and they want to read about modern man and women. They are interested in problems, rather than stories; in characters rather than in types. No doubt the time has come for the realistic Yoruba novel, and in fact writers like Delano, Babalola and Faleti have made a vigorous beginning in this direction. But this hardly detracts from the merits of Fagunwa's writing. It is true that he does not deal with contemporary social problems, that he does

203

not 'analyse' characters and is completely disinterested in the 'African Personality'. But then he makes up for this by his charm, his humour, his vividness, his baroque imagery. And it is not quite true to say that Fagunwa is not realistic. His plot, of course, is fantastic, and so are many of his characters, but Fagunwa is extremely realistic in much of his detail. He knows how they speak. He knows how they laugh, how they flirt and how they flatter. In his description of people's manners and mannerisms, of their greed, their weaknesses, their humour, Fagunwa is more realistic than many 'modern' Yoruba novelists. As an observer of the Yoruba mind at work Fagunwa is still unsurpassed. This is also where he surpasses Tutuola. It is true that Tutuola rivals him as a story-teller, that the stories he tells are in fact more authentically Yoruba and traditional. But in a passage like the following, Fagunwa is without rival. Here he tells how the hero has got himself on the top of a high tree through his own carelessness. Now he cannot descend and all the animals of the forest to whom he appeals for help walk past without stopping. At last the rat passes and he knows that this is his last chance and he *must* make it stop and listen and *must* secure its help: what a beautiful piece of flattery Fagunwa invents for the purpose; what a shrewd beating about the bush:

'After a little while I saw a rat passing by. I could hardly recognise it was a rat, because I was sitting perched so high off the ground. I shouted to it and said: "You rat!" He answered and said:"Who is calling me a rat? I who dwell in the forest, I who dwell in the bush, who am living among the trees and the creepers." And I replied again: It was I, Olowo-Aiye, calling you. The son of Akowediran. I, the elephant hunter, the husband of Ajediran, who came to hunt in this forest and whom you see squatting on this tree. Please help me, you rat, playing about. Nobody is little, before the Almighty. The only one who is small in the eyes of god is the dishonest man who invited the thief to steal on the farm and still asked the farmer to watch his farm. The farmer thanks him, and the thief also thanks him—but his judgement will happen in heaven—from where the rain falls. You rat of Olodumare. Some people may think you are little, and yet you are bigger than rabbits in other places. There is only one thing I want you to know: you are not little in the eyes of God, the king. You are not like the dishonest man, who has blood in his belly and spits out white saliva. My dear rat, let me tell you a little story:
"One day I and a dishonest man sat in the same meeting. Later we realised that he wanted to ruin our society. We had all agreed together that a certain man was to be banned from our meeting. But when we had scattered, this dishonest fellow secretly went to tell the man that he had no hand in our decision. But finally all of of us heard about the matter and the man was put to shame. When we queried him, he answered like a stammerer. He looked as if we were about to cut off his head. My dear rat: you are not like one of these, and I beg you not to leave me without showing me your truth today. I want you to let me see the truth you have

in your belly. To tell me openly now the way that I can take, to escape from this prison, into which I got through my own foolishness.'''

Fagunwa does not attempt to solve any problems in his books. He has two simple aims as a writer: he tries to delight and to entertain; he also tries —alas—to instruct and improve his reader. But he succeeds so excellently well in his first aim that we willingly forgive him the second.

It is high time that Fagunwa was translated into English, so that more people can share the pleasure he has to give.

Camara Laye's Symbolism

An Interpretation of: "The Radiance of the King"

J. A. RAMSARAN

The chief character in this novel,[1] which is set in Africa, is Clarence, a white man in quest of the king whose service he wishes to enter. Clarence has been staying at a good European hotel before he moves into an African caravanserai because he is unable to meet his bills at the former place where, as a result, he was despised by his fellow white men. Reduced to looking for some kind of work, he is willing to do anything honest as long as he receives 'adequate remuneration' for his services. It is in this frame of mind that he, the only white man, joins the huge crowd awaiting the appearance of the King on the esplanade at Adrame. He fails to get to the King because of the crush, and is advised by a haughty beggar to travel South where the King is due to appear next. Clarence invites the beggar and two impudent boys into the caravanserai where the African innkeeper demands payment of Clarence and receives his coat in settlement. Shortly after the company of four has left the caravanserai, the innkeeper appears in the street with public guards and accuses Clarence of having stolen back the coat. He is arrested and tried in a court where he is the victim of a gross travesty of justice. He manages to run away from the courtroom, through a number of intricate passages, led by a young woman who turns out to be the daughter of the judge. There are several other dreamlike incongruities. However, he finally rejoins his companions, the beggar and two impudent boys, and they travel through the forest of thorns and odours, coming upon villages where they feed on the alms given to the beggar. (It is interesting to note the correspondence between this journeying South and Amos Tutuola's stories, especially his *Simbi and the Satyr of the Dark Jungle*, where Simbi, like Clarence, is in search of something.) Clarence and his companions arrive at Aziana, where he chooses to remain—or rather, is left by the beggar in exchange for a donkey and a woman given him by the old *naba* who has a harem of many wives. Clarence prefers staying in Aziana to leading a strenuous life with the beggar. There ensues a period of waiting which one fears is going to be as futile as waiting for Godot. He is treated well, and his woman, Akissi, provides for all his physical needs, while he keeps on hoping to be of some use to the village, for he is not engaged in any 'creative' work as he understands that epithet, but seems to be frittering away his life in sensuality. In time Clarence comes to realise his own unworthiness, and finally, in utter humility, he knows that there is no service he can offer to the King; if he is lucky he may be the recipient of some favour from the King. Such is the story in brief, but the meaning of the allegory is not so simple.

Translated from the French by James Kirkup, London, Collins, 1956.

206

The fleeting vision which Clarence caught of the King on the crowded esplanade, his experiences at the inn and court trial, his wandering through the forest of the South, and his life at Aziana where he ultimately saw the full radiance of the King and was received by him—all have the quality of a troubled dream, in parts reminiscent of Tutuola's nightmare world, and in parts of Kafka's world of semi-consciousness between dreaming and waking—especially the wall of thorns, the persistent odour, and the haughty behaviour of the beggar.

He walks for a long time in the forest, struggling against the odour, and against his desire for sleep. He has never tried so hard to keep his eyes open: he would like to see the wall of thorns. And he would like to get to the roots of another mystery—why the beggar behaves as he does. He would like not to fall asleep before solving the mystery. But the mystery is very hard to solve. Each time Clarence is on the point of solving it, sleep plunges everything into darkness again. Yet Clarence is never nearer to a solution than at the moment before he falls asleep. Then there is a moment, only a second perhaps, or perhaps infinitely less, in which it seems everything is going to be made clear at last. But then slumber intervenes, and Clarence falls asleep before he has had time to grasp . . . What? Who knows?

He has come to Africa in search of something, he knows not what, until he joins the throng on the esplanade at Adrame to catch a glimpse of the King. From that moment he is never at peace until he is received by the King at Aziana. In spite of his assertion: 'I am not "just anybody", I am a white man', Clarence is Everyman, but Everyman in search of something; having realised that he is lacking that something, and that he does not know all the answers, perhaps will never know all the answers. The beggar's observation: 'The white men think they know everything. And what do they know when all's said and done?' is to be taken as a rebuke to any man wise in his own estimation, and spiritually dormant. Clarence and his companions journey painfully towards the South, yet seem to go round in a circle; and, paradoxically, the beggar says, 'The South is everywhere.' 'Yes,' Clarence reflects, 'the inferno of the senses is everywhere.' This should give them pause who think that West Africa, or any torrid land, is the natural clime for riotous passions and unlicensed sexual indulgence, as depicted in some novels of today.

After the forest wanderings Clarence settles in the Vanity Fair of Aziana where the *naba*, the eunuch Samba Baloun, and the Master of Ceremonies become the centre of interest along with the domestic affaires of Clarence. Stripped of his shabby western clothes he dons the native *boubou*, and sometimes goes naked without any sense of embarrassment—the veneer of civilisation, as it were, is stripped and Clarence appears as he really is; and it is in his nakedness that he finally approaches the King. But before this Clarence's repressed desires are given full rein and he lives a Jekyll and Hyde existence without realising it, until the end. But even in Aziana there are people like Diallo, the blacksmith, who is dedicated to his craft. He

207

would make an axe as perfect as he possibly can to offer as his gift when the King does come.

'Will your axe be ready by the time he comes?' asked Clarence. 'Probably,' Diallo replied. 'Anyhow, I hope it will be. But what is an axe? I have forged thousands of them, and this one will undoubtedly be the finest of them all. The others will have been no more than experiments I made in order to forge this one perfect one. So that this will be the one of everything I have ever learnt; it will be like my life, and all the effort I have made to live it well. . . . He will accept it, at least I hope he will accept it, and perhaps he will even deign to admire it; but he will accept it and admire it only in order to give me pleasure. After all, what sort of pleasure could he take in it? There will always be axes that are finer. . . . Yet I go on forging it. . . . Perhaps I can do nothing else, perhaps I am like a tree which can bear only one kind of fruit. . . . And perhaps, in spite of having so many faults, because I am like that tree and lack the means to do anything but this; in spite of everything, the King will give me credit for my good will.'

It is this last sentence that sticks in Clarence's mind. Half hoping, half despairing, he murmurs, as the King's glance falls upon him in the final scene,

'Alas, Lord, I have only my good will, and it is weak! But you cannot accept it, My good will condemns me: there is no virtue in it.'

Yet he moves forward and falls upon his knees before the King, but is still not near enough. He is at the end of his seeking, at the end of all seekings, when he is held in the King's embrace and enveloped by the mantle of his love. So the quest of Clarence ends in this mystic union after the long struggle between the sensual and the spiritual.

Camara Laye's novel is a strange mixture of these two qualities, the sensual and the spiritual. It may be that the explanation lies in the forces that have shaped his present philosophy. The allegory bears some obvious resemblances to Christian thought, yet one must bear in mind that in *The Dark Child*[1] Laye says that he comes of a Muslim family—his scholarly uncle was a devout reader of the Koran in Arabic. One wonders how much of the mysticism of the Sufis contributes to the allegory of *The Radiance of the King*. It is as though the author is asking whether a synthesis of man's intellectual questioning, spiritual yearning, and an uninhibited enjoyment of life is not possible. In the process of presenting this possibility, however, he confronts the reader with so many paradoxes and contradictions that the result of a first reading is likely to be somewhat confusing. The allegory is not consistently maintained but the main threads can be picked up, as I have tried to show. In my attempt to do this I make no pretence that I am right, or that there is only one meaning.

[1] *Translated from the French by James Kirkup, London, Collins, 1955.*

It seems to me that Camara Laye instinctively understands the search for an answer on the part of those who undertake a journey into Africa: Clarence is the seeker, both on the conscious and sub-conscious levels; and through all his bewildering experiences he does not realise the full impact of his learning until the final revelation. The fertility dances, the drumming, insistent as the pounding of the sea waves, the all-pervasive odour of the forest of primitive urges, the ecstasy of the priestess Diolu—all these, partly or wholly inexplicable aspects of Africa, become the symbol of the inscrutable forces in man, regardless of colour or creed. So *The Radiance of the King* may be seen as a tentative approach to the mystery of our being—an approach which suggests that a journey into the primitive, and apparently utterly strange, can result in a self-discovery altogether startling but none the less illuminating. For, as Sir Thomas Browne wrote in his *Religio Medici* 300 years ago, 'We carry within us the wonders that are without us: there is all Africa and her prodigies in us.'

Camara Laye

Another Interpretation

JANHEINZ JAHN

J. A. Ramsaran has given an interpretation of Camara Laye's symbolism in *The Radiance of the King* in which he relates Laye's symbolism to Kafka, and he looks to Christianity and Islam for further comparisons. But I think that we could find a more convincing explanation nearer home, in *African* thinking. I should like to consider here Camara Laye's two books, because the first is a key to the second. In *The Dark Child* Camara Laye shows his understanding and respect for African traditions, and in *The Radiance of the King* he makes this tradition work on a stranger.

In *The Dark Child* Camara Laye shows the new spirit of French West Africans towards tradition. He did not consider his African childhood as something remote, primitive, something to be ashamed of. On the contrary: looking back on it from a distance, and having learned the technical skills European education had to offer, he discovered these skills had been animated, and had been more closely related to man, in his native civilisation. In his novel he describes lovingly the work of his father, a goldsmith, who was in his way a technician, but who is helped by the praise-singers while he works.

See how Camara Laye describes the actual smelting of gold:

> 'My father used to utter actual words at this time, I know that he was uttering them in his mind. I could see it by his lips. What were the words my father's lips were forming? I do not know, I do not know for certain: I was never told what they were. But what else could they have been, if not magical incantations? Were they not the spirits of fire and gold, of fire and air, of fire born in air, of gold married with fire—were not these spirits he was invoking? The operation that was going on before my eyes was simply the smelting of gold, but it was something more than that: a magical operation.
>
> During the whole process of transformation the praise-singer had kept on singing his praises, accelerating his rhythm, increasing his flatteries, as the trinket took shape, and praising my father's talents to the skies. Indeed, the praise-singer participated in a curious—I was going to say direct, effective—way in the work. He too, was intoxicated with the joy of creation, he declaimed his rapture, and plucked his harp like a man inspired: he warmed to the task as if he had been the craftsman himself, as if the trinket had been made by his own hands.'

This scene illustrates and emphasises the importance and the quality of the word in Africa, the effective power of the creative word, which has such

210

importance in African philosophy. Senghor, the famous poet and philosopher from Senegal, in one of his essays comments on the scene:

'Laye's father is forging a golden jewel. The prayer, or rather the poem, which he recites, the song of praise which the Griot sings as he works the gold, the dance of the smith at the end of the operation, it is all that—poem, song and dance—which, more than the gestures of the craftsman, accomplish the work, and make it a work of art.

Thus finally all human doing and creating is a kind of magic, and a formula of chemistry, a calculation of statistics, what else is it than a magic formula, the right word in the right moment to accomplish a creative mystery? Camara Laye, although an engineer, remained related to his African tradition and thus did not lose his soul in the technical environment because he was able to give to those abstract formulas a spiritual meaning, the living meaning of a symbol.'

In his second book, *The Radiance of the King*, he does even more. The whole book is full of symbolism. It is usually considered as an ingenious allegory about man's search for God. But I think that the book cannot be seen in this sense only; it is ambivalent, even multivalent, as Senghor says of all African art. Clarence, a European, finds himself without the help and support of his countrymen in an African environment. He is without money, without hope of outside help. He is thrown exactly into that position in which many Africans often find themselves in the European world. He has to conform. And thus he gradually becomes initiated. The whole book can be considered as a lesson in African wisdom.

Clarence concentrates his hopes on the African king. He stands in the dust of the street and watches the King pass. A beggar who is also watching promises to put in a good word for him, so that Clarence might get a job. When the beggar reappears, Clarence was trying to read the beggar's face, but he could make out nothing at all: he had been too short a time in this country to be able to decipher the expression on the black men's faces.

'Well,' he asked.
'I am sorry,' said the beggar, 'there is no post available for you.'
'But I would have accepted any post whatsoever!'
'I know, but there are no posts available.'
'I should have been satisfied with the humblest situation,' said Clarence. 'I could have . . .' he said. But what could he have done? Had he the least idea? 'I could have been a simple drummer boy . . .'
'That is not a simple occupation,' said the beggar. 'The drummers are drawn from a noble caste and their employment is hereditary. Even if you had been allowed to beat a drum it would have had no meaning. The white men think they know everything, and what *do* they know, when all's said and done? Perhaps I should not have announced that you were ready to accept any kind of employment whatsoever, perhaps they were suspicious of a

211

man who was ready to accept just *any* kind of employment, feeling that such a one would be incapable of doing anything.'

Thus is the beginning of this European's education. He gets one lesson after the other, most of them painful. At a Law Court he is treated like Africans were at times treated in colonialist Law Courts: his evidence has no value and he cannot get justice. Only the beggar helps him on: his art of begging supplies enough food while they go South where the King is expected. Clarence does not see that they move on; he believes he is tricked, that they go the same way every day, so unchanged is the landscape to him, the forest that never ends. In a village Clarence does not want to go on; the beggar sells him there, getting a woman and a donkey for him. Clarence does not know that he has been sold, his life is comfortable, he is not supposed to work and gets a nice companion to sleep with him in his hut. But sometimes he has the impression that his woman is different, that the woman he has in the night is not his woman. He worries; he wants to find out, though he is told that it is better for him not to know. But as a white man he cannot leave any secret untouched, he wants to know the truth. He finally finds out that he is used as a stallion to mate with the wives of the *naba*, the chief. Knowing it makes him more unhappy than before, seeing his pride in his white race reduced to nothing but a biological difference whimsically used by a *naba* to make his offspring look different from other offspring.

Even his humanitarian ideals, his Christian pity, are shown to be worthless and harmful. The Master of Ceremonies has done wrong in letting Clarence into the secret, and as a punishment the Master of Ceremonies gets whipped. Clarence, attending the scene, is torn by his conscience, mutters 'Savages!' and stops the whipping. But not even the whipped Master of Ceremonies thanks him for his interference, because the Master of Ceremonies will enjoy no respite now. If the display had been allowed to pursue its rightful course, he would have been able really to enjoy the respite, the sense of relief that the conclusion of a well-regulated torture always affords. Whereas now he has to drag himself around as if he had never received a single stroke.

Clarence's preconceived ideas are altered, his prejudices torn. None of the persons who surround him is wholly reliable, but all are human, neither good nor bad but both.

Noaga and Nagoa, the two boys who accompany Clarence all the time, are neither good nor bad. At any time they take their chance; they steal where there is an opportunity. Clarence is often worried about them, at times he is shocked, at times compelled to admire. They never consider life too seriously. There is no question whether they are to be redeemed by the King or not. 'Tomorrow we go with the King', they say. Their redemption is not a question of good or evil, they cannot be rejected by the King, because already they live life as a unity. Clarence on the other hand can only be redeemed after he has learned that his moral problems are not essential. This is one of the strongest arguments against the Christian interpretation of the end of the book.

212

Clarence learns, and learns gradually, to become one of those around him; human himself, humble at last when all his preconceptions are gone. It is again a smith, Diallo the blacksmith, who gives him the most worthy lessons. One morning he learns about the essence of African art: Diallo's reflections on the axe he is making for the King, which Mr. Ramsaran has quoted, make clear that not the purpose of the axe is important, but its meaning. The process of creation is more important than the created object. In itself it is not worth much, its worth lasts as long as the artist creates it, doing his best to justify his own life. And as soon as it is finished he starts to forge a new one, a better one again, and each one is the sum of everything he has ever learnt. And the former axes are destooled works of art, they are of no value to him, they become mere tools which now the farmer may use.

Finally Clarence is redeemed after he has learned that all his former scales of values are wrong. When finally he has learned to have visions, when he has understood that what he thought to be sin is not sin but life, that by all his errors there is nothing that really counts but his good will, then the king draws him to his breast. Like everything in this novel this king is a symbol too. He is fortune, merit, favour, mercy, he is king and redeemer. Camara Laye gives the sum of all religion, of all humanity, in this novel. And he shows that here, finally, all religion is one. Various symbols of different religions are used to fuse them into a unified concept of religion.

Mr. Ramsaran sees the novel as a 'strange mixture of two qualities, the sensual and the spiritual'. But the sensual and the spiritual are one in African thinking. It is Clarence, the European, who separates the two. For Clarence the mixture is strange. He tries to split these forces, until he is redeemed and has learned that there is no split. Unity is not a final synthesis for Laye, it is the original state.

The end of the novel, often misunderstood, means that even the white man in Africa can be redeemed and accepted when he shows his will to learn and not only to teach. And that Camara Laye in all his lessons does not consider the African way of faith and redemption the only one imaginable and superior. He wants to say that it is the only right way for Africa and that it is of equal value with any other way of mankind.

Symbolism in 'The Radiance of the King'

J. A. RAMSARAN

I find Mr. Jahn's interpretation of Camara Laye's novel most interesting though not entirely convincing. His close study of African life obviously gives him an advantage over any reader with no knowledge of African thought. But I would suggest, with due deference to his experience of things African, that he is perhaps a little uncritical about what he calls 'African thinking' when he implies that such a philosophy is common to all Africans,

213

and that Monsieur Laye has written a novel the meaning and implications of which he himself was conscious of all the time even before he set pen to paper. When Mr. Jahn says that the book is 'ambivalent, even multivalent' I am in perfect agreement with him, if he will admit that the ambivalence derives from the author's own search for self-knowledge, his own questionings of both European and African values as they appear to the twentieth-century intellectual of either culture; for the African intellectual is as much a 'split' personality as his European counterpart, is as much in need of integration, on a different level from the unity that obtains, if it does obtain, in the unsophisticated African society.

Camara Laye, sensitive and percipient, has realised with the acuteness of a poet that mankind as a whole is suffering from a spiritual malaise and that a nostalgia for what seems a lost innocence infects the intellectuals of today. *The Radiance of the King* is Monsieur Laye's expression of this awareness in a work which is, like all art, 'multivalent'—it can mean several things the author himself might not have been conscious of when he embarked on the novel; it disturbs, it excites, it holds out some promise of a vision that will explain the mystery of our being; but it does not fulfil that promise. Mr. Jahn seems to think it does, but I am still not sure, although his interpretation helps me in the enjoyment of the novel.

George Lamming

HELMUT GÜNTHER

In a German newspaper I read an essay by the English writer, Harold Champion, entitled *The West Indies—A Growing Nation*. It says: 'On the 22nd of April 1958 Princess Margaret opened the first Federal Parliament of the West Indian Federation. On this day a constitution passed into law that closely resembled the previous constitution of the individual islands and even the constitution of Great Britain itself. The islands Jamaica, Barbados, Dominica, Grenada, Monserrat, Antigua, St. Kitts, Nevis, Anguilla, St Lucia, St. Vincent, Trinidad and Tobago have formed a new state. A long development was needed to achieve this degree of political maturity on the islands.' The article gives an exact outline of the political structure of the new state. But nothing is said about the people and their culture. For the author, the West Indian Federation is just an English-speaking part of the British Commonwealth. In reality this is a state of Indians, Chinese and above all, black people. It is an Afro-American state. The people of these islands have achieved a new spiritual and political confidence. Their culture is already influencing the rest of the world.

The wave of calypso music that has recently swept over the world is only the harbinger of the cultural encounter between the West Indies and the rest of the world. Music and dancing, the most basic and human of all the arts, usually come first. Afro-American culture first affected the Western world through jazz, then through Afro-Cuban music, the tango and the rumba. Since 1940 literature from the West Indies has been making its mark. At this moment the islands are becoming part of world culture.

One of the most important representatives of West Indian literature is George Lamming, who was born in 1927 in Barbados. He writes in English, his mother tongue, and he is a film and book critic on the BBC.

English critics see in Lamming a sort of phenomenon. They praise his new vision (which in reality is very ancient), the power of his language, the richness of his poetic imagination. From a European point of view Lamming is indeed something new and strange: both a volcano and a source of lyrical fairy tales. Lamming writes magnificent English, the kind of English that has not been written since Francis Thompson, whose poem *The Hound of Heaven* he once quotes. Yet Lamming does not really belong to English literature, but to those Afro-American authors in whom the African spirit has rediscovered itself. Lamming is a product of the highest contemporary education. He has absorbed Faulkner and Sartre. He also knows the French surrealists. But the wealth of his imagery has nothing to do with surrealism. His images have not been stuck together artificially; they form a whole and spring from a common source. The agitated world of Lamming's novels is not the arbitrary, torn world of civilisation. In Lamming we find the whole

215

world, and for Lamming the world is a whole. Everything is related to everything else. For Lamming, therefore, there is no such thing as absolute freedom; freedom is ecstasy and bliss; and he means to be part of a whole, to be receptive to the breath of the world.

It is true that Lamming fights against suppression and colonialism, and for the political and social freedom of his people. He is a rebel and a nationalist. But political freedom is only a means to achieve the great freedom of man as such.

In Lamming's novel *Of Age and Innocence*[1] the black writer Mark says:

> 'Nationalism is not only frenzy and struggle for the destruction of those forces which condemn you to the status we call colonial. The national spirit is deeper than that, It is the private feeling you experience of possessing and being possessed by the whole landscape of the place where you were born, the freedom which helps you to recognise the rhythm of the winds, the silence and aroma of the night, rocks, water . . . the temper of the sea and the mornings arousing nature everywhere to the silent and sacred communion between you and the roots you have made in this island. . . . And the freedom you sing . . . freedom . . .'

Lamming is an important novelist, because he is a modern individual and at the same time lives as part of all things and all forces. African culture has comprehended what is the supreme happiness of man. The basis of African culture is the dance; the mysterious union of ecstasy and form, of ego and world, the experience of the great freedom. Lamming has described the happiness and freedom of the dance in the following words:

> There was only the body which was the dance itself, regulated, informed, nourished and dictated not only by its blood, but by some pervasive, measureless source of being that was its own logic of receptivity and transmission, a world that could be defined only through the presence of others, yet remained in its definition absolute, free, itself. The body was part of the source of its being and at the same time its being. It was within and outside itself simultaneously. Free, yet subject to the compulsion of its freedom, it strained beyond the limit of its resources.'[2]

Humanity and love are the powers behind any kind of poetry. That is why Lamming is both rebel and dreamer, politician and poet, like all the great modern African poets (Césaire and Senghor, for examples). The poet is the voice of world *and* of man. Politics and poetry are one and the same thing for Lamming. Politics creates the space in which man can be a human being, that is a free being in contact with all the forces of the world. Politics without religious and poetic roots is meaningless. But poetry without topical human and social reference is empty. If we separate poetry and politics in the following we merely show two sides of the same thing.

Lamming's theme is of extraordinary simplicity: it is the West Indies and

---

[1] London, Michael Joseph, 1958.   [2] *The Emigrants*, Michael Joseph, 1954.

England, black and white. Lamming describes the rise of his people. His novels form a trilogy. In his first book, *In the Castle of my Skin,*[1] Lamming describes his childhood: a legendary world, mythical, biblical without a sense of history. On the one side the feudal landlords, on the other the black people who own nothing but fairy tales, the myths, and the biblical hope.

> Like children under the threat of hell fire they accepted instinctively that the others, meaning the white, were superior . . . This world of the others' imagined perfection hung like a dead weight over their energy. If the low-down nigger people weren't what they are, the others couldn't say anything about us. Suspicion, distrust, hostility.

But already there is a lightening on the horizon: unrest strikes, first, political leaders. The War opens the eyes of the black people. Up till then they had been ashamed to be black. But a man who had emigrated to the United States brings home the new message: the message of the great Jamaican Marcus Garvey, who proclaimed the unity of the African peoples. He is the first man on the island who speaks of black man as 'My people, the negro race . . .'. But he had to emigrate to discover himself.

The second novel, *The Emigrants,* describes the mass migration of West Indians to London. They seek their fortune there. They know no hatred against white people. England is their hope, their dream. Barbados has always been proud to be called 'Little England':

> Barbados or Little England was the oldest and purest of England's children, and may it always be so. One day before time changed for eternity, Little England and Big England, God's anointed on earth, might hand-in-hand rule this earth. . . . Big England had only to say the word and Little England followed. Big England had the strongest navy, and Little England the best fishermen in this God's world. Together they were mistresses of the sea, and whenever, wherever, the two met on the same side, war or peace, there was bound to be a victory.

England is the big friend, the educator, the helper. The coloured West Indians want nothing but understanding and love. England is their rightful heritage. England, oh England! But England turns out to be the enemy. England, oh England? They live in caves and holes under the ground, but they do not give up their hope. They have ceased to look for England now. They want to discover themselves. What they are really looking for is not merely material fortune, but recognition as human beings. Thus England becomes merely a diversion on the road home; it becomes the school in which they are taught to prove that they are West Indians and want to be West Indians. That is why they don't give up. There is a conversation between the emigrants on the boat. Somebody says:

[1] Michael Joseph, 1953.

'West Indies people, whatever island you bring them from, them want to prove something. . . . Me serve in the R.A.F. three years, an' de only thing that West Indians in de R.A.F. din't want to prove is his capability wid a bottle or a blonde. . . . In everything else, him feelin', him searching. An' if you ask what it is them want to prove the answer sound a stupid answer. Them want to prove that them is themself. Them is West Indians.'

Lamming's third novel, *Of Age and Innocence*, is located on an island called San Cristobal. The name is invented but the island is real enough. The coloured people on this island, Negroes and Indians, are fighting for victory. The world has changed radically. The old people, particularly the mothers, are still living in a world of dreams, of legend and the Bible. But the two men who are the real heroes of the book have just returned from England. They have both lost contact with their people. Mark, the black writer, has experienced the isolation and solitude of the modern European. The woman he loves is English. After twenty years of absence he is returning home: and here at last he rediscovers his identity, his objective existence. In the same way Shepherd, who becomes hero and saviour of his people, was driven into politics only by the disappointment of a 'white' love. Colonial rule is coming to an end. Its last weapons are terror and murder. Shepherd arouses his people to 'a new conception of itself'. Now everything is Politics. The individual fate of the various characters is tragic. The last chapters tell of violence and fear, of death and tombs. Shepherd is dead. The bayonets and the tanks rule once more. There is a state of war. But the young generation will continue the fight and the victory is certain.

Lamming writes novels, but he is not a novelist in the European sense of the word. Of course he describes an historical world that is fixed in space and time and he has action. In *Of Age and Innocence* he even has a sort of plot. There are quite realistic scenes and discussions, very many in fact. But Lamming is never satisfied merely to tell a story and to copy reality. He does not merely want to report, he wants to conjure the world in words, like a true African. In European terms, Lamming is an epic and a lyrical writer and a novelist all at once. He is an excellent story-teller. His books abound with humorous anecdotes and tense adventures. He can tell real thrillers, with murder and flight. He can also create the individual fate of his various characters with great mastery. But these individual characters are merely parts of an all embracing lyrical-epic world. That is why the author must again and again break through the framework of realistic prose. Lamming fully masters the technique of the modern novel. But he knows that in this way he can only touch the surface of the world. What he really wants is to conjure the world in its entirety in pictures. In pictures he reveals the unity of the world, the interrelationship of all things. That is why Lamming's language is often heightened into poetry, for example in the description of Paddington Station in London. That is why Lamming's most beautiful characters are the mothers who are still living in myths and images. In *In the Castle of my Skin* there is Ma, the oldest woman on the island. But the

218

most beautiful of all Lamming's characters is that other Ma, the pious mother of the rebel Shepherd. All these women carry on an unhistorical existence, being part of the whole. Their language is therefore always poetical and mythical and conjuring in the African sense.

'Their language seemed to give everything the sound of ritual, and there was no end of ritual in San Cristobal' (*Of Age and Innocence*). Pa and Ma (*In the Castle of my Skin*) speak in biblical language about the first leader of the island. Thus says Ma:

> 'Seems to me you see Yuh salvation in Mr. Slime. He's get a chance to go to Yuh head like rum to a next man's an now you hear the shout you can't think or say nothing that ain't bound up with him. But I tell you already, an' I tell you again, I won't store no riches here on the earth, Pa. I won't store no riches here where we see when we least expecting flood, famine an' all the pest'lence that God 'flict the earth with. It ain't no place to store riches, Pa.'

Or listen to this old fisherman:

> 'I enter the ocean at an early age, a strip of a boy beside my father, helpin' to raid the fish of the sea, all class of fish in every kind of sea-water. No fish none of you can name that I din't down with harpoon or hook or haul flyin' in with these said same hands you see here. . . . Night and day is two sides of the same coin, one side maybe is heads, the next side maybe tails, but the same coin, an' 'tis the same with every man who chase fish. maybe 'tis night-light, maybe 'tis daylight, but there's only one time, that's fishing time.'

That is the world, the language, the poetry, from which Lamming has come. Even for him, the modern intellectual, the world is still mythical and magical, a world of images and secret relationships. Everything is alive, full of divine power. The boldest example is perhaps in *The Emigrants*. There he says of the newly gained freedom of a young colonial:

> 'I felt this freedom. It was a private and personal acquisition, and I used it as a man uses what is private and personal, like his penis.'

For the true poet, who thinks in images and in contexts, there is nothing individual, nothing separate. The world is a stream of powers. Lamming does not merely give a series of images, nor does he merely draw on the African mythical world of mothers, but his novels move on in large general images into which the individual characters have been woven. The progress of time is expressed through the change of images in space. Time is expressed through space. Space and time thus appear as the manifestations of a single living force. Even the human beings, who are acting in this time-space, are cosmic forces, who are endowed with spirit and freedom. But a plot that progresses merely in time can never exist in Lamming's work, because a plot dissolves the unity of the world into single actions and

219

moments. Lamming always presents large images. Within these images there is no chronological progression of action. Always an entire world is presented—the ship, or London—a world in which everything forms a unity. Even modern London becomes in Lamming's work a magical space, a space in which everything is united by basic links. A separate individual action cannor exist here. The action is jerky. But the unity of space and time is never destroyed. Of course, even in Lamming's novels the different images must succeed each other in time. But that merely follows from the technique to which every writer is subjected. A painter like Picasso can represent the different aspects of a subject and a picture simultaneously. The writer must present a sequence of time and space. But Lamming tries again and again to dovetail the different images and scenes in order to create the impression of a uniform, compact world. Past and present overlap. All spaces in the world are simultaneous. Everything is eternal, in the same time and the same space. This is just like the poetry of the great contemporary Negro poets, for example Césaire. Everything is ever present. The poet is master of the world and at the same time its smallest part. In Lamming's work, therefore, the political fight in time is 'a great and extreme change' but in reality everything amounts to a return to the deepest sources of the world. For the Afro-American writer Lamming, poetry is politics and politics is poetry. That is why he can live simultaneously in the most modern forms of modern civilisation, and in the age-old myths and images of his Afro-American homeland.

Fiction by Black South Africans

LEWIS NKOSI

With the best will in the world it is impossible to detect in the fiction of black South Africans any significant and complex talent which responds with both the vigour of the imagination and sufficient technical resources to the problems posed by conditions in South Africa.

Where urban African music, for instance, has responded to the challenges of the disintegrative tendencies of city life with an amazing suppleness and subtlety, black writing shows the cracks and tension of language working under severe strain. Where African music and dance have moved forward, not through renouncing tradition but by fusing diverse elements into an integrated whole, black fiction has renounced African tradition without showing itself capable of benefiting from the accumulated example of modern European literature. To put it bluntly: nothing stands behind the fiction of black South Africans—no tradition, whether indigenous, such as energises *The Palm Wine Drinkard*, or alien, such as is most significantly at work in the latest fiction by Camara Laye.[1]

If black South African writers have read modern works of literature they seem to be totally unaware of their most compelling innovations; they blithely go on 'telling stories' or crudely attempting to solve problems to which European practitioners, from Dostoevsky to Burroughs, have responded with greater subtlety, technical originality and sustained vigour; and black South Africans write, of course, as though Dostoevsky, Kafka or Joyce had never lived. Is is not possible, without sounding either superior or unpatriotic, to ask how a fiction written by people conversant with the history of the development of modern fiction can reveal no awareness of the existence of *Notes From Underground*, *Ulysses* or similar works? For make no mistake about this; it is not an instance of writers who have assimilated so well the lessons of the masters that they are able to conceal what they have learned; rather is it an example of a group of writers operating blindly in a vacuum.

This primitiveness or mere concern with *telling* the story may be supposed to have its own virtues. In contrast with Europe, for instance, where it is impossible to write without being conscious of the fossilised examples of literary tradition, this lack of self-consciousness may seem a welcome liberation from the burden of tradition: it could even be supposed to allow for a certain freshness and originative power in the writing; yet these are virtues which would be very difficult to find in fiction by black South Africans. We certainly have nothing to counterpoise against the imaginative power of Chinua Achebe's *Things Fall Apart* or the placid grace of its

---

[1] See his story: *The Eyes of the Statue* in 'Black Orpheus': an anthology of New African and Afro-American stories, London, Longmans, 1964.

style. Nor do we have anything to equal the teeming inventive genius of Amos Tutuola's *The Palm Wine Drinkard*. To read a novel like Richard Rive's *Emergency*[1] is to gain a minute glimpse into a literary situation which seems to me quite desperate. It may even be wondered whether it might not be more prudent to 'renounce literature temporarily', as some have advised, and solve the political problem first rather than continue to grind out third-rate novels of which *Emergency* is a leading example, a novel in which the author falls far short of the promise of his earlier fictional pieces such as *Rain* and *Willieboy*, and altogether fails in characterisation and imaginative power to do justice to the desperate human situations with which he is dealing.

What we do get from South Africa, therefore—and what we get most frequently—is the journalistic fact parading outrageously as imaginative literature. We find here a type of fiction which exploits the ready-made plots of racial violence, social *apartheid*, interracial love affairs which are doomed from the beginning, without any attempt to transcend or transmute these given 'social facts' into artistically persuasive works of fiction. Thus a story like *The Situation* by Bloke Modisane relies mainly on the 'inside' information about the exciting underground life of the Johannesburg township of which the author happens to be in possession; and through the limited power of the documentary technique we are taken on a tour of the Johannesburg *shebeen*; we are offered glimpses of the motley company of thugs, pimps and their 'nice-time' girls; and we are made to feel the tension between rival gangs which is as gratuitous as the tension generated in a Western film by the presence of two fast draws in the same saloon; yet, even with the exploitation of the earthiest detail the story still flounders on a general lack of ideas; it collapses finally because both in its method and in its theme the story is a stereotype and the excitement is external— part and parcel of a dangerous social stratum—and does not come from the inner tension of creative talent confronting inert matter. At the end there is neither impact nor revelation but a kind of cessation. Yet without this power for so re-ordering experience, and for so transmuting the given social facts that we can detect an underlying moral imagination at work, it is difficult to see why we should give up the daily newspaper in favour of creative fiction. The newspapers would tell us just as much about life.

In an interesting essay called *The Function of Criticism*[2] Robert Langbaum ably states the case for creative literature; but in reading him I seemed to be reading a carefully inscribed charge-sheet against the kind of fiction I am describing. Mr. Langbaum writes:

> The imagination ... remains for us the faculty which accounts for literature as revelations, as a maker of values.

Quite obviously literature as 'revelation' or as a 'maker of values' is not likely to result from a type of writing which relies on the technique of *cinéma-verité*—a technique which consists largely in training the camera

[1] London, Faber & Faber, 1964.   [2] See 'The Yale Review', Winter, 1965.

long enough on the passing scene in the desperate hope that art may result by accident. It might very well be that the vitality of African writing in South Africa lies mainly in the area of non-fiction. Certainly the picture of the Sophiatown ghetto in Bloke Modisane's book *Blame Me On History*,[1] or passages in Ezekiel Mphahlele's autobiographical essay *Down Second Avenue*[2] are far superior to anything these writers have attempted in creative fiction.

Even the way Bloke Modisane structures the book shows a dedication to a superior form of realism which succeeds partly because the author is alive to the fact that reality itself is elusive to the process of Time as an orderly sequence of events. Thus the events narrated are in no way chronological; Modisane shuffles them about like a pack of cards, allowing only their emotional intensity to dictate their sequence in time. It seems to me a pity that Bloke Modisane has not exploited his potential talent for satire which he exhibited to advantage in his story *The Dignity of Begging*:[3]

> One of these days, when I am on my annual leave, I hope to write a book on begging, something like a treatise on the subject. It will be written with sensitivity and charm, brimful with sketches from life and profusely illustrated with coloured photographs, with easy-to-follow rules on the noblest and oldest occupation in the world.

Ezekiel Mphahlele has so far produced no profoundly moving work of fiction, but he differs from the other black South African writers in his preoccupations which, in his most recent fiction, reveal how keenly aware he is of the intractable nature of South African experience when it has to be contained within an artistic form; and this intractability has something to do both with the over-melodramatic nature of the political situation and the barrenness and infertile nature of tradition. It has always amazed me that bad writers should consider racial conflict a God-sent theme, when prudent writers know how resistant this theme has proved to be to any artistic purpose. This is not only true in Africa; American Negro fiction, with the exception of James Baldwin's *Go Tell it On the Mountain* and Ralph Ellison's *The Invisible Man*, has proved incapable of revealing half the depth and richness of Negro life as expressed by American Negro music, especially the blues. The main hope for Ezekiel Mphahlele as a writer is that he is aware of all these things, and latterly he has been moving in the direction of saying something positive about black experience in South Africa instead of writing, as many of our writers do, as though everything the blacks did in the country was a reaction to white oppression.

He had already begun to do this, of course, in some of his stories based on quirky Newclare characters, though these stories were often little more than sketches; and of course his small volume of collected stories 'The

[1] London, Thames and Hudson, 1963.
[2] London, Faber & Faber, 1959.
[3] In Rutherfoord, P. (ed.) 'Darkness and Light; an anthology of African Writing', London, Faith Press, 1958.

Living and Dead',[1] has some good examples of this type of fiction in *The Suitcase* and *He and the Cat*. However, it is in his most recent story published in the Johannesburg quarterly, *The Classic*, that Ezekiel Mphahlele has given the best account of his talent.[2]

Now the most remarkable thing about Africans—this is not always to their benefit—is hardly their conservatism; on the contrary, it is their ability to absorb alien influences and manners and to adapt them to their particular tradition. In a city like Johannesburg, for example, a study of the African languages as they are spoken today would reveal a great deal about this African willingness to borrow and to adapt foreign words and concepts, which are thereafter given a new dimension altogether. I am thinking of words like 'situation', which is a term of abuse for members of the African middle-class trying to 'situate' themselves above the masses. And so is *sitshuzimi*, which is an adaptation of the phrase 'Excuse me', also used in a satirical vein to refer to pretentious half-baked Africans trying to ape the ways of white folk by a repetitive use of similar phrases.

So far as I have been able to gather, from such evidence as I possess, what Ezekiel Mphahlele has been trying to do is reclaim some of these words from the African languages back into the English where they have their origin anyway; and simultaneously he exploits the new connotative element they have since acquired by their association with the African languages: in so doing he manages to give them a slightly ambivalent satirical content which they would otherwise not possess. Or he merely makes African idioms and speech rhythms stand behind his English, something which Nigerians do all the time. The re-arrangement of syntax, for instance, often achieves a comical effect similar to that arrived at by American Jewish writers, most notably Bernard Malamud. For instance, Africans in South Africa seem unable to think of a government as a faceless bureaucratic institution; they always seek to personify it before they can properly conceive it. Thus in Ezekiel Mphahlele's story an old woman rebukes a policeman who is only too ready to hide behind the vast nameless authority of the Government:

> 'Is this how you would like your mother or your wife to be treated, I mean your own mother?'
> 'I am doing the government's work.'
> Go and tell that government of yours that he is full of dung to send you to do such things. *Sies. Kgoboromente kgoboromente!* You and him can go to hell where you belong.'

This is as close as you can get to the quality of African speech in English transposition, and the effect of course is always slightly comical.

In his story *In Corner B* Ezekiel Mphahlele has gone further; he successfully exploits that vein of tragi-comedy which has been so fruitfully mined in African song and dance and in the rudimentary urban African theatre, but which has not, to my knowledge, been usefully tapped in

---

[1] Ibadan, Mbari, 1961.   [2] 'The Classic', Vol. One, No. 3, 1964.

African writing. By situating a number of episodes within the framework of an African funeral he also achieves a number of ironies. Firstly, he does this by juxtaposition; those who come to such funerals, still largely traditional, are often there to enjoy a ceremony which is not without some festive gaiety, as well as to mourn. The juxtaposition is one between the African's very profound sense of piety in the face of death as well as the well-known African tendency to turn sad religious occasions into moments not of self-abnegation but of sensual expression whose orgiastic force and redemptive lust are anti-Puritanical in spirit. Protracted as the traditional period of mourning is, in these African funerals, they have become notorious occasions for exploiting the hospitality of the bereaved family. They have also become happy hunting-grounds for sex-starved matrons and the iniquitous young, as well as helping to bring together numerous relatives from various parts of the country who use the funeral as an occasion for prosecuting familial matters. Thus during the mourning we see surreptitious groups of carousing drinkers 'drowning de sorry'; there is a family quarrel between rival cousins of the dead man over the right of disposing of the body; there is copulation in the yard between a young couple who quietly rejoin the singing after the brief release of sexual tension, a need which is just as pressing, if not more so, than the need to express grief.

> 'Shh!' The senior uncle of the dead man cut in to try to keep the peace. And he was firm. 'What do you want to turn this house into? There is a widow in there in grief and here you are, you haven't got what the English call respection. Do you want all the people around to laugh at us, think little of us? All of us bury our quarrels when we come together to weep over a dear one who has left; what nawsons is this?'

In the past what had always put me off Ezekiel Mphahlele's writing was a certain dullness of tone, much like the ponderous speech of a dull-witted person so that it was often difficult to pursue the story to its ending. The gems were often embedded in a thick mud of cliché and lustreless writing: a succession of simple clauses, for instance, linked together by semi-colons. The texture of the prose had the feel and look of sweaty labour much like the stains of honest sweat on the cloth-cap of the toiling proletariat. For instance, in order to expose the inner thoughts of his characters, Mphahlele would often reflect in this clumsy manner:

> Now she was ill. She was about to have a baby; a third baby. And with nothing to take home for the last two months, his savings running out, he felt something must be done. Not anything that would get him into jail. No, not that . . .

And so it would go on. Somewhere along the line the monologue of his hero becomes merged with that of the author. The danger with this kind of writing is that it can often become a substitute for action in the story, or a substitute for a more ingenious solution to the problem of flashbacks. At his slowest it contributed to a considerable amount of dullness in

225

Mphahlele's writing. Yet some of these problems of style were clearly attributable to external causes: the strain of maintaining an equilibrium in a dangerously melodramatic situation. If one went too far the other way in an effort to match with language the violence of the streets, the prose became strained, brittle and frayed; so that the flatness in Mphahlele's writing was sometimes due to an honourable attempt to remain 'cool under fire'. It seems to me that in the latest work Mphahlele's writing has become tighter, more solid and assured as he acquires a more properly synthesised vocabulary to deal with the stresses of South African life. He has achieved greater authority and a better grip on his own particular idiom: the result is a happier fluency of tone.

Alex la Guma, the Cape coloured writer, most assuredly deserves wider notice abroad for his novella *A Walk in the Night*[1]. Paradoxically, of all the black writers who have suffered the most at the hands of the South African Government, La Guma has been longest on the receiving end. He was one of the defendants in the protracted Treason Trial; he has been banned from attending gatherings of any kind and detained in prison several times. He is now under house arrest in Capetown; his writings cannot, of course, be published or quoted in the country. This means he has been virtually denied the right to earn a living, as he has always done, through journalism.

Alex la Guma tills the same *apartheid* plot which the other writers have so exhaustively worked up, but what distinguishes him as a true novelist is his enthusiasm for life as it is lived. He has the artist's eye for the interesting detail; his stories and novels are sagging under the weight of real people waging a bloody contest with the forces of oppression; and credibly they celebrate their few moments of victory in sex, cheap Cape wine and stupid fights. The rooms they inhabit smell of decay, urine and sweat; they share them with 'roaches, fleas, bugs, lice'. Their only triumph is that they are human—superlatively human; and this is their sole claim upon our imagination.

Another quality of La Guma as a writer is the suggestive power of his prose. *A Glass of Wine*,[2] for instance, is a superbly observed story with an appropriate dialogue that relies on the speech idioms of the Cape Malay folk. The boy who was 'tall and young and thin as a billiard cue' is really white though he comes to the *shebeen* to visit one of the coloured girls. As for the girl, instantly she comes to life before us as La Guma discreetly observes her: 'She did not look at the boy, but knew that he was there, and looking at him in turn I could see the deep flush of his own face and the gentle lowering of the eyelids as he watched her.' There is marvellous irony here which is beautifully sustained, when one of the drunks, unaware that the boy is really white, gently mocks the young couple: 'With such love, blushing and all, these two must marry.'

---

[1] Ibadan, Mbari, 1962.
[2] In 'Quartet; New voices from South Africa', Rive, R. (ed.) London, Heinemann Educational Books, 1965.

At the end of the story there is revelation, not only of the tragedy of the young lovers who cannot marry, but of the absurdity of life itself.

> 'You and your wedding,' I told him as we went up the street. 'You know that white boy can't marry the girl, even though he may love her. It isn't allowed.'
> 'Jesus,' Arthur said in the dark. 'Jesus. What the hell.'

In *A Walk in the Night* La Guma follows the progress of Michael Adonis, a coloured boy thrown out of his factory job for talking back to the white foreman; and a supporting cast of thugs, derelicts, spivs, neurotic cops 'doomed for a certain term to walk the night'. By the end of this night Adonis has killed under an impulse a harmless old man; a neurotic police-man has shot a small-time thug; a penniless man has been 'rolled' for money; but incontestably life has also been celebrated in the cheap bars, speakeasies and wretched slumhouses along the Harlem-like ghetto of Cape Town's District Six. This impressive short work has distinct Dostoev-skian undertones, which, I hope, is not too large a claim to make for it. It is inexcusable that European and American publishers who are in such indecent haste to put into print any mediocre talent from Africa have ignored this novel.

There are a few other black South African writers like Arthur Maimane, Casey Motsisi, Dugmore Boeti, Harry Mashabela, Can Themba, whom I have not mentioned, though some of them write much abler prose than many writers on the continent . This is because the work of these writers has been largely in the area of non-fiction or because they have produced only one or two short stories upon which it is impossible to make an esti-mation of their talent. Of these Can Themba has perhaps the liveliest mind and the best command of the English language; but apart from his recent story published in 'Modern Stories from Africa'[1] he has been annoyingly shiftless, throwing off cheap potboilers when magazines demanded them. Casey Motsisi has perhaps our wiliest satirical talent in South Africa but his success so far has been in the area of sketches which owe a great deal in inspiration to Langston Hughes' *Simple Speaks His Mind*. I have seen only one story by Dugmore Boeti,[2] which was extraordinarily witty, power-ful and ironical, if also brutal; one would like to see more writing by him. It also had the tough pitiless nerve which one has come to associate with the sensibility of modern literature.

[1] Komey, E. A. and Mphahlele, E. (eds.), London, Faber & Faber, 1964.
[2] *The Last Leg*, in 'The Classic', Johannesburg, Vol. One, No. 2, 1963.

The African Personality in the African Novel

ROBERT W. JULY

During the past few years much has been said, both inside and outside Africa, about *négritude* and the African personality. The discussion has been carried on in a variety of ways—by anthropologists and sociologists concerned with the structure of a changing African society, by African statesmen intent on rallying their people behind the new independence movements, by journalists and political commentators, and by artists and writers in Africa seeking new means of expression to match a new social order. Though the artistic and literary world has been increasingly active in pursuing the debate—witness the voluminous proceedings of the two congresses of African artists and writers sponsored by *Présence Africaine* in 1956 and 1959—very little attention has thus far been given to the evidence of an African personality as presented through literary and artistic works. Yet these offer a great deal, not only in the form of sociological or political reporting, but in the perceptive insights which art can sometimes provide where more analytical methods fail.

To illustrate the richness of this source of information, let us examine four novels which have appeared in Africa within the recent past, and which are concerned with exploring the quality of the contemporary African mind and how it operates.[1] Each work presents a major character and a number of lesser figures whose lives are made by the world they live in, and whom we can see as authentic modern Africans, presenting the rich detail of internal mental stress, external physical action, and environmental force whose tensions balance to form these particular African personalities. Two of these novels come from Nigeria—*Jagua Nana* by Cyprian Ekwensi, and *Blade Among the Boys* by Onuora Nzekwu. The third, more strictly a long short story, is *A Walk in the Night* by the South African writer, Alex La Guma. The fourth, *L'Aventure Ambiguë*, is by the Senegalese writer and public servant, Cheikh Amidou Kane. What kind of person emerges?

A Walk in the Night presents a few hours of one day in an African district of Capetown. A young African, Michael Adonis, has just lost his job because he was 'cheeky' to his white foreman. He roams the neighbourhood, meeting acquaintances with whom he bitterly discusses his plight. He soon gets drunk on cheap wine, returns to his lodging where he unpremeditatedly and senselessly kills a neighbour, an old Irishman dying of alcoholism. By

[1] *A Walk in the Night*, by Alex La Guma, Ibadan, Mbari, 1962.
Jagua Nana, by Cyprian Ekwensi, London, Hutchinson, 1961.
Blade among the Boys, by Onuora Nzekwu, London, Hutchinson, 1962.
L'Aventure Ambiguë, by Cheikh Amidou Kane, Paris, Julliard, 1961.

chance Adonis escapes detection and all suspicion falls on Willieboy, a footloose young drifter, unemployed and with a record of petty crime. Willieboy is hunted down and killed in the street by the police. Michael at the same moment is to embark on a criminal career by participating in a robbery.

These are the bare bones of a story on which is built a picture of such vividness and verisimilitude that one can almost taste and smell the air, the streets, the buildings against which the characters move in sure and full three-dimensional reality. The world of these Africans is an urban slum —narrow garbage-filled streets, grimy tenements with vestibules smelling of urine, dark stairs leading to narrow corridors and eventually to cheerless rooms where rats and roaches compete with the human inhabitants for possession. They eat their meals in greasy cafés that smell of rancid oil, of sweat, of stale smoke. They seek their recreation gambling in clandestine pool halls which exist only through police corruption, and they find some escape from their sordid meaningless lives in the local pub where cheap wine offers a momentary false courage against the forces which are grinding them down to hopeless dreary extinction. Bit by bit the author adds to the picture. Here a shabby store window containing 'rows of guitars, banjoes, mandolins, the displayed gramophone parts, guitar picks, strings, electric irons, plugs, jews'-harps, adaptors, celluloid dolls all the way from Japan, and the pictures of angels and Christ with a crown of thorns and drops of blood like lipstick marks on his pink forehead.' Down the street the entrance to a tenement where a row of dustbins 'exhaled the smell of rotten fruit, stale food, stagnant water and general decay', while 'a cat, the colour of dish-water', tried to paw 'the remains of a fishhead from one of the bins'. Inside 'the staircase was worn and blackened, the old oak banister loose and scarred. Naked bulbs wherever the light sockets were in working order cast a pallid glare over parts of the interior, lighting up the big patches of damp and mildew, and the maps of denuded sections on the walls. . . . From each landing a dim corridor lined with doors tunnelled towards a latrine that stood like a sentry box at its end, the floor in front of it soggy with spilled water', while in the air was the smell of 'ancient cooking, urine, damp-rot and stale tobacco'.

And what of the people living in this slum? There are the 'derelicts, bums, domestic workers, in-town-from-the-country folk, working people, taxi-drivers, and the rest of the mould that accumulated on the fringe of the underworld: loiterers, prostitutes, *fah-fee* numbers runners, petty gang-sters, drab and frayed-looking thugs', the gangsters at once identifiable by their 'lightweight tropical suits with pegged trousers and gaudy neckties, yellowish, depraved faces and thick hair shiny with brilliantine'. Despite the plethora of apparently exotic types, it is the ordinary people who form the majority of this population—'the worn, brutalised, wasted, slum-scratched faces of the poor', hardworking, ignorant, little understanding their losing fight for existence against forces they cannot control. Typical is the stevedore who 'worked like hell in the docks' all day only to come

229

home to his dingy, dirty, crowded room occupied by himself, his wife, and their five children.

> He wore a singlet and a pair of old corduroys shiny with wear, and there was coal dust in the grooves where the furry cotton had not been worn away. He had an air of harassment about him, of too hard work and unpaid bills and sour babies. . . . His wife had a few minutes earlier announced that she was once more pregnant and he was trying to decide whether it was good news or bad.

The drabness and hopelessness of such lives drove many to seek romantic fulfilment in criminal unsettled lives which, if they inevitably ended in tragedy and futility, at least gave a momentary illusion of success and a small measure of personal distinction. Thus we have the lookout for a bawdy house, 'an old decrepit ghost of a man . . . [who] nursed a sort of pride in his position . . . which raised him a dubious degree out of the morass into which the dependent poor had been trodden'.

Thus too, Willieboy, who is perhaps the author's major protagonist.

> Willieboy was young and dark and wore his kinky hair brushed into a point above his forehead. He wore a . . . crucifix around his neck, more as a flamboyant decoration than as an act of religious devotion. He had . . . an air of nonchalance, like the outward visible sign of his distorted pride in the terms he had served in a reformatory and once in prison for assault. . . . He was also aware of his inferiority. All his youthful life he had cherished dreams of becoming a big shot. He had seen others rise to some sort of power in the confined underworld of this district and found himself left behind. . . . He had affected a slouch, wore gaudy shirts and peg-bottomed trousers, brushed his hair into a flamboyant peak. He had been thinking of piercing one ear and decorating it with a gold ring. But even with these things he continued to remain something less than nondescript, part of the blurred face of the crowd, inconspicuous as a smudge on a grimy wall.

This then is the backdrop and these the people. We can see how their world acted upon them and what their reaction was. But how self-conscious are they, how aware of their predicament? What motivation, if any, stirs them to action? There appears to be very little—a narrow range from total unawareness to adolescent dreams. At one extreme is the unselfconscious amorality of the gangsters, implicit in their actions and, of course, never articulated. The middle ground is occupied by the ordinary citizen—decent, hard working, vaguely aware that his life lacks something but unable to understand what it is and how to go about getting it. The younger people, hopelessly unable as they are to deal with their lives and encumbered with values which only a lunatic might find of service, at least do have some conscious standards and the warped courage to live by them. Michael Adonis, freshly out of a job, full of bitter self-pity, gets drunk, sees himself as the romantic hero of the escapist Westerns which are his constant emotional diet—'Okay, trouble-shooter. You're a mighty tough *hombre*.

230

Fastest man in Tucson'—kills a man. With difficulty he overcomes an urge to confess, to discuss all the details, an urge born not of remorse or a sense of wrong, but from a desire to achieve status. In the end he sinks into a life of crime. Willieboy lives by similar values and if they lead him to a violent end it is not so much because he doubts them as because he is less well equipped to survive. Only one person in the whole cast of characters seems able to see the futility of this way of life. And he is cast in a minor role as Joe, a nondescript homeless beggar, a half-insane boy who yet has some vision of human dignity. Vainly begging Adonis to stay clear of criminal entanglements, his pitiful cry goes unheeded, 'Jesus, isn't we all people?'

The scene is Capetown, South Africa, the people African, but where is the African personality? The conditions we see, the actions and motives of the characters could fit with equal authority a city slum in Europe or America. Chicago, St. Louis, New York, London. Willieboy with his hollow bravado is at once reminiscent of young Studs Lonigan, similarly undernourished physically and psychically, moving across the urban squalor and meanness of South Side Chicago with a swagger which never quite makes up for the sense of inadequacy and ultimate failure. East Harlem in New York City today contains blocks which are at once recognisable in La Guma's powerful narrative. The similarity between Harlem and Cape-town, however, does not result from the fact that they are both Negro quarters, but that they are both city slums. People living in crowded tene-ments amidst dirt and disease, lacking the means for a normal family life with its security, its childhood pleasures and adult satisfactions, constantly brushing against the brutalised amorality of criminals, develop character-istics and attitudes of identifiable similarity. These people are authentic Africans without question, but they belong to the new Africa of the indus-trial city. If none of the ways of tribal Africa shows through, it may be because consciously or otherwise they have left that world far behind. Joe, the strange young drifter, puts it best when he describes how his father deserted his family, forcing his mother to sell her few things and go back to live with his grandmother in the country. 'Me, I ran away when I heard they were going . . . I wasn't going to the outside. To the country. Man, that would be the same like running away . . . . My old man, he ran away. I didn't want to run, too.'

Jagua Nana provides another view of the new urbanised African. The details are different: Lagos is not Capetown and the Nigerian is not to be confused with the South African, but the essential identity is unmistakable. Both display the African city with its way of life, its physical appearance and its values so different from those of the traditional village. Both tell the story of how these forces have shaped the African city dweller, making him in turn equally different from his country cousin. The plot of this novel need not detain us; it is the characters who interest us as they already exist when we first encounter them: vibrant, bawdy, optimistic, unmoral, opportunistic, living from day to day in the noisy, crowded, yeasty, lusty West African city of Lagos where the heat and the dampness never seem to deprive the Nigerian of his energy and his enthusiasm for living.

Jagua Nana might be called an amateur prostitute, not in the sense of lacking skill or eschewing remuneration, but in the sense of loving her work. Physically impressive, she found as a girl that village life was much too restrictive to one of her talents and enthusiasm and, like many others similarly affected, came to Lagos to live. There she carries on a bewildering succession of affairs, living on the favours of the men she sleeps with, guided by a code of ethics derived from the *Tropicana*, a nightclub which serves as her base of operations and source of spiritual refreshment. This is the world of the fast sports car, the tired business man, the crooked politician, the hoodlum, and packaged sex. The girls wear undersize dresses designed to make men ogle, their faces are masked with powder, pencil, and lipstick, their hair is combed straight and heavily oiled, and their feet are clad in high-heeled sandals through which can be seen the tips of lacquered nails. And Jagua is always the best of the lot. 'She lowered the neckline of her sleeveless blouses and raised the heels of her shoes. She did her hair in the Jagua mop, wore ear-rings that really rang bells, as she walked with deliberately swinging hips.' This is the standard for the Lagos demi-monde and possible for others as well. When Jagua is about to enter the *Tropicana* on one occasion, she is examined with approval by a woman selling cooked yams near the entrance, who bursts out, 'Heh! . . . One day ah will ride motor car and wear fine fine cloth.'

Others from this boisterous world attract our attention and hold our interest. There is Uncle Taiwo, the indefatigable politican, who drives an enormous Pontiac and pursues his career of misleading the voters and misappropriating his party's funds to his destiny of death in the streets, a twisted swollen corpse in a muddy gutter. There is Freddie who combines infatuation for Jagua with a fondness for the dignified westernised respectability of a British Council lecture, who studies law in England as a means to wealth, power, and esteem, but who also falls victim to the corruption and violence of Lagos politics. There is Dennis, a young hoodlum, and his gang who live their violent lives briefly but with no sense of regret that they might have had something better. There are others, anonymous but no less sharply defined:

> The influential men of Lagos. Private business men . . . dabblers in party politics . . . men in their early fifties, and what they lost in youthful virility and attractiveness they made up by lavishing their money on women like Jagua Nana. . . . Jagua saw them now as with white collars off they struck a different mood from the British Council: the 'expatriate' bank managers, the oil men and shipping agents, the brewers of beer and pumpers out of swamp water, the builders of Maternity Block, the healers of the flesh. German, English, Dutch, American, Nigerian, Ghanaian, they were all here.

232

Like Jagua, most of the Africans in Lagos have come from small villages, driven to the city by boredom, ambition, or circumstance. Like her, they occasionally return home either actually or figuratively. Jagua may be firmly attached to city ways but she has brought with her a heritage of beliefs and attitudes which disappear slowly. She is not above belief in witchcraft and juju, particularly where affairs of the heart are concerned. Neither, for that matter, is the ostensibly better-educated Freddie. He broods over his affair with Jagua and wonders at her powers.

> Could it really be . . . that Jagua was resorting to black magic to torture him? Was she a witch with black powers over his soul? Only that morning he had been telling the pupils at the College that there was no such thing as black magic or witchery, only the imagination. Scientific facts, he held, could be demonstrated; but these extra-sensory qualities depended too much on vague circumstances and conditions.

But ultimately these are city people wedded to city ways and guided by the values that rule the city. 'Like Freddie she was an Ibo from Eastern Nigeria, but when she spoke to him she always used pidgin English, because living in Lagos City they did not want too many embarrassing reminders of clan or custom. They and many others were practically strangers in a town where all came to make fast money by faster means, and greedily to seek positions that yielded even more money.' In the end Jagua goes home to her village to live, but this is the weakest part of the book and remains unconvincing. More likely, she, 'like many women who came to Lagos [was] imprisoned, entangled in the city, unable to extricate herself from its clutches. The lowest and the most degraded standards of living were to her preferable to a quiet and dignified life in her own home where she would not be "free".' And so with greed and lust comes also freedom for the individual to pattern his life as he himself may wish, not according to outdated customs and superstitions. The fact that some might use this freedom unwisely need not deter others from achieving a more meaningful emancipation.

The world of Jagua Nana is an authentic part of the African city, but it is only one part. At the same time Lagos is only one part of Nigeria. Beyond the city, for all its importance, its growth and its foreshadowing of the future, lies the country where the vast majority of the people of Africa still live under conditions far removed from what is to be found in the industrial, urban centres. If we are to understand the full dimension of the African personality, we must look into these villages where Onuora Nzekwu has set most of the scene for his novel, *Blade Among the Boys*. This is an interesting story which says much about the face of Africa. In the first place it deals with the African's deep sense of religion: a universal and timeless quality of traditional African society. Secondly, it poses the power of traditional African values and practices against Western 'enlight-

233

enment', and concludes that the individual who chooses the latter and flouts the former does so at his peril.

The novel deals with the fortunes of a young Ibo, Patrick Ikenga. As a boy, Patrick is reared on a strict diet of Roman Catholic doctrine and practice and, not surprisingly, he early harbours ambitions of becoming a priest. His father dies when Patrick is only eleven years old and his mother brings him back to live in the village of his paternal uncle. The rest of the novel is concerned with the struggle between Christianity and paganism for Patrick's allegiance. Powerful psychological and material forces are brought to bear by both sides. The Church offers education—the necessary ingredient for worldly success—while standing for progressive ideas and modern thought. But belief in the traditional religious hierarchy of spirits and ancestors is deep-seated, and life in a village can be markedly uncomfortable for the non-conformist who makes light of time-honoured custom, and refuses to partake in accepted social and religious practice. Patrick displays unusual courage in finally turning his back on the village and entering a seminary to prepare for the priesthood. In the end, however, he is discovered to have committed adultery and is dismissed from the seminary.

Throughout this work the impact of modern Western ideas and standards as exemplified by the Catholic faith is blurred and softened by the virility of the traditional beliefs and customs. Patrick's father and mother are devout and active Christians. They are deeply involved in the affairs of their local parish, and they see to it that Patrick is early introduced to rigorous religious indoctrination so that by successive stages baptism is followed by first communion, regular church attendance, and service as an altar boy. Patrick's initially expressed desire to become a priest causes them no surprise or concern. But,

> had the priests gone behind the scenes they would have discovered ... the numerous charms John Ikenga hid behind photographs hanging on the walls. ... His was a different brand of Christianity ... that accommodated ... principles and practices of his tribal religion. For one thing, he never could drop the primary aim of tribal worship: to reinforce life by means of prayers, sacrifices and sympathetic magic. ... He was certain that some envious ones were jealous ... and were working magic on him. He ... believed that the Church did not understand such matters and could not therefore give effective counter-measures. ... To protect himself and his family he resorted to magic. ... He consulted fortune-tellers, made and wore charms and even sponsored sacrifices to placate his tribal gods and his ancestral spirits.

As for Patrick's mother, his decision in favour of the priesthood eventually destroys her, despite her genuine devotion and loyalty to the Church. She pleads with him with growing desperation to meet his obligations to his family. 'I am trying to save you from committing the worst crime anyone can commit in Ado—that of letting one's family fold up as if there is no one to keep it going. . . . I want John Ikenga's family to continue. It must continue. . . . I need a son to continue the work of reproduction in the family.' When he refuses, she renounces him as her son and goes home to die.

Other pressures brought to bear on Patrick to make him conform to traditional ways give us further insight into the mind of the Ibo villager. Patrick is the ward of his uncle, Ononye, who supports him and pays for his schooling, and who will suffer no heretical Christian doctrine in his family. When Patrick falls ill with suspected malaria, Ononye forbids any utilisation of Western medicine. The boy is given hot baths and a concoction of herbs to drink. 'His neck, wrists and waist were ringed round with charms which would keep witches, evil men and evil spirits from interfering with the efficacy of the treatment he received. A series of sacrifices, seeking the aid of his ancestral spirits in his recovery and warding off evil spirits . . . were offered.' Some relatives, to be sure, suggest hospitalisation, but their advice lacks conviction for they basically mistrust Western medical practice. 'Their desire to demonstrate that they belonged to the new generation of literate gentlemen had made them attend the hospitals . . . in which they themselves had little faith, for the old order still had a firm grip on them.'

Patrick recovers and goes on to spend his adolescence and early manhood living in the traditional African world, learning its practices and absorbing its values. At the same time he continues his mission-school education for, as his uncle says, 'Literacy is the hallmark of a gentleman these days. . . . The teaching of reading, writing and arithmetic . . . we have now learned to value as the passport to future wealth and power.' Nonetheless, guided by his uncle's careful tutelage, he participates in the activities of appropriate age-groups in his lineage, attends religious ceremonies involving ritual purification and sacrifices to the ancestors, listens to detailed descriptions of the ways of spirits and the best means for detecting and combating witchcraft, is inducted into a masquerade cult, and on achieving adulthood begins building a large house in his home village. Through tribal custom it has long since been decided that he is to succeed to the headship of his patrilineal lineage and his training has therefore been unusually thorough. Though still harbouring a latent allegiance to the Church, Patrick comes to accept much of the traditional teaching. He abandons thoughts of the priesthood, and begins to think about marriage, possibly with the girl to whom he had been betrothed as a child. During the several years he had spent away from home working in the railroad system, he dealt heavily in bribery as a means for meeting the burdensome but proper levies on his resources made by his people in the village. 'For in times of stress, and in his old age, he would fall back on the lineage whose bounden duty it would then be to minister unto his needs, the degree of ministration being determined by his contribution to their well-being now that he had the means to do so.' After a brief exposure to the free-thinking ways of Lagos, he explains his philosophy and his reasons for abandoning Christianity and returning to his traditional faith,

235

'You realise . . . how enjoyable it is to be free. Gradually you stop going to church. . . . Simultaneously, you find that the traditional elements are gone too from your life, though not as distantly as the Christian ones. . . . Traditional religion, by virtue of its hold on the society in which you live, because it permeates all phases of the life of that society, and offers an explanation and a solution to the problems which confront you daily, appeals to you and attracts you to itself . . . You find it easier to go back to traditional religion whose agents have not antagonised you the way the Christian missionaries have done. Traditional worship, in view of your nearness to nature, suits you. For even on sorrowful occasions it consists of ritual feasts held in a lively atmosphere which conjures up within you the right emotional feelings.'

Somewhat inexplicably and unconvincingly, Patrick ultimately revives his plans for the priesthood and breaks with his family and lineage. They are outraged by his heresy. Not only is he making a mockery of their religious faith and way of life, but he is threatening the very existence of the family—the ancestors and the living as well as the yet unborn. Our children, observes Ononye, 'are the links that will carry our traditions, which distinguish us from all other peoples, to future generations. If . . . they fail to take part in our rituals, time will come when we can no longer identify one man from another. And if, as we do believe, the dead do see and have power, I will be one of those who will rise from the dead to take revenge on those who let our traditions die away.' Patrick is ostracised by his family and left to defend himself as best he can against the inevitable wrath of the gods and ancestral spirits. The girl to whom he was pledged years earlier at the time of her birth manages to administer a love potion to him and shortly thereafter he seduces her. When his action is discovered, his clerical ambitions are brought to an abrupt end. Who knows what caused his downfall? Was it lust or was it magic? As Patrick himself observed on another occasion concerning another mystery, 'Looks like what a charm alone can accomplish. Or could it be mere coincidence?'

Religion, the ancient virtues, and modernity are themes which have been brought together eloquently by Cheikh Kane in *L'Aventure Ambiguë*. Here is another view of Africa which extols the simple traditional way of life, emphasises the fundamental religiousness of the African people, and questions the validity of modern western culture. The conclusion is inescapable. If the world is to be saved, it can only be done by cleaving to the basic verities revealed through love of God, and it is Africa and not the West which has within it the power of salvation.

Samba Diallo is a young nephew of the chief of the Diallobé of Senegal, and on him the future leadership of the tribe appears likely to fall. He is given the most careful of religious instruction by his old and wise Muslim religious teacher, and is then sent off to France to gain a western education, for the tribe is not prospering—its numbers are decreasing, its people are

236

sickly, and its properties are in disrepair. After some years at the university in Paris, he returns to his people only to find that he can no longer reach them: he has become too Westernised. Finally, in effect, he kills himself.

The individuals in the book are types rather than flesh-and-blood characters, symbols for a series of attitudes which reflect the African view of the world. There is the old religious teacher who embodies the belief that only ceaseless asceticism and total absorption with the word of God can lead to a life of the highest attainment. Frail, and emaciated from long years of fasting, his body is as feeble as his home and property are run down. But his spirit is bright with the love of God.

> In many ways the master was a formidable man. His life was concerned with two occupations: cultivation of the spirit and the soil. To his fields he devoted the strictest minimum of his time and asked nothing more of the soil but what was needed for the barest nourishment for him and his family. . . . The rest of his time was given over to study, to meditation, to prayer and to the formation of the young people entrusted to his charge. . . . The master believed deeply that the love of God was not compatible with human pride. . . . Pride means a sense of superiority, but faith is above all humility, if not humiliation. The master thought that man had no reason to exalt himself except precisely in the adoration of God.

He was passionately serious and never laughed, at least not outwardly. But occasionally at prayer he found himself amused by the rheumatic misery of his joints which no longer moved where and how he wanted them to. 'Was this impious? "Perhaps it is some evil vanity which fills me thus." He thought for a minute. "No . . . my laughter is innocent. I laugh because my old friend jokes about his creaking joints. But his will is better than ever. Even when he can't move, he will keep trying, and he will continue to pray. I love him well." '

The old master is afraid that the chief of the tribe is going to yield to the desires of the people to send their best young men to France for training and education. His apprehension is shared by Samba Diallo's father who, like the master, can see no point to a life of material prosperity if it lacks spiritual fulfilment. And Samba's father feels that the West has lost sight of this ultimate objective in its pursuit of materialism. Work and its fruits need justification through God.

> If a man believes in God, the time he takes from prayer for work is still prayer. Indeed, it is a very beautiful prayer. . . . But if a life is not justified in God . . . it is in this case not a pious work. It is only a life, no more than what it appears to be. . . . The West is in the process of overturning these simple truths. It began, timidly, by putting God in quotation marks. Then, two centuries later, having gained more assurance, it decreed, "God is dead". On that day began the era of frenzied work. Nietzsche is contemporary with the industrial revolution. God was no longer available as a measure and justification. . . . After the death of God

comes the death of man. . . . Life and work are no longer in tune
. . . . Formerly, the work of one life could only sustain a single
life. . . . But now the West is on the point of being able to do without man as a producer of work. . . . And to the extent that work
transcends human life, man ceases to be its ultimate goal. Man
has never been so unhappy as in this moment when he has
accumulated so much. Nowhere are these things more scorned
than where they have been most accumulated. Thus the history of
the West seems to reveal the poverty of the doctrine that man is an
end in himself. Human happiness requires belief in the existence
of God.

But the problem of survival for the Diallobé still remains unresolved,
and the chief, however sympathetic he may be with the view that God must
be served, still has the responsibility for the welfare of his people. They
want to learn how better to build their houses, to care for their children,
to increase their holdings, and gain the strength to re-establish their independence from foreign domination. These things can only be learned
through western education, but is this to the ultimate advantage of the
people? ' "If I tell them to go to the new school, they will go in mass. They
will learn all the methods of building which we do not know. But in learning they will also forget. Will what they learn be worth what they forget?" '
The master has no doubt; in his school they learn about God and forget
about man. Another voice is heard, ' "Give them their chance, my brother.
If you don't, I assure you there will soon be no more people in the
country." ' It is the sister of the chief, the dowager princess whose practical
energy and wisdom have long directed the affairs of the tribe through the
nominal authority of her brother. Imposing in her full blue robes and the
white veil wound voluminously about her head and neck, she is the essence
of Fulani nobility and only her Muslim faith has ever succeeded in taming
the imperiousness of her spirit. She goes on to point out that their royal
grandfather and his warriors had been defeated by the foreigners a hundred
years earlier. To defeat them in turn, ' "it is necessary to go and learn from
them the art of conquest without justification. . . . The struggle has not yet
ended. The foreigners' school is the new form of the war which we wage
against those who came here, and we must send our élite to it, and eventually all of our people." '
Samba Diallo thus becomes the instrument for reconciling the conflicting
views of the master and the dowager princess, and in his success or failure
lies personal survival and perhaps the salvation of his people. Certainly as
he sets out on his journey he is much of the same opinion as his father and
his master teacher. Under the master's guidance he has become a serious
devoted Muslim, deeply involved in study of his texts, in prayer, in fasting,
in mendicancy. He lives close to the soil and to God, and he finds this life
rewarding. As his studies in France proceed, he gradually masters Western
thought and culture. The process is an exhilarating intellectual adventure,
but with it comes growing doubt as to the essential wisdom of Western
238

values, and fear that he personally may lose touch with the truths he had learned during his childhood years. He still feels himself in close touch with nature. ' "The greatest dignity to which I still aspire today is to be her faithful son. I dare not fight her for I am part of her. Never do I seek nourishment from her breast without first asking humble pardon. I cannot cut down a tree and use its timber without begging its brotherly forgiveness." '

Still, in Paris he feels strangely void, like the city which, for all its crowded busy streets, gives the impression of emptiness and lifelessness. Perhaps it is because Western culture has developed an artificial world which has buried nature and cut itself off from the primal source of life. Back home in Africa ' "the world was like my father's house: everything was revealed in its essence as if nothing could exist except through my experience. The world was not silent and sterile. It was alive. It was aggressive. . . . Here . . . the world is silent and I no longer vibrate. I am like a burst balloon, like a dead musical instrument. I have the impression that nothing touches me any more." '

The West may feel that it has much to teach the rest of the world, and some Africans may agree. To Samba Diallo this is a mistake. The West is different, not because the fundamental nature of its people is different, but because it has surrounded itself with artificiality. Those Africans who feel strangely uncomfortable while living in the West need not ascribe this sensation to the fact that they are not needed by the West.

> On the contrary, this feeling establishes our necessity and points up the urgency of our task which is to clear away the rubbish and excavate nature. This is a noble task. If we allow ourselves to be convinced that all we need is to acquire the West's mastery of the material world, we will fail. For the West has become a world of things, not people. In order to move from place to place, a vehicle is needed; walking is no longer sufficient. For eating, iron utensils are required; the fingers will not serve. Flesh and blood have disappeared.
>
> With the same action the West colonised us and gained mastery over the material world. If we do not make the West aware of the difference which separates us from this phenomenon, we will not be worth any more than it is, and we will never learn to master it. And our defeat would be the end of the last human being on this earth.

Samba Diallo sees Africa's destiny with clarity but at the same time he has become unable to play a personal rôle in carrying it out. ' "I am not clearly of the Diallobé, facing a clearly defined West, and appreciating with a cool head what I can take and what I must leave as counterpart. I have become both. I am not a clear head deciding between two parts of a choice. I am a single strange nature, in distress at not being two." ' And so, repelled by western culture but trapped by its teaching, wanting to return to the life of simple piety he once lived but unable to reach it, he returns home. He

239

has learned how to teach his people to rebuild the houses they live in but he has forgotten how to live.

These four works present widely different aspects of the African personality, and in their very variety give some indication of the complexity of a vast continent and the differences that exist among the many people who dwell there. Consequently, generalities are risky; yet there seem to be certain qualities shared by the characters in these novels, as well as common reactions to forces in the world around them, which may constitute the essentials of the unique personality which many Africans insist is theirs. Alternatively, as other Africans maintain, these may simply be human beings acting characteristically in situations which could be, and are, reproduced daily in other parts of the world.

Let us look first at the backdrop. Here, one is struck immediately in all these works by the enormous influence which the outside world appears to have exerted on the traditional way of African life wherever contact has been made. More than any other continent, Africa had been isolated and inward-looking over many hundreds of years, but when outside influences came, their impact was far-reaching and their acceptance enthusiastic. For historical reasons these influences have varied widely from place to place. Thus in the South Africa of *A Walk in the Night*, the Westernisation of background and personality is virtually complete—the Capetown slums and their population are indistinguishable from what might be found in any industrialised city the world over. Even the race issue does not seem to be as fundamental as the struggle of human beings against the forces of poverty, ignorance, and psychic starvation.

Poised against the total Westernisation of the South African city, the Ibo village of *Blade Among the Boys* appears at first to have succeeded in its resistance to outside ways. Yet, despite the self-belief and self-satisfaction of traditional Ibo life, new ideas from the outside are gaining acceptance. Patrick Ikenga's uncle may belong to the old school but he sees the value of a Western education. Patrick himself is already profoundly affected by his mission training and his experience with urban living. His destruction comes not so much from personal shortcomings as from his inability to reconcile the old Africa with the West, and one is left at the end with the conviction that, though Patrick has failed, in welcoming ideas from the outside he has displayed a foresight superior to that of his elders.

As for the mystics of Cheikh Kane's tale, they are at least as much a product of Muslim ethics and metaphysics as of the traditional tribal way of life, while the pessimism and hostility displayed towards Western values reflects attitudes not entirely foreign to European existentialist thought. Finally, it is the modern Westernised Lagos of *Jagua Nana* which is the natural habitat of the novel's characters, and they cheerfully accept its perils and corruptions in return for the excitement, the novelty and the stimulation of taking part in the birth of a new Africa.

Though it is clear that outside forces have profoundly affected the African and his world, commanding his acceptance of alien ways, it does not mean that he has absorbed foreign ideas uncritically or turned his back on his own culture and traditions. The greater has been the influence from Europe, the more the African has felt compelled to reassert his own values. Onuora Nzekwu sets forth in precise detail the tough resilience of an ancient well-tried way of life with its ordered world and its tested solutions to human situations and needs. Patrick Ikenga's difficulty arises precisely from the fact that he can see the value of the traditional customs as well as the western concepts which he has come to respect and to need. Cheikh Kane goes much further than Nzekwu in arguing the moral superiority of rural traditionalism over the soulless materialism of a technically superior culture. The tragedy lies not in a confusion of choice but in the necessity for the sake of survival of accepting Western ways. When the chief of the tribe asks whether the new learning is worth what is lost in forgetting the old, the question seems rhetorical—the choice is forced and the result foredoomed. The world of Jagua Nana is populated with characters who are neither analytical nor introspective; yet their allegiance to the city is tempered by an inarticulate urge to go back to sources, to the simple village life where the real world and the ideal coincide in a romantic idyll.

The case of the protagonists of *A Walk in the Night* is more complex. All are rebels and failures in the world that surrounds them. All hate it and struggle against it. Yet none seems prepared to solve his problems by default in returning to the old life in the villages. In the end, death and moral destruction standing one's ground in the city are considered preferable. Once again the reasons are historical. In the first place, the Africans in the cities of South Africa have had a longer experience with urban life and are much more deeply committed to its ways and its possibilities than Africans in other parts of the continent. More important perhaps, they cannot afford to look back to the tribal ways, for it is precisely in this direction that the *apartheid* and Bantustan policies of the South African government are trying to force the people. In the effort to avoid being frozen culturally while the rest of the world moves on, they are compelled to turn their backs, at least temporarily, on values and viewpoints which otherwise might be treated more sympathetically. It may well require nothing less than a political revolution to persuade the Africans of South Africa to look to their traditional culture with a more kindly eye.

The reaction to outside forces, however, does not stop with mere resistance and the counterpoising of traditional values. The rise of independent states in Africa since 1957 has led to a search for an independence perhaps more subtle and difficult to achieve even than political freedom. Thoughtful Africans realise that political independence and economic development must be accomplished sooner or later by a true cultural emancipation which not only gives a fresh contemporary definition to the African character and its aspirations, but also makes possible a uniquely African contribution to world progress and civilisation. This is the basic meaning of the philosophy of *négritude* and the concept of the African personality.

The search for cultural identity expresses itself in several ways amply illustrated by the four novels under examination. First of all, there is the need for historical roots and a modern culture based not on foreign ideas but on native African values. This view is most clearly expressed by Cheikh Kane, the only one of the four authors clearly committed to the doctrine of *négritude*. The emotional appeal of his whole argument is to the past— the beauty and simplicity of the traditional life, the nobility of the ancestors and the glories of the old empire, the sublimity of the ascetic man. Against the serene perfection of this world, the West comes out a very poor second with its artificiality and ugliness, its amorality and godlessness, and its divorce from the living pulse of the real world. Of the others, it is Nzekwu who comes closest to Kane in allowing the traditional society to speak for itself, though he leaves the reader uncertain at the end as to how the modern Nigerian can make most effective use of traditional customs and values.

A second aspect of African cultural identity is the need to establish and express a sense of human dignity. Political freedom, satisfying as it is, needs to be followed by a world-wide acknowledgment that the new nation has earned its independence on its merits, not through some hand-me-down charity arising from international politics. The volumes we have been examining do not neglect this aspect of the African psychology. It is not surprising that *L'Aventure Ambiguë*, reflecting Gallic logic, is most precise in presenting characters of a lofty moral and ethical superiority. Diallo Samba, his father, the old master, the dowager, and the chief of the Diallobé all move through the action with a stoic detachment and devotion to higher principles that transcends the peccadillos of the everyday world, even while their fates are being settled by these trivia. On the other hand, the few Europeans who appear are remarkable perhaps for their cleverness and cynicism but never for nobility of character or largeness of spirit.

Alex La Guma treats the theme of dignity no less fully, if completely differently. His subjects meet the test on the white man's ground, only dimly aware of the inevitability of their defeat, but in refusing the sanctuary of the tribe and the village they succeed in living out their lives as best they know how and so achieve their measure of human dignity. The humanity of *Blade Among the Boys* is realised primarily through the sympathetic treatment given to the traditional village life, while Jagua Nana, for all her moral shortcomings, is a warm, vivid, three-dimensional character.

The third element of cultural identity springs naturally from the search for roots and the wish for the approbation of one's fellow man. This is the desire to make some positive contribution to contemporary world culture. Again it is Kane whose *négritude* is most didactic—the African lives in close sympathy with the natural forces of the world, his religious instinct brings him into surer touch with the infinite, and his higher morality is the only hope for a world out of touch with its own rhythm, lacking faith in God, and apparently bent on self-destruction. Ekwensi and Nzekwu describe rather than instruct—their characters exhibit the earthiness, the religious sense, the quick humour, and the personal warmth of the African and by implication suggest that these are qualities worthy of emulation the world over. La Guma makes no effort to convert. His case study of the South African city slum is none the less an eloquent plea for a better way of life than what has been brought from Europe to that unhappy part of Africa.

One more comment might be added about these four novels. It may seem curious that the authors selected failure and personal shortcoming as their vehicle because the prevailing mood in Africa today is clearly one of great buoyancy and faith in the future. South Africa may be burdened with *apartheid* and urban slums but the African in that land gives no indication of being downhearted or beaten. Similarly, West Africans do not seem to be greatly disturbed by the many problems thrust upon them by their rapidly changing world; this is just part of the business of building new nations. As for the African villager, is he not the very person whose drive, shrewdness, and pastoral virtue will be enlisted to ensure the success of these new states? Finally, in French-speaking Africa, where the doctrine of *négritude* has received its widest support, there appears to be no doubt as to the importance of Africa's future in the world. We may conclude, therefore, that if these writers speak in sober tones, it does not mean despair, but only that the way may be difficult even though the goal is secure.

African Writers of the Eighteenth Century

Ignatius Sancho; Ottobah Cugoano; Olaudah Equiano

O. R. DATHORNE

Africans were not unusual in eighteenth-century England; indeed there were so many of them who had come up via the West Indies, that they were given the name of 'St. Giles' black birds', since they congregated around St. Giles Circus. Most of them were employed in the households of prominent people and were simply chattels; three managed to become more than this and wrote and published during their lifetime.

Little, in his *Negroes in Britain*, quotes a letter that the Duchess of Devonshire sent to her mother in which she referred to her servant as 'a cheap servant' whom she 'will make a Christian . . . and a good boy'.[1] This attitude, partly a mixture of ideological paternalism and domestic necessity, was the basic actuality of what was called humanitarianism:

> In turning to the eighteenth century we discover that one of the broader aspects of the thought of this period was that of humanitarianism. In a sense it was merely one of the aspects of the romanticism of the period; and its over-all aim was to make the best of all possible worlds in which to live.[2]

This accounts in large measure for the concept of the century—they could see the African as partly savage and partly noble. The Africans who wrote also saw themselves in just this same way.

Among the better-known servants who lived during this period were Soubise and Francis Barber. Soubise was apparently something of a fop. Henry Angelo wrote of him.

> Fancying he was admired by the ladies, he boasted much of his amours and his epistolary correspondence.[3]

It was the intention of Soubise's employer to send him to University but he apparently proved to be too superior and they changed their minds. Soubise then went to teach fencing in India and he died there. Francis Barber, on the other hand, was Dr. Johnson's servant. He came to England in 1750.[4] Johnson sent him to school and taught him Latin, and in a letter dated 25th September, 1770 he wrote to him:

[1] Little, K., *Negroes in Britain*, London, 1948, p. 167. Sypher adds that by 1770 there were 14,000 Negro slaves in England; Sypher, Wylie, *Guinea's Captive Kings*, Chapel Hill, 1942, p. 2.

[2] McCullough, N. V., *The Negro in English Literature*, Ilfracombe, 1962, p. 52.

[3] Angelo, Henry, *Angelo's Pic Nic or Table Talk*, London, 1834, p. 61. For a further account v. Angelo, Henry, *Reminiscences of Henry Angelo*, London, 1828, pp. 447–53.

[4] For more details of Francis Barber, v. Boswell's *Life*, London, 1888 ed, Vol. I, p. 145.

244

I am very well satisfied with your progress, if you can really perform the exercises which you are set. . . . Let me know what English books you read for your entertainment. You can never be wise unless you love reading.[1]

The more liberal at the time would have liked to believe that the African, if given the chance, would be able to become a cultured man. There were a few who believed that he was even capable of writing; some, however, doubted this, and around Francis Williams, an African who had been educated at Cambridge and who had returned to Jamaica, this argument raged. Hume thought:

In Jamaica, indeed, they talk of one negroe as a man of parts and learning but 'tis likely he is admired for very slender accomplishments.[2]

Edward Long, on the other hand, conceded that he did write and 'was fond of a species of composition in Latin'[3] but added this warning about an example of his verse that Long quoted:

To consider the merits of this specimen impartially we must endeavour to forget in the first place that the writer was a Negroe; for if we regard it as an extraordinary production, merely because it came from a Negroe, we admit at once the inequality of genius which has been before supposed and admire it only as a rare phenomenon.[4]

It is against this background that the literary contributions of Ignatius Sancho, Ottobah Cugoano and Olaudah Equiano can best be understood.[5] They were all West Africans who had been enslaved and who had managed to get to England only as servants. That they survived is a testament to their fortitude. That they could write at all proves considerable ability.

Sancho was the first to be published. His *Letters of the Late Ignatius Sancho, an African* was published in London in 1782, two years after he died. In the Introduction we are told something of Sancho's life. He was born in 1729 on a slave ship; his mother died soon after and his father committed suicide. He was baptised at Cartagena and given the name Ignatius, Sancho being added afterwards. At the age of two he came from the West Indies to England and was given to two sisters. The Duke of Montagu liked him and used to give him books; when he died, Sancho became a butler in the Duchess's household until her death. After this, we are told, he lived a wild life; then he returned to Montagu House but illness forced him to retire in 1773. By then he had married and he started

[1] *Ibid.*, Vol. I, p. 388.
[2] Hume, David, *Philosophical Works*, ed. Green, T. H., and Grose, T. H., London, 1875, Vol. III, p. 252 n.
[3] Long, Edward, *History of Jamaica*, London, 1774, p. 478.
[4] *Ibid.*, p. 484.
[5] I omit Phyllis Wheatley. She is more properly 'American' although her *Poems on Various Subjects* was published in London in 1773.

a small grocery store in Westminster. After his death one of his six children carried on the business and, indeed, edited the fifth edition of his letters in 1803.

He was well known in polite and literary circles. He was an acquaintance of Garrick's as we can tell from his correspondence, and wrote to, and admired Sterne. From his letters one can glimpse the personal nature of the man—his sense of humour, his love for his family, his concern with the predicament of his fellow Africans. One sees also something of his raw love of life and his conceit.

Slavery is only one of the concerns in his letters; in a letter to Sterne he thanked him for condemning slavery in one of his sermons and thought 'that subject handled in your striking manner would ease the yoke (perhaps) of many'. In another letter to a friend he condemns the 'most diabolical usage of my brother Negroes'. But he did not sentimentalise his African past, as some of his contemporaries did. He wrote about the 'horrid cruelty and treachery of the petty kings—encouraged by their Christian customers'. He could frequently write in a detached way about another African and an acquaintance; so, in a letter, he warns a friend in India about Soubise's coming:

> If he should chance to fall in your way, do not fail to give the rattle-pate what wholesome advice you can; but remember, I do strictly caution you against lending him money upon any account, for he has everything but—principle.

Occasionally, as in a letter to Soubise, he becomes sanctimonious, and sometimes one wonders if he did not completely forget that he was an African. He recommends a Mr. B as:

> a merry, chirping, white tooth'd . . . and light little fellow; with a woolley pate—and face as dark as your humble. . . . I like the rogue's looks or a similarity of colour should not have induced me to recommend him.

Sancho showed himself interested in the political matters of his day. He did not like the American war and wrote frequently to the press about it. Under the name of 'Africanus' he wrote to the *General Advertiser* outlining at times various improbable schemes. He was obviously well known and was caricatured in the anonymous *Memoir and Opinions of Mr. Blenfield* (1790). Little adds that Sancho wrote verse and music and that some of his poetry was published in 1803. He also mentions that Sancho wrote two stage pieces for the theatre.[1]

Less the artist but the greater documentarian was Ottobah Cugoano whose *Thoughts and Sentiments on the Evil and Wicked Traffic of the Slavery and Commerce of the Human Species* was published in London in 1787. His book is partly biographical and partly propagandist. It tells the story of how he was captured and sold into slavery. He was taken to England from the West Indies; there he applied himself 'to learn reading and writing,

[1] Little, K., *op cit.*, p. 199.

which soon became my recreation, pleasure and delight.' His later description of the rigours of his capture and the Middle Passage is suspect, if only because he admits that he was only two when it happened, and one wonders to what extent he was dependent on another source for his information:

> I saw many of my miserable countrymen chained two and two, some hand-cuffed, and some with their hands tied behind.

His injunctions frequently have the heavy sententiousness of biblical exhortations, as for instance when he is denouncing the slave-trade:

> It is surely to the great shame and scandal of Christianity among all the Heathen nations that those robbers, plunderers, destroyers and enslavers of men should call themselves Christians, and exercise their power under any Christian government and authority. I would have my countrymen understand that the destroyers and enslavers of men can be no Christians; for Christianity is the system of benignity and love, and all its votaries are devoted to honesty, justice, meekness, peace and goodness to all men.

This method of writing frequently causes him to attitudinise and in his description of his misery at being captured he combines a personal predicament and an externalised woe:

> All my help was cries and tears and these could not avail; nor suffered long till one succeeding woe and dread swelled up another. Brought from a state of innocence and freedom, and in a barbarous and cruel manner, conveyed to a state of horror and slavery. This abandoned situation may be easier conceived than described.

Like Sancho he too makes the point about the chiefs being bad:

> Though the common people are free, they often suffer by the villainy of their different chieftains and by the wars and feuds which happen among them.

But, unlike Sancho, his desire to strike attitudes often makes him seem anti-European. He advances this theory about the origins of the English:

> Many of the Canaanites who fled away in the time of Joshua, became mingled with the different nations, and some historians think some of them came to England as far back as that time.

But occasionally he can achieve something of the private warmth of Sancho, as in his description of his capture while out hunting birds and the confusion that followed. The language here, while still having a biblical ring about it, nevertheless expresses bewilderment:

> Next morning there came three other men, whose language differed from ours, and spoke to some of those who watched us all the night, but he that pretended to be our friend with the great man, and some others, were gone away.

247

Indeed the whole style of the book varies so much between the 'experienced accounts' of the author and his exhortations against the slave trade that one is tempted to suggest that the simpler, more actualistic accounts are probably his and the long diatribes against slavery the work of probably some well-intentioned hack or, if his own, heavily dependent on some secondary material. Indeed Cugoano does mention Ramsay's *An Essay on the Treatment and Conversion of the African Slaves in the British Sugar Colonies*, Clarkson's *Essay on the Slavery and Commerce of the Human Species* and an *Historical Account of Guinea*. In addition he makes frequent references to and quotations from the Bible and much of his imagery owes its origin to the Bible. In fact he admits that his account is partly experiential and partly derivative:

> What I intended to advance against the evil, criminal and wicked traffic of enslaving men are only some thoughts and sentiments which occur to me, as being obvious from the scriptures of divine truth, or such arguments as are chiefly deduced from thence, with other such observations as I have been able to collect.

Equiano on the other hand draws more on his own recollected experiences. This was in itself an achievement, for most of the anti-slavery as well the pro-slavery propaganda of the time was written by Englishmen, and this is also true of the expression of the anti-slavery campaign in imaginative literature. Day's *Dying Negro* is a good example here; the dying Negro makes a long impassioned speech in which he says:

> And thou, whose impious avarice and pride
> Thy God's blest symbol to my brows deny'd,
> Forbade me or the rights of man to claim
> Or share with thee a Christian's hallowed name,
> Thou, too, farewell!—for not beyond the grave
> Thy power extends, nor is my dust thy slave.[1]

As we have seen with Cugoano, sentimentalising of the African predicament was all in order; it was the greater craftsman who sought to get away from this, even though it might make him into an unpopular writer.

The Interesting Narrative of the Life of Olaudah Equiano or Gustavus Vassa was published in London in 1789. It was a very popular book and by 1794 had had eight English editions and one American. Equiano was forty-four when the book was published and was obviously caught up in the romanticising of the African; he even quotes from Day's *Dying Negro*. Equiano traced his life back to the days of his childhood. He was not sold into slavery until he was twelve, after which he was taken to the West Indies and later became a servant in London. Like Cugoano he too refused to eat for several days after his capture and narrowly missed death in the Bahamas. At one time he was stranded in the Arctic circle during an expedition to seek a North-East passage to India. In 1787 he was appointed a 'Commissary of provisions and Stores for the Black Poor going to Sierra Leone'—a testimony to his worth as a citizen.

[1] Day, Thomas, *Dying Negro* in 'The Monthly Review', Vol. XLIX, July 1773, p. 63.

He shows a more universal human compassion than either Sancho or Cugoano. During the voyage of the Middle Passage he describes how a white sailor:

> was flogged so unmercifully with a large rope near the foremast, that he died in the consequence of it; and they tossed him over the side as they would have done a brute.

He is not free from idealising his African past and, emancipationist though he was, he could still write that West Indian planters preferred the Ibos as they were full of 'hardiness, intelligence, integrity and zeal'. But like both of the others he criticises the Africans who sold their tribesmen into slavery and exchanged 'the price of their fellow creature's liberty with as little reluctance as the enlightened merchant'. But he is without the censorious self-righteousness of Cugoano and writes respectfully of indigenous African religious rites, even though he was a Christian. He can write with a touching and humane tenderness, as for instance when he relates the story of how he was lost in the forest when trying to escape from his enslavers:

> I heard frequent rustlings among the leaves and, being pretty sure they were snakes, I expected every instant to be stung by them. This increased my anguish, and the horror of the situation became now quite unsupportable. I at length quitted the thicket, very faint and hungry, for I had not eaten or drunk anything all the day; and crept to my master's kitchen, from whence I set out at first, and laid myself down in the ashes with an unconscious wish for death to relieve me from all my pains.

Frequently he can write with an irritating sense of patronage, as when he describes the inhabitants of the Isle of Wight as 'very civil'; but he was obviously a man who, in spite of his education away from his own culture, still managed to maintain a fierce energetic pride in his race:

> Let the polished and haughty European recollect that his ancestors were once, like the Africans, uncivilised, and even barbarous.

In his account he writes with ease and dignity. His religion never obtrudes, although he must have been very Christian, for he even wanted to become an ordained minister of the Church of England and to go to Africa as a missionary. (He tells us, however, that the Bishop of London refused 'from certain scruples of delicacy'.) Perhaps it was this essential humanity that endeared him to John Wesley, and Bready gives the account of how, on his death bed, Wesley asked two friends to read aloud to him from Equiano's book.[1] What frequently makes the style so easy is the sense of humour, absent in Cugoano and less sure in Sancho. For instance, he laughs at his own unsophisticated gullibility when he first sees a watch in his master's house in Virginia:

[1] Bready, J. W., *England Before and After Wesley*, London, 1938, p. 229.

I was quite surprised at the noise it made and was afraid it would tell the gentleman anything I might do amiss.

On the ship when he first sees white people he speaks to his companions:

I asked them if we were not to be eaten by those white men with horrible looks, red faces and long hair. They told me I was not.

This is a sophisticated way of telling the traveller's tales of cannibal orgies from a different point of view, and one feels that he was sufficiently integrated into English society to be able to take an occasional swipe at it. The 'Gentleman's Magazine' of April 1792 reported his marriage:

at Soham, co. Cambridge, Gustavus Vassa, the African, well known in England as the champion and advocate for procuring the suppression of the slave trade, to Miss Cullen, daughter of Mr. C of Ely, in the same country.

By education, adoption and marriage he was of England, so when he writes, tongue in cheek, that by fourteen or fifteen he had seen so much terror that he 'was in that respect at least, almost an Englishman', he is stating more than half a truth.

All three of these writers were to a great extent absorbed in eighteenth-century English society. This, paradoxically, helped to make them more completely themselves, for it was a century that was concerned with the great humanitarian fervour for emancipation. But because their society encouraged them to extend themselves in this public way—to proclaim their most private tensions—one must ask just how genuine their responses were to the matters, which, though very close to them, nevertheless required certain kinds of stock responses. One must therefore be wary of ascribing too much to them as individuals; they had to react in a certain way to these issues and this tended to mould their thought and to colour their language. Any knowing hack could have attempted to imitate them or indeed to re-cast or simply write whole passages. Consequently the edition of Sancho's letters two years after his death, the long anti-slavery diatribes in Cugoano, and some of the more splendiferous effusions of Equiano and Cugoano, where they seem to have grown completely outside their skins, make one doubt their authorship at times, and at other times feel that perhaps they had attained an alarming degree of liberal emancipation. But their heavy adherence to the Bible, their weighty sermonising, and their care with the language, give us no reason to doubt that their writing was to a large extent genuine. They were expressing the thought and attitudes of liberal Englishmen which they had fully adopted. Consequently they managed to create an interesting ancestor to the *Kunstlerroman*: not only giving an embryo life of the artist, but also exploring the significance of their own development within a foreign culture. In a very special way, they were privileged insiders who shared all of the licence but none of the prejudices of outsiders; this is why their work is a valid commentary on the entire cycle of eighteenth-century enquiry and resolution.

250

Public Opinion on Lovers

Popular Nigerian Literature sold in Onitsha Market

ULLI BEIER

It has been said that the market of Onitsha on the east bank of the river Niger is the largest in the world. I have no means to verify the claim, but walking along the endless rows of stalls that seem to offer more goods than all the department stores put together one is inclined to believe it. Not only the variety of goods is staggering, but more so is the enormous number of stalls which seem to be duplicating the same wares. The large majority are imported manufactured goods. The tourist on the lookout for objects of Nigerian origin will be a little disappointed. But to his surprise his curiosity will be richly rewarded on the bookstalls. Though the booksellers mostly stock school textbooks, they also display fascinating local novels and plays which have been written, printed and published in Onitsha itself and a few other towns of the Eastern region. Mostly they are small pamphlets selling very cheaply indeed and seldom more than 48 pages thick. Any day in Onitsha market one can buy at least a hundred different titles.

Usually the printers are also the publishers. They buy manuscripts at varying prices according to the popularity of the author. An advertisement at the back of one pamphlet offered '2/6 to £5. 5s. for a good tortoise story'. But a popular novel writer can easily fetch £10 or more for a manuscript. The usual edition of these pamphlets is one to two thousand copies, but there are best sellers that keep reprinting year after year and they go to five thousand or more. Most publishers are emphatic about copyright: yet there is a fair amount of plagiarism.

The titles of the books are attractive and revealing in themselves:

> *Saturday Night Disappointment*
> *Rosemary and the Taxi Driver*
> *Romance in a Nutshell*
> *Disaster in the Realms of Love*
> *Public Opinion on Lovers*

Sometimes the pamphlets have elaborate explanatory subtitles:

> Our Modern Ladies Characters towards Boys
> (The most exciting Novel with Love letters, drama, telegrams, and campaigns of Miss Beauty to the teacher asking him to marry her.)

or

> Husband and Wife who Hate Themselves
> (It was a forced marriage made by Chief Monger, as a result of this everyday so so quarrel, so so talk, so so fight, no peace.)

There is another type of pamphlet which is neither a novel nor a play but a

251

kind of moralising book of advice or admonition. The titles are no less revealing:

> Money Hard to Get but Easy to Spend.
> Why Harlots hate Married men and Love Bachelors.
> The Half Educated Court Messenger.
> Drunkards Believe Bar as Heaven.
> Money Hard, But some Women don't Know.
> What is Life?
> (A Complete, general book of life, dedicated to the high, the average, the low and for all sitters of life, with a speculatory guide of living.)

The authors of these pamphlets often give themselves fancy names, like: Money Monger; Strong Man of the Pen; Money Hard and Master of Life, who obtained the title M.L. at the Commonsense College, where he passed very hard lessons in money mastery and Life Problems.

Sometimes the publisher uses one name to cover various authors. (Several people have written under the name Highbred Maxwell, for example, which is the publisher's own name.)

The authors are seldom very educated in English. Many have only primary school education. One or two are known to be secondary school boys. Thus the introduction to one 'novel' says:

> 'Cletus is one of the Nigerian schoolboys who delight in the attempt of things that are bold. When he asked me to write a foreword to his book, I was surprised, because I never expected that he could hold his studies in one hand and use the other in compiling a book so wonderfully exciting.'

Many authors are apologetic about their imperfect English, but nevertheless feel the urge to write. The following are two charming sentences from author's prefaces:

> '. . . and readers should mind very little the poor English it contains, which is hoped to be amended when this book will celebrate her publication.'
> 'It has been practically impracticable to avoid some minute typographical errors and may the readers not be embarrassed where they occur.'

One author, in his preface, says he welcomes 'mild but constructive criticism from the public'.

Some of the more accomplished authors are journalists, usually correspondents of small provincial papers. It is also worth noting that one intellectual author, Cyprian Ekwensi, made his debut with an Onitsha pamphlet ('When Love Whispers'). His full-length novels *Jagua Nana* and *Beautiful Feathers* were published by Hutchinson in London.

In the following, however, we shall not be concerned with the exception, who made his way to become an intellectual writer with an international market, but we shall try to examine the works of those popular Nigerian authors who write for and are read by Nigerian schoolboys, junior clerks, taxi drivers and petty traders.

The language of these pamphlets owes its peculiar charm and vitality partly to the fact that most of the authors do not really master the language. Their ideas about syntax and grammar are extremely hazy, though their vocabulary can be surprisingly large. The writers are not too familiar with English idioms and often new and charming expressions are coined, simply because they have misheard and reinterpreted an English phrase. Like:

> . . . head over feels in love.
> . . . means of lovelihood.
> . . . you are the apple of my heart.
> . . . he is the sort of boy who would sell his mother for a dirty mess of pottage.

Often the language is extremely awkward, because the author writes about things he has apparently not been talking about:

> she gave him three strokes of kiss.

On the other hand some rather attractive new words are created occasionally by the authors, who are wrestling with the language, groping for the right expression, and they formulate without having any regard for the conventional parts of speech:

> Her father messaged me.
> I daggered the idiot to death.
> He is a lovely someone.
> It was headaching.
> There were great bemoanings.
> He tried to show his bigmanity.
> Money sweets women more than men.
> He endeavoured to find the unfindings.

Much of this writing has the freshness of innocence. The writer has no idea of what is conventional in English language or thought, and he can be startling without intending to:

> 'Darling, you don't look normal to day,' said Obiageli. 'You look as if you have been thinking. You look miserable.'
> 'The bridegroom wasn't so happy with the bride for he had tasted the feminine stock of her love before the wedding.'

A general characteristic of all this writing is the uninhibited *vigour* of the expressions:

> She liquidated her husband and left him.
> (in a love scene) She hurled him into her knees.
> He could scarcely vomit a word.

253

Most writers are fond of expressing themselves in superlatives:

> It was the highest eccentric subtle ever experienced.

There are some, particularly Miller O. Albert, who practise a kind of studied toughness in their speech, probably stimulated by American gangster films:

> (Girl rejecting a suitor) 'You aren't the only man of instinct.'
> (Couple of boys making up to a girl) 'What are you sure you can do to have us fully embraced?'
> (Blasé lover) 'Yes, girls are the most comfortable things we can get alright, for a happy cuddle.'

Even though the language is often clumsy, these Onitsha pamphlets are full of the most striking and original images:

> (Drinking scene) 'They swilled all round, extending the waistband of their pants.'
> 'That Elizabeth, they nodded, is another girl of diversified scarlet colours.'
> (A girl has become pregnant) 'She walked away with an additional pound of flesh.'
> (Admission of failure in life:) 'My name is written in white ink on white paper.'

Some writers are extremely fond of big words, sometimes to the extent of becoming completely incomprehensible. Here is a passage from 'What is Life':

> 'Life been mistaken, men away of existence, people dangling in an empty full of creation, immoral depiction now an expansion of monumental reasonings, movements a habitude of an unsoundly survivor, and in sense that very genuineness and rightness of living are left to disgustments, what a contempt!'

There are some 48 pages of this same stuff, and some people apparently attempt to read it all. On the other hand there is an awareness of this among other Onitsha writers, who occasionally make fun of it. Ogali Ogali, 'dramatist and novelist' and one of the most gifted and skilful Onitsha writers, introduces funny characters into his plays who speak a stilted type of language taken straight out of the Oxford dictionary. In 'Mr. Rabbit is Dead' one of these characters is paraphrasing the 23rd Psalm thus:

> Deity is my pasture, I shall not be indigent.
> He maketh me to recompense the verdant lawn
> He leadeth me beside the rippled liquidities,
> And he conducteth me in the avenues of rectitude
> For the celebrity of his appelation.
> Undoubtedly, though I shall not be perturbed
> By any catastrophe for thou art present.

Thou preparest a refection before me in the presence of my
    enemies
And quench my ungroshonological revevelence
My commiseration shall continue all the lutony on my vitality
And I shall eternalise my habitation in the metropoles of nature.

Although many West African idioms have crept into these Onitsha
pamphlets, the authors carefully avoid pidgin English and on the whole
aspire to write what they think is standard English. Pidgin is used, however,
deliberately in plays to characterise and ridicule illiterate characters. Here
is a sample, again from Ogali Ogali. The character, Chief Jombo, com-
plains to his wife about his daughter Veronica, who is running after a boy
called Mike (pronounced by him Mikere):

> Chief Jombo: 'What kind trouble dis be. My daughter get strong
> ear too much. I flog'am tire, no change. I talk tire, no change.
> Dis boy Mikere go killi my daughter. What do you talk for dis
> your daughter way want cut my hair for strong ear sake? I do
> everything I tire, Veronica no listen. Any place Mikere dey,
> Veronica dey. I tell Veronica, leave Mikere, Veronica say no.
> Weting you say make I do? Talk! Talk all the grammarian you
> sabi.'
> ('sabi' = know).

The subject matter of these novels and plays can best be described with
the West African term 'Highlife'. Highlife is a reaction against the austerity
of traditional African life. It is a way of life that believes in pleasure, music,
drinking, free love, and ostentatious spending of money. The Onitsha
writers speak about this new generation: schoolboys, teachers, drivers,
clerks—people who have not yet gone very far in being 'westernised', but
who already find themselves in sharp opposition to traditional ways of life.
It is significant that where traditional people occur in these books they are
always the villains and always ridiculed. One of the favourite stock situations is the old illiterate father who wants to marry off his daughter in the
traditional manner to some wealthy old friend of his. He does not see that
the daughter should have any say in this. But the 'enlightened' daughter
revolts. She wants to marry the man she loves, and she usually gets her way.
In one way or another all these books are concerned with the concept of
'romantic love'. This does not mean, however, that these stories are as stale
as 'True Stories' or fiction in 'Woman's Own' (even though some of the
authors have read both). It is not stale, because many of these authors
represent the first generation who have escaped from the dignity and
austerity of traditional African life—a first generation of bars, highlife,
music, tarts, cinemas and a considerable degree of individual freedom. This
new freedom to choose between different ways of life, the freedom to make
individual decisions without consulting one's family, are things that excite
and stimulate these authors.

The idea of 'romantic love' is clearly new, to some of them, and though they have taken over all the clichés of the cinema they see it all with fresh and innocent eyes. The influence of the cinema is self-evident in the stories, and in addition there are also a number of direct references to it:

> Usually while the film was on, and there was a part where there was kissing, Jerry would kiss Obiageli as well. But today Jerry was so absent-minded that he forgot to kiss Obiageli during a kissing part of the film. Obiageli turned sharply to Jerry and asked him why he didn't kiss her. Jerry was unable to answer.
> 'Jerry, I think you don't love me any longer,' said Obiageli.
> (from *Boys and Girls of Nowadays* by C. C. Obiaga)
> 'Okoro was a Film goer. He knew himself that to change a car was an English method of bringing confusion into crime.'·
> (From *Rosemary and the Taxi Driver* by Miller O. Albert.)

Most of the authors profess that they are teaching young people what they need to know about love; that they give them useful advice as to how to handle these new situations. Here are some passages from authors' prefaces:

> 'I have written this booklet named "The Work of Love" in order to help many youths to know more of the work of love and how it penetrates. Whether this my work is earthly or a morbid interest I did not pretend to determine. My only concern is to satisfy that curiosity which like the impulse to write about the work of love is nothing new, and just to advise hasty youths and to give them corrections. Marriage is really made in Heaven before on Earth.'
> 'Actually it is not possible for a young man whether married or unmarried to live happily without at first knowing how to get round our modern, mendacious and honey tongued girls who are the squeezers of the scanty sum usually paid to my dear gentlemen as their monthly income.'

Some of the writers are real prophets of gloom. Their books are not really fiction, but books of advice, in which young men are warned that most women are evil and that drink and women are the ruin of men. Subtitle on a cover:

> 'This book is worth owning. It arms the buyer against hardship and generates in him the courage to deal wisely with world-difficulties. Advise a friend to buy one. — Publisher.'

'WIFE BROUGHT LEPROSY TO HER HUSBAND AFTER COMMUNICATING WITH A SECRET FRIEND. — READ PAGE 4.'

On the other hand there are some writers who try to be simply realistic, and apologise to the readers for not describing the world better than it is:

> 'Books on human life do not give explanations of things as things should be, but as some people see them. It is how men see women, and how women see men at this present age.'

The most vigorous of the writers, however, are not didactic. They write for entertainment. One advertises his book as a 'griping novel'; another says 'it entertains more than two bottles of beer'. The case of the Onitsha writer who writes for pleasure and entertainment is most ably put by Thomas Iguh in the preface to his book *John in the Romance of True Love*.

> 'This drama is one of the best love intricacies ever exposed in this part of Africa. It is a good thriller and it tells us of a boy called John who only for the sake of love killed his twin brother — Dixon. After this bloody deed of his, he proceeded to the secondary school with his girl friend Agnes.
> 'Who can guess how they met their end? Well, Agnes was pregnant and not wanting her parents to know, she took some drugs to procure abortion which later made her to bleed profusely after which she was rushed to the hospital where she died. But before she died, she of course confessed to her parents why she was dying prematurely.

> 'John having been told of his lovers death wasted no time rushing to hospital where he saw Agnes dead. He then kisses her for the last time and daggered himself to death.
> 'This drama, with all its mistakes, I hope ,will be a good thriller and I hope it too will serve as a good lesson to some of our boys and girls who are always mad about love.
> 'Finally I may say that all the names used in the play are fictitious ones, hence the drama itself is a fiction.'

Even here there is lip service being paid to a moralistic attitude—but then these pamphlets are chiefly sold to schoolboys.

Like Thomas Iguh, most of the authors take great care to point out that all their characters are fictitious and that any resemblance to people alive or dead are purely accidental. Often they use delightfully fresh language to say so:

> 'All characters in this novel are all round imaginary. Note, none is real. It is not a true story, and therefore concerns nobody in any way. Whoever hits his head at the ceiling does it at his own personal risk.'
>
> (Miller O. Albert.)

Thomas Iguh's introduction gives a good idea of the type of wild plot the authors indulge in. Most of them have no difficulty in inventing plots and in holding the attention of their readers.

The authors' main difficulties arise from their struggle with the language and also from the fact that they have to write about new concepts and new ideals, and that they are constantly formulating new ideas and have to try and do so with the limited vocabulary at their disposal.

Such is for example the concept of beauty. Obviously, in traditional Ibo life there were very precise concepts of what constituted female beauty, but the Onitsha writers deal with a new type of girl, with the smart city girl who

257

does all she can to look *different* from a traditional beauty, and they write about 'modern' boys who expect something different from a woman.

The writers often resort to impossible clichés when trying to describe the beauty of their heroines. One can read about 'snow-white teeth', 'scarlet red lips' and once even 'blond hair' (!) Usually the ideal is 'slim'.

But there are also some more original notions. One writer speaks about the girl's 'cannon ball head', another about her 'burst shape', and several refer to her 'hairy hands' and one even to her 'hairy body' as a mark of beauty. One mentions 'the round fact that nature has awarded her as a scholarship'.

The writers find it easier to describe the girl's accomplishments: 'she was a beautiful certificated lady', 'She had a laughing character', 'the damsel loomed large on the social horizon of Nigeria'.

They are fairly eloquent in describing the heroine's impact on the men: 'Another peculiarity that goes to her credit is the undue satisfaction one feels and receives in merely seeing her.' And '. . . she provoked the impetus of glaring at sexual menace below the belt.'

Virginity is seldom praised in the girls, though once we hear that 'She was in her maiden form and remained untampered, since her generate days. Even to meddle with her zestful glamour of beauty nobody had ever succeeded.' However, they never stay virgins for long and a quality is preferred in the women which Miller O. Albert has called 'her glamorous beautiful guts of life'. On the whole they like them gorgeously dressed: 'Her violet gown with vibrant colours and heavenly patterns vested below her knees. She wore a dazzling gold necklace, shiny earrings and a botanical veil, stained all over with jet colours.' Usually also the 'lip-painted ladies' are preferred to plain country beauties, and it is said of one girl that she powdered her nose 'making it a more beautiful article from nature'.

There are many touching scenes of courtship in these books:

> Rosemary drifted to him, loving him and loving him the more. She flashed her romantic eyes, bending down for shamefulness. A little of a time she made her character to be:
> 'How is it?'
> 'It is quite well.'

And almost immediately they 'delved into a torrential downpour of speeches, making their introductions'.

Here is another passage from a book where three boys intercept a girl on the street all proposing love to her at once. She replies with decorum:

> 'Is that how I shall fall in love with three of you? You can come privately and let me consider within myself. At present your request is too childish, though of great worth. Just put it in writing. Please, I beg you to leave me if I waste more time here my parents will ask me questions if I reach home.'

The girls are not always as shy and modest. In *Saturday Night Dis-*

appointment it is the girl, 'gentle Eliza', who is proposing to the boy in no uncertain terms:

> Soon gentle Eliza mettled up and said: 'Chima I think you ain't feeling very comfortable.' 'Well,' Chima hummed.
> 'Say on with certainty. Play your rough. Assume this is an opera. Calling on for your own art. Aren't you a generate male?'

Much of the courting is done by letter, and there are in fact several books entitled *How To Write Love Letters*. All novels contain love letters as some special kind of attraction.

> 'Men had now indulged in the habit of despatching floods of letters to me. The battle for love, who to love and how to make it in the natural way became blooming.'

The letters themselves are often quite touching:

> 'We are just like babes in love making and have not known the disadvantages and advantages of it.'
> 'I would like to make a suggestion. Let us become engaged, what do you think darling? You see, I want to buy you a ring so that people may feel that you are engaged and will stop worrying for the same purpose.'
> 'I love to buy you a ring now, so that people know you are mine. Will you allow me to do that? For your information the ring will mean that we are engaged which is a thing I devoutly desire. In fact it would bring us nearer to our marriage. Think of the joy of it all, darling.'

The Onitsha writers can often convey touches of real tenderness. They find it a little harder when they attempt to express the big passions and violent emotions; too often they end in bathos:

> For a while after reading the letter not a word is spoken by Galinda.
> The roaring noise from the public field of the village was drawing under the setting moon of a perfect June night. She started baiting her nails and comforting herself with songs.
>   (*Disaster in the Realms of Love* by J. N. C. Egemonye)
> She did not only want Ema to enter into the rite wholeheartedly, but he should, if possible, take the initiative. Then at last, she said justly, I love you. Don't you in turn love me? Ascending the highest step of the staircase of feelings, Ema, with emotion and exposed white teeth, said softly but impressively: Why? I love you Rosie. Rose was maddened. She became wild with joy. She became restless in her seat. She has done what Napoleon found difficult. With every nerve in her body tingling she rose up and walked towards their refrigerator.
>   (*Miss Rosie in the Romance of Love* by N. O. Madu)
> 'What a life for the female element,' Dora said, wiping her tears on the flowers she had used on her wedding day.
>   (from *The Work of Love*)

Some of the emotions do not ring true, but when the writers get down to brass tacks and describe real love-making they sound a lot more convincing. Here is Miller O. Albert again, in a scene from *Rosemary and the Taxi Driver*:

> They rocked each other, hugging themselves together, feeling the transfer of flirtation and fervourism, through the sending over of the warmth which God had wasted time in giving over to any living belong, excepting the reptiles. Their intentions were deep, mostly that of Okoro. His sexual instinct was in its worst intensive urgent. Startled were the leaves around, mourning under the roary wind. The scaring desert winded over with tremor. They like doing the lot, the life they played was as the first day of a virgin in a honeymoon. How beautiful it is to toss oneself with ones wife, how lovely it was for Rosemary to feel very shy and sophisticated. Her youthful fidelity was exhausted and they delved into a romantic blast. It was a nice day for men to marry. If it hadn't been that there was no responsible adult, it could have been a honeymoon.

And another good passage from *Nancy in Blooming Youth* by an anonymous author:

> When, as it was often the case, the marriage ceremony was only a couple of days ahead, Welly came to spend two jolly nights with me. We set aside these two nights as 'Special Period of Romance.' In deed and indeed they really were! Not to exaggerate matters, it was a FIRST CLASS ASPECT OF LOVE YOU CAN IMA-GINE. I freely allowed Welly to satisfy his EMOTIONAL FEELINGS AS MUCH AS HE WISHED; and to be brief, I made him feel as if he were in Paradise. He confessed it! On kissing my soft lips Welly beckoned, 'You see darling, that the love climax you've begun to play with me is one that intoxicates me as if I'd had two bottles of aromatic Schnapps. How I wish life were like that all the time? Are you, honestly speaking, mine for aye?' 'Why not, if not?' I nodded.

The Onitsha authors are seldom so explicit about love making, but their books are studded with little gems and brief remarks like this: 'Come nearer darling and let me touch those soft balls on your chest, for they are always an invigorating cordial to me.'

The relationships between men and women are not always that romantic. Many of the pamphlets deal with unhappy marriages. They are always the result of an old rich but illiterate man marrying a young schoolgirl.

Typical of these quarrels is the opening scene from the play 'Husband and Wife Who Hate Themselves':

HUSBAND RETURNS FROM WORK
(meets wife doing nothing)
Mark: This woman, have you cooked finish?
Victoria: I have not.

Mark: This woman why have you never finish the cooking by this time?
Victoria: Z.
Mark: You say what?
Victoria: What heard you?
Mark: I heard about your head.
Victoria: You can hear about your nose.
Mark: Nonsence woman, who are you talking to?
Victoria: Nonsense I am talking to your father.
Mark: To my father-a! To my father-a!

                    (THE SITUATION IS PROVOKED)
(Hon. Mark now becomes provoked and handles the wife, Victoria at her right hand and asks her to repeat what she has said. Victoria struggles to release her hand and pushes Mark back strongly with her left, and free fight starts.)
Mark slaps Victoria, and pushes her down. Victoria manages to get up and gets hold of the nearest plate and breaks it into pieces upon Mark's head. (Blood rushes out.) She begins to damage properties, radio broken, cupboard pushed down, plates broken, wall clock damaged also.

And a few pages further on the final separation:

Mark: I will not marry you further you are a useless, hopeless, stupid disobedient and nonsense wife. (Victoria begins to pack her properties and talks as she packs.)
Victoria: Bad man, bokom man, silly man, wicked man, foolish man, bush man, I am packing quick quick and must move today. You could remember that I refused to marry you but my illiterate father forced me. You deceived and corrupted him with a bottle of White Horse.

Fights are not missing in any of the books and usually they are among the most vigorous and colourful bits of writing. Here are two quotations again from the inimitable Miller O. Albert:

The fight became too rigid Okoro manoeuvred the second time, blasting a punch on the man's belly, beer rushed out forming a little rivulet, to mark the great occasion. He knocked the scoundrel down. After noticing the catastrophe as very unbecoming he set out on Olympic game with Rosemary, heading off to Onitsha, creating the worst record of event, ever recorded, in the annals of such an occasion.
He knew wrestling strategem. Then he let go the twisting leg type and hurled him up in the air and left him to land anyhow he likes, even if with his head broken; it was equally good. Soon, after a few minutes, all the heaviness of his body landed with a hefty noise of beer, from his stomach, like a parcel of sand.

Gilbert Nwankwo also rises to the occasion when he describes a blood-thirsty scene in *The Woman from Nowhere.*

And what did the chief do? He got up slowly holding on to his knees. His eyes were unnatural and bloodshot, and at that moment he was really mad; deliberately he put his hand inside his wrapper and brought out a dagger and in one swift movement he plunged it into the chest of his son. Blood burst out as if from a fountain—Have you ever seen a fountain of blood? I have seen it twice. One was when old Eke cut his leg and the blood flew to the heavens. This was the second one. The Chief's face was covered with rich, red blood, it entered his mouth, his eyes, his nostrils. The Chief stood where he was crazed and dazed. Then he opened his eyes and fainted.

Much of the humour in these pamphlets is involuntary. But this does not mean that they are lacking in deliberate humour. Ogali's plays are full of comical characters. We have already quoted a passage of Chief Jombo. Here is another piece of humour from Albert's *Saturday Night Disappointment*:

'I wish I could hear a word from you, on how you conducted the interview.'
'Well, as my father told me that English people like people who are bold; when I reached there, I made a bold noise making the European fall from his chair. He felt my boldness. When I was told to be quiet, I kept mute even when he asked me questions. I then stood attention, making chest five inches fat and thickness over a yam mound. Haven't I tried?'
'You have fallen yourself.'
'Well, it is practical psychology.'
'What next did the European tell you.'
'He said: "Go, Idiot! You are too energetic for me." Then I nodded and went off breaking the steps leading downstairs.'

The Onitsha authors are clearly interested in human beings and in the relationships between them. As one of them put it: 'This book deals mainly on the requirements of love and particularly the type existing between men and women.' The writers are not interested in the moods of nature and the changing of the season. Some of them appear to have noticed that descriptions of nature appear in European love stories and make efforts to introduce this element into their books. Mostly they are as incongruous as this passage from *Romance in a Nutshell* (E. Euba).

The faint sweet music of the cooling wind coupled with the song of birds and the piquant rustle of leaves helped her to give birth to her child when the time came.

An even better example is the following one from 'Our Modern Ladies Characters towards Boys'.

She set out one bright sunny winter morning with thoughts of love and marriage scattered in her shallow troubled mind. She travelled through sand, stones, and foggy, deserted places where

even the voice of an insect was not heard. Cannibals and wild flesh eating animals hunted her, but she was delivered by the Almighty. Hardship was hers. No any kind of hardship was purchased. She nearly died of hunger, thirst, and loneliness. Lamentation was inevitable. . . .
She bore all these hardships in pursuit of a husband.

The majority of Onitsha writers enjoy telling a good tale of passionate love, of seduction and lust, with some good fights thrown in. Even where they profess to tell their tale in order to help and warn the young, it is easy to see that they simply relish the description of 'Highlife'.

But there are some who see the gloomy side of the picture throughout. Their books of advice or wisdom, in which they warn all honest men of the wickedness of women, are often tedious and repetitive, but they also contain quite a few gems. The most prominent writers of this kind are Okenwa Olisa (alias Master of Life) and 'Money Hard'. Both have more than a dozen booklets to their name.

Olisa is fond of telling his readers very short stories with an obvious moral. Here are a couple:

MR. OFO-OGELI RUNS AWAY
Mr. Ofo-Ogeli of Lagos ran away after having a nice time with his harlot. In the morning the harlot demanded the amount agreed by Mr. Ofo-Ogeli to pay, and Mr. Ofo-Ogeli said: 'Let me urinate.' From there he ran away as a madman. The harlot shouted: 'Catcham! Catcham!'

RENEW MY BODY AS IT WAS BEFORE
A wife by name Nwanyioma argued before her husband at Aba, when the husband told her to pack away. 'You caused my breasts which pointed as nails to collapse. I shall not pack away as you request, unless you renew my body as it was before.'

'Strong Man of the Pen' freely offers advice to all who want to hear about all kinds of 'life problems'. Here is some on his advice on whom to marry:

SHORT GIRLS.
Too much beautiful girls are not advisable to be married, for they bring trouble to their husband. They are arrogant and too loose to boys. Very ugly girls are not recommended by me for marriage, because they hardly give romantic happiness. Very short girls 'should not also be married', because naturally or generally they are wicked and do not endure anything.

These books are also full of 'wise sayings' and maxims:

Man do suffer till sweat comes out before he eats.
Man no go pass his fellow man in two ways; if you pass me tall, I pass you short, if you pass me white, I pass you black.
(Olisa.)
Love is like measles. We all have to go through it.
Marriage is like a book, where the hero dies in the first chapter.

263

The first to fall sick is not the first to die.
When you are away, the best lock against burglers is a wife in the house.

Tongue oftenly becomes more active and effective in getting a woman than money.

(N. O. Njoku, *How to write Love Letters*)

These writers are particularly hard on women. 'Strong Man of the Pen' claims (in his book *Money Hard but Some Women don't know*) that women are harlots and 'money mongers' and he levies ten serious accusations against all women. He agrees, however, to accept an apology from women on condition that 'before tendering an apology, they must organise and hold a meeting of girls and ladies and pass a vote of no confidence in themselves to serve as public confession'.

The most amusing harangues against women are found in 'Money Hard's' delightful pamphlet: 'Why Harlots love Bachelors and Hate Married men.'

> Why harlots, independent women, mostly lip-painted ladies love bachelors is because they know that the bachelors have a long way to go with them, and they will have to see them, and also will have to take care of their pride. They come to remember what they use to get from the bachelors and salo the money they got from them to buy their needs such as rekyi-rekyi, popo-cloth, velvet, ejecombe lawyer, sasarobia scent, fine pomade, gold and silver, headtie, handkerchiefs, umbrella, shoes, shirt and blouse, sandals, iron beds, blankets and bed seets, pillows and pillow cases, sleeping gowns, cushion chairs and covers, door blinds, window blinds, mosquito nets, tables and table cloths, carpets, bed curtains, ladies handwatches, looking glass, powder, ladies sewing machine, portmanteaux, trunk box, bicycle, grammophone and so many other things a woman could use.

Complaints about the greediness of women occur over and over in these booklets and in 'Public Opinion on Lovers' Highbred Maxwell is even prompted to write the following poem on the theme:

> Love is a walking shadow
> Maria who has deserted me
> All I spend no refund
> Rice and beans all I cooked
> Meat and bread, butter and milk
> Coffee and tea now and then
> Theatre with taxi all I paid
> Cloth or powder all my expense
> Come and go transport I paid
> Business I left for Maria's sake
> Legal action will pay the debt.

All these examples have, I hope, conveyed some idea as to what this writing is like. Nobody could call it great literature, but these books have qualities that can give pleasure to a wider range of readers than they were intended for: there is the freshness and vigour of the language, the colourful and virile plots, and the all-pervading sense of humour.

Onitsha literature is important above all as a *symptom*. This literature symbolises the tremendous vitality of these newly literate classes. Here are people who have had little chance of education, but who nevertheless grab hold of the new life with both hands. The self-taught Onitsha writers must be seen together with the self-taught Highlife musicians who play in the night clubs of Onitsha, Enugu and Port Harcourt. They are to be seen as part of the same culture that produced the self-taught artists, who under the name of 'sign writers' design barber's signs, decorate lorries, paint behind glass and produce rubber cuts as illustrations to the Onitsha books.

It is a new social class that within a single generation has been able to create its own popular art forms and which constitutes a vast reservoir of untrained but creative talent in modern Nigeria.

Part 4

Drama

Yoruba Theatre

ULLI BEIER

There is no conventional theatre in Yoruba tradition. The dramatic re-enactments of historical events, which often form part of religious festivals, involve acting but they are not meant as entertainment, nor have they produced a professional class of actors.

Closer to theatre are the two societies of masqueraders known as *Gelede* and *Egungun*. Both these are extremely serious and partly secret societies. The *Gelede* society is run by women and its prime function is the placation of witches. It is assumed that all women are potential witches, because 'the mothers'—as the witches are called—can control them through the flow of blood.

Gelede accepts the existence of witches as an integral part of the universe. They are not entirely evil forces, as in European mythology, but they are extremely dangerous and *Orisha* worship is not always considered sufficient protection. The function of the *Gelede* cult therefore is to appease them. There are two aspects to the masqueraders' performances: a ritual one and an entertaining one.

The ritual dance always takes place at night. It is preceded by sacrifice and accompanied by praise songs and prayer. It culminates in the appearance of *Efe*—a powerful mask—preceded by a young girl who carries a witch in the form of a bird in a calabash. But from a theatrical point of view the dance that usually follows the next afternoon is more interesting. For the avowed purpose of this dance is to provide entertainment to the witches and keep them in good temper and—of course—at the same time entertain the townspeople at large who had been excluded from the night ceremony.

The masks always come out in pairs. The mask consists of a face mask that is worn *on top* of the head, thus giving the dancer the appearance of a very long neck. This face mask usually has a superstructure and on this almost any subject under the sun can be represented. Here is a list of masks seen by me in Pobe in Dahomey:

> a war chief; a man smoking a pipe; a black nurse with two white children; four men fighting with guns and matchets; a catholic priest; a monkey with elephantiasis of the scrotum; four skulls; a jackal and birds eating a snake; a Hausaman; *Aroni*, a one-legged forest spirit; two snakes and a bird trying to eat the same tortoise; a python; a copulating couple; two wrestlers; a *Sango* priest; a woman exposing her sex which is painted bright red; a tree with fruit dangling from it and a snake curled round it.

There is no specific order or sequence in their appearance and the dancing of the mask is not related to the subject matter of the mask. This *Gelede* dance is therefore more like a carnival procession than a theatrical performance. One might speak of the beginning of a puppet theatre, however, because sometimes the limbs of the superstructure can be moved by the masquerader with the help of a string that is hidden inside the masquerader's costume. Particularly the copulating couple can be 'animated' in this way to great effect.

Closer to theatre is the *Egungun* society known as *Agbegijo*.

The *Egungun* society is also a very serious affair. Its main function is to deal with the worship and appeasement of the dead. The great masks are impersonations of ancestors. They are sacrosanct and to touch them could mean death.

The *Agbegijo* group (literally, 'we take wood to dance') are again entertainers. Here we have a relatively clear-cut division between the sacred and the profane, because though the *Agbegijo* are members of the cult, and though they have to be initiated and learn how to deal with the dead, they are not allowed to carry the serious masks.

They have their own head and lead a fairly independent existence, often travelling far and wide as professional entertainers. They do not necessarily dance on religious occasions but come out whenever they are called by people who are able to pay them.

Their own dance involves acting: the *Egungun* dancer does not merely display the mask; he acts the part. The mask he uses is usually a face mask and it is supported by the appropriate costume. The masks imitate leopards, monkeys, crocodiles, snakes, tortoises and other animals. Each animal has to act its part: the monkey scratches; the leopard climbs on the roof of a house and pounces down on a chicken. Often there is a whole scene between a hunter and a leopard. Others imitate people. These may be funny because of abnormal features: the beak-nosed man, or the bucktoothed woman. Or else they may make fun of ethnic groups: the Hausaman, the Fulani woman; the Dahomey warrior. One of the most amusing masks is usually the European. They wear masks with long pointed noses, their smooth black hair is made from a Colobus monkey skin. They walk around, stiffly shake hands and say 'Howdoyoudo'. In Abeokuta I have seen 'Prince Philip' and 'Queen Elizabeth'. Members of other cult groups also come in for fun: the *Sango* worshipper, the *Gelede* Mask, the *Agemo* masquerader are common figures. In each case the masquerader has learned the appropriate dance and style of singing.

In some groups little stories are enacted. The *Sango* worshipper begins his display, is interrupted by policemen and finally bribes his way out of trouble. The harlot often does a kind of strip-tease act—displaying long cloth breasts and embroidered pubic hair—and she may frequently do a mock copulation with the policeman or some other character.

A form of puppet theatre is also known to these masqueraders. There is a mask called *Fafa* that consists of a dancing raffia mat. This mat finally comes to a standstill and two carved dolls emerge. They seem supported by sticks, but these are not visible because they are hidden in a long hose

270

of cloth. The dolls rise up into the air on their invisible sticks—some twenty feet high—and usually amuse themselves up there to everybody's delight.

Thus the *Agbegijo* dancers come rather close to theatre. They are mimes, and often very good ones. But I have not yet seen a longer story with a complicated plot acted out by one of these groups.

When theatre finally developed in Yoruba country it came from an entirely different source: the Church.

It was, I believe, the split-away African Churches, the Seraphim and Cherubim, the Apostolic Church and others who began to perform Biblical stories in and outside the church as a means of instructing their members, and also as a fund-raising device. I do not know when this activity actually started, but I am told that it existed in the 'thirties. Among the favourite subjects treated were 'Adam and Eve'; 'Joseph and his Brethren', the 'Nativity' and 'Nebuchadnezzar'. Usually the Biblical texts are treated quite freely. I can remember a performance of 'Adam and Eve'—some fifteen years ago—in the old Glover Memorial Hall in Lagos, where Adam and Eve, both dressed in black swimsuits, indulged in ribald remarks on discovering their nudity in Paradise.

The music of these Biblical plays was—and still is—based on Yoruba hymns and it is attractive but monotonous. E. K. Philips, the famous organist of Lagos, used to call Yoruba the missing link between speech and music. What he meant was that the music is so highly tonal that one merely has to increase the intervals between speech tones to turn speech into music. The relative position of speech tones must of course be observed in writing Yoruba music in order to preserve the sense, but this naturally imposes very severe restrictions on the composition of melody. The richness that traditional Yoruba music derives from its rhythmic structure, from the different *colour* of the large variety of drums and flutes; and from the complicated and varied methods of voice production, were not exploited in these plays.

Professional theatre in Yoruba begins with Hubert Ogunde, who recently celebrated his twentieth anniversary as a professional dramatist. All these years he has managed to keep a company going. Yoruba theatre is of course a better commercial proposition in Nigeria than English-speaking theatre. On the one hand, a Yoruba theatre will find a large number of audiences within a very short travelling distance. On the other hand it is possible to form a Yoruba company with primary school leavers, which means that they can be maintained for less than a hundred pounds a month. The living standard of actors who can perform in English would be infinitely higher.

Ogunde's major problem was to find actresses to keep them in the company. Acting is not a very respectable profession in Nigeria. Many parents will not allow their daughters on the stage. Then, of course, the girls tend to marry young and after many months of training the company director is apt to lose them to their husbands. But Ogunde is the kind of thoroughly professional showman who is not easily put out. At first he experimented with boys taking girls' parts—as in the Elizabethan theatre. But in the end he found a more satisfactory and gallant solution: he married all his actresses. Thus today the female section of his company is the most stable; and I can remember that, not so long ago, when his boys quarrelled with him and left him suddenly before a performance which was already advertised, Ogunde put on the show with girls only.

Ogunde secularised Yoruba theatre. He moved away quickly from Biblical themes, though King Solomon, Nebuchadnezzar, the Garden of Eden and Israel in Egypt still figure in his repertoire.

Many of his most successful plays indulge in a mild form of social satire. Ogunde's tunes are still basically hymn tunes—particularly as far as the dialogue is concerned—but he has jazzed up the whole show and he opens most of his performances with a crazy number called the opening glee, in which lightly dressed girls go wild on saxophones. The plays rely heavily on horseplay and sex appeal—but Ogunde told me recently that he had once been writing more ambitious plays.

Ogunde explained to me: there are two types of play in Yoruba. The cultural play and the 'jeun-jeun' (or bread-and-butter) play. One of his earlier plays had been the *Black Forest* (which unfortunately I have not been privileged to see). Ogunde describes it as a Yoruba cultural play, with traditional dance music and the rest. But when he took this play on tour to Ghana and the Ivory Coast he returned with 7/6d. in his pocket, and he owed his cast a month's salary and the lorry owner the fare. After this experience he decided that he must give the people what they want to see. He learned to play the saxophone and he began his long series of 'bread-and-butter' plays. Ogunde's plays are popular even outside the Yoruba language area. He performs all over West Africa with equal success. Only the songs of the play are written down and rehearsed. Most of the dialogue is improvised on broad outlines previously laid down. This, of course, enables Ogunde to keep his finger on the pulse of the audience all the time.

Recently Ogunde gained fame with a political play, *Yoruba Ronu*, that caused him to be banned from the Western Region. He tells the Yorubas that the loss of prestige they have suffered was the result of quarrelling among their leaders:

> Yorubas undo themselves because of money.
> Yorubas conspire against each other because of jobs,
> They turn the guilty to the innocent
> And the innocent to the guilty.
> They call the thief to break the house
> And they call the owner of the house to catch him.
> Once wisdom carried them to a high place of honour,
> Now they lie flat on the ground.
> Those who were once the masters
> Are now people to be pushed around.
> Yo! Yo! Yo!

Yoruba as bright as fire in the evening
Yoruba rising high like waves of the sea—
Yo Yo Yo!
Yorubas think!
Yorubas have turned themselves into a football
They kick you up,
They kick you down.
A tribe already small,
But now reducing to nothing.
Lazily you squat on your haunches,
Patient like goats led to the slaughter.
Yo Yo Yo!
Yorubas think.

Ogunde quickly cottoned on to the fact that topical plays bring in the crowd. He has since produced another political play in which a mock election is held on the stage, and another play has dealt with the general strike.

Ogunde's main achievement is that he has made theatre a commercial proposition in Nigeria and that he has created theatre audiences all over the country for others to draw on.

It was left to E. K. Ogunmola, one of Ogunde's colleagues from Ekiti, to develop Yoruba 'Opera' as a serious theatre form.

Ogunmola cut out the music hall element from Ogunde's plays: the horseplay, the sex appeal, the saxophones; and he tried to substitute all these by serious acting. His music is more purely Yoruba than Ogunde's—he still does not make full use of Yoruba instruments, relying mostly on Bongo drums, but he has developed a kind of nervous, electric rhythm that underlies all his singing and spoken dialogue and gives considerable unity to his plays.

Ogunmola's *forte* is his acting—his mime in particular; I can remember certain moments from performances seen as long as a decade ago. As an actor, and even as a director, he can reach great heights. As a playwright he is less interesting. Many of his plays are still in the Biblical tradition: Nebuchadnezzar, Joseph and his Brethren and so on. Others again are fairytales, reminiscent of the fantastic plots found in Fagunwa's novels, where spirits usually appear as the *deus ex machina* to save the hero from his plight.

He is most successful when he attempts social satire and in this field *Love of Money* is probably his greatest play. It tells the story of the downfall of a happy man through foolish ambition. The opening of the play presents Adeleke, a comfortably wealthy man, husband of a pretty wife and father of two children. But already he is tempting his fate by pestering his wife and querying her loyalty:

'If the world is turned upside down,' he says, 'if I should be poor; if money is finished and you have no cloth to wear—whom will you recognise as your husband?'

Morolayo, his loyal wife, gives him no cause for complaint. She continues to profess her loyalty, and so do his children. Adeleke is satisfied: 'It is the head that brings you luck,' he says 'and good reputation.'

However his friends appear with sinister warning—like a Greek Chorus:

> Our friend—don't you know,
> That if the world rewards you, you must live wisely;
> Money does not stay in the same place for generations to come.
> Fear the son of man!
> When people look at the bush fowl—
> It is because they want to eat it with *okro* soup.
> When the earthworm is swaggering about, the hen gets annoyed.
> The people of the world don't like us when we get rich.
> Don't trust your luck:
> The girls of nowadays are bad—you know;
> The girls of nowadays are hard.
> They merely come to eat you clean,
> They shave your head and paint it black.
> Beware of them!
> If the world rewards you, live wisely!
> Money does not stay in the same place for generations to come:
> Fear the son of man!

Sure enough, temptation comes Adeleke's way very quickly in the form of Mopelola, a loose girl who declares bluntly that she intends to marry Adeleke. Adeleke is confused but pleased. When his wife returns, she immediately notices that there is something wrong, and Adeleke confesses:

> Ah—there is something. There is something, there is something.
> Come here and sit down.
> Since I have come into the world
> and since I married and had children
> My eyes have not seen,
> my eyes have not heard
> that a woman wakes up early in the morning
> and goes to man's house
> and chooses him as her husband!
> Ha! It is like a dream! I cannot understand—
> Mopelola came to my house—she wants to be my wife.
> Love covered all her body when she came to my house.
> She says I am the only one she wants to be her husband.
> When the yam seller refuses to be paid—
> When the child refuses to eat maize gruel—
> What is one to do?
> Morolayo, please enlighten me.

But Morolayo is a good wife. She sees nothing wrong with the proposition: or so she pretends.

274

Ah—what you say is good. It is good.
There is nothing wrong in my eyes.
Remember the proverb of our elders,
The proverb of our fathers:
An orange that fails to fall into the hands of good people
Will surely be eaten by the birds.
Let us get ready then,
So that we may be two in your house.
If Mopelola is your wife
I shall be happy.

Needless to say the new wife soon quarrels with the senior one. Adeleke, blinded with love, sides with Mopelola and drives away his first wife: Morolayo and her children sing a pathetic farewell:

Adeleke, we are ready to go.
If you want to find an elephant—you must go to the bush.
If you want to find a buffalo—you must go to the savannah.
If you want to find another wife like me—you will be looking
    forever.

Mopelola, the new wife, soon turns out to be a source of trouble. Other men come and claim a refund of the dowry paid on her. The friends keep turning up periodically with their sinister warning. But Adeleke pays no heed.

Eventually Mopelola's boy friend appears—he is a hooligan with the mysterious name R.S.K. He comes with a group of crooks—money doublers—and they fool Adeleke out of all his money. The moment he is poor, Mopelola, who is in league with R.S.K., packs her load.

Mopelola reveals her true character in her farewell:

Ha, listen, Adeleke's friends, wait.
Listen, be my witnesses, wait and listen to me.
My father who begot me was a rich man.
My mother who brought me up was a rich woman.
A goat cannot give birth to a sheep!
I am ready to leave—I am going!

This simple summary of the text or even a reading of the complete text cannot give one even a faint idea of the pleasures of the performance. Ogunmola's capacity for mime, his eye for detail, his intimate knowledge of the Yoruba people—all these add to the delight of the performance. Ogunmola does not seem like a writer who is at the beginning of a tradition. He has no axes to grind, he does not attempt to change the world. He has the tolerance that springs from wisdom, and he can laugh at human follies without bitterness. In European theatre nothing comes closer to him than the degenerate *fin de siècle* Viennese comedies by Nestroy and Raymund. There is the same sophisticated feeling of resignation in both.

275

Love of Money is still Ogunmola's favourite play—even though he gained greater fame with *The Palm Wine Drinkard*. This play owed most of its success to the colourful and splendid production rather than to the subtleties of the text. Mr. Nwoko's costumes and *décor* were a big attraction and Ogunmola's personal acting was, as always, a delight to watch. But the text—based on Professor Collis's adaptation—was poor. Not only was the whole sense of Tutuola's book perverted by the happy ending (the palm-wine drinkard discovers at the end that everything was merely a dream!) but the play consists of a series of loosely connected episodes and there is neither development nor tension. One could speak of a pageant rather than a play.

In his most recent play, *Conscience*, Ogunmola goes back to the realism and social satire of *Love of Money* in which he is at his best. In this play, however, Ogunmola has gone beyond his earlier work in both the music and the dancing, and there seems to be an indication here of new developments lying ahead.

Ogunmola's most recent colleague is Duro Ladipo. Though he has been involved in theatre work for a number of years now, it is only three years since he directed a professional theatre company.

Ladipo started his career as a musician. Even in the days when he was a primary school teacher he composed Yoruba music for the local church in Oshogbo. He soon got into trouble with the church authorities, because he insisted on bringing drums into the church. He then began to perform his Easter and Christmas Cantatas in schools and clubs and this finally led him into drama.

Ladipo was the first Yoruba composer and dramatist to break with the hymn and highlife tradition in the theatre. He uses music for dramatic effect—not as a mere fluid in which the words can swim. He has made the whole wide range of classical Yoruba music available to Yoruba theatre: the hard metallic sound of the *bata* drums, the subtle *dundun* talking drum, the muffled sound of the *okiti* pottery drums, the little wooden flute—all these instruments and many more are played by Ladipo's small orchestra and are used to obtain specific dramatic effects. In plays like *Oba Koso* (The King does not Hang) one can speak of composition in the true sense of the word. The rich musical texture of these plays goes hand in hand with complex dancing and singing. Here again Ladipo has studied the different singing techniques and dancing steps of Yoruba hunters, Sango worshippers, masqueraders and so forth.

The language of these plays draws heavily on traditional Yoruba poetry: When Sango's wives in *Oba Koso* sings:

> You think the worm is dancing—
> But that is merely the way it walks.
> You think Sango is fighting you—
> But that is merely the way he *is*

then they are reciting the ancient praise names of the God that have been

276

handed down for generations. On the other hand, when Timi in the same play opens his incantation with the beautiful lines:

> I come gently like rain in the evening
> I come swiftly like rain in the morning
> I come suddenly like rain in bright sunlight . . .

then Ladipo writes his own poetry in the classical manner.

Oba Koso is the story of a Yoruba king who was ambitious and incited his generals to go to war and enlarge his kingdom. When his people finally persuaded him that they needed peace, he found that he could no longer control the generals he had created. Desperate at having failed his people he decides to go into exile, and finally hangs himself. But the people of Oyo —his kingdom—worship him as a God after his death. The king never died, they say, and one of his defiantly paradoxical praise names becomes 'The king does not hang.'

> *Kabiyesi o!*
> *To to to to to Fuuuun!*
> Fire in your eyes,
> Fire in your mouth,
> Fire on the roofs!
> The kite was lost in the sky
> And returned to its nest.
> The banana was cut down
> But bears a new fruit.
> You will speak to us
> Through the *bata* drum.
> You will dance for us
> With the *dundun* drum.
> Two hundred glowing embers
> Must bow down to the fire.
> One thousand warriors
> Must succumb to death:
> Two hundred stars
> Must worship the sun.
> *Kabiyesi o!*
> The king does not hang!

Oba Koso has the feeling of Greek tragedy, and its poetry comes across so well in translation that it was possible for Klaus Stephan to turn it into a very successful German radio play.

In *Oba Waja* Ladipo takes up the familiar West African theme of the 'conflict of cultures'. But there is much less theorising here than in many West African novels. Ladipo treats the theme as one individual's personal tragedy and his play is based on fact. It was only in 1946 when the *Alafin* (king) of Oyo died that the Commander of the King's Horse prepared to

277

follow him to the grave, according to the custom, because the king must not cross the river of death unattended:

> Shall the owner of the palace cross the
>   river alone?
> Shall he confront the gate-keeper of
>   heaven unaccompanied?
> Ojurongbe Aremu, Commander of the
>   King's Horse,
> You will row him across the river;
> You will enforce his entry into heaven.
> Ojurongbe Aremu,
> Tomorrow you will be a burning sun, like
>   Alafin,
> Tomorrow your eyes will gleam in the
>   shadows,
> Tomorrow you will shine like a red-hot
>   iron.

As tradition demands, the Commander of the Horse prepares a big feast. He dances through the town attended by friends and family in order to die in the evening by an act of willpower. But the District Officer suddenly appears on the scene and arrests the Commander of the Horse in order to stop the 'barbaric custom'. The Commander of the Horse is bewildered and confused. He knows that he has failed his people. He could kill himself with a matchet. But what would be the use? The magic charm is broken and the glorious death by willpower is forfeited:

> My head whom I worshipped in the
>   morning,
> My head whom I praised in the morning,
> Why did you allow this to happen in my
>   time?
> The white man rendered my charms im-
>   potent,
> He drained the power of my medicine.
> He has deprived me of a glorious death.
> Now I can die of the matchet
> like a cow slaughtered in the market.
> I can bleed to death.
> Now I can burn myself alive
> smouldering away like a rubbish dump.
> But the glorious road to heaven is closed.
> The elephant has been beheaded like a
>   common hyena,
> The elephant has been trapped like a
>   common antelope.

> People of Oyo,
> Help me to repair the life that was spoiled
> By the white man's rule.

But his son, who heard the news of the *Alafin*'s death, rushes home from the Gold Coast, in order—as he thinks—to bury his father. When he sees his father alive he is so overcome by shame that he kills himself.

Suddenly the District Officer, whose 'good deed' has been turned into horror, has become a tragic figure, a 'sport of the Gods':

> What mockery is this!
> Can good intentions turn to evil?
> Can justice turn into crime?
> Must the son pay, because the father was
>   saved?

But the people's judgement on him is harsh:

> We speak—you do not hear us.
> We shout—you turn away.
> We beat the drum—you do not understand.
> Look now—the evil of your work has been
>   exposed.
> The unspeakable has happened.
> The unpronounceable has come to pass.
> The head of the family is shitting like a
>   teething child.
> The palm tree should die, being weighed
>   down by his fruit
> See now the old stem erect, and his fruit
>   rotting on the ground.
> Oyinbo Ajele—this is your work.

In the District Officer's world there is neither comfort nor an explanation for the terrible events which he caused to happen. But Yoruba philosophy knows about Eshu, 'confuser of men', the unpredictable God of fate who orders things his own way. Thus to the people of Oyo the tragedy is not meaningless—things fall into place:

> White man, bringer of new laws,
> White man, bringer of new times,
> Your work was confounded by Eshu,
>   confuser of men.
> Nobody can succeed against the will of
>   Eshu
> The god of fate;
> Having thrown a stone today—he kills a
>   bird yesterday.

Lying down, his head hits the roof—
Standing up he cannot look into the
   cooking pot.
With Eshu
Wisdom counts for more than good inten-
   tions,
And understanding is greater than justice.

Duro Ladipo's latest production is *Eda*, an adaptation of *Everyman* by a former member of his cast, Obotunde Ijimere. In this play the Christian mythology of Heaven and Hell has been replaced by the Yoruba concept of reincarnation. The production proves that Ladipo is capable of comedy as well as tragedy and that his intellectual approach has carried these plays far beyond the limits of 'folk opera'.

In September 1964 Ladipo's *Oba Koso* had a triumphant success at the Berlin Theatre and Music Festival, where it was listed as one of the three highlights of the season, alongside with Stravinsky's concert and Genet's *The Blacks*.

At the time of writing Ladipo prepares to present *Oba Koso* at the Commonwealth Festival and he will tour Europe and Israel with both *Oba Koso* and *Eda*. Yoruba theatre has gained international recognition.

Two Nigerian Playwrights

MARTIN ESSLIN

Wole Soyinka, *Five Plays*, O.U.P., 1964
J. P. Clark, *Three Plays*, O.U.P., 1964

I must, at the very outset, disclaim any special knowledge of the social and cultural background from which these plays spring. Indeed, I presume that must have been the reason I was asked to review them in these pages—to provide, for once, the corrective of a change of perspective, as it were; of focus, of viewpoint; to submit them, like organisms in a laboratory, to a survival test *in vacuo* by seeing how they appear to someone who, in the course of his professional work, has to read an endless succession of plays from totally different backgrounds and who will therefore, almost automatically, apply to them the same general yardstick; who will judge them not as African plays but as plays pure and simple.

Having said this, I am bound to add that I think such a test hardly possible. It may be so with poetry, which deals with the basic human emotions on a purely individual plane: affection, loneliness, joy, sorrow and the skills with which they are expressed, might be truly universal. But drama deals with the basic human emotions and predicaments in a social context, both in the interaction of several characters on the stage, and in the even more important interaction between the stage and the audience. The basic human emotions are still involved, but they are expressed through social conventions which may be totally different from one society to another. The *Antigone* of Sophocles, for example, depends for its impact on the consequences that followed, in the belief of the Greeks, from a corpse left unburied. Antigone's action in burying her dead brother can appear in its true light, as an expression of death-defying sisterly love, only in that social context. To a modern European audience that particular social convention is almost meaningless. If the play is still performed, and still has an impact, this is almost entirely due to the fact that the audiences concerned have been taught about Greek beliefs at school and are therefore able to make a special effort to translate the Greek convention into an expression of a basic human emotion. Because the poetry of Sophocles is so great, but also because it is one of the social conventions of the European world that Greek drama *must* be appreciated (being part and parcel of a more or less mythical cultural heritage) this special effort is sometimes made by some people (who are only a tiny minority, anyway). But equally great works of Indian or Chinese drama remain totally unappreciated and unperformed in the West, simply because those special factors are not operative. This is not to say that universal, or almost universal, drama is wholly impossible. There may, after all, be social conventions that are

281

shared by very large sections of humanity, if not by all mankind. The prohibition of incest, for example, is one of these; hence Sophocles' *King Oedipus* comes as near to universal drama as can be imagined. Its subject-matter is universal; and this allows the supreme craftsmanship of the play's construction and the greatness of its poetic expression to make an equal appeal to all epochs and all nationalities. In other words: in order to reach truly universal acceptance a play must fulfil both conditions—it must have a subject-matter that is accessible to the maximum number of different societies; and it must be an example of supreme craftsmanship in construction and language. This dependence of drama on social contexts explains, on a much humbler level, why so few French or German plays ever achieve success in the English-speaking world, and why, even within the English-speaking world, the great success in the West End of London so often proves a dismal failure on Broadway, and vice versa. It is only occasionally that the very strangeness of the social context is a factor *in favour* of an imported play which allows it to cash in on its exoticism. But, alas, experience shows that delight in exoticism almost invariably fastens on superficial, external factors (like the bare bosoms of African dance companies) and therefore tends to favour the most shallow importations which concentrate on such surface elements.

These considerations should make it easier to understand why the work even of major dramatists, past and present, is less easily acclimatised in different social environments than the work of poets or even novelists.

But, it might be argued, the work of the two playwrights we are here discussing, Wole Soyinka and J. P. Clark, should be largely exempt from these considerations; for, after all, *they* are writing in English. Far from being an advantage, in my opinion, this is a further handicap. Not that these two playwrights are in any way at a disadvantage in using the English language. On the contrary: both are real masters of all its nuances and, indeed, very considerable artists in English. Here again the problem arises from the nature of drama itself. These plays are by Africans about Africans in an African social context. And they are, largely, about Africans who, in reality, speak their own African languages. It is here that the problem lies. We are here presented with African peasants, African fishermen, African labourers expressing themselves in impeccable English. Of course in reality they speak their own languages equally impeccably and the playwrights have merely translated what they would have said in those languages into the equivalent English. Precisely! Which is to say that these original plays labour under the universal handicap of all translated drama. And anyone who has to deal with the problems of plays in translation, as I have to almost daily, will know what an enormous handicap that represents! How should a French peasant in a play by, let us say, Pagnol, speak in English? If one translates him into an equivalent rustic dialect—from Provençal into, say, West-country—the character will be completely changed. The Southern French are hotblooded; Wessex yeomen slow and puritanical. So the translation into a roughly equivalent English idiom will not work. But if you translate the French peasant dialect into standard English, the peasant will cease to be a peasant altogether. In other words: realism in translations of this kind is quite impossible. Realistic plays in non-standard idioms are untranslatable. Only highly stylised poetic drama has a chance in translation. And that surely is the reason why J. P. Clark writes entirely in a highly stylised free verse, while Wole Soyinka's prose (which only occasionally is heightened to verse) also remains on a strictly formalised, stylised level. The question arises however: would it not have been more effective and easier for J. P. Clark to deal with his subject-matter in realistic, vernacular, prose terms? To me this certainly is true of his play *The Raft* which deals with the plight of four Nigerian lumbermen helplessly drifting to perdition downstream. This is tragedy, but it is realistic tragedy; much here depends on the differentiation between the townsman and the peasant, the old man and the younger generation. The free verse submerges rather than emphasises these differentiations; it also detracts from the purely technical side of the tragedy, the men's various attempts to salvage their craft. To deal with such a subject in verse would be justified only if the situation could be raised up to the level of an eternal poetic symbol. Thus the very fact that verse is used constitutes a programme of tremendous ambitiousness; and I don't think that this particular play can live up to such a high ambition. It is therefore literally crushed under the load of its poetic objective. As a realistic play in realistic prose it would have been most gripping. But for such prose in the mouths of African working men there is no equivalent in English. These are the horns of the dilemma on which a playwright like J. P. Clark can be impaled.

I am, in my own mind, not quite clear as to the reasons that prompt African playwrights to use English in preference to their own rich and highly poetic languages.

Is it that they themselves are more at home in English? In that case there might be very strong arguments for their concentrating on a realistic treatment of the life of English-speaking Africans. This would enable them to use an actual language, or different shades and idioms as spoken by different strata of that particular—and surely immensely important—segment of their society. Or is it that African playwrights use English because they want a larger, more universal audience? This has been the motivation of European playwrights belonging to language communities of restricted size; for example, a Hungarian (Julius Hay) who has written in German, or a Rumanian (Eugene Ionesco) who writes in French. But in that case the subject-matter must also be of universal comprehensibility and validity. Ionesco, for example, never refers to Rumanian conditions in his plays. Hay's German output is largely concerned with historical subjects of general European character.

Or is it that, English being the language of the educated classes in Africa —or at least in ex-British Africa—and education spreading ever wider, English will become the *lingua franca* of educated Africans in those countries regardless of national borders? If that is so, the playwrights concerned are faced with the task of evolving a new, truly African brand of English which will eventually be able to embody the emotions, customs and daily life of the people concerned as efficiently and beautifully as West Indian English expresses the character of the people who use it in daily life as well as in literature. I, personally, don't know which of these assumptions is true. I merely throw them out as possible starting points for debate in a situation which clearly is in need of some very thorough discussion of a number of basic issues.

Having listed the handicaps and dilemmas inherent in J. P. Clark's and Wole Soyinka's work, I should like to emphasise that I have done so merely to highlight the magnitude of their achievement. Despite the limitation that, for a European reader, the social context of their subject-matter is often difficult to savour in its full emotional implications and impacts, and despite the limitation that their use of English restricts them to stylised poetic, or at best semi-poetic, treatment of that subject-matter, they have in a considerable number of cases succeeded in moving and uplifting a reader who is a hardened professional not easily moved or uplifted by plays he reads and (as a professional producer) re-enacts and re-produces in his mind's eye.

Of John Pepper Clark's *Three Plays* it was *The Masquerade* which came nearest to achieving this effect on me. It is a simple tale of fisher-folk in the Niger Delta. A stranger has won the hand of a beautiful girl. The wedding is in progress when the rumour spreads that he is the issue of an adulterous relationship and that his mother died in childbirth. Thus he is accursed and the girl's father insists the marriage cannot be consummated. When the daughter persists in clinging to her bridegroom, the father kills her. And the bridegroom, too, trying to avenge his love, falls victim to the father's wrath. Choruses of neighbours and priests comment on the events of the play, and —as in Greek tragedy—relate crucial incidents of violence that have happened off-stage. The central issue of the play, whether it is indeed sacrilege for a young girl to get married to the son of a adulterous mother who died in childbirth, is difficult for an outsider to grasp. But the atmosphere of relentless doom is so strong; the father, Diribi, acts with such utter conviction, that I, for one, was carried along. Indeed the high degree of stylisation which springs from the author's need to relate his tale in a timeless free verse tends to obliterate the local colour to such an extent that the European reader is constantly reminded of similar doom-laden wedding incidents among simple people in Spanish, French or German literature or, for that matter, in the equally stark and relentless world of Scottish Ballads. Lorca's *Blood Wedding*, more elaborate and quite differently motivated, has a similarly balladesque character.

Clark's language is remarkable for what I can only describe as highly sophisticated simplicity. This is how one of the priests relates the heroine's last struggle with her father, who found her playing marbles, with her baby brother on her lap:

284

> . . . With a bound
> She was running, kneeling, presenting the baby
> As a shield although clutching it back
> From harm and all this in one motion—
> Do forgive my running nose.

How subtle the description of the conflicting motives that drive the girl to use the baby as a shield and to protect it at the same time! And how brilliant the insertion of the physical effect on the speaker of having to relate this terrible incident. The translation of emotion into its physical expression is of the very essence of drama. How enviable, for any European, is the African playwright's ability to refer to any aspects of the physical side of the human condition without shame or self-consciousness. In a European play, the line about the running nose would have been hopelessly sentimentalised into something like

> Forgive me, grief has overcome me quite . . .

or

> Tears, bitter tears prevent my going on . . .

—clichés that drown the immediacy of physical sensation in empty phrasemaking.

Although this is never expressly stated, *The Masquerade* clearly forms the second part of a diptych, of which the first play in this volume is the other half. For, in describing the curse under which Tufa, the bridegroom, labours, the angry father says:

> . . . Did he tell you also his father
> Usurped the bed of his elder brother, yes,
> Brazenly in his lifetime, and for shame
> Of it after hanged himself in broad daylight
> While this unfortunate abused husband
> Walked of his own will into the sea?

This passage in *The Masquerade* is a concise and accurate synopsis of *Song of a Goat*. So, in fact, J. P. Clark has here attempted something in the nature of a cycle of plays on the working out of a family curse, no less than a Nigerian *Oresteia*. It is an ambitious undertaking. And it nearly succeeds. Not completely though. For, unaware of this intention at first reading it, I found *Song of a Goat* not quite convincing. The motivation of the tragedy, which is simply the husband's inability to engender a child, is far too simple and unoriginal to support the weight of full-scale tragedy across the generations. Moreover, the wife's seduction of the husband's younger brother, is also, at least for my admittedly quite differently conditioned feelings, far too clumsily straightforward. Instead of primeval tragedy (of which the second part of the diptych undoubtedly has the atmosphere) we are, in this crucial first part, merely left with a rather predictable incident from the pages

285

of any popular newspaper. But here too the stark, timeless and almost place-less simplicity of the language invests the trivial event with the dignity of near tragedy.

I have already pointed out why the very timelessness and placelessness of J. P. Clark's language seems to me to militate against his own intentions in the third play in the volume, *The Raft*. The four men on the raft could only be individualised and fully motivated by being treated far more realistically. Left as stylised and generalised figures their actions seem unnecessarily arbitrary. But here, too, a very ambitious objective—the raft as as image of human life and man's dependence on his fellow men and sheer chance—is very boldly and imaginatively pursued.

If J. P. Clark is clearly inspired by a classical ideal of austere archetypal characters and events, Wole Soyinka is of a far more romantic turn of mind: he revels in variety and diversity, alternating between farce (*The Trials of Brother Jero*), tragedy (*The Strong Breed*) and romantic mythology (*A Dance of the Forests*), changing from prose to verse within one play and employing the full panoply of the great African tradition of dance and mime. And whereas J. P. Clark's verse removes his plays into an almost timeless sphere, Soyinka's are firmly set in the present—a very recognisable independent Nigeria with its corrupting town life set against superstition and backwardness in the countryside (for example in *The Swamp Dwellers, The Lion and the Jewel*) and ambitious members of Parliament falling for the career prospects held out to them by fraudulent sectarian cultists (*Brother Jero*).

Undoubtedly the most ambitious of Soyinka's plays[1] is *A Dance of the Forests*, a kind of African *Midsummer Night's Dream*, in which a group of three guilty people is lured into the woods by a group of nature gods and spirits and confronted with their own guilt, which at the same time is shown to be identical with the guilt of previous incarnations of the same human beings in one of the great golden ages of the African past that have in recent years been rediscovered to such good purpose. Ogun and Oro and the Forest Head (greatest and wisest among the rulers of the forest) have been asked to supply some illustrious spirits of the past for the celebration of the gathering of the Tribes at which the rulers of the present want to demon-strate the continuity of the history of their newly independent states. But the spirits, while they are obliging, produce not heroes but two dead people, a man and a woman, who are embodiments also of the guilt and violence of the past. So the three sinners see themselves involved with these two ghosts in a re-enactment of a moment of past history, an incident at the court of Mata Kharibu. Here the guilty woodcarver Demoke, who was instrumental in the death of his apprentice at the top of the mighty tree he was carving into a totem for the celebration, recognises himself in the equally guilty court-poet; Rola, the prostitute is revealed to herself as the legendary Mother Tortoise, Mata Kharibu's heartless man-eating consort;

---

[1] Since this essay was written the following play has been published: Soyinka, W., *The Road*, London, O.U.P., 1965.

286

and Adenebi, the Council Orator who took a bribe by which a truck was licensed to carry a vast overload of passengers who fell victim to an accident, reappears as Mata Kharibu's Court Historian who also took a bribe to facilitate the sale of a company of valiant men into slavery. Chastened by the recognition of their true natures, but unpunished, the three guilty human beings return from the forest. This is only one, if (in my opinion), the principal strand in a many-layered poetic texture which the author handles with consummate skill.

And the basic philosophy behind it all? It is, for a citizen of an emerging, developing country in a truly revolutionary situation, strangely conservative and resigned. As Forest Head says towards the end of the play:

> 'The fooleries of beings whom I have fashioned closer to me weary and distress me. Yet I must persist, knowing that nothing is ever altered. My secret is my eternal burden—to pierce the encrustations of soul-deadening habit, and bare the mirror of original nakedness—knowing full well it is all futility. Yet I must do this alone, and no more, since to intervene is to be guilty of contradiction, and yet to remain altogether unfelt is to make my long-rumoured ineffectuality complete; hoping that when I have tortured awareness from their souls, that perhaps, only perhaps, in new beginnings . . .'

Here speaks the creator of the universe; but also, and most feelingly, the human creator, the poet and playwright, whose purpose it is indeed to pierce the encrustations of soul-deadening habit and to hold the mirror of their original nakedness up to his readers and spectators.

The Lion and the Jewel, in a much lighter mood, again contrasts the present and the past; the forward-looking moderns and the upholders of past traditions. Here it is a beautiful girl, Sidi, the village belle of Ilujinle, who stands between the two warring worlds. Lakunle, the school-teacher, tries to introduce mechanical civilisation to the village; the *Bale*, Baroka, who lives lazily in his harem and exercises his prowess with a daily bout of wrestling, stands for the tribal past of chieftainship and old-world ways of life. When Sidi is discovered by a photographer from the big city and appears on the front page of an illustrated magazine, the *Bale* wants to make her his latest wife. At first she rejects him. But when the *Bale* confesses to his senior wife that he has lost his manhood and this secret is immediately leaked by her to her young rival, Sidi decides to tempt him. And, of course, the confession of impotence was merely a ruse. Having tasted the old man's mature love, Sidi contemptuously rejects her progressive suitor and casts her lot with the traditional past. This is a gay, light-hearted play, with much mime and dance. But it surely also has an allegorical meaning. Is Sidi the Nigerian people who might believe in the impotence of the past but will nevertheless experience its powers? Wole Soyinka seems indeed a romantic!

And yet in two of the three shorter plays in the volume, he joins in attacking the superstitions and obscurantisms of that same past. In *The Swamp*

Dwellers a young farmer whose fields have been flooded in spite of his having done all the priest demanded to propitiate the Serpent which is the spirit of the swamps, takes his revenge on the priest by making him believe he will cut his throat while he is shaving him. But then, to balance the account, that same young farmer has returned from Lagos, where he wanted to make his fortune, having been cheated and exploited by his wealthy twin brother, who has also taken his wife away from him. And indeed: the mother of the twins persists in claiming that the brother who disappeared into the big city has in fact been swallowed by the swamp. So the backward swamp, ruled by superstition, is somehow equated with the equally murderous modern city of Lagos. In *The Strong Breed*, however, the hero is clearly on the side of the new ideas. Eman lives as a schoolteacher in a village where he is a stranger. What he does not know is that each New Year's Day the villagers make an outsider the carrier of their sins whom they beat and harry to distraction. When he realises that this year's choice has fallen on an idiot boy whom he has taken under his wing, Eman offers himself instead and is cruelly sacrificed. The only gleam of hope lies in the fact that the majority of the villagers is horrified when it becomes clear how brutally the upholders of the old tradition have acted. Is this 'the tortured awareness' in men's souls that might perhaps, in the Forest Head's words in that other play, result in a new beginning? 'Perhaps, only perhaps...'.

Wole Soyinka is a highly accomplished playwright. My only criticism of his dramatic technique concerns his somewhat overfree, and somewhat confusing, use of flash-back scenes. In practice the flash-back (which is largely a cinematic technique) does not work very effectively on the stage which does not possess the subtle fade-outs of the screen; so that flash-backs as a rule involve clumsy sceneshifting in the dark, loss of continuity and easy flow of the action. This is not to say that the flashback should not be used; merely that it should be used with caution and be introduced with the utmost degree of clarity (Brecht, for example, announced his flash-backs quite boldly as demonstrations of past events, as evidence which the author, or one of the characters wanted to present).

But this is a minor technical criticism of Soyinka's work. I have no doubt whatever that he is a master-craftsman of the theatre and a major dramatic poet.

I have, at the beginning of these remarks, expressed some fundamental considerations which, in my eyes, make the endeavour to create an English-language African drama a difficult and problematical enterprise. But *if* the social conditions exist which will make such an enterprise possible, if an African English-speaking culture is indeed emerging, then Wole Soyinka and J. P. Clark have every right to be regarded as two of the pioneers who in the field of drama have achieved the first, decisive breakthrough.

Selected Bibliography of Scholarship and Criticism

Bernth Lindfors

So much has been written about African literature since the first edition of this anthology appeared in 1967 that it has been necessary to revise completely the bibliography accompanying it. The original bibliography listed articles and other brief studies related to the topics discussed; this one lists only the major books that have appeared on the same range of subjects. The remarkable increase in the number of full-length studies published in recent years reflects the growing interest in the verbal arts of the black world.

Bibliographies and Reference Works

African Book Publishing Record: quarterly journal. (Running bibliography of books published in Africa.)

Journal of Commonwealth Literature: triannual journal. (Annual bibliography of criticism and creative works from Anglophone areas.)

MLA International Bibliography of Books and Articles on the Modern Languages and Literatures. Modern Language Association, New York. (Annual critical bibliography.)

BARATTE-ENO BELINGA, THÉRÈSE, *Bibliographie: Auteurs africains et malgaches de langue française*, 3rd ed. Office de Radiodiffusion Télévision Française, Paris, 1972.

BEETON, RIDLEY, *A Pilot Bibliography of South African English Literature (from the Beginnings to 1971)*, University of South Africa, Pretoria, 1976.

FERRES, JOHN H., and TUCKER, MARTIN, eds., *Modern Commonwealth Literature*, Ungar, New York, 1977.

HERDECK, DONALD E., *African Authors: A Companion to Black Writing. Vol. I: 1300–1973*, Black Orpheus Press, Washington, D.C., 1973.

JAHN, JANHEINZ, and DRESSLER, CLAUS P. *Bibliography of Creative African Writing*, Kraus-Thomson, Nendeln, Liechtenstein, 1971.

JAHN, JANHEINZ, SCHILD, ULLA, and NORDMANN, ALMUT, *Who's Who in African Literature: Biographies, Works, Commentaries*, Erdmann, Tübingen, 1972.

MOSER, GERALD M., *A Tentative Portuguese-African Bibliography: Portuguese Literature in Africa and African Literature in the Portuguese Language*, Pennsylvania State University Libraries, University Park, 1970.

NEW, WILLIAM H., *Critical Writings on Commonwealth Literature: A Selective Bibliography to 1970, with a List of Theses and Dissertations*, Pennsylvania State University Press, University Park and London, 1975.

POPKIN, MICHAEL, ed., *Modern Black Writers*, Ungar, New York, 1978

RAMSARAN, JOHN A. *New Approaches to African Literature: A Guide to Negro-African Writing and Related Studies*, Ibadan University Press, 1965; 2nd ed. 1970.

SAINT-ANDRÉ-UTUDJIAN, ELIANE. *A Bibliography of West African Life and Literature*, African Studies Association, Waltham, Mass., 1977.

SCHEUB, HAROLD. *African Oral Narratives, Proverbs, Riddles, Poetry and Song*, G. K. Hall, Boston, 1977.

SCHMIDT, NANCY J. *Children's Books on Africa and Their Authors: An Annotated Bibliography*, Africana Publishing Co., New York and London, 1975.

UNITED STATES LIBRARY OF CONGRESS. *Africa South of the Sahara: Index to Periodical Literature, 1900–1970*, vol. 4, G. K. Hall, Boston, 1971.

ZELL, HANS M. *African Books In Print*, vols. 1 and 2, 2nd ed., Mansell, London, Meckler, Westport, Conn., 1978.

ZELL, HANS M., and SILVER, HELENE. *A Reader's Guide to African Literature*, Heinemann, London; Africana Publishing Co., New York, 1972.

General Studies

ACHEBE, CHINUA, *Morning Yet on Creation Day: Essays*, Heinemann, London; Anchor/Doubleday, Garden City, N.Y., 1975.

AWOONOR, KOFI, *The Breast of the Earth: A Survey of the History, Culture and Literature of Africa South of the Sahara*, Anchor/Doubleday, Garden City, N.Y., 1975.

BROWN, LLOYD W., ed., *The Black Writer in Africa and the Americas*, Hennessey and Ingalls, Los Angeles, 1973.

CARTEY, WILFRED. *Whispers from a Continent: Writings from Contemporary Black Africa*, Random House, New York, 1969.

COOK, DAVID, *African Literature: A Critical View*, Longman, London, 1977.

COOK, MERCER, and HENDERSON, STEPHEN E., *The Militant Black Writer in Africa and the United States*, University of Wisconsin Press, Madison, 1969.

DATHORNE, O. R., *The Black Mind: A History of African Literature*, University of Minnesota Press, Minneapolis, 1974; rpt. in abridged ed. entitled *African Literature in the Twentieth Century*, University of Minnesota Press, Minneapolis; Heinemann, London, 1976.

ECHERUO, MICHAEL J. C., and OBIECHINA, EMMANUEL N., eds., *Igbo Traditional Life, Culture and Literature*, Conch Magazine Ltd., Owerri, Nigeria, 1971.

FEUSER, WILLFRIED F., *Aspectos de literatura do mundo negro*, Universidade Federal da Bahia, Centro de Estudos Afro-Orientais, Bahia, 1969.

GORDIMER, NADINE, *The Black Interpreters: Notes on African Writing*, SproCas/Ravan, Johannesburg, 1973.

GURR, ANDREW, and ZIRIMU, PIO, eds., *Black Aesthetics: Papers from a Colloquium Held at the University of Nairobi, June 1971*, East African Literature Bureau, Nairobi, Kamala, Dar es Salaam, 1973.

HEYWOOD, CHRISTOPHER, ed., *Perspectives on African Literature: Selections from the Proceedings of the Conference on African Literature Held at the University of Ife 1968*, Heinemann, London; Africana Publishing Co., New York, in association with the Universty of Ife Press, 1971.

HEYWOOD, CHRISTOPHER, ed., *Papers on African Literature*, Sheffield Papers on Literature and Society, No. 1, Department of English Literature, University of Sheffield; University of Texas Press, Austin, 1976.

JAHN, JANHEINZ, *Muntu: An Outline of the New African Culture*, Faber and Faber, London; Grove Press, New York, 1961.

JAHN, JANHEINZ, *A History of Neo-African Literature: Writing in Two Continents*, Faber, London, 1968; Grove Press, New York, 1969.

KILLAM, DOUGLAS G., ed., *African Writers on African Writing*. Heinemann, London; Africana Publishing Co., New York, 1973.

KING, BRUCE, ed., *Introduction to Nigerian Literature*, University of Lagos; Africana Publishing Co., New York; Evans, London, 1971.

KING, BRUCE, and OGUNGBESAN, KOLAWOLE, eds., *A Celebration of Black and African Writing*, Ahmadu Bello University Press and Oxford University Press, Zaria and Ibadan, 1975.

KLÍMA, VLADIMÍR, FRANTIŠEK RŮŽIČKA, KAREL, and ZIMA, PETR, *Black Africa. Literature and Language*, Dordrect, Netherlands; Reidel, Boston, 1975.

LINDFORS, BERNTH, ed., *Critical Perspectives on Nigerian Literatures*, Three Continents Press, Washington, D.C., 1976.

LINDFORS, BERNTH, and SCHILD, ULLA, eds., *Neo-African Literature and Culture: Essays in Memory of Janheinz Jahn*, B. Heymann, Weisbaden, 1976.

LO LIYONG, TABAN, *The Last Word: Cultural Synthesism*, East African Publishing House, Nairobi, 1969.

MELONE, THOMAS, *Mélanges africains*, Editions Pédagogiques Afrique-Contact, Yaoundé, n.d.

MEZO, S. OKECHUKWU, ed., *Modern Black Literature*, Black Academy Press, Buffalo, N.Y., 1971.

MOORE, GERALD, *Seven African Writers*, Oxford University Press, London, 1962; rev. ed., 1966.

MOORE, GERALD, ed., *African Literature and the Universities*, Ibadan University Press for the Congress for Cultural Freedom, 1965.

MOORE, GERALD, *The Chosen Tongue: English Writing in the Tropical World*, Longman, London, 1969.

MPHAHLELE, EZEKIEL, *The African Image*, Faber, London, 1962; revised 2nd ed., 1974.

NGUGI WA THIONG'O. (JAMES.) *Homecoming: Essays on African and Caribbean Literature, Culture and Politics*, Heinemann, London, 1972; Lawrence Hill, New York and Westport, Conn., 1973.

NKOSI, LEWIS, *Home and Exile*, Longman, London, 1965.

NORDMANN-SEILER, ALMUT, *La Littérature néo-africaine*, Presses Universitaires de France, Paris, 1976.

OKPAKU, JOSEPH O., ed., *New African Literature and the Arts.*, vol. 1, Crowell and Third Press, New York, 1970; vol. 2, 1970; vol. 3, 1973.

OLNEY, JAMES, *Tell Me Africa: An Approach to African Literature*, Princeton University Press, 1973.

PÁRICSY, PÁL, ed., *Studies on Modern Black African Literature*, Center for Afro-Asian Research of the Hungarian Academy of Sciences, Budapest, 1971.

P'BITEK, OKOT, *Africa's Cultural Revolution*, Macmillan Books for Africa, Nairobi, 1973.

RIRICARD, ALAIN, *Livre et communication au Nigéria: Essai de vue généraliste*, Présence Africaine, Paris, 1975.

SCHILD, ULLA, *Storia della letteratura africana*, Fratelli Fabbri Editori, Milan, 1971.

SMITH, ROWLAND, ed., *Exile and Tradition: Studies in African and Caribbean Literature*, Longman and Dalhousie University Press, London, 1976.

SOYINKA, WOLE, *Myth, Literature and the African World*, Cambridge University Press, 1976.

TAIWO, OLADELE, *An Introduction to West African Literature*. Nelson, London; Humanities, New York, 1967.

USTVEDT, YNGVAR, ed., *Stemmer fra den tredje verden*, Gyldendal Norsk Forlag, Oslo, 1970.

WANJALA, CHRIS L., ed., *Standpoints on African Literature: A Critical Anthology*, East African Literature Bureau, Nairobi, Kampala, Dar es Salaam, 1973.

WÄSTBERG, PER, *The Writer in Modern Africa: African-Scandinavian Writers' Conference, Stockholm 1967*, Scandinavian Institute of African Studies, Uppsala, 1968; Africana Publishing Co., New York, 1969.

WÄSTBERG, PER, *Afrikas moderna litteratur*, Wahlström and Widstrand, Stockholm, 1969.

WAUTHIER, CLAUDE, *The Literature and Thought of Modern Africa: A Survey*, Pall Mall Press, London, 1966; Praeger, New York, 1967.

Oral Traditions

AWOONOR, KOFI, *Guardians of the Sacred Word: Ewe Poetry*, Nok, New York, 1974.

BASCOM, WILLIAM R., *Ifa Divination: Communication between Gods and Men in West Africa*, Indiana University Press, Bloomington, 1969.

BASCOM, WILLIAM, R., *African Dilemma Tales*, Mouton, The Hague, 1975.

BIEBUYCK, DANIEL, and MATEENE, KAHOMBOC., eds., *The Mwindo Epic from the Banyanga (Congo Republic)*, University of California Press, Berkeley and Los Angeles, 1971.

CALAME-GRIAULE, GENEVIÈVE, *Le Thème de l'arbre dans les contes africains*, Klincksieck, Paris, 1970.

DENG, FRANCIS MADING, *Dinka Folktales: African Stories from the Sudan*, Africana Publishing Co., New York, 1974.

DORSON, RICHARD, ed., *African Folklore*, Anchor/Doubleday, Garden City, N.Y., 1972.

EVANS-PRITCHARD, E. E., *The Zande Trickser*, Clarendon Press, Oxford, 1967.

FINNEGAN, RUTH, *Limba Stories and Storytelling*, Clarendon Press, Oxford, 1967.

FINNEGAN, RUTH, *Oral Literature in Africa*, Clarendon Press, Oxford, 1970.

GOODY, JACK, *The Myth of the Bagre*, Clarendon Press, Oxford, 1972.

HERSKOVITS, MELVILLE J. and FRANCES S., *Dahomean Narrative*, Northwestern University Press, Evanston, 1958.

INNES, GORDON, *Sunjata: Three Mandinka Versions*, School of Oriental and African Studies, University of London, 1974.

SCHEUB, HAROLD, *The Xhosa Ntsomi*, Clarendon Press, Oxford, 1975.

SKINNER, NEIL, ed., *Hausa Tales and Traditions: An English Translation of Tatsuniyoyi na Hausa Originally Compiled by Frank Edgar*, Cass, London; Africana Publishing Co., New York, 1970.

Anglophone Africa

CLARK, J. P., *The Example of Shakespeare*, Longman, London; Northwestern University Press, Evanston, 1970.

DUERDEN, DENNIS, *The Invisible Present: African Art and Literature*, Harper and Row, New York, 1975; Heinemann, London, 1977.

292

DUERDEN, DENNIS, and PIETERSE, COSMO, eds., *African Writers Talking: A Collection of Radio Interviews*, Heinemann, London; Africana Publishing Co., New York, 1972.

GOODWIN, K. L., ed., *National Identity: Papers Delivered at the Commonwealth Literature Conference, University of Queensland, Brisbane, 9th–15th August, 1968*, Heinemann, London and Melbourne, 1970.

GURR, ANDREW, and CALDER, ANGUS, eds., *Writers in East Africa*, East African Literature Bureau, Nairobi, Kampala, Dar es Salaam, 1974.

LAURENCE, MARGARET, *Long Drums and Cannons: Nigerian Dramatists and Novelists, 1952–1966*, Macmillan, London, 1968; Praeger, New York, 1969.

LINDFORS, BERNTH, *Folklore in Nigerian Literature*, Africana Publishing Co., New York, 1973.

MAES-JELINEK, HENA, ed., *Commonwealth Literature and the Modern World*, Didier, Brussels, 1975.

MPHAHLELE, EZEKIEL, *Voices in the Whirlwind and Other Essays*, Hill and Wang, New York; Macmillan, London, 1972.

MUTISO, GIDEON-CYRUS M., *Socio-political Thought in African Literature: Weusi?*, Macmillan, London; Barnes & Noble, New York, 1974.

NAZARETH, PETER, *Literature and Society in Modern Africa: Essays on Literature*, Nairobi, Kampala, Dar es Salaam: East African Literature Bureau, 1972; rpt. as *An African View of Literature*, Northwestern University Press, Evanston, Ill., 1974.

NIVEN, ALASTAIR, ed., *The Commonwealth Writer Overseas: Themes of Exile and Expatriation*, Didier, Brussels, 1976.

NKOSI, LEWIS, *The Transplanted Heart: Essays on South Africa*, Ethiope Publishing Corp., Benin City, Nigeria, 1975.

OBIECHINA, EMMANUEL N., *An African Popular Literature: A Study of Onitsha Market Pamphlets*, Cambridge University Press, 1973.

PRESS, JOHN, ed., *Commonwealth Literature: Unity and Diversity in a Common Culture*, Heinemann, London, 1965.

ROSCOE, ADRIAN, *Mother is Gold: A Study in West African Literature*, Cambridge University Press, 1971.

ROSCOE, ADRIAN, *Uhuru's Fire: African Literature East to South*, Cambridge University Press, 1977.

RUTHERFORD, ANNA, ed., *Common Wealth*, Akademisk Boghandel, Aarhus, 1972.

TUCKER, MARTIN, *Africa in Modern Literature: A Survey of Contemporary Writing in English*, Frederick Ungar, New York, 1967.

WALSH, WILLIAM, *Commonwealth Literature*, Oxford University Press, London, Oxford, New York, 1973.

WALSH, WILLIAM, ed., *Reading in Commonwealth Literature*, Clarendon Press, Oxford, 1973.

Francophone Africa

BLAIR, DOROTHY S., *African Literature in French: A History of Creative Writing in French from West and Equatorial Africa*, Cambridge University Press, 1976.

BONN, CHARLES, *La Littérature algérienne de langue française et ses lecteurs*, Naaman, Ottawa, 1974.

CHEVRIER, JACQUES, *Littérature nègre: Afrique, Antilles, Madagascar*, Colin, Paris, 1974.

CORNEVIN, ROBERT, *Littératures d'afrique noire de langue française*, Presses Universitaires de France, Paris, 1976.

DÉJEUX, JEAN, *Littérature maghrébine de langue française*, Naaman, Ottawa, 1973.

GÉRARD, ALBERT, *Études de littérature africaine francophone*, Nouvelles Editions Africaines, Dakar and Abidjan, 1977.

GORÉ, JEANNE-LYDIE, ed., *Négritude africaine, Négritude caraïbe*, Universite Paris-Nord, Centre d'Etudes Francophones, Paris, 1973.

KESTELOOT, LILYAN, *Les Écrivains noirs de langue française: Naissance d'une littérature*, Université Libre, Brussels, 1963; 5th ed., 1975. Translated by Ellen Conroy Kennedy as *Black Writers of French: A Literary History of Negritude*, Temple University Press, Philadelphia, 1974.

MERAD, GHANI, *La Littérature algérienne d'expression française: Approches socio-culturelles*, Oswald, Paris, 1976.

NANTET, JACQUES, *Panorama de la littérature noire d'expression française* Fayard, Paris, 1972.

Lusophone Africa

ARAUJO, NORMAN, *A Study of Cape Verdean Literature*, Boston College, Boston, 1966.

BURNESS, DONALD, *Fire: Six Writers from Angola, Mozambique and Cape Verde*, Three Continents Press, Washington, D.C., 1977.

CÉSAR, AMÂNDIO, *Novos parágrafos de literatura ultramarina*, Sociedade de Expansão Cultural, Lisbon, 1971.

HAMILTON, RUSSEL G., *Voices from the Empire: A History of Afro-Portuguese Literature*, University of Minnesota Press, Minneapolis, 1975.

MOSER, GERALD M., *Essays in Portuguese-African Literature*, Pennsylvania State University, University Park, 1969.

Literatures in African Languages

GÉRARD, ALBERT S., *Four African Literatures: Xhosa, Sotho, Zulu, Amharic*, University of California Press, Berkeley and Los Angeles, 1971.

HARRIES, LYNDON, *Swahili Poetry*, Oxford University Press, Oxford, 1962.

HISKETT, M., *A History of Hausa Islamic Verse*, University of London School of Oriental and African Studies, 1975.

JORDON, A. C., *Towards an African Literature*, University of California Press, Berkeley and Los Angeles, 1973.

KANE, THOMAS LEIPER, *Ethiopian Literature in Amharic*, Otto Harrassowitz, Wiesbaden, 1975.

KUNENE, DANIEL P., *Heroic Poetry of the Basotho*, Clarendon Press, Oxford, 1971.

Fiction

ACHIRIGA, JINGIRI J., *La Révolte des romanciers noirs de langue française*, Naaman, Ottawa, 1973.

HAMNER, ROBERT, *Critical Perspectives on V. S. Naipaul*, Three Contine
Press, Washington, D.C., 1977.

HARRIS, WILSON, *Tradition, the Writer and Society*, New Beacon, London
Port-of-Spain, 1967.

MCDOWELL, ROBERT E., *Bibliography of Literature from Guyana*, Sal
Arlington, Texas, 1975.

MUNRO, IAN, and SANDER, REINHARD, eds., *Kas-Kas: Interviews with Th
Caribbean Writers in Texas: George Lamming, C. L. R. James, Wilson Har*
African and Afro-American Research Institute, University of Texas, Aus
1972.

RAMCHAND, KENNETH, *The West Indian Novel and Its Background*, Fat
London; Barnes and Noble, New York, 1970.

RAMCHAND, KENNETH, *An Introduction to the Study of West Indian Literatu*
Nelson Caribbean, Middlesex, Nairobi and Kingston, 1976.

ANOZIE, SUNDAY O., *Sociologie du roman africain: Réalisme, structure et
détermination dans le roman moderne ouestafricain*, Aubier-Montaigne, Paris,
1970.

BÖTTCHER, KARL-HEINZ, *Tradition und Modernität bei Amos Tutuola und
Chinua Achebe: Grundzüge der westafrikanischen Erzählliteratur englischer
Sprache*, Herbert Grundmann, Bonn, 1974.

BRENCH, A. C., *The Novelists' Inheritance in French Africa: Writers from Senegal
to Cameroon*, Oxford University Press, London, 1967.

GAKWANDI, SHATTO ARTHUR, *The Novel and Contemporary Experience in
Africa*, Heinemann, London; Africana Publishing Co., New York, 1977.

GLEASON, JUDITH, *This Africa: Novels by West Africans in English and French*,
Northwestern University Press, Evanston, Ill., 1965.

ISCHINGER, ANN-BARBARA, *Der antikolonialistische Roman im frankophonen
Schwarzafrika*, Peter Lang and Herbert Lang, Frankfurt and Bern, 1975.

KHATIBI, ABDELKABIR, *Le Roman maghrébin*, François Maspero, Paris, 1968.

KLÍMA, VLADIMÍR, *Modern Nigerian Novels*, Academia, Prague, 1969.

KLÍMA, VLADIMÍR, *South African Prose Writing in English*, Academia, Prague,
1971.

LARSON, CHARLES R., *The Emergence of African Fiction*, Indiana University
Press, Bloomington and London, 1972.

LARSON, CHARLES R., *The Novel in the Third World*, Inscape, Washington,
D.C., 1976.

NEW, WILLIAM H., *Among Worlds: An Introduction to Modern Commonwealth
and South African Fiction*, Press Porcepic, Erin, Canada, 1975.

OBIECHINA, EMMANUEL N., *Culture, Tradition and Society in the West African
Novel*, Cambridge University Press, 1975.

PALMER, EUSTACE, *An Introduction to the African Novel: A Critical Study of
Twelve Books by Chinua Achebe, James Ngugi, Camara Laye, Elechi Amadi,
Ayi Kwei Armah, Mongo Beti and Gabriel Okara*, Heinemann, London;
Africana Publishing Co., New York, 1972.

TAIWO, OLADELE, *Culture and the Nigerian Novel*, Macmillan, London;
St. Martin's Press, New York, 1976.

YETIV, ISAAC, *Le Thème de l'aliénation dans le roman maghrébin d'expression
française de 1952 à 1956*, Centre d'Etude des Littératures d'Expression
Française, Université de Sherbrooke, 1972.

Drama

ANON, *Actes du colloque sur le théâtre négro-africain*, Présence Africaine, Paris,
1971.

BANHAM, MARTIN, and WAKE, CLIVE, *African Theatre Today*, Pitman, London,
1976.

CORNEVIN, ROBERT, *Le Théâtre en Afrique noire et à Madagascar*, Le Livre
Africain, Paris, 1970.

GRAHAM-WHITE, ANTHONY, *The Drama of Black Africa*, Samuel French,
New York, 1974.

RICARD, ALAIN, *Théâtre et nationalisme: Wole Soyinka et LeRoi Jones*, Présence
Africaine, Paris, 1972.

SCHIPPER-DE LEEUW, MINEKE, *Toneel en Matschappij in Afrika*, Van Gorcum,
Assen, Amsterdam, 1977.

TRAORÉ, BAKARY, *Le Théâtre négro-africaine et ses fonctions sociales*, Paris: Présence Africaine, 1958. Translated by Dapo Adelugba as *The Black Theatre and its Social Functions*, Ibadan University Press; Africana Publishing Co., New York, 1972.

Poetry

EGUDU, ROMANUS N., *Four Modern West African Poets*, Nok, New York, 1977.
PRETO-RODAS, RICHARD A., *Negritude as a Theme in the Poetry of the Portuguese-Speaking World*, University of Florida Press, Gainesville, 1970.
UDOEYOP, N. J., *Three Nigerian Poets: A Critical Study of the Poetry of Soyinka, Clark and Okigbo*, Ibadan University Press, 1973.

Literary Criticism

BAKER, HOUSTON A., JR., ed., *Reading Black: Essays in the Criticism of African, Caribbean, and Black American Literature*, Cornell University Africana Studies and Research Center, Ithaca, N.Y., 1976.
SCHIPPER-DE LEEUW, MINEKE, ed., *Text and Context: Methodological Explorations in the Field of African Literature*, special issue of *African Perspectives*, No. 1, 1977.
SOCIÉTÉ AFRICAINE DE CULTURE, *Le Critique africain et son Peuple comme producteur de civilisation*, Présence Africain, Paris, 1977.
WRIGHT, EDGAR, ed., *The Critical Evaluation of African Literature*, Heinemann, London, 1973; Inscape Corp., Washington, D.C., 1976.

Studies of Individual Authors

Abrahams
WADE, MICHAEL, *Peter Abrahams*, Evans, London and Ibadan, 1972.

Achebe
CARROLL, DAVID, *Chinua Achebe*, Twayne, New York, 1970.
KILLAM, G. D., *The Novels of Chinua Achebe*, Heinemann, London; Africana Publishing Co., New York, 1969; revised ed. published as the *The Writings of Chinua Achebe*, 1977.
MELONE, THOMAS, *Chinua Achebe et la tragédie de l'histoire*, Présence Africaine, Paris, 1973.
RAVENCROFT, ARTHUR, *Chinua Achebe*, Longmans, Green, for the British Council and the National Book League, 1969.

Beti
MELONE, THOMAS, *Mongo Beti: l'Homme et le destin*, Présence Africaine, Paris, 1971.

Césaire
CAILLER, BERNADETTE, *Proposition poétique: Une lecture de l'oeuvre d'Aimé Césaire*, Naaman, Sherbrooke, 1976.
JUIN, HUBERT, *Aimé Césaire: Poète Noir*, Présence Africaine, Paris, 1956.
KESTELOOT, LILYAN, *Aimé Césaire*, Seghers, Paris, 1962.

NGAL, M. A M., *Aimé Césaire: Un Homme à la recherche d'une patrie*, Nouvelles Editions Africaines, Dakar, 1975.

Ekwensi
EMENYONU, ERNEST, *Cyprian Ekwensi*, Evans, London, 1974.

Mphahlele
BARNETT, URSULA A., *Ezekiel Mphahlele*, Twayne, New York, 1976.

Okigbo
ANOZIE, SUNDAY, O. *Christopher Okigbo: Creative Rhetoric*, Evans, London; p'Bitek, Africana Publishing Co., New York, 1972.
HERON, G. A., *The Poetry of Okot p'Bitek*, Heinemann, London; Africana Publishing Co., New York, 1976.

Sembène
VIEYRA, PAULIN SOUMANOU, *Ousmane Sembene: Cinéaste*, Présence Africaine, Paris, 1972.

Senghor
BA, SYLVIA WASHINGTON, *The Concept of Negritude in the Poetry of Léopold Sédar Senghor*, Princeton University Press, 1973.
HYMANS, JACQUES LOUIS, *Léopold Sédar Senghor: An Intellectual Biography*, Edinburgh University Press, 1971.
LEBAUD, G., *Léopold Sédar Senghor ou la poésie du royaume d'enfance*, Nouvelles Editions Africaines, Dakar, 1976.
MARKOVITZ, IRVING L., *Léopold Sédar Senghor and the Politics of Negritude*, Atheneum, New York, 1969.
MEZU, S. OKECHUKWU, *The Poetry of L. S. Senghor*, Heinemann, London, 1973.

Soyinka
BÖTTCHER-WÖBCKE, RITA, *Komik, Ironie und Satire im dramatischen Werk von Wole Soyinka*, Helmut Buske, Hamburg, 1976.
JONES, ELDRED, *The Writing of Wole Soyinka*, Heinemann, London; Twayne, New York, 1973.
MOORE, GERALD, *Wole Soyinka*, Evans, London; Africana Publishing Co., New York, 1971.
OGUNBA, OYIN, *The Movement of Transition: A Study of the Plays of Wole Soyinka*, Ibadan University Press, 1975.

Tutuola
COLLINS, HAROLD R., *Amos Tutuola*, Twayne, New York, 1969.
LINDFORS, BERNTH, ed., *Critical Perspectives on Amos Tutuola*, Three Continents Press, Washington, D.C., 1975.
DUSSUTOUR-HAMMER, MICHÈLE, *Amos Tutuola: Tradition orale et écriture de conte*, Présence Africaine, Paris, 1976.

Caribbean Literature

BAUGH, EDWARD, ed., *Critics on Caribbean Literature*, St. Martin's Press, New York, 1978.
COULTHARD, G. R., *Race and Colour in Caribbean Literature*, Oxford University Press, London, 1962.
GILKES, MICHAEL, *Wilson Harris and the Caribbean Novel*, Longman, London and Trinidad, 1975.

Notes on the Contributors

GEORMBEEYI ADALI-MORTTY Educated at Achimota College and graduate of Cornell University; formerly director of the Writers' Workshop (Ghana) and joint editor of *Okyeame*; now Senior Lecturer in Business Management, University of Ghana; poems published in *Black Orpheus* and other journals and anthologies; co-editor (with Kofi Awoonor) of *Messages: Poems from Ghana* (London, 1971).

YAHAYA ALIYU Graduate of University of Ibadan; formerly Lecturer in English at Zaria Teachers' College, Nigeria; co-author (with A. H. M. Kirk-Greene) of *A Modern Hausa Reader* (London, 1967).

ADEBOYE BABALOLA Educated in Nigeria, Ghana and Cambridge, England; Ph.D., University of London; formerly Principal of Igbobi College, Lagos; now Professor and Head of the Department of African Languages and Literatures, University of Lagos; author of *The Content and Form of Yoruba Ijala* (Oxford, 1966).

ULLI BEIER Born in Germany. From 1951–67 he taught in the Department of Extra-Mural Studies, University of Ibadan; now serving as Director of the Institute of Papua New Guinea Studies at the University of Papua New Guinea. Founder and former editor of *Odu*, a journal of Yoruba studies, and of *Black Orpheus*; currently editing *Gigibori: A Journal of Papua New Guinea Cultures*. In Oshogbo, Nigeria, he founded a museum of popular African art and was associated with Duro Ladipo's theatre group. His many books include *Yoruba Poetry* (Ibadan, 1959), *Art in Nigeria, 1960* (London, 1960), *African Mud Sculpture* (London, 1963), *The Origin of Life and Death: African Creation Myths* (London, 1966), *Not Even God is Ripe Enough: Yoruba Stories* (London, 1968), *Contemporary Art in Africa* (London, 1968), *Words of Paradise: Poetry of Papua New Guinea* (Santa Barbara, 1973), and *The Return of the Gods: The Sacred Art of Susanne Wenger* (Cambridge, 1975).

O. R. DATHORNE Born in Guyana. Formerly a lecturer in English at the University of Ibadan; now Professor of English at Ohio State University. Editor of *Caribbean Narrative: An Anthology of West Indian Writing* (London, 1966) and *Caribbean Verse: An Anthology*, and co-editor (with Willfried Feuser) of *Africa in Prose* (Baltimore, 1969). Author of two novels, *Dumplings in the Soup* (London, 1963) and *The Scholar Man* (London, 1964), and of a critical study, *The Black Mind: A History of African Literature* (Minneapolis, 1974).

ARTHUR DRAYTON Born in Trinidad. Formerly a lecturer in the Department of Extra-Mural Studies, University of Ibadan; now Senior Lecturer in English and Dean of Arts and General Studies at the University of the West Indies, Kingston.

ROMANUS EGUDU is Associate Professor of Modern Languages at the University of Benin and author of *Four Modern West African Poets* (New York, 1977).

MARTIN ESSLIN Formerly Head of Drama at B.B.C.; now Professor of Drama at Stanford University. Author of many works on drama, including *Brecht: The Man and His Work* (Garden City, N.Y., 1960), *The Theatre of the Absurd*

(London, 1962), *Reflections: Essays on Modern Theatre* (Garden City, N.Y., 1969), *The Peopled Wound: The Work of Harold Pinter* (Garden City, N.Y., 1970), and *An Anatomy of Drama* (London, 1976).

HELMUT GUNTHER Teacher in a German secondary school, critic of dancing (European and African), and writer on African literature and affairs.

ABIOLA IRELE Graduate of the University of Ibadan; completed his doctoral dissertation at the Sorbonne on Aimé Césaire; now Senior Lecturer in French at the University of Ibadan; author of numerous critical articles and *Literature and Ideology in Martinique: René Maran, Aimé Césaire, Frantz Fanon* (Buffalo, 1971); editor of *Lectures Africaines* (London, 1969) and *Selected Poems of Léopold Sédar Senghor* (Cambridge, 1977).

JANHEINZ JAHN Late German author of *Muntu* (London, 1961), *Through African Doors* (New York, 1962), *A History of Neo-African Literature: Writing in Two Continents* (London, 1968), and *Leo Frobenius: The Demonic Child* (Austin, 1974); translator and editor of numerous anthologies of African literature published in Germany; compiler (with Claus Peter Dressler) of *Bibliography of Creative African Writing* (Nendeln, 1971) and (with Ulla Schild and Almut Nordmann) of *Who's Who in African Literature: Biographies, Works, Commentaries* (Tübingen, 1972).

ROBERT W. JULY Former Assistant Director for the Humanities, Rockefeller Foundation, and Visiting Research Associate at the University of Ibadan and the University of Nairobi; now Professor of History at Hunter College, New York City. Author of *The Origins of Modern African Thought* (New York, 1967), *A History of the African People* (New York, 1970), and *Precolonial Africa: An Economic and Social History* (New York, 1975).

JAN KNAPPERT Ph.D., University of London; Lecturer in Bantu languages, School of Oriental and African Studies, London; amassed large collection of Swahili literature, now deposited in University of Dar es Salaam Library. Author of *Traditional Swahili Poetry* (Leiden, 1967) and *Swahili Islamic Poetry*, 3 vols. (Leiden, 1971); editor of *Myths and Legends of the Swahili* (London, 1970), *Myths and Legends of the Congo* (London, 1971), and *A Choice of Flowers: An Anthology of Swahili Love Poetry* (London, 1972).

BERNTH LINDFORS is Professor of African Literature at the University of Texas and in 1978-9 Visiting Professor at the University of Nairobi. He is the editor of *Critical Perspectives on Amos Tutuola* (Washington, 1975), and of *Critical Perspectives on Nigerian Literature* (Washington, 1976), co-editor (with Ulla Schild) of *Neo-African Literature and Culture* (Weisbaden, 1976), and author of *Folklore in Nigerian Literature* (New York, 1973).

W. S. MERWIN American poet, playwright and translator; graduate of Princeton. University. His numerous published volumes of poetry include *A Mask for Janus* (New Haven, 1952), *The Dancing Bears* (New Haven, 1954), *Green with Beasts* (London, 1956), *The Drunk in the Furnace* (New York, 1960), *The Moving Target* (New York, 1963), *The Lice* (New York, 1967), *The Carrier of Ladders* (New York, 1970), and *Writings to an Unfinished Accompaniment* (New York, 1974). He has also adapted plays by Corneille, Marivaux, Garcia Lorca and others, and has translated poetry by Pablo Neruda, Osip Mandel'shtam, Jean Follain and others.

300

GERALD MOORE Formerly Director of Extra-Mural Studies, Makerere University College, Kampala, and Senior Lecturer in English, School of African and Asian Studies, University of Sussex; now Professor of English at the University of Port Harcourt, Nigeria. Author of numerous translations and studies of African literature, including *Seven African Writers* (London, 1962), *The Chosen Tongue: English Writing in the Tropical World* (New York, 1969), and *Wole Soyinka* (London, 1971); editor of *African Literature and the Universities* (Ibadan, 1965) and co-editor (with Ulli Beier) of *Modern Poetry from Africa* (Harmondsworth, 1963).

EZEKIEL MPHAHLELE South African writer, now an Inspector of Schools in the Nothern Transvaal; formerly Director of Chem-Chemi Cultural Centre, Nairobi, and Professor of English at University of Denver and University of Pennsylvania; early literary editor of *Drum* and co-editor of *Black Orpheus*. Author of three collections of short stories: *Man Must Live and Other Stories* (Cape Town, 1946), *The Living and the Dead and Other Stories* (Ibadan, n.d.), *In Corner B* (Nairobi, 1967); an autobiography, *Down Second Avenue* (London, 1959); a novel, *The Wanderers* (New York, 1971); and numerous critical essays as well as two studies, *The African Image* (London, 1962; rev. ed. 1974) and *Voices in the Whirlwind* (New York, 1972).

J. H. KWABENA NKETIA Director, Institute of African Studies, University of Ghana; author of numerous articles on African music and culture and of *Funeral Dirges of the Akan People* (Accra, 1955), *African Music in Ghana* (London, 1962), *Folk Songs of Ghana* (London, 1963), *Drumming in Akan Communities of Ghana* (Edinburgh, 1963), *Ethnomusicology in Ghana* (Accra, 1970), and *The Music of Africa* (New York, 1974).

LEWIS NKOSI Born in Johannesburg; worked on *Drum* and other magazines until he left South Africa for England in the mid-1960s; was literary editor of *The New African*; now a free-lance writer and working on a doctorate in African literature at the University of Sussex. Author of a play, *The Rhythm of Violence* (London, 1964), a collection of autobiographical and critical essays, *Home and Exile* (London, 1965), and a book entitled *The Transplanted Heart: Essays on South Africa* (Benin City, Nigeria, 1975).

HENRY OWUOR Born in Kenya; formerly a teacher at Friends' School, Kamusinga, during which time he made a collection of Luo songs; read English Literature at Cambridge.

J. A. RAMSARAN Born in Trinidad; graduate of London University; formerly Lecturer in English and African Literature, University of Ibadan; now Senior Lecturer in English Language and Literature at the University of Swansea; author of *New Approaches to African Literature: A Guide to Negro-African Writing and Related Studies* (Ibadan, 1965).

DON SCHARFE Graduate of Harvard College and University of California; formerly Lecturer in English at Zaria Teachers' College.

PAUL THEROUX American novelist and critic; has taught at universities in Italy, Malawi, Uganda, Singapore and Virginia; currently living in England. His writings include novels: *Waldo* (Boston, 1967), *Fong and the Indians* (Boston, 1968), *Girls at Play* (Boston, 1969), *Jungle Lovers* (Boston, 1971), *Saint Jack* (Boston, 1973), *The Black House* (London, 1974), *The Family Arsenal* (Boston,

1976); short stories, *Sinning with Annie, and Other Stories* (Boston, 1972), and *The Consul's File* (Boston, 1977); a travel book, *The Great Railway Bazaar* (Boston, 1975); and a critical study, *V. S. Naipaul: An Introduction to His Work* (London, 1972).

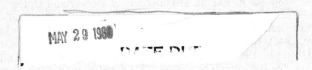